American Writing Today

810.904
T 48 a
59627
Nov. 1967

AMERICAN
WRITING
TODAY

Its Independence
and Vigor

Edited by ALLAN ANGOFF

Washington Square
New York University Press
1957

ACKNOWLEDGMENTS

Even the assembling of other people's writing presents knotty editorial problems and certainly entails considerable time, planning, and effort. My burden has been lightened substantially by the assistance of my colleagues of the New York University Press, particularly Wilson Follett and Ruth Almond. I am also grateful to Alan Pryce-Jones, editor of the *Times* (London) *Literary Supplement,* for preparing at my request in the midst of his heavy schedule a preface that explains the unique origin of the articles in this book and adds to their value for American readers. I must note finally my great debt to my wife, Florence Angoff, who assisted me in all aspects of the work, including the reading and correcting of proof and the making of the index.

ALLAN ANGOFF

Preface

By the editor of THE TIMES (London) LITERARY SUPPLEMENT

THE CONTENTS of this book comprise a special number of the London *Times Literary Supplement*—a literary weekly in which all critical contributions are unsigned. This has often been criticized, in England and elsewhere. The editorial staff is told, very reasonably, by dissident readers that they like to know who is telling them what. They like to follow their chosen critics, to discount the opinions of others whom they have learned to distrust, and to sense, behind the signatures, what editorial policy governs the doctrine of the paper.

Rightly or wrongly, we defend our habit notwithstanding. To begin with, we can give it a historical background. Since *The Times Literary Supplement* came into existence at the beginning of this century it has always followed what used to be common practice in the days when literary reviews were at the height of their influence; and although it would be absurd to assert that a habit is any the better for being an established habit, it is also likely that what lasts for a hundred years and more will have some positive merit in it. And then, looking round the literary world of modern England, we have become convinced that there is a place for unsigned criticism, just as there is a much larger place for signed criticism.

For one thing, the editor of a review in which the criticism is anonymous has an important advantage over his competitors: he can avoid literary snobbery. Not only in England, most writers and all publishers would sooner expose themselves to criticism from a great name than to good criticism. And over the years a

small group of pundits accumulate under recognizable banners—
the leading critics of the leading papers—whose opinion, from the
snobbish point of view, makes or mars a book. Thus, the chief
critic of a Sunday book page may find himself in the position of
having to turn out a column of lively prose on any subject from
climbing in the Himalayas to the private life of Louis XV; and
he will do so, not because he knows anything much of the subject,
but because he is expected to write about the book of the week.

The opposite method is to try to marry each book, good or bad,
to the best critic available to discuss its subject. Most of these
critics will not be famous. They will be working in provincial universities or quiet country libraries; they may be (in the best sense)
amateurs; they may have fallen from fashion; they may be too
young for fame. But if they are properly chosen, they will bring
a far fresher approach to their subject than any literary journalist,
however gifted and popular.

And then, too, there are the critics who, for quite legitimate
reasons, prefer to remain anonymous. Statesmen, for instance, and
diplomats; workers in fields so specialized that they are unwilling
to discuss publicly the work of their one or two rivals; writers—
Virginia Woolf is a case in point—so well-known in one sphere
that they do not wish to plunge directly into the role of critic. All
these can be persuaded—with luck—to write unsigned criticism,
and by doing so they will help to achieve something that the overt
critic can seldom manage except by some sacrifice of his personality: they can build a college of opinion, not too rigid, not too
exclusive, containing within itself those tensions that keep a paper
alive.

The lack of rigidity is important, if only because it implies a
proper mixture of care and diffidence on the part of the editorial
staff. They might, of course, lay down a strict canon for themselves,
on the assumption that they are always right; they might, on the
other hand, give rein to such qualities as tenderness of heart or
malice or jealousy (since even editors are human) which totally
bedevil judgment. By using a very large number of anonymous
contributors, however, they can avoid both too constant a repeti-

tion of the same views and a natural tendency to dogmatism. And so long as they receive letters from subscribers in approximately equal numbers accusing them of being hirelings of the Vatican or of the Kremlin they can be fairly sure that they are pursuing an argumentative course which is working forward sensibly by a normal dialectical process.

Every now and again, however, we feel the need to pause and take stock. A weekly critical paper has its nose pressed so tightly to current books that it is all too easy to overlook the larger patterns into which those books—most of them very temporary books, too—have to be fitted. We print a special number, then, from time to time, in order to draw together the loose strands that have been offered week after week to those willing to be interested. And it soon became clear that, among such special numbers, one must be devoted to the literature of the United States today.

This is not the place to recapitulate what will be found in the following pages. But it is perhaps worth stressing the very special part that American writing plays in the rest of the English-speaking world, and, in particular, noting the paradox that although a great deal is written and talked about its influence and its vitality, very little indeed is generally known about the practical side of the writer's life in the United States, about the nature of the American literary public, or about the feel of creative work in a country so singularly unlike any to be found in Europe.

It is true that the ordinary intelligent Englishman (or Australian or South African) believes himself to be fairly well at home in American writing today. A mass of names are familiar to him, and he has had a number of routine attitudes copiously explained. Apart from the inconvenience that both names and attitudes are generally several years out of date, he will be able to hold his own in conversation about those books and writers that have been accepted abroad as representative of American culture. He will not, however, have any first-hand knowledge of the American literary scene. And almost certainly he will be unable—having no dollars —to verify for himself on the spot what he has been told by others.

In consequence, he is likely to be seriously misled in his ideas of what America is like. For in the last resort, books are nothing but the record of a community at a given time: the stories it tells itself, the ideas that circulate among its members, the facts it finds useful, the interpretations of history and life and art and religion that give it its own flavor. Unless, therefore, outsiders can check their vague notions of a community against personal contact with it, they are likely to become more and more perplexed by what they read. They will hear large assertions: such as a reproach often leveled against American scholarship by European critics, to the effect that it has been paralyzed by too Germanic an attitude towards the *minutiae* of learning. But they will almost certainly be unable, for lack of first-hand evidence, to accept or to reject this charge. And among works of the imagination they may lose their way altogether: unsure whether Edmund Wilson's Princeton is still just as it was, whether Faulkner's South is a reality or a personal legend, whether Greenwich Village really exists or not outside a world already as dispersed as that of Bloomsbury in London, whether it is false or true that all American poets teach literature in women's colleges—as, from a distance, they seem to.

And yet, against this background of uncertainty or plain mis-statement, the fact of American literature has become immensely important to European readers. They find in it a directness, a vitality, a poetry, often lacking in their own. If they are honest with themselves they may well experience also a contrasting sense of lassitude and overrefinement in much of what is being written in England. And they must be aware that in other languages—particularly in French—the influence of English percolates now not from across the Channel but from across the Atlantic.

This fact alone leads to some sensitivity on either side. The English feel that they are giving constant proofs of a beautiful sensitivity that is not sufficiently appreciated; and the Americans, sensing the strength of their position, suspect the motives of any criticism that may come their way. In such circumstances, then, we decided a little time ago that the moment was ripe for laying before a public primarily British as accurate a picture as we could paint of the state of writing in America today. We were surprised that so hazardous a venture was so generally applauded; and we are particularly pleased that a New York publisher and editor should wish to give our special number this permanent form.

At first it seemed somewhat coy to withhold the names of the contributors; but then a difficulty arose. Many of them have deliberately adjusted their style of writing to the impersonal manner required of them, and some did not wish to break out of their anonymity unless they were given the opportunity of redrafting what they had written. Others, again, would never have consented to write at all but for the cover given them by our lack of signatures. And finally, it seemed on reflection that for better or for worse the very nature of the book required the absence of personality. It must stand or fall as the best the London *Times* could do, using mainly British writers, but occasionally (when no British writer could be found to carry out an assignment) turning for help to the United States. With all the saddening brightness of hindsight it is possible to see now one or two ways in which the book could have been better. More attention, for instance, might have been paid to some of the little reviews in America, to experimental writing, and to the youngest poets. Nevertheless, we had to bear in mind that there was a danger of losing the main outline if we went into too much detail in too many directions. After all, we were trying to produce a picture, not an encyclopedia. And since the picture we unfolded has already gained many fresh adherents to the cause of understanding better what is being written in the United States, we have at any rate had the satisfaction of achieving the main part of our purpose in undertaking the work at all.

ALAN PRYCE-JONES

Contents

Introduction

THE BEST vantage point for a good view of American writing is probably the editorial office of a general magazine or of a book publishing house. The multitude of manuscripts that come to these offices daily from all over the country reveals turbulence and ferment on every level. There is hardly a corner of American life that our writers fail to explore: the Boston Irish and the Boston Brahmins, the Negro of the South and of the big cities of the North, the sharecroppers, the academic life, big business. Every national, religious, racial, social group is represented in that never-ending rush of manuscripts. Every writing form is represented: the poem, play, short story, novel, history, biography. No editor can fail to be moved by it, and indeed no editor ever wearies of it or quite accepts it as routine. For one thing, he cannot if he is to survive as an editor and if his magazine or publishing house is to continue as a vital force in the community. But a more compelling reason is the expectancy and quiet excitement with which that daily manuscript mail is greeted. If, as happens all too often, most of the manuscripts have little quality and must be returned, the time they require is well spent. For they do reveal an unmistakable vitality in the land, they do reveal the country's innermost thoughts and hopes in more effective fashion than any of the highly publicized scientific polls.

The articles in this volume cover almost the entire range of American writing. Like the daily manuscript mail of the editor, they reveal an impressive quantity of writing about almost every aspect of living in the United States. Some figures of very great stature, perhaps of world stature, are discussed here, but even they are incidental to the larger underlying theme of the book: that a dynamic democratic spirit has permeated every form of American writing far more rapidly and genuinely than it has affected the political and social body of the United States. This is a phenomenon that is understandably the envy of writers and editors and of some statesmen in all countries. Even the editors of the *Times Literary Supplement* of London, who first conceived of this portrait of American writing and tribute to it and first published it in their pages, pointed out in editorial columns never given to overstatement that "it is now generally recognized that nowhere in the modern world is there a more rewarding literature than that which America has to offer."

It is a rewarding literature because it has vigorous spokesmen for every stratum of American life in every part of the country. These spokesmen, to be sure, are rarely great poets, great novelists, great journalists. But they are frequently men of imagination and they all have their audiences, thanks in large measure to an unexcelled system of communications and a printing and publishing industry of astounding efficiency. Here perhaps are "the vigorous, yet unsuspected literatures" of which Whitman spoke almost a century ago.

But it was not always so, as these pages point out, and as they should. Whitman was shunned by many of his most eminent contemporaries as an indecent poet. Melville wrote a book that many now regard as one of the peaks of world literature, but the United States of 1851 ignored it or found it a bore, and the author of *Moby Dick* lived out his remaining years in pathetic obscurity. Emily Dickinson, it is true, imposed obscurity on herself during her lifetime, but it is often forgotten that much of her magnificent verse was published in 1890, 1891, and 1896, and that she was regarded as a minor poet until well into the 1920's. Nearer our own day there was the lonely figure of Theodore Dreiser, accurately described in this volume as "the first major non-Anglo Saxon novelist" and as the storyteller who first voiced the fears and dreams of the "cheated immigrant," and yet this man's own publisher attempted to sabotage so important a book as *Sister*

Carrie by issuing it in an insignificant edition in 1900. Fourteen years were to elapse before the book was reprinted and distributed on the scale it so obviously warranted. Those were hard days for unconventional novelists, and Dreiser later recalled them in these bitter words: "I think it nothing less than tragic that these men, or boys, fresh, forceful, imbued with a burning desire to present life as they saw it, were thus completely overawed by the moral hypocrisy of the American mind and did not even dare to think of sending their novel to an American publisher. . . . You couldn't write about life as it was; you had to write about it as somebody else thought it was."

All these instances and many more recall Whitman's lament in *Democratic Vistas* that feudalism and caste still held our literature in bondage and that democracy could never prove itself until it founded its own art forms. Even so scathing a critic as Whitman was careful to point out, nevertheless, that feudalism and caste were retreating, and indeed they retreated so far that Whitman was a revered national and world figure during the last years of his life. And as for the author of *Sister Carrie*, Sherwood Anderson prophesied accurately that "because of him, those who follow will never have to face the road through the wilderness of Puritan denial, the road that Dreiser faced alone."

Since Dreiser, as the article in this volume, *A Search for the Conscience of a People*, points out, two generations of novelists from Sinclair Lewis to Norman Mailer and James Jones have arraigned and exposed American life mercilessly, but—and most important—in defense of the great promises held out by the Founding Fathers, promises that are frequently perverted and falsified.

It is this spirit, this self-criticism that has given our literature such vitality. We do not have a Shakespeare, a Dante, a Tolstoy, but we do have a variety of literatures in which the whole population participates. American writing today would seem to be on the verge of fulfilling Whitman's hope. His words, rather than those of any living critic, seem particularly appropriate in introducing this view of American writing at the mid-twentieth century. "The problem of humanity all over the civilized world is social and religious," he said, "and is to be finally met and treated by literature. . . . At all times, perhaps, the central point in any nation, and that whence it is itself really swayed the most, and whence it sways others, is its national literature. . . . Above all previous lands, a great original literature is surely to become the justification and reliance (in some respects the sole reliance) of American democracy."

ALLAN ANGOFF

Part 1. POETRY AND DRAMA

The Rising Generation, by Edith Sitwell

How Cruel Is April? by W. H. Auden

Poetic Background

The Three Realms of the Young Poet

Thirty Years of Theatrical Enterprise

EDITH SITWELL

The Rising Generation

OF ALL recent statements on the subject of poetry, one made by
Robert Frost is among the most valuable, that a poem "begins
in delight and ends in wisdom." The American poetry of our time
is, for the most part, fertile in delight—

> As the immense dew of Florida
> Brings forth
> The big-finned palm
> And green vine angering for life
> . . .
> So, in me, come flinging
> Forms, flames, and the flakes of flames.

Those lovely lines from Wallace Stevens's "Nomad Exquise" seem
to embody the life of the best American poets of our age, whose
poetry "angers for life" and moves with an entirely natural ease,
an inborn athleticism. There are, of course, in America as elsewhere, self-conscious, "invented" poems. But the literary scene is
not cluttered up by gentlemen and ladies assuming postures of a
strained difficulty—strong men straddling under the burden of
seemingly enormous weights which, when examined, will prove
to be constructed of colored paper—bladders containing exactly
nothing.

(American poets, like English poets, have undergone that phase
of "showing-off," incidental to youth, and have survived it.) Nor
do they suffer from the self-conscious simplicity that, in the past,
showered upon us such benefactions as Whittier's

> Blessings on thee, little man,
> Barefoot boy, with cheek of tan!

> With thy turned-up pantaloons,
> And thy merry whistled tunes;

(Oh, certainly bless him! I quite agree! But unfortunately the benediction was not translated into good poetry.)

In America, as in England, there are earnest-minded people bent on improving the world by means of poetry. But to do this we must, in the words of the Oracle, "have heard the light speak." Many who have not heard that mighty voice are in the habit of fitting everything into a preconceived groove. (An English critic, recently, saw in Gray's Elegy a "plea for decentralization, recalling the over-urbanized ruling class to its roots in a rural society.")

I do not find the American poetry of the time given over to the silly dictates of a temporary fashion (this state exists in America as elsewhere, but not to a great extent): What *might* become a danger to poetry in the English language is a misunderstanding of the uses of concentration—a quality which, when used properly, is among the most valuable and necessary qualities in poetry. We read, in Maurice Bucke's *Cosmic Consciousness,* that "the race began with a few, or, as Geiger says, 'a single word.' " "It can be proved by examination of language that as late as the time of the primitive Aryans, not more than fifteen or twenty thousand years ago, man was only conscious of, or perceived, one colour." It is to this state, wherein concentration is only a narrowing of perception and experience, not a condensation of essence, that poetry might return if the dangers inherent in this misunderstanding continue.

What we see in the first American poetry of our time is the quality that Emerson called "a genial radiation, skilful to discriminate power from form, essence from accident, and opening, by its terminology and definition, high roads into Nature." These poets will have none of the

> Albino man, bleached from the mortal clay,
> Mild-mannered, gifted in your master's ease
> While the sun squats upon the waveless seas.
>   (Allen Tate: *Christmas Sonnets.*)

They see that poetry is, in one sense, "the animalization of God." They give us poetry full (as Whitman said poetry should be) "of strong sensual germs," "a language fann'd by the breath of Nature, which leaps overhead, cares mostly for impetus and effects, and for what it plants and invigorates to grow"—a poetry acutely living in its texture. (Take, for instance, the varying transparencies and densities of Marianne Moore's poems: we find in these all variations, from the beech bark, like the surface of the elephant's skin, to the sweet warmth and softness of feathers.)

But it is not of the poets who have long been famous in England —Mr. Eliot and Mr. Pound, Miss Moore, Mr. Frost, Mr. Tate, Mr. Ransom, Mr. Cummings, "H.D.," Mr. Stevens—that I intended to write, but of poets known here for but a short time, or who have not as yet been published in England. If the English people do not realize that Robert Lowell's "The Ghost" is a great poem, I shall despair of them. (His poems have been published in England.) It seems to me one of the most magnificent short poems of our time.

And Lethe oozes from her nether lip.

Does not that line call to mind the naked majesty of Tourneur or of Middleton?

Theodore Roethke is another young poet who has been published, already, in England. Almost the last time I saw Dylan Thomas he told me he regarded Roethke as one of the most remarkable and original of the younger poets writing in America or England in our time. And I agree. His poems are strange, and have an entirely original physical beauty, as in these verses, from a poem about a child in a greenhouse:

The roses kept breathing in the dark
They had many mouths to breathe with.
My knees made little winds underneath
Where the weeds slept.

There was always a single light
Swinging by the fire-pit,

> Where the fireman pulled out roses,
> The big roses, the big bloody cinders.

At this time, there seems to be a rebirth, among the younger American poets, of "pure poetry." Now amidst the other grumbles about modern poetry, two loud howls arise. One camp of howlers complains that certain poetry is "pure poetry"—contains no philosophy or "message." The other camp howls about the complete absence of "pure poetry" in this age. When, however, the latter complainants are brought face to face with "pure poetry"—such as many of José Garcia Villa's poems—they do not recognize it. Mr. Villa is a young poet who, Filipino by birth, now lives in New York. "All absolute sensation is religious," said Novalis. And this absolute sensation is known by Mr. Villa, shines and burns alike in his love poems and his poems about God. These have much physical beauty, the religious poems seem born of a joyous combat between the poet's spirit

> Ferocious and beautiful leopard that thrives
> On the rose-imagination

and his God. His love is not for the meek Christ, but for Christ the Lion:

> Much beauty is less than the face of
> My dark hero. His under is pure
> Lightning. His under is the socket
>
> Of the sun. Not Christ the Fox, not
> Christ the Lord, His beauty is too
> Sly, too meek. But Christ Oppositor,
>
> Christ Foeman: The true dark Hero.

(Christ conquering us against our will—the Christ known, perhaps, to such men as Blanco Posnet.)

"The Anchored Angel," a poem of great beauty, is very strange and, I must admit, difficult. (No critic, however determined, could find in it a "plea for decentralization.") But take the lines with which the poem begins:

And lay he down, the golden father
(Genesis' fist, all gentle now)
Between the Wall of China and
The tiger tree (his centuries, his
Aerials of light). . . .

"Genesis' fist" means that the Angel holds the beginnings of all
things in his hand. "The Wall of China" is that wall that separates
the Living from the multitudes of the Dead. "The tiger tree" is
the Tree of Life. By "sanskrit of love," a phrase that occurs later
in this poem, he means the language, uniting Man with his brother
Man, whose meaning is now almost lost to us.

Charles Henri Ford, like Mr. Villa, has not as yet found an
English publisher for his poems. The general demand, at present,
seems to be for what an American critic called "flannel-mouthed,
rock-garden ruggedness," for bun-tough, bun-stale whinings about
personal grievances, and for autumnal Kensington Gardens medita-
tions on the Infinite. ("Gray," said Dr. Johnson, most unfairly in
that particular case, "was dull in a new way, and that made people
think him great.")

I believe, however, that the following poem did, years ago,
appear in book form in England. But unfortunately, I possess the
American edition only, and do not know who was the English
publisher, to whom I must apologize for this ignorance.

Plaint before a mob of 10,000 at Owenboro, Ky.

I, Rainy Betha, 22,
From the top branch of race-hatred look at you.
My limbs are bound, though boundless the bright sun
Like my bright blood which had to run
Into the orchard that excluded me.
Now I climb death's tree.

The pruning hooks of many mouths
Cut the black-eyed boughs.
The robins of my eyes hover where
Sixteen leaves fall like a prayer.

Sixteen mouths are open wide,
The minutes, like black cherries,
Drip from my shady side.
Oh, who is the forester must tend such a tree, Lord?
Do angels pick the cherry-blood of folk like me, Lord?

In this beautiful and profoundly moving poem, the boughs of the tree of death, the dark limbs of the martyred boy, are seen as one. The phrase "the robins of my eyes" seems strange at first, but it is exact and real: the poet is speaking of the red congested eyes of the dying boy. As for the lines

Sixteen leaves fall like a prayer
Sixteen mouths are open wide

the sixteen mouths are, of course, wounds and from each wound falls a prayer.

The poets mentioned here are only a few among the many young men of considerable achievement now writing in America.

W. H. AUDEN

How Cruel Is April?

THE DIFFERENCE between any two poets of the same nationality, between, say, Robert Frost and Marianne Moore or William Empson and Dylan Thomas, is immediately obvious and fairly easy to describe, but I very much doubt if it is possible to say what qualities the American or the British pair have in common which they do not share with their cousins, even though a sensitive reader may feel sure that such qualities exist. One can only approach the problem indirectly by asking if there are any experiences peculiar to each country but common to all its inhabitants, irrespective of temperament, occupation, or social status. Anybody who has visited both countries can think of two: Englishmen live in a mild climate of "weather," Americans in a climate of violent extremes; in England there is no primitive wilderness left and no uninhabitable area, but within fifty miles of New York City you can get fatally lost in the woods, and a breakdown of the irrigation system would turn most of Southern California into desert within a few days.

The Arcadian conception of Nature as friendly and humanized is as natural to all Englishmen (except, perhaps, the very poor) as it is incomprehensible to any American. I am quite prepared to be told that the first line of *The Waste Land* is adapted from the French, but I shall continue to think that Eliot's reaction to the fourth month is as American as Browning's is British. In his story "The Domain of Arnheim" Poe describes an American Arcadia, but its construction and upkeep require the total resources of the richest man in the world; in any British detective story the same kind of scenery is within the means of the village curate. In England, even when, as in Thomas Hardy's poem "Yellham Woods' Story," the message of Nature is a stern one, "Life offers—to deny!", her voice is still human and intelligible; she may have read Darwin and Schopenhauer but she is still recognizably Rhea: in the United States she is apt to become either Adams's Dynamo or Melville's White Whale, the inhuman Other against which he must pit his manhood. There are millions of devout Catholics in the States, but I doubt if any of them anticipate a day when there will be pilgrimages to the shrine of, say, Our Lady of Kalamazoo.

American Nature may be numinous, but she is not to be propitiated by prayers or rites, and he who loves her must learn stoically to endure her indifference and not confuse courage with a romantic lack of caution; if she is in a temper he had better arm himself with an unchivalrous bulldozer or hide. The same attitude, Frost suggests in his poem "A Drumlin Woodchuck," is the wisest one for the individual to adopt towards our modern egalitarian society.

All we who prefer to live
  Have a little whistle we give,
And flash, at the least alarm
We dive down under the farm . . .

. . . And if after the hunt goes past
And the double-barreled blast
(Like war and pestilence
And the loss of common sense),

I can with confidence say
That still for another day,
Or even another year,
I will be there for you, my dear,

It will be because, though small
As measured against the All,
I have been so instinctively thorough
About my crevice and burrow.

If America is a land of heat waves, cold waves, tornadoes, droughts, floods, it is also, as a land only half full and half domesticated, still a land of the Open Road, where the openness of the future does not seem wholly dependent on technological advance and political wisdom. It is true that Huckleberry Finn can no longer light out for a Wild West, but he still feels that if today he fails, he can make a wholly new start somewhere else tomorrow; he can remember the past if he likes, but he doesn't have to, and its only meaning to him is its relevance to the present.

Literature of any value cannot, of course, be written without reverence for the past, but an idolatry of the past as past can be equally stultifying, and from that Americans are spared. Her best writers and critics have been able to look at our common literary heritage with a freshness and lack of provinciality that Europeans must envy. The latter may laugh, and rightly, at the anachronisms of Hollywood movies (*Cleopatra:* "Take a letter to Caesar. To Caesar, Rome. Dear Caesar . . ."), but in a country where such things were impossible, the creative use of tradition by such poets as Eliot and Pound, to which Europe owes so much, would probably have been impossible too.

Poetic Background

A PERIOD OF CONSOLIDATION

POETS AND their audience in America, as in other Western countries, form a small group compared with the population as a whole. In the United States this small body has not only grown appreciably in size during the last twenty years, but has gained in insight and what may be called a consolidation of resources. Standards have been established and a new sense of perspective has brought about a new confidence. The situation at present is by no means a completely happy one; drawbacks and frustrations of one kind or another still block the way towards deep and effective accomplishment on the part of poets and complete understanding on the part of their hearers. But in spite of these obstacles it may safely be said that listeners and readers in general, if they are interested in poetry at all, have become interested in the poetry of this century. A time lag that existed far too long and far too generally has been at least partially overcome.

The fact that modern poetry, like modern art as a whole, has become a respectable subject for academic attention and scholarly research has helped to bring about this change. The role of the enlightened amateur is an important one in any society, and it is especially important in a country like the United States, where wide geographical extent produces special kinds of provincialism, and where a sharply marked middle-class insistence on business or professional "success" leads into a tendency to treat the arts either as play or as decoration. Special methods of mass education which have recently sprung up have spread the good and important "cultural" word. To the foreigner there has always been something rather awkward and touching in the American desire for "culture," as well as in the ways and means that Americans have evolved to satisfy this desire. The days of dependence upon the visiting lecturer, the era of passive studies in "appreciation" of this or that, are now on the wane. Poets and critics of proved standing now function as teachers in colleges and universities throughout the land, and the "summer writing conference" has rapidly developed into an educational phenomenon. At these conferences not only the young, but men and women of all sorts of background and vocation now make some effort to write (for the summer conference places emphasis upon "workshop methods") in prose or verse, in direct contact with, and guided by, professionals. Much of this activity takes place in connection with the programs of state universities—in areas, that is, formerly cut off from the life and interests of the larger cities—in those same regions whose provincial complacency and ignorance were not long ago a common target for satirical derision.

For a poet to hold either permanent or temporary tenure as a member of an academic faculty has become usual since the war. Opinion is at present divided, both in academic and literary circles, as to the final use and importance of this new development. Teachers who adhere to the older, historic methods of ordering and presenting information have been known to resent intruders armed with the tenets of "the new criticism"; and fears have been expressed concerning the drying up of individual talents confined to the limits of this campus or that. Can poetry be taught, in any case? While these questions remain unsolved the facts remain: that a large proportion of postwar youth—including the veterans, who proved to be the most serious and diligent of students—has had the opportunity of observing living poets in the midst of working careers. Added to this experience of association, gifted young people have recently been encouraged and rewarded through fellowships (the Fulbright traveling fellowships stemming from government aid have been particularly generous), grants, and scholarships that far exceed any bounties, public or private, previously known. The prizes given to mature accomplishment have also multiplied: the Bollingen Award of the Yale University Library and the Harriet Monroe Award, administered through the University of Chicago, now equal or exceed the Pulitzer Prize in amount and importance; and these prizes in general have, of late years, been given to poets whose claims to them were long overdue.

The advance into this relatively kindly and appreciative intellectual climate has not been easy; frequent and sharp skirmishes have been fought, since the beginning of the thirties, over every inch of now gained ground; and if the public have had their moments of blankness and irritation, the poets themselves have at times seemed clouded in intention and confused in thought. Twenty years ago the pressures of Marxian ideology began to produce eddies in the "creative" atmosphere, and a kind of poetry by means of which one could state and argue convictions was about to be condensed out of the general tension. A kind of sentimental regionalism was also rather prevalent. The older experimentalists —Marianne Moore, William Carlos Williams, and Wallace Stevens —were in print, but critical enthusiasm for these remarkable talents was sparse and grudging. Miss Moore's *Selected Poems,* with an introduction by T. S. Eliot, first published in England in the spring of 1935, appeared in America in the following autumn and found few readers. Mr. Eliot's own *Collected Poems: 1909–1935,* published in the United States in 1936, received a cool welcome from reviewers and the public alike. In contrast, Carl Sandburg's *The People, Yes* (1936) and Stephen Vincent Benét's *Burning City* of the same year—the first a strong "populist" affirmation of the vigor and virtue of "the common man" and the second containing a set of nightmare visions of the imminent collapse of modern civilization—had a marked success.

If certain poets, young and middle-aged, were quickly drawn into a "faith" that seemed to offer a workable solution, in a time of economic depression, for pressing social ills, they were as quickly disillusioned by unexpected shifts in Marxian policy and escaped from the ideological trap as suddenly as they had entered it. Marxist influence began to fall off after 1938, but the brief passage of some American writers through fields of extreme materialist thought was not entirely without positive results. Poets were brought face to face with the grim facts of their period, and many were able to reach and seize upon sections of reality that had heretofore been closed to them. The early poetry of the young British triad of Auden-Spender-Day Lewis, published in America in 1934 and thereafter, contributed new technical means and suggested new subject matter. Auden's influence soon became very strong indeed, and the poetry written during the war years by Karl Shapiro and others was often factual and edged with satire in the early Auden manner.

The history of *The Partisan Review* illustrates how an ultimately valuable liaison between aesthetic and political controversy came into existence, during the process of this magazine's withdrawal from an extreme position. Founded in 1934 with a definite left-wing program, the magazine shifted its policy abruptly in the course of three years, so that by the end of 1937 a new set of editors announced their "independence of doctrinal control." In immediately subsequent years *The Partisan Review* published some of the most interesting writing of the period—British, American, and in translation from European languages—as well as criticism of a high and provocative order. A series of symposia in which writers and "intellectuals" expressed their opinions (political and otherwise) became a feature; and it was to *The Partisan Review* that Eliot sent two sections—"East Coker" and "The Dry Salvages"—of *Four Quartets* for a first American publication. *The Partisan Review* still appears and has kept much of its vitality intact through various erosions of opinion and morale during the war years and shifts of aesthetic and critical bias since. It has been joined by other reviews; the noncommercial *Literary Quarterly* has now become a permanent feature of the American literary scene.

As the 1930's advanced experimental poetry in America went through a rather peculiar set of changes. For although the impulse towards experiment seemed to have come to a natural dead end, certain scattered enthusiasts were determined to keep it alive. The most tenacious champion of the *avant-garde* through the years has been James Laughlin, whose New Directions Press has published modern (chiefly experimental) poetry in quantity, from 1926 to the present. Mr. Laughlin's conviction that literary experiment "is absolutely essential to the healthy evolution of literature" contains an element of truth; and if his choices have shown unevenness in quality, he has without question helped to keep one channel of modern writing open to the future, displaying a great deal of courage along the way. The *avant-garde* received some refreshment after 1936 in a growing enthusiasm for surrealism; a small group of Americans began to echo the beliefs and emulate the practice of Paul Éluard and André Breton. But even this transfusion of new energy was not enough permanently to revivify experimentalism as a whole. By the early 1940's Laughlin was being forced (in a new *Poet of the Month* series), through sheer lack of interesting material, either to reprint traditional poetry that had some bearing on modern taste or to turn to translations. His choices in the first category included, interestingly enough, Herrick as well as Donne, and Rochester and Melville, along with Hopkins; and the translations ranged from Hölderlin, Baudelaire, Rimbaud, and Pushkin through Rilke and Berthold Brecht.

This introduction of European writers through translations was a marked development of the war years and one that persists into the present. The influence of French symbolism was broken through by an interest in two poets of a later period: Rainer Maria Rilke and Federico García Lorca. Translations by Americans—many of poets by poets—ranged back from modern to classical times, and the majority were competent and sensitive. Contemporary French poetry continued to receive attention in versions of Valéry, Apollinaire, and others. Critical appraisals of European poetry have also appeared in some quantity during the past ten years.

The recent increase of critical writing in the United States has drawn the ironic comment of native and foreign observers. Randall Jarrell, himself a poet and critic of the younger generation, recently outlined a situation in which criticism seems to have taken on more importance, in current literary journals, than the creative material with which it deals. It would sometimes appear, Mr. Jarrell points out, that critical articles actually outnumber works of the imagination in these highly serious publications, and that a rather bleak criticism *of* criticism has become usual. There is truth in these remarks, but the reasons for the present seeming surplus of critics and of criticism are less artificial than one might at first suppose. We have noted that the present period, in the field of the arts as a whole, is one of stasis. Owing to the fact that the modern "style" has become the official style, analysis, or even codification of kind and quality, is a natural undertaking at the moment. It is a time of repetition, of formulation, of absorption, of (perhaps excessive) discrimination—a kind of period that, historically, usually follows a highly creative era and precedes a revolt against too firmly established patterns. There is, it is true, little evidence just now of a movement away from current clichés in art and literature, but that such a movement will come is certain.

Meanwhile, in America, some victories may be said to have been permanently won. Poet and audience alike have come, as indicated above, into a new understanding of quality and aims. The line between serious formal poetry and sentimental middle-class verse has been drawn, and there is little likelihood that one will again be completely mistaken for the other. An often delightful flowering of the suburban turns up in light verse, which is now competently written and frequently joins mild satire with a "zany" humor—as in Ogden Nash. A continued diversity in subject and approach, on the formal level, seems to be assured, for the possibility always exists, in America, of paradoxically opposed kinds of temperament existing in the same generation. American writers of the nineteenth century, D. H. Lawrence states in the introduction to his *Studies in Classic American Literature,* "reached a pitch of extreme consciousness . . . without *trying* to be extreme." American poetry at the moment has no Poe, Whitman, or Emily Dickinson, just as American prose lacks a modern counterpart of Melville or Hawthorne, but there is no reason to believe that the tendency towards the excessive is gone for good. In Robinson Jeffers and E. E. Cummings we find remaining traces of the strain; and in Ezra Pound American die-hardism and nonconformity were pushed to tragic limits.

Today young poets writing in English are fully equipped to write about anything, in a variety of manners; the experiment and explorations of their elders have extended both technical flexibility and range of subject. Few poets of the newest generation, however, have been able to grasp and utilize this freedom. There is no doubt that the stiffening mark of writing learned by rule— even by the best modern rule—has begun to show up in the work of young men and women who, in the United States, have passed through English Departments. A kind of graduate school poetry has come into being: well written, beautifully organized, and nicely centered at some "norm" of excellence, but at the same time dead, dry, and without a spark of either feeling or originality. The fading out, in the postwar generation, of the spirit of controversy, the becalming of political and social opinion, has also had its effect. All is not completely standardized, however. Theodore Roethke, who won the Pulitzer Prize in 1954, has recognized that power can be released by an effort to make contact with subconscious processes; and Roethke and others have recently attempted to express the vulgarity and violence usual in modern life—which cannot be approached or utilized in literature except in the simplest and sincerest terms. W. H. Auden of recent years has indicated a method of combating sterility of feeling and shallowness of subject by his revival of the "occasional" poem that makes little demand upon the reader either in form or meaning but celebrates the everyday person and event with appreciative warmth.

The American arts are beginning to feel the effects of a new decentralization in American life. The movement is away from the cities, and even away from the more deadly forms of commercial entertainment. A new feeling for the "region" has become active, shorn of almost all sentimentality; and outlands that at one time were thought to be benighted provinces have begun to enjoy themselves in their own way, on their own terms. The amateur theater, the "theater-in-the-round," the special festivals of the arts, the square dances, the pleasure felt in dressing down and not up —all are manifestations of a break with former hampering conventions. It is all to the good that recordings have been made both officially (by the Library of Congress) and commercially of contemporary poets reading their own poems; that the poetic "little theater" shows signs of vitality; that visiting poets draw large and appreciative audiences (the popularity of the late Dylan Thomas on his coast-to-coast tours is a case in point). It is good for poet and poetic amateur alike to know that Eliot has drawn deeply upon his native sources in his later work, and to have Auden (an American citizen since 1946) functioning as a hard-working teacher and *chef-d'école*. Perhaps a future is within sight when the American poet need no longer feel complete alienation from his society, with the maiming results that such alienation brings. Perhaps a time will come when the poets will again be free of the universities, having given enough training in taste and discrimination to the public at large; when Americans will have become so confident in the rightness of their critical appraisals that they need no longer mistake poetic—or other—geese for swans.

The Three Realms of the Young Poet

THE YOUNG poet in America generally finds three courses open to him, the Bohemian, the journalistic, and the academic, all three of which contain pitfalls for the creative talent. But this is not news. Poetry has always been a dangerous occupation. In America as in England, most poets spring from the respectable middle class of professional and business men. Most of them attend, but —as the careers of Edwin Arlington Robinson and Robert Frost attest—sometimes do not graduate from, institutions of higher learning. Thus far and no farther can they depend at least partially on family support. Thereafter, unless they come from affluent backgrounds, the three ways already mentioned fan out before them.

The rumor that Greenwich Village, the threadbare neighborhood thirty blocks south of Times Square, the forcing house of so much American talent in the twenties, has grown moribund and commercialized is groundless, though it remains true, as it was true in the twenties, that there is an "inner" and an "outer" Village, the Village of the workers and the Village of the poseurs. This is the true Bohemia; and it has extended its dominion through many of the larger cities of America since the Left Bank of the Seine, once Bohemia's world capital, has gone into existentialist deep-freeze. Since the war Mexico, Arizona, and that terribly beautiful part of California inhabited by Robinson Jeffers, Henry Miller, and Kenneth Rexroth have added to its bounds. It is a country mostly inhabited by the young and penurious. How they live from day to day they themselves hardly know, but odd jobs of one sort or another—posing for artists, clerking in bookshops, "bussing" in restaurants, and journalistic work of various kinds— keep them going. More prosperous friends give them handouts at times or allow them to occupy their city apartments when they go north in the summer or south in the winter. They do hack work for Western, detective, and science fiction magazines. Older citizens of this kingdom whose work gives promise of permanence are Kenneth Fearing, Kenneth Patchen, Tom Boggs, and Robert Clairmont. The list might be extended a good deal without gaining much in accuracy; for as soon as a name becomes "known" it acquires a certain aura of respectability and sloughs its Bohemian overtones.

Vachel Lindsay remained a citizen of Bohemia to the end. Carl Sandburg has long since resigned his freehold there. But Bohemia endures partly at least because it represents a still vital tradition in American poetry, the tradition of Walt Whitman. Whether it has been a very fruitful tradition remains a matter of opinion. Geoffrey Moore in his recent Penguin anthology takes on the whole a dim view of it. Yet much of the present rich yield of American verse would have been impossible without it. Hart Crane, for example, was a Whitmanite Bohemian, even to the extent of dispensing with any formal university education and of earning his precarious living as a copywriter in a New York advertising agency. It is true, of course, that his longest and most magnificent poem, "The Bridge," would probably never have been written if Otto Kahn, the New York philanthropist, had not paid Crane's living expenses while he was writing it. Sustained poetry is the fruit of sustained contemplation, and this is generally not possible within the hand-to-mouth purlieus of Bohemia.

Young poets emigrate from this kingdom, marry, and establish a family as soon as they can possibly afford it. Yet money, or the lack of it, is not the only consideration that keeps Bohemia peopled. Whitman himself preferred to dwell there long after he reached comparative affluence (enough, at least, to erect a large and ugly tomb to his own memory). And memory recalls John Wheelwright, a socialist millionaire and poet, camping out in the kitchen of his Beacon Street mansion, insisting that the noblest modern expression of the Jungian mandate was the Red Square in Moscow; the story is told, too, of his address to a meeting of striking workers, which began: "Your main job, gentlemen, is to do away with people like me."

The second kingdom in which the young poet may take up citizenship, that of professional journalism, enjoys more solid respect from the general public, and is perhaps in closer touch with it, than either of the others. It has many ramifications nowadays, including not only newspapers but the whole complex realm of advertising and public relations, script writing for radio and television, Hollywood scenario work, and a whole host of "trade" magazines (boots and shoes, automobiles, etc.), as well as the glossy news magazines, *Life, Time,* and their competitors. The staffs of the superglossy fiction magazines seldom include poets among their number—with the exception of *Harper's* and the *Atlantic,* which cannot afford to pay very much, and the *New Yorker,* which pays so well that its staff members generally cannot afford to go on writing poetry. This second kingdom arouses mistrust. Too many young poets of promise have disappeared into it, become proficient in their specialty, and never been heard from again—mute, widely published Miltons. It might even be argued that journalism is a form of poetry, for it requires every one of the skills and a good deal of the sensitivity to language that poetry requires. It is also true that the modern world as we know it could not exist for twenty-four hours without it. The question is, can we have this and a flourishing poetry, too? Journalism, especially at the higher and more fascinating levels, demands so much and pays so well for the very imaginative gifts that poetry lives by that its citizens retain little time or inclination for the writing of serious verse. There are honorable exceptions. Archibald MacLeish was at one time attached to the staff of *Fortune,* and James Blish, a young poet and critic of considerable promise, writes science fiction and edits a wholesale grocers' magazine for a living.

There remains the third kingdom, a risky, yet, as events have proved, a surprisingly fertile terrain. The American university is not, of course, quite the carefree pleasure dome that jealous and grumpy journalists and Bohemians sometimes imagine it to be. The preparation of lectures, the marking of papers, and active membership on the usual committees consume a surprising amount of time. Karl Shapiro, the editor of *Poetry* (Chicago), who since the war has been associated with university work at Johns Hopkins, the University of Iowa, and Loyola, has expressed more than once the opinion that most of the poetry composed in the universities is written on stolen time. Furthermore, no poet can be very happy in his mind or remain long attached to the staff of a reputable university who does not have a genuine vocation for teaching—quite another thing, after all, from the writing of poetry. How long would Milton have lasted, one wonders, as an instructor of freshmen? And though Shakespeare would no doubt have been popular with the undergraduates, would the dean and the departmental heads have approved?

The marriage between poetry and the American universities remains an uneasy one on both sides; and criticism from Bohemians and journalists without and exact scholars within is not lacking. Yet in the sheer quantity of production of first-rate work it has justified itself remarkably over the past decade. A brief listing of poets together with the colleges to which at one time or another they have been attached is impressive. There are Frost (Amherst), Ransom (Kenyon); Allen Tate (University of Minnesota); Robert Penn Warren (Yale); Theodore Roethke (University of Washington); John Ciardi (Rutgers); Archibald MacLeish and Richard Wilbur (Harvard); John Malcolm Brinnin (University of Denver); Karl Shapiro (Johns Hopkins and Loyola); John Frederick Nims (Notre Dame); Robert Lowell (University of Iowa); Randall Jarrell (University of North Carolina); Winfield Townley Scott (Brown); James Hall (University of Washington); Peter Viereck (Mount Holyoke); and others, many others. Not all the younger American poets are citizens of these three realms. Some, of course, have private means and move above the battle. James Merrill is one of these, one of the most delicate and extraordinary talents to appear in America in recent years. Richard Eberhart is a business executive, and Wallace Stevens was one. Merrill Moore and William Carlos Williams belong to the medical profession. Nevertheless, it seems that more good poetry has come from the universities of America during the last decade than from anywhere else.

Whether the poet-in-residence at the American university results in more student poetry of the first quality may be doubted. Teachers have seen too many of their most promising students swallowed up in advertising, journalism, and public relations to feel any certainty in the matter. The only certainty is that more young people are learning to read poetry with greater insight, pleasure, and discrimination. For many years *Poetry* (Chicago) carried on its back the motto from Walt Whitman, "To have great poets, you must have great audiences too." As usual, Whitman overstated the case. Blake, Hopkins, and Emily Dickinson are witnesses to the contrary. But the wholeness of poetry opposes of its very nature the absolute passions of the passing hour.

> Split the lark and you'll find music
> Bulb after bulb in silver rolled.

The nation that cannot hear its best singers is not only deaf: it is in danger. The lark's song outlasts the lark, but surely whatever facilitates our hearing it serves human freedom.

Thirty Years of Theatrical Enterprise

THE AMERICAN claim to have produced in the last three decades more good drama than any other country usually has appended to it a disquieting footnote. This rich flow of drama, it is pointed out, has had to force its way through the veins of a theater afflicted with an apparently fatal disease.

Three thousand miles from Broadway there is a natural disinclination to take the footnote at its somber face value. We reflect that theatrical health, though sometimes surprisingly good, depends on too rare a set of coincidences, economic, social, and artistic, ever to be good for long. Theaters the world over spend much time on sick beds. Their normal state is to be always dying, but never quite dead. It remains true, nevertheless, that the professional theater of the United States has been in a bad way for a very long time. According to the more pessimistic observers it has never really got over the shocking discovery in 1927 that films could be made to talk. There have been little spurts of recovery as trends regarded as inexorable were checked by war or by other unexpected happenings, but the general decline has gone on, and today—though a particular season may raise some flickers of hope —its dependents and well-wishers are still deeply worried.

There is no doubt that Broadway has had to put up with a great deal. No sooner had the talking film begun to lure actors to faraway Hollywood and turn audiences to mechanical entertainment than the stock market crash came to complete the disaster. The effects of this body blow were more lasting than is commonly supposed. They were hardly spent before the second war enveloped the theater in a heady atmosphere of prosperity that was plainly ephemeral and ultimately detrimental to health. Costs of everything went up at a rate that nobody noticed at the time, and when the customer again became selective it was found that the gamble of financing a Broadway production required the assembly of a whole stable of backers who must be prepared to expect a substantial loss on any run of less than six months. The headlong expansion of television during the first half of 1949, involving an increase in the number of stations to a total of seventy, was perhaps more of a headache for radio and film concerns than for Broadway, but Broadway also was conscious of a painful throbbing in the temples.

Besides these more or less external troubles there are plenty of troubles within the professional theater itself. One diagnostician has found that they have a common basis in greed:

There is the greed of the actors—particularly the stars—who, after being exploited for centuries, have during the past three decades demanded higher and higher salaries, using in recent years the inflated salaries of Hollywood and radio networks as measuring sticks. There is also the demand of playwrights for higher royalties and a larger share of subsidiary (particularly film) rights on their work. There is the appalling and ruthless attitude of the stage hands' and musicians' unions, both of whom have on occasion tied productions in such economic knots that strangulation was the result.

There is scarcely need to dilate on the "crass materialism" of those who have a direct or indirect financial interest in Broadway. The picture is dark enough. And a severely statistical approach to the general theatrical problem is no less discouraging. Today there are only thirty-two theaters in New York. There were more than twice that number twenty-three years ago. Whereas in the twenties there would be usually well over two hundred new productions a season, this figure is now never expected to rise higher than seventy and was as low in 1949–50 as sixty. For the past two years the aggregate losses in Broadway productions have exceeded three million dollars in each season.

The economic health of Broadway would call for less attention if there were any signs that American contemporary drama is yet ready to make a life for itself. There exists almost no professional theater outside New York. The stock companies have dwindled to a handful. There are the road companies that take the Broadway plays through the country, and these also have dwindled. The summer theaters, an unexpected improvisation of the thirties, still do good business. They mostly inhabit permanent buildings, give performances that are only professional in parts, charge fairly high admission prices, and are patronized by well-to-do and more or less sophisticated holiday makers. But many cities, not to mention small towns, never have the chance of seeing a play put on by professional players. Interest in the living theater is largely left for amateurs to maintain.

The amateur movement has grown at a prodigious rate in recent years. There are some three hundred university and civic playhouses, some of them far better equipped than the more old-fashioned houses on Broadway. They do much useful work. They bring plays to audiences that might otherwise see no plays at all. They contribute to the professional stage some actors and even more technicians. Without doubt there is here a tremendous potential force for the reinvigoration of the theater. So far, unfortunately, this force has not found a sense of direction. The amateur theaters in general are even less inclined than Broadway

to experiment; indeed, in many centers anxious thought is given
not so much to serious experimentation as to securing at the
earliest possible release date the latest New York hit. Of the four
hundred productions put on by 126 colleges and universities in a
single year only eleven were original plays, and most of these were
revues. The very flexibility of the up-to-date stages in possession
of these noncommercial organizations has tended to put too great
a stress on the visual appeal of production; and this is having its
influence on apprentice dramatists even in those areas where a
serious effort is made to encourage local writing talent. While
this nation-wide movement, so busy and on the whole so well-
meaning, remains dependent on Broadway all concerned with the
making of contemporary drama must perforce keep watchful eyes
on the fluctuating temperature chart hanging at the bedside of the
perpetual invalid.

However dark may be the future, the American claim to have
produced in the steadily worsening theatrical conditions of thirty
years more good drama than any other country is everywhere
accepted as valid. Whether any of it belongs to the highest order
of art is no part of the claim. That is another question, and the
answer to it must turn on the critical estimate of Eugene O'Neill.
But the flow of plays since the early twenties exacts respect by the
sheer weight and thrust of its theatrical impact. Its sudden beginning took the world by surprise, for the professional theater of
Broadway, however actively and profitably it had employed its pro-
longed nonage, contributed nothing of importance to theatrical
literature till about 1914. By the mid-twenties the names of its
plays and playwrights were echoing clearly across the Atlantic. It is
good now to recall the halcyon days of O'Neill's *All God's Chillun
Got Wings* and *Desire under the Elms,* Elmer Rice's *The Adding
Machine,* Maxwell Anderson's *What Price Glory?,* Paul Green's
The Scuffletown Outlaws, Marc Connelly's and George S. Kauf-
man's *Beggar on Horseback,* Sidney Howard's *The Silver Cord,*
Robert Sherwood's *The Road to Rome,* and Dubose Heyward's
Porgy.

These were plays in many different styles. It was from the first and it has always remained the habit of playwrights of this theater to borrow styles and to depend on individual accomplishment to make the borrowed styles their own. But they were plays that left no doubt that a new and powerful dramatic impulse had been released on to the international stage. Till the end of the thirties this impulse gave no conspicuous signs of exhaustion. The same dramatists continued prolific and adventurous and they were joined by others, such as Clifford Odets, William Saroyan, Lillian Hellman, and Thornton Wilder, with fresh things to say and their own distinctive way of saying them. Yet with all this exciting record of varied achievement the end of the two decades brought a somewhat puzzled sense of disillusionment. It was given judicial expression by Mr. Joseph Wood Krutch, who remarked that

> the surviving corpus of dramatic writing seemed not to justify entirely the sense one has had from year to year that excellent plays were being produced in considerable number. Too many of these plays seem to have fulfilled their function of keeping alive a vital and interesting theater without actually achieving any permanent place in dramatic literature. The "best play of the year" has very often owed its popularity to some novelty of theme or dramatic method which seemed exceptionally interesting at the moment but which failed to remain so for very long, and some of these "best plays" have already been almost completely forgotten.

No doubt much the same thing could be said of any dramatic period that stops short of greatness, but the poignancy of its application to American drama between the wars is that this was a drama that seemed to be always hurrying with powerful strides towards greatness and never getting there.

Eugene O'Neill, from as early as 1914 onwards, led the way, and his leadership was not seriously challenged till the day of his death. "Since 1920," Arthur Miller has said with truth, "American drama has been a steady year-by-year documentation of the frustration of man"; and the frustration to which he refers is that implicit in the victimization of the individual by society. O'Neill must be partly excepted from this generalization. He alone among his contemporaries sought to come to grips with the larger problem of man in relation to God. The problem was always at the back of his mind, and he made several attempts to treat it, but always his radical defects as an artist stood between him and his purpose. The one play in which he might have achieved tragic greatness, *Mourning Becomes Electra,* slipped from his hands to the lower level of psychological drama. He cuts a strange figure in theatrical history. Most of the qualities found in the greatest dramatists are found in one or other of his works, but the missing few are apparently indispensable. He could never adjust his ideas to his medium, asking with restless impatience more from the stage than he could compel it to yield him. He could never wholly carry the conviction that his ideas sprang from something deeper than a mood. And he was so little a master of words that he was prone to fall back helplessly on exclamation marks, leaving again and again scenes of crisis crying out for the clinching expression that he was unable to produce. Some of the power once thought to be in his work is to be felt there still, but its unevenness is more marked. His passing left the theater that he dominated no single play that can be put in the highest class.

This omission his contemporaries among the older American dramatists have often seemed about to make good, but none of them has. Maxwell Anderson's two poetic plays of the early 1930's held great promise, and *Elizabeth the Queen* and *Mary of Scotland* have been followed by much bold experimentation that has interested and often impressed audiences but has largely left the early promise unfulfilled. Clifford Odets raised with *Awake and Sing* and *Golden Boy* hopes that the confused *Rocket to the Moon* and the mixed brutality and triviality of *The Big Knife* have done nothing to satisfy, though *Night Music,* which failed instantly in the theater, haunts the memory with its touching presentment of eager youth baffled by the futility and hopelessness of the times. Elmer Rice has kept his place in the higher ranks, though his plays now inspire more admiration for the skill with which they manipulate techniques new to him than hope that anything big will come of the latest experiment. It is, indeed, the fate of all who made the American drama between the wars and are still writing to feed admiration rather than hope. Hope has turned to Arthur Miller and to Tennessee Williams, the two major playwrights to emerge during the 1940's, and in a lesser degree to William Inge. Miller's reputation rests on three plays. *All My Sons* makes fine indignant melodrama of a father's realization that to make money dishonestly for the sake of his son may be to ruin the life of a sensitive son. *The Death of a Salesman* turns into immensely effective theater the truism that even an unsuccessful salesman ruined by his brash belief in the mystique of salesmanship is a human being. The third is *The Crucible,* a piece that, with more evidence of an outraged political sensibility than of art, dramatizes the witch hunt in Salem at the end of the seventeenth century, leaving audiences to find the contemporary parallels. Miller at his best is a powerful writer, but he seems always in danger of being run away with by his own fierce indignation. Tennessee Williams has so far developed in three of his plays— *The Glass Menagerie, A Streetcar Named Desire,* and *Summer and Smoke*—the theme of the inability of those who live on dreams to stand up to modern America. He has a delicate sense of the pathos of fragile minds; and all these three plays are, for all their sentimentality, based on genuine observation of character. In his more recent plays he has seemed to become less uncontrolled emotionally and to make exorbitant demands on his actors. *The Rose Tattoo,* in its alternately ribald and pathetic passages, is like a design for stage virtuosity, and *Camino Real,* a phantasmagoria of decadence, appears to aspire to a sort of playwriting that will be able ultimately to dispense with words altogether and pass into a condition of feverish mime. William Inge is lighter in weight than either Miller or Williams, but *Come Back, Little Sheba* and *Picnic* have at least the virtue of recommending popular themes to the discriminating. The works of these dramatists are, of course, much hemmed in with musicals. The successful and most of the unsuccessful have one thing in common: they are all musical versions of something else. The more unlikely the source, the greater the esteem in which they are held. But it must be admitted that the attempts to repeat the radiant *Oklahoma!* by copying its formula have become progressively duller.

Part 2. CRITICAL APPRECIATION

Literary Criticism

The Living American Classics

Expressive Voices

The Passing of English Influence

The Southern Revival

Rival Approaches to History

Recollected in Tranquillity

Negro Writing

Literary Criticism

THE MINDS BEHIND THE WRITTEN WORD

IF WE in England go back to American criticism in the nineteenth century at all, it is to Poe and Henry James. Emerson and Lowell, grand figures as they are in the history of American letters, have not so much to offer us, and William Dean Howells, too, is of more interest in connection with American literature. But Poe and James are interesting on the subject of literature itself. They exhibit tendencies that can be traced in American criticism of the present century, for whereas Poe tried to formulate his impressions into general theories and aesthetic principles, Henry James—although he was led at times to make general statements —is chiefly valuable as a critic of delicate and specific personal perceptions. On the whole, it is the Poe example that has triumphed in America, for there seems to be something in the Roman atmosphere of the United States that encourages critics or would-be critics to cry constantly for an ideal method or set of watertight categories.

It is only comparatively recently, however, that this preoccupation with method has become so noticeable. Since the beginning of the present century we have had reason to be amazed at both the variety and the quality of American criticism, and although, to be honest, we do not find ourselves consulting the critics of the first two decades, William Crary Brownell, James Gibbons Huneker, George Edward Woodberry, Randolph Bourne, or even the acid Mr. Mencken very much these days, this is certainly not true of Ezra Pound and T. S. Eliot. It was Mr. Pound more than anyone who was responsible for bringing into modern criticism a most refreshing outspokenness and a refusal to accept the standards and pronouncements of the past unless their relevance and truth could be tested by personal experience and practical application.

Since both he and T. S. Eliot have been read and quoted widely in Britain during the past thirty years, however, it will perhaps be more helpful if we pay more particular attention to those American critics who are important yet insufficiently known or appreciated here. One of these is Joel Elias Spingarn, sometime Professor of Comparative Literature at Columbia University, author of *The New Criticism* and *Creative Criticism*.

The New Criticism (a term now more generally associated with the colleagues and pupils of John Crowe Ransom, who published a book with the same title in 1941) came out in 1911, and in it Spingarn emphasized that it was the poem and not the critic that we ought to be interested in. The impressionistic critics brought us back always to themselves. The historical critics took us "in search of the environment, the age, the race. . . ." The psychological critics deflected our interest to the poet. Purely aesthetic criticism led us into philosophy. Like Goethe and like Carlyle, Spingarn would have us decide what the poet's aim was, and how far, using the materials at his disposal, he has fulfilled that aim. Only Croce, of all the critics of his time, Spingarn found, had kept this aim strictly before him. In his insistence on "the work and nothing but the work" Spingarn can be seen as the forerunner of that school of criticism that insists on the close examination of the "words on the page" and evaluates the poem on this basis—a school that includes, in England, I. A. Richards, William Empson, and F. R. Leavis, and, in America, Mr. Ransom, Mr. Warren, and Mr. Brooks. It is a kind of criticism peculiarly acceptable to our time, since it makes us feel that the critic is being honest and exact. A work of art, we tend to believe, should, if good, stand on its own merits. This method does not, however, as Spingarn thought, demand that we abandon all our other interests. We frequently have to know something about the poet's time in order to discover the connotations of an important word.

We are sometimes interested in the relation a particular work bears to other works and to the age. We are sometimes—as with Shakespeare's tragedies—even interested in noting how well they fit Aristotle's theory of tragedy. Most of us, in fact, are interested in different kinds of approach at different times and find no one method consistently satisfactory. But even though we cannot go all the way with Spingarn we have reason to be grateful to him for bringing our attention back to the thing that matters most, the work of art, and for stating bluntly and clearly what most good critics had already been coming to believe.

There are two figures from among the V. F. Calvertons, the Ludwig Lewisohns, the Granville Hickses, and the Waldo Franks of the twenties and thirties who ought to be singled out. They are Irving Babbitt and his friend Paul Elmer More. Both Babbitt and More were humanists, or, as T. S. Eliot might have put it, their standards were the standards of Christianity with the Christian part taken out. They both believed in the dualism of man's nature and were violently opposed to Romanticism. Wise self-control, they thought, would help man to subdue his animal nature (which led to naturalism) and lead him to the highest. The critic, Babbitt said in *Rousseau and Romanticism,* should judge "by some standard set above both his temperament and that of the creator." More, who was on the whole a more considerable figure, concentrated much more on literature itself. He distrusted and opposed scientific thought—perhaps because he knew only the science of the nineteenth century. He became a Platonist, which was only one step forward from his humanistic ideas, but in the end, unlike Babbitt, he entered the Anglo-Catholic Church. It will be seen how much these two Harvard critics (and particularly More) have in common with T. S. Eliot. They represent only slightly differing facets of the New England mind, More being a sort of halfway point between Babbitt and Eliot.

Of the critics who dominate the American scene today, one of the most outstanding is R. P. Blackmur. A scholar without formal university training, Mr. Blackmur began writing for *Hound and Horn* in the late twenties. He later lectured at the Institute

for Advanced Study at Princeton and is now a Fellow in Creative Writing there. His *Double Agent* came out in 1935, *The
Expense of Greatness* in 1940, and *Language as Gesture* in 1952.
His criticism is a perfect illustration of what Spingarn had in
mind. Here, working with the precision and the trained effort-
lessness of a great athlete, is a powerful and discriminating intelligence brought to bear on the work itself. Only those matters
that arise out of the work itself are considered, and Mr. Blackmur spares himself nothing in his attempt to find out just what
the author intended. In this capacity for taking pains and considering the minutest details he is typical of the majority of American critics and unlike a great many English critics, who are too
often inclined to be impressionistic and to begin an essay with
some such phrase as: "It is twenty years since I read this book,
but if I remember rightly . . ." One is reminded of a well-known
English poet and critic who, at a private literary meeting at one
of the older universities, replied to a searching question with a
disarming smile and the classic remark: "Well, it seems like the
sort of thing that ought to be true." One cannot imagine Mr.
Blackmur ever making a remark like that. He gives the impression of being courteously able and willing to consider whatever
comes his way, and to treat it to the best of his intelligence.

Unlike some other American textual critics, he always makes a
judgment, either directly or indirectly, and so thorough is his examination, so high the standard he sets, and so fascinating the
mind brought to bear on the work that this judgment is always
impressive, even where it is at odds with the personal conviction
of the reader. His criticism of E. E. Cummings is a good example of this. He takes Mr. Cummings's work book by book, poem
by poem, and examines the language. Although he believes that
"words bring meanings to birth" he does not believe that the poet
can attach arbitrary meanings to words and still write well. It is
the meanings that words have acquired during the development of
the language that combine to make connotations. The private experience of the poet must be translated into terms that fully convey the poet's emotion, for without that there is only nebulous

feeling. Mr. Blackmur notes the constant reappearance of Mr. Cummings's favorite word, "flower," and in a withering analysis shows that few of the varying meanings that the poet obviously attaches to the word are conveyed to the reader.

Like his own ideal critic, Mr. Blackmur endeavors to keep himself "in a steady startled state: as if one were about to be haunted: as if one were never to get used to, and hence never to let down, one's powers of vision, one's resources of feeling, and had yet, in such suspense, to judge, to decide—and so to express—the actuality of the job in hand." Since this ability to look freshly at any given piece of work is combined with a quite remarkable (and not merely classical) learning, with wit and with a dry style that expresses the minutest responses of a fine sensibility, the resulting piece of criticism is not only an act of illumination but a work of art in itself. Perhaps this is what has made some people a little shy of Mr. Blackmur. At times he is almost too brilliant, and at times, too, it must be admitted, a little super-Jamesian in the convolutions of his style. He will never have the broad appeal of Van Wyck Brooks, or even of Edmund Wilson. But his difficulty is not the difficulty of Kenneth Burke. He is not esoteric; he has common as well as extraordinary sense, and he never gives the impression that he is parading his knowledge in order to dazzle the reader, or using literature for an extraliterary purpose.

The fact that there is a Burke vogue rather than a Blackmur vogue in the United States at the moment is disappointing but to some extent understandable. Mr. Burke is primarily interested in the writer's imagination, and he uses literature for psychological analysis and for philosophical and sometimes sociological speculations. Mr. Burke's field is "ideas," and since there seem to be far more people in the United States interested in "ideas" than in literature it is Mr. Burke's name that is now on every tongue. It has not always been so, however. A member of *The Dial* circle since the 1920's, Mr. Burke has been publishing in comparative obscurity since 1931. *Counter Statement,* the title of his first book, indicates both his method and his consciousness of his own position. If he undertakes to write of Remy de Gourmont or of André

Gide it is to investigate the supposed effect of de Gourmont's disfigurement and Gide's concern with homosexuality on the direction of their work. In *Permanence and Change* Mr. Burke was concerned with such topics as the "abyss-motive" in Milton, T. S. Eliot, and Hart Crane, the symbol of the mountain in *The Magic Mountain,* and Ernest Hemingway's deliberately incongruous descriptions of violence.

The idea of "perspective by incongruity," in fact, interests Mr. Burke a great deal. It is his term for such phrases as Thorstein Veblen's "trained incapacity" and seems to be connected with his interest in the deliberate iconoclasm and upheaval of the surrealist method. Mr. Burke thinks it should be "deliberately cultivated for the purpose of experimentally wrenching apart all those molecular combinations of adjective and noun, substantive and verb, which still remain with us." In his third and fourth books, *Attitudes Towards History* and *The Philosophy of Literary Form,* Mr. Burke developed his theory of literature as "symbolic action." He categorizes literature under "frames of acceptance" (*e.g.,* Whitman and Emerson) and "frames of rejection" (*e.g.,* Marx and Nietzsche). In between comes what Mr. Burke rather misleadingly terms the frame of the "comic," and his description of it will give the reader some idea of what he is faced with in this critic's style. The "comic" frame of motives shows us

> how an act can "dialectically" contain both transcendental and material ingredients, both imagination and bureaucratic embodiments, both "service" and "spoils." But it also makes us sensitive to the point at which one of these ingredients becomes hypertrophied, with the corresponding atrophy of the other. A well-balanced ecology requires the symbiosis of the other two.

In *The Philosophy of Literary Form* Mr. Burke proposes a distinction between "strategies" and "situations." Literature means the adoption of "various strategies for the encompassing of situations. These strategies size up the situations, name their structure and outstanding ingredients, and name them in a way that contains an attitude towards them." Mr. Burke then develops various

techniques for studying poetic strategies. The "dramatic align-
ment" must be isolated and component "equations" separated out,
associated clusters of words must be noted, and "watershed moments," and, finally, the "differentia" that gives each piece of
literature considered as a symbolic act its intrinsic nature. The
most recent books, *A Grammar of Motives* and a *Rhetoric of
Motives* are part of a trilogy, the third of which is to be *A Symbolic of Motives,* in which the aim is to explore human motives
in life and literature and to relate the two. The metaphor for the
first work is "drama," and the constituent parts are Act, Scene,
Agent, Agency, and Purpose. There is much more to come.

Such tireless ingenuity is magnificent, but it is also monstrous.
We are used to occasional psychological interpretations of literature, which can often (if we make the reservation that they do
not "explain" a poem or novel) be extremely interesting. But Mr.
Burke reduces literature entirely to the level of material for psychological analysis, to a mere biological function. He experiments
with the artist's personality as Pavlov experimented with his dog.
Those things that are intrinsic to literature, the insights and felicities that make it memorable, are treated as secondary. It is prose
"meanings" and the Freudian connotations of words that interest
Mr. Burke, and he reduces us all, the mean and the noble alike,
to the same raw, wriggling mass. If we feel anything for literature at all, we cannot read Mr. Burke without distrust and, very
often, nausea. (He calls Mr. Eliot's well-known play, for example, *"Merdes" in the Cathedral,* or *"ecclesia super cloacam."*)
And yet we cannot help being impressed by the vast, if shapeless
and unco-ordinated, labors of this mind, which for the past thirty
years has been laboring at what is no less than an attempt to explore and to order the whole of human nature. If only Mr. Burke
had never heard of Freud, or better still of literature!

It is a relief to turn from Mr. Burke to those critics who not
only consider that literature can have nobility and dignity (Mr.
Burke considers dignity merely "a subjective adjustment"), but
who also write clearly and well. Some of them are sufficiently

well-known in England by now to need very little comment. Of this number are Van Wyck Brooks, Edmund Wilson, the late F. O. Matthiessen, and Lionel Trilling. Mr. Brooks and Mr. Wilson seem to be despised by the American psychological-methodological school as being, respectively, "biographical" and "interpretative" critics, but they may rest assured—if they need any reassuring—that they will be read in England as long as there are any people who take pleasure in literature itself, rather than in the complexes it may be suspected to reveal. The progress of Mr. Brooks from *The Wine of the Puritans* to *The Opinions of Oliver Allston* is in a sense our own progress from ignorance to understanding of the American literary tradition. We comprehend the slow maturing of his present opinions. But it is perhaps for the series *Makers and Finders*—the latest of which is *The Confident Years*—that we have reason to be most grateful. These entertaining and highly informative studies of the literary background in America have taken us into the American scene as no other books have. With Mr. Brooks we can feel at home in what for so many Englishmen is an unknown country.

Mr. Wilson too, in spite of some anti-British prejudice, has perhaps had as much honor in this country as in his own, mainly because of *Axel's Castle*, which came out in the same year as Mr. Burke's *Counter Statement*. But he has published several other books of criticism since then, the most outstanding of which are *The Triple Thinkers, To the Finland Station, The Wound and the Bow*, and *Classics and Commercials*. Mr. Wilson has the valuable ability to communicate the sense of a cultural pattern and yet not to make extreme claims or fantastic analogies. If he finds it necessary to talk to someone like Vico, he will not throw off the name as if everyone knew, or ought to know, exactly who Vico was and what he said; he will tell us about him, not condescendingly but with subtlety, grace, and clarity, so that even those who already know all about him will possibly find some point of illumination in his remarks. Such critics as Edmund Wilson are vitally necessary in an age such as ours, in which the primary need is not for the correction of taste but for sheer elucidation. Given the whole story, the complete background, we ask leave these days to form our own taste.

F. O. Matthiessen was another "interpretative" critic. *The Achievement of T. S. Eliot, The American Renaissance,* and *The Responsibilities of the Critic* did much to make British readers conscious of the workings of the American literary mind. But perhaps the most outstanding of the "general" American critics today—from an English point of view—is Lionel Trilling, whose *The Liberal Imagination,* published in 1950, came as a delight and a surprise to those who were not familiar with his books on Matthew Arnold and E. M. Forster and who had not read his essays in the *Kenyon* and other reviews.

Mr. Trilling is a good illustration of another difference between American and English critics. English critics seem, in the main, not to be able to consider science or politics or psychology without denying them or being dominated by them. Mr. Trilling has come to terms with them and takes them into account without ever losing his high sense of literary values. Like Mr. Blackmur, but in a more measured way, he makes us feel not merely his brilliance but his essential common sense.

A well-known American critic who, in spite of the number of books he has published, has very understandably not burst on England with such éclat as Mr. Trilling is Yvor Winters. His *Primitivism and Decadence* came out in 1937, *Maule's Curse* the year after, and *The Anatomy of Nonsense* in 1943 (all republished, with an additional essay, under the title *In Defense of Reason* in 1947). Mr. Winters is a moral critic, and he evaluates literature—mainly American literature—in the light of his conviction that there are absolute truths and absolute values. Mr. Winters will have nothing to do with the words-on-the-page technique of the textual critics. He calls for historical and biographical information in order to throw light on the author's mind and method, for the analysis of any literary theories he may hold, for a paraphrase of the poem, for consideration of technique, and, finally, for a judgment taking into account all these things and the general impression that the poem conveys.

Mr. Winters's temper may be conveyed by citing some of the authors he admires. These are: Edith Wharton (whom he considers superior to James because of the precision with which she puts a moral point), Robert Bridges, Thomas Sturge Moore, and Miss Elizabeth Daryush. Some of those he dislikes are W. B. Yeats, T. S. Eliot, and Ezra Pound. Yet Mr. Winters has a clear, logical intelligence. He is worth reading because one knows where one is with him, even if one seldom agrees with his evaluation. It would be tempting to call him the Dr. Johnson of modern American criticism, but the analogy is apt only on a very superficial level, for whereas Dr. Johnson, for all his fierce personal opinions, was secure in the knowledge that his deepest convictions were shared by the society of his day, Mr. Winters cannot be sure of the same thing. Generally speaking today it is only those who know little about literature who attempt to judge it on a purely moral basis. Mr. Winters is therefore a striking and salutary, if exasperating, anachronism, and the American critical scene would be poorer without his bad-tempered fulminations. At least he stirs up controversy and by irritating his confreres into rebuttals helps them clarify their own not quite so well-defined opinions.

If Mr. Winters believes in absolutes, Allen Tate—whose best-known book is probably *Reactionary Essays on Poetry and Ideas* —believes in the absoluteness of poetry. He has a very high opinion of the poet as the creator of order out of chaos, and he does not want poetry to be contaminated by the irrelevant standards of science. He believes that the world of the poet is autonomous. In *Reason in Madness* Mr. Tate emphasized the need for tradition and his distrust of science, romanticism, and humanism, and in his essay entitled "The Present Function of Criticism" he called literature "the complete knowledge of man's experience, and by knowledge I mean that unique and formed intelligence of the world of which man alone is capable." There are very few critics, either in America or in England, who would claim quite so much for literature.

As a Southern critic, Mr. Tate is usually coupled with Messrs. Ransom, Cleanth Brooks, and Robert Penn Warren, and he was associated with them in the editing of *The Fugitive* and *The Southern Review* and in the agrarian symposium *I'll Take My Stand*. Mr. Ransom, the doyen of the group, also dislikes science and romanticism. In *The World's Body* he adapted Mr. Eliot's dictum to fit his own beliefs—"In manners, aristocratic; in religion, ritualistic; in art, traditional." Mr. Ransom does not approve of the moral judgment of poetry; he places his faith in the cultural heritage that he, as a Southerner, feels perhaps more strongly than other Americans. For the rest "each critic must be his own authority." In *The New Criticism,* his study of T. S. Eliot, I. A. Richards, and Yvor Winters, Mr. Ransom called for a criticism that would concern itself with technique, with structure, with the text itself, with, in fact, the sort of thing that Dr. Leavis had been insisting on in England and that Mr. Ransom's colleague Cleanth Brooks had so successfully demonstrated in his *Modern Poetry and the Tradition* and showed again later in *The Well-Wrought Urn*.

Mr. Brooks is in many ways the most attractive of the Southern critics. He is vehemently against the idea that there is any set body of subjects that are properly "poetic." He is an especial champion of the metaphysical poets and can appreciate and expound the quality of wit better than most critics. Like Mr. Ransom, he is very much against the idea that there is a specific "truth" or message embedded like a plum in the poem. He cannot be called an original critic, but he has applied the methods inherent in the work of I. A. Richards, F. R. Leavis, and William Empson to areas that these critics have not covered. If there is a paradox or an ambiguity within striking distance Mr. Brooks will strike it, and his diligence and intelligence in dealing with such poems as "Sailing to Byzantium" have revealed treasures even for those who imagined they already appreciated the poem to the full. With Mr. Warren he has applied his methods very successfully to the elucidation of literature for college and university students, and their *Understanding Poetry* and *Understanding Fiction* are models of what is now called "explication."

There ought finally to be mentioned—of at least a dozen calling for comment—the names of Alfred Kazin, Harry Levin, and Richard Chase, all of whom are outstanding in their detailed appreciations of individual authors, and also those young and not quite so young critics now publishing in the *Kenyon, Sewanee, Hudson, Partisan,* and other reviews. To pick up one of these magazines is to be at once delighted and confounded—delighted by the skill of the writing and confounded by the fact that we have nothing to equal them in this country. To some extent their columns have been invaded by the jargon critics, of whom Mr. Burke is not by any means the worst example; but on the whole the contributors to these magazines, though writing for an extremely specialized audience, do so with a refreshing lack of ceremony as well as a remarkable depth of insight. One thinks of Delmore Schwartz and Philip Rahv, who are most often seen in the *Partisan Review,* Arthur Mizener, who in *The Kenyon Review* had the courage to tell Marianne Moore (a present deity) that her translations were bad—and prove it—and Randall Jarrell, the best of whose articles over the past few years were recently collected in *Poetry and the Age.*

This book, second only to R. P. Blackmur's in the quality of its response to modern American poetry, is in the best tradition of American criticism—urbane, witty, intuitive, written from a broad cultural background, and above all sensible, giving the reader the impression that the critic has looked clearly and originally at his subject matter and has not been afraid to say exactly what he thinks. Mr. Jarrell is in the tradition of Henry James rather than of Poe. It would be pleasant to think that his example might encourage other young critics in America.

The Living American Classics

IN THE search for those qualities that go to make the typical American, both native and foreign observers, and indeed the American people themselves, have been inclined to concentrate their detective powers on two aspects of American life, the physical and the sentimental. On the one hand it is American comfort, American economic and military might, and the ever wonderful ingenuity of the Americans that give the native cause to crow and the foreigner cause to gasp. On the other hand it is such traits as American idealism, generosity, and hospitality that force adulation even from the most reluctant Europeans and make eager patriots swell with pride.

There is, in any nation, a third aspect of national life: the national mind—national intellectual and artistic achievement—and it is from consideration of this part of American life that we in Europe have learned many of our doubts about American stability. Indeed, if Europe is skeptical of America's powers of leadership—and it undoubtedly is—then the skepticism springs, in part at least, from our poor opinion of American cultural achievement. Europe has the feeling that, in 180 years of opportunity (350 if one includes the colonial period), America has produced fewer great artists and philosophers than many a small European country, fewer than Sweden, for example, or Switzerland. Such creative leaders as have appeared in the United States—so runs European comment—have either, like Professor Einstein and Mr. Auden, arrived in America for the sake of their physical comfort, or else, like Henry James and Mr. Eliot, have been forced to desert America for the sake of their mental health. In fact, America has produced little that is both worthwhile and indigenous, and has sacrificed much of the little to her own folly.

The comment is, of course, an exaggeration, and is based as much on ignorance as on reality. In considering the European, and particularly the British, response to American cultural influences, lack of knowledge must be taken into the equation. If American literature, American music, the American fine arts, or for that matter American religion, is used as an expression of the American mind, then the x of ignorance is a powerful factor. Until the last few years the number of American writers, for example, whose names were what is called household words in Britain could be counted on the fingers of one hand. Writers of the colonial period, with the one possible exception of Benjamin Franklin, we in Britain have never known, and even the exception is of doubtful validity, for Franklin's fame hardly includes his authorship. Jonathan Edwards, that most untypical champion of Puritanism, had his moment of influence over Scottish Presbyterians, but the growth of antipathy to severe Calvinism has deprived him of posthumous power and has at the same time, but far less justifiably, taken from him the reputation that he deserves, for his lucid, compact, and eloquent style. Anne Bradstreet is unknown except as a footnote to the works of du Bartas, Herbert, and Spenser, her simple grace stilted by the academic habit that is forced upon her. The discovery in 1937 at New Haven of four hundred pages of unpublished poetry after the fashion of Crashaw or Quarles seems to have passed almost unnoticed in Britain, and even the name of America's finest poet of the seventeeth and eighteenth centuries, Edward Taylor, is virtually unknown on this side of the Atlantic.

Though literature is in analysis more permanent than revolution, it is as revolutionaries and not as authors that Jefferson, Jay, Madison, and Hamilton have entered the European consciousness. And in this at least the European judgment is correct, for, certainly until the middle of the nineteenth century, the great thinkers of America devoted their energies to developing organization and ideal rather than theory and idea; the outstanding achievements of the American people were in practical and American politics. Even John Marshall was an organizer first and a jurist, in the philosophical sense, only for his own delight. When transcendentalism gripped the minds of Europeans it lured them away from public affairs. Channing, Bronson Alcott, Theodore Parker, Emerson, even Thoreau were notorious for their urgent and much-proclaimed desire to right social wrong, and it is significant that the one book produced by the American transcendentalists that was, and still is, regarded as a classic in Britain is a description of an escape from social responsibility. *Walden,* for all its discursiveness, contains a close-knit and universal argument for a rebellion against the conventional pattern of social organization.

From the experience that British taste has fixed to early American literature certain generalizations are possible as to what makes an American book "live" in Britain. It must not be too derivative, and it must be able to stand in comparison with European equivalents. For this reason Washington Irving has been stripped and now stands revealed, without his careful corseting of long outmoded and imitative style, a flabby and unworthy heir to German and Abbotsford Gothicism, and for this reason the American transcendentalists could not long hold favor with a public brought up on Coleridge or Kant. But, at the same time, the American book must not be concerned, to the exclusion of all else, with problems that seem peculiarly American.

Thus James Fenimore Cooper, whose social criticism was always tolerant and usually well-written and perspicacious, has become for most of us a one-book author, and his work, once admired by critics as far apart as Balzac and Karl Postl, is now represented by *The Last of the Mohicans* on the same nursery shelf that contains the books of Henty, Ballantyne, Percy F. Westerman, and Baroness Orczy. At such a level it is possible to attain and maintain classic proportions by narrative skill. The other four novels of the Leatherstocking series, like *The Spy* and *The Pilot,* have moments of excellent description and some magnificent characterization; Natty Bumppo, particularly in *The Deerslayer,*

belongs with Huck Finn and Captain Ahab among the great characters of American fiction. But only in *The Last of the Mohicans*
is the excitement of the action unbroken by miserably stilted dialogue, and only in *The Last of the Mohicans* does Cooper succeed in drawing minor characters who can live in the same world
as his heroes. Consequently Cooper, who set out deliberately to
engineer the Americanization of the American novel, built instead
—and almost by accident—for this one book a permanent place
among boyhood classics.

Hawthorne, the first American to be flattered by inclusion in
the English Men of Letters series, has suffered a fate very like
Cooper's, but whereas *The Last of the Mohicans* flourishes in the
schoolroom atmosphere Hawthorne's "pale flowers that blossomed
in too retired a shade" wither and die because he, who told a
story badly, is made to serve as storyteller, because the symbols
that are the true strength of his work go all untended, and because his two principal themes—isolation and reunion—are too
vital for schoolroom exposition. Nominally *The Scarlet Letter* and
Twice-Told Tales are among the living American classics, both
are still found on many British bookshelves, and the Hawthorne
cult, which, in America, has succeeded to the Melville cult, may
yet follow its predecessor across the Atlantic, but still for us Hester
Prynne, Arthur Dimmesdale, the Pyncheons, and Donatello live
only in the suburbs of the city peopled with the great characters
of classical fiction.

Books live not by their literary quality alone, and the bargain
basements of literature have sold more "classics" than the respectable stores. *Uncle Tom's Cabin, Little Women,* and "Hia-
watha" seem destined for a permanent place both in the British
and the American repertoire, while even the greatest writers are
often held in affection for works that are hardly worthy of their
authors. Poe was a considerable poet; his verse is now less read
than analyzed. In his lifetime he was most respected as a critic;
his criticism is now for the most part decently reserved for the
pleasures of pedants; his much-proclaimed standards were limited
standards; his principles now seem to have been designed to prove

that there are few supreme artists, but that one of them is Edgar Allan Poe. Yet as a writer of short stories Poe almost lived up to his own conceit. There was shrewdness in his use of Gothicism —horror sold well in 1840 as in the 1950's—but "Ligeia," "The Cask of Amontillado," and "The Fall of the House of Usher" have seldom been surpassed as short stories. But Poe's position among the classics is secured in the bargain basement. "The Murders in the Rue Morgue," "The Mystery of Marie Roget," "The Gold Bug," and "The Purloined Letter" are all good short stories; they are indeed among the best of detective stories, because criminals and detectives alike are human beings with human motives and not merely expressions of the author's cleverness; but the fact remains that Dupin is a genius in a profession that convention has peopled with near-morons acting like genius, and Poe is now much read because he invented a detective. Precedence in this field has done more for his fame than ability in fiction, poetry, or criticism.

In recent years Herman Melville has been edited, re-edited, psychoanalyzed, commented upon, subjected to all the battery of critical tricks that go with rediscovery. Yet, for Britain at least, and for one book, Melville had needed no revival. *Moby Dick* sweeps aside all chauvinism and convinces us of the value of American literature. It is only part of Melville; without the whole of his work it is impossible to appreciate his place in the American war of independence against European cultural domination. But a sense of the classic is independent of literary history and independent of origins or influences; it is *Moby Dick* that lives. All the rest of Melville's achievement, the desperate struggle to achieve perfection demonstrated by the earlier books, the faltering success of *Pierre,* and (after Melville's twenty years of bitter silence) the fineness of *Billy Budd,* seem to suffer with time from the damning fact that a writer who writes a masterpiece can never write an ordinary good book without its being judged as something less than ordinary.

American authors before Melville's generation must be judged by European standards, and by those standards most of them seem midgets. After Melville many Americans use a philosophical idiom that is to Europe foreign. Melville belonged to a phase in American history when America was to itself complete, but when Europe was still part of the completeness. Some of his American contemporaries have held the affection of Europe because they turned an essentially European eye upon an essentially American circumstance; few books translate to European readers the supreme significance of that supreme fact in American life, the Frontier, so successfully as Francis Parkman's historical cycle and his superb adventure story, *The Oregon Trail*. Some of his contemporaries and near contemporaries, like Prescott, Motley, and Henry Adams, turned an essentially European blind eye on all things American, and thus have become part of European rather than American literature. Melville, like Parkman, was obsessed with the notion of completeness. He too looked out to the Frontier, but saw it not as the geographical setting for an historical sequence, nor yet as a symbol of the struggle for America and Americanism; his frontier was on the seas and his symbols for all mankind and all time.

In this *Moby Dick* is more secure with time than even *Leaves of Grass,* for Whitman protested his Americanism so often and so violently that the protest convinces, becomes a principal theme of the poems for many readers, and so reduces the true value of the poetry. Nationalistic self-consciousness is but a petty trait in a poet; Whitman was far greater, far more concerned with the universal than his pretense would allow. *Leaves of Grass* is a classic, not because Whitman saw himself as the arch-priest of Americanism, nor yet because he imagined that Americanism was the apotheosis of man's achievement, but because, in his wisdom, he could but realize by what awful lapses America had fallen from its ideals—and if America, then also the rest of the civilized world. It is Whitman and not Thoreau who is the great American critic of the civilized life, Whitman and not the expatriates who is the great American critic of America.

There remains for consideration at least one American author of the nineteenth century—essentially American and essentially nineteenth-century—who, perhaps, of them all is the only one who in the twentieth century and even outside America can be certain of finding his way for more than one book into any list of living literature. Mark Twain, in his lesser books, was the American as the American loves to know himself: energetic, uninhibited, and inventive. The accents of Britain give those words a different sound, and for us the Mark Twain of *Innocents Abroad* is bustling, brash, and a most awful liar, thus comfortable to British prejudices. *Tom Sawyer* and *Huckleberry Finn* are set in a place undeniably American and seem to be created out of the rich mine of American mythology, but the permanence of these two novels depends (even for Americans) upon something more vital. In them Mark Twain sees through the eyes of youth and creates, for youth, a mythology that is universal. *Huckleberry Finn,* above all, is the book for youthful reading underneath the bedclothes, the book that parents confiscate—and then reread.

Judged for classic achievement few national literatures can produce many representatives; judged by such standards, America can show nothing in drama and little in poetry. But, from a nation that was in its first centuries absorbed inevitably with the problems of survival and expansion, the American record in creative literature is by no means poor. Prejudice has stood between American authors and cisatlantic prestige; those who have climbed the barrier can move freely and without shame in any congregation.

Expressive Voices

THE EMERGENCE OF A NATIONAL STYLE

THE FIRST question the term "American style" provokes is doubtless the same retort that was raised as late as forty or fifty years ago by the phrase "American literature" itself: "Is there one?"

Which in turn raises further questions: Is there an English style? A French, a German, an Italian? Forty years ago the English author of a short study of French literature attempted in his closing sentences an inclusive formula. Seeking to define the "essential spirit" of that literature, Strachey proposed its "devotion to truth," its "love of rhetoric," its "clarity," its "generalizing power," all of which he believed to be "truly its own," only to find that there was another quality "which controls and animates all the rest":

> The one high principle which, through so many generations, has guided like a star the writers of France, is the principle of deliberation, of intention, of a conscious search for ordered beauty; an unwavering, an indomitable pursuit of the endless glories of art.

The generalization is wide enough to apply without much question to Racine, Molière, La Fontaine, Voltaire, Chénier, Flaubert, Mallarmé, Valéry, Gide, and a long line of other masters, and few will resent its broad validity. But are we sure it applies to Rabelais, to Chateaubriand, Balzac, and Zola, to Hugo and George Sand, to Lautréamont, Rimbaud, and Apollinaire, to Claudel, or to Jean Genet? How many of these can be called with any fitness exponents of deliberation, of controlled intention, of consciously ordered beauty? Foreigners often describe Russian literature in terms that Russians themselves find close to parody; and we have only to attempt a similar simplification of English literature, not only in its entirety but in any given century, to realize the difficulty, perhaps the futility, of the effort. It is a task that three hundred years of American writing makes no easier today.

Nevertheless, and in spite of the great number of factors and derivations—racial, linguistic, religious, literary, perhaps even physical and climatic—that have gone into the shaping of the American character, the adjective "American" will always be made to do duty as a label and shibboleth. That appears to be its special historic destiny. No temporary disappointment, no discouraging regression, seems to prevent most Europeans from expecting the American nation to live up to what she promised to be in her first years of settlement and independence—the ideal or model of an ancient Western hope: the promise scrutinized by Burke, Tocqueville, Bryce, and D. H. Lawrence, and declared in the radical American scriptures themselves, all the way from Franklin, Jefferson, and the founding fathers, through Emerson's "Nature" and "The American Scholar," Cooper's novels, Whitman's *Leaves of Grass* and *Democratic Vistas,* to such later sermons as Van Wyck Brooks's *America's Coming of Age* and Ezra Pound's *Patria Mia.* Equally, no amount of complexity, hybridizing, or sophistication in American writing seems to discourage the foreign reader—or, of course, the American—from expecting an American book or poem to speak with a recognizable American voice.

That expectation has generated an extensive line of native apologetic. Whitman's, echoing Emerson's in "The American Scholar," is doubtless the most celebrated:

> Swiftly, on limitless foundations, the United States too are founding a literature. . . . The lists of ready-made literatures which America inherits by the mighty inheritance of the English language . . . have made, and still continue to make, magnificent preparations for that other plainly signified literature, to be our own, to be electric, fresh, lusty, to express the full-sized body, male and female—to give the modern meanings of things. . . . Of course we shall have a national character, an identity. As it ought to be, it will be. That, with much else, takes care of itself, is a result, and the cause of greater results.

Henry James's view of the case is perhaps less familiar. The character Darcy, who speaks for him in the dialogue called "An Animated Conversation" (*Essays in London*), answers the question, "Haven't we a right to have a language of our own?" by asserting:

> It is inevitable. . . . A body of English people crossed the Atlantic and sat down in a new climate on a new soil, amid new circumstances. It was a new heaven and a new earth. They invented new institutions, they encountered different needs. They developed a particular physique, as people do in a particular medium, and

they began to speak in a new voice. They went in for democracy, and that alone would affect—it *has* affected—the tone immensely. *C'est bien le moins* (do you follow?) that that tone should have had its range and that the language they brought over with them should have become different to express different things. A language is a very sensitive organism. It must be convenient—it must be handy. It serves, it obeys, it accommodates itself.

What T. S. Eliot and Wallace Stevens have lately said on this score echoes these earlier claims: Mr. Eliot when, in his introduction to *Huckleberry Finn,* he said of "the consistency and perfect adaptation of the writing" that "This is a style which at the period, whether in America or in England, was an innovation, a new discovery in the English language. Other authors had achieved natural speech in relation to particular characters . . . but no one else had kept it up through the whole of a book. . . . In *Huckleberry Finn* there is no exaggeration of grammar or spelling or speech, there is no sentence or phrase to destroy the illusion that these are Huck's own words"—this appearing in turn to echo or apply to what Mr. Eliot said long ago in *The Sacred Wood* in a criticism of Swinburne: that the language important to us is "that which is struggling to digest and express new objects, new groups of objects, new feelings, new aspects, as, for instance, the prose of Mr. James Joyce or the earlier Conrad." And when Wallace Stevens, a poet far removed from the vernacular or popular tradition, replied to a questionnaire from England several years ago, he made the point even more directly:

At bottom this question is whether there is such a thing as an American. If there is, the poems he writes are American poems. . . . Would you be likely to mistake *Leaves of Grass* for something English? "Snowbound" is a typical American poem. The poems of *Leaves of Grass* are typical American poems. Even if a difference could not be found in anything else, it could be found in what we write about. We live in two different physical worlds and it is not nonsense to think that that matters.

The tenet assumed by these statements is clear. There is an American experience, an American character. They have expressed

themselves in an American language and an American style. They
issue from a complex historical process of emigration, assimilation, physical adaptation and climatic adjustment, institutional
bents and habits, the absorption of a great number of racial,
ethnic, and linguistic strains to a native mode of speech and expression, with a consequent re-creation of sensibility and an effort, unconscious as much as conscious, to "digest and express"
a new form and mode of life in the words, cadences, and inform-
ing spirit of the language.

That the language itself is involved in this process is inevitable.
H. L. Mencken's immense exploration of its growth in the four
editions of *The American Language* and its two bulky supple-
ments provides a chapter of linguistic history to which a horde
of scholars have devoted themselves. It is exhaustively documented
in Sir William Craigie's and Professor Hulbert's great dictionary
of American English; and English observers have admitted the
growth as vital to the future of the tongue—Robert Bridges and
Bernard Shaw as much as Virginia Woolf ("The Americans are
doing what the Elizabethans did—they are coining new words.
They are instinctively making the language adapt itself to their
needs. . . . It is significant that when we want to freshen our
speech, we borrow from American. . . . All the expressive, ugly,
vigorous slang which creeps into use among us, first in talk, later
in writing, comes from across the Atlantic.")

What especially distinguishes the phenomenon and makes it,
even today, the cause of so much contention, is the first fact about
it: the American language and literature have their immediate ancestry in English. No other European parent has bred so large a
progeny, or a more intractable and physically estranged one—not
France and French with their offshoots in Belgium and Canada,
not Germany in the satellite literatures of Austria and Prague, not
even Russia in the more complex but still contiguous provinces of
her empire. No admixtures from other European countries, no
blend of bloods and temperaments, no assimilation of aboriginal,
Indian, Negro, Mexican, or Oriental strains, can minimize the fact

that the American language is English before it is anything else, that the dominant influences on American style have been English influences, and that there has always existed both a consciousness of that source and all the resistance of a rival culture to it. No two other literatures using the same language have ever existed in so lively a state of attraction and rivalry.

Yet it is equally obvious that, whatever we mean by American character, literature, style, have become something as radically different from those of England as the American accent differs from the English. Edmund Wilson has asked how have the

> different rhythm and tempo of American speech, how have the different values given the English vowels, affected the writing of poetry? And how is it that the prose styles of writers so different as, say, Mark Twain, Henry James, and Dreiser are all, in their several ways, modes of expression characteristically American which could never have been produced by the English?

He believes that "two things, certainly, would be plain from such a study": first, that "at a time when prose style in England was growing more and more ornate and elaborate . . . American prose was reverting to something more like the colloquial directness of the seventeenth century" ("it would be impossible," he thinks, "to bring the language of literature any closer to the language of ordinary talk than has been done by Mark Twain and his successors"); and, secondly, that "another feature of our literature has been its readiness to resort to other sources. . . . Our culture is polyglot in its elements: in spite of the English basis of our language, we are culturally almost as close to other European countries as to England."

Once we admit these arguments in even a general way (they have formed the basis of the modern movement in American writing that dates from around 1912); once we admit that the experimental impulse in contemporary American writing has coincided with an almost universal tendency to renovate the language and modes of literature in the twentieth century; once, moreover, we reject Arnold's claim of a monolithic English heritage and accept the existence of the American "voice," an American style, the question becomes: Where do we find these?

This is where the problem becomes formidable. Is it in the plain man's speech of Franklin? In the fluently oracular discourse of Emerson? In Hawthorne's carefully designed, elegantly homely sentences, or in Cooper's clumsy persistence? In Emily Dickinson's angular eccentricity, or in Whitman's dithyrambic, solemnly fraternal, strenuously polyglottic oratory? In Mark Twain's instinctive casualness and realism, or in Henry James's rich and complex assimilation of English and French qualities to those consciously native and earthy elements that permitted Constance Rourke to devote a chapter to him in her *American Humor,* where he kept company with Mark Twain, Artemus Ward, and the frontier buffoons?

Or, to come down to more recent cases, is it in Stephen Crane's scalpel-like precision, or in Dreiser's cumbrous, Germanic, ponderously Zolaesque strain of personal honesty that could admit so many spurious "philosophical" and pseudo-scientific adulterations? In Sinclair Lewis's racy journalese, or in Scott Fitzgerald's lyric honesty? In Willa Cather's lucid shapeliness, or in Faulkner's tumid density of language and historical sensibility? In Hemingway, Gertrude Stein, Dos Passos, James T. Farrell? In Katherine Anne Porter or Carson McCullers? Or—arriving at the more complex sphere of modern poetry—in continuators of the Whitman tradition like Lindsay, Masters, Sandburg, and MacLeish, or in strongly intellectual, Europeanized, and yet insistently American poets like Ezra Pound, John Crowe Ransom, Hart Crane, Allen Tate? In Marianne Moore's subtle adaptations of prose process and idiom, or in the lyric manners, now rhetorical, now "metaphysical," now closely schooled and disciplined, of Edna St. Vincent Millay, Elinor Wylie, Léonie Adams, and Louise Bogan? Or in that latest generation of poets—Lowell, Jarrell, Schwartz, Roethke, Eberhart, Wilbur—who, with an inevitable clue from Auden and a large consciousness of European experiment, have tried to assimilate all they learned from Eliot, Pound, and the stylistic radicals to new modes of personal sincerity and realism?

Some of the writers named are certainly not American in any easily identified sense. Some of them have deliberately schooled themselves in European models. Merely to name them is to realize the condition of diversity at which the American style has arrived, a condition virtually equivalent to the tradition-riddled, restlessly experimental, personally and historically distracted condition of modern writing itself. It is inevitable that American literature, even more than English, should be the exponent of that condition. The susceptible, responsive character of American life throughout its history has been, even in the face of its strenuous efforts at self-determination, the reflector of the enormously diverse forces that have shaped it. The reluctance (not invariably successful) of American writers to tolerate literary "rules" or dictators has had its cognate in this equivalent eagerness to welcome every possible style and manner that has offered itself for their use. Whether a common denominator can be found in their work is a problem that has baffled more than one critic and historian. But the effort to find it persists, and any serious student of American literature must make it.

Any effort of this kind must cut boldly across the lines and conventions of literary form. It must, necessarily, simplify. It must above all tune itself to those basic tones and qualities in writing that are perceptible only to a native ear. The attempt would be easiest if applied to the explicit kinds of native expression that appear in dialogue, dialect, slang, the oddities, jargons, and neologisms of folk speech. But to put these in evidence would make the task too easy, and in a sense misleading. It is not by diction or dialect, but by the whole complex of sensibility, cadence, rhythm, and structure that authentic style is arrived at. Any demonstration, even a tentative one, must come down to concrete cases. The following are taken from fiction:

(1) Two or three days and nights went by; I reckon I might say they swum by, they slid along so quiet and smooth and lovely. Here is the way we put in the time. It was a monstrous big river down there—sometimes a mile and a half wide; we run nights, and laid up and hid daytimes; soon as night was most gone, we stopped

navigating and tied up—nearly always in the dead water under a towhead; and then cut young cottonwoods and willows and hid the raft with them. Then we set out the lines. Next we slid into the river and had a swim, so as to freshen up and cool off; then we set down on the sandy bottom where the water was about knee-deep, and watched the daylight come. Not a sound anywheres—perfectly still—just like the whole world was asleep, only sometimes the bullfrogs a-clattering, maybe.

(2) A man stood upon a railroad bridge in northern Alabama, looking down into the swift water twenty feet below. The man's hands were behind his back, the wrists bound with a cord. A rope closely encircled his neck. It was attached to a stout cross-timber above his head and the slack fell to the level of his knees. Some loose boards laid upon the sleepers supporting the metals of the railway supplied a footing for him and his executioners—two private soldiers of the Federal army, directed by a sergeant who in civil life may have been a deputy sheriff. At a short remove upon the same temporary platform was an officer in the uniform of his rank, armed. He was a captain.

(3) None of them knew the color of the sky. Their eyes glanced level, and were fastened upon the waves that swept toward them. These waves were of the hue of slate, save for the tops, which were of foaming white, and all of the men knew the colors of the sea. The horizon narrowed and widened, and dipped and rose, and at all times its edge was jagged with waves that seemed thrust up in points like rocks. . . . As the boat bounced from the top of each wave, the wind tore through the hair of the hatless men, and as the craft plopped her stern down again the spray slashed past them. The crest of each of these waves was a hill, from the top of which the men surveyed, for a moment, a broad tumultuous expanse, shining and wind-driven. It was probably splendid. It was probably glorious, this play of the free sea, wild with lights of emerald and white and amber.

In these three specimens, all written before 1900, a certain process can be seen at work. In the first and most famous the break with formal diction and convention is outright. A native voice is speaking. The structure is relaxed, instinctive, uninhibited. No single literary phrase or turn is allowed. The language is directed wholly by physical sensation and instinctive cunning. A rhythmic principle operates, but it operates at the simplest possible level of intimacy and communication. On closer scrutiny one sees in the placing of the "ands," the shrewd use of grammatical crudities, the enhancement of poetic suggestion through vulgarisms and local allusions, that a balance is being struck between uncensored realism and literary craft. In the second example this balance reappears, but it is much more highly calculated. The sentences are still mostly simple, but they are more obviously plotted. The laconic tone is braced by several formal terms: "closely encircled," "supplied a footing," "at a short remove." We are being prepared for something momentous in studiedly objective language, and the dramatic irony that will be the story's chief point is anticipated in the detachment with which a violent occasion is put before us. In the third quotation the sentences are still declarative, simple in structure, and the words are again braced firmly against any suspicion of formality or artifice. Again a laconic objectivity is aimed at. But from the first phrase to the last a heightening is at work, a calculated sense of drama, an underlining of dramatic as well as verbal irony that leads from the opening sentence to the grim, half-rhetorical desperation of "probably splendid," "probably glorious," at the end. Though the passage bristles with resistance to literary mannerism, such mannerism has nevertheless taken charge, introducing an extreme consciousness of effects into direct sensory reporting, and resulting in a kind of writing that is stylistically self-conscious in every syllable.

In the first quotation, by Mark Twain, a whole tradition of rhetoric, rhetorical method, and instructed effect—the tradition of Melville, Hawthorne, James—is rejected in favor of the simplest prose naturalism. In the second, by Bierce, this naturalism, though still insisted on, has become objective, toughened, reportorial. In the third, by Stephen Crane, it has become calculated, heightened, stylized, complicated by poetic intention and dramatic casuistry, even while it insists on its realistic basis. That this development was to be further disciplined in the twentieth century can be seen in what followed:

(4) The tradesmen of Bridgepoint learned to dread the sound of "Miss Mathilda," for with that name the good Anna always conquered.

The strictest of the one-price stores found that they could give things for a little less when the good Anna had fully said that "Miss Mathilda" could not pay so much and that she could buy it cheaper "by Lindheims."

Lindheims was Anna's favorite store, for there they had bargain days, when flour and sugar were sold for a quarter of a cent less for the pound, and there the heads of the departments were all her friends and always managed to give her the bargain prices, even on other days.

Anna led an arduous and troubled life.

Anna managed the whole little house for Miss Mathilda. It was a funny little house, one of a whole row of all the same kind that made a close pile like a row of dominoes that a child knocks over, for they were built along a street which at this point came down a steep hill. They were funny little houses, two stories high, with red brick fronts and long white steps.

(5) An old man with steel-rimmed spectacles and very dusty clothes sat by the side of the road. There was a pontoon bridge across the river and carts, trucks, and men, women, and children were crossing it. The mule-drawn carts staggered up the steep bank from the bridge with soldiers helping push against the spokes of the wheels. The trucks ground up and away heading out of it all and the peasants plodded along in the ankle-deep dust. But the old man sat there without moving. He was too tired to go any further.

It was my business to cross the bridge, explore the bridgehead beyond, and find out to what point the enemy had advanced. I did this and returned over the bridge. There were not so many carts now and very few people on foot, but the old man was still there.

(6) In sleep she knew she was in her bed, but not the bed she had lain down in a few hours since, and the room was not the same but it was a room she had known somewhere. Her heart was a stone lying upon her breast outside of her; her pulses lagged and paused, and she knew that something strange was going to happen,

even as the early morning winds were cool through the lattice, the streaks of light were dark blue and the whole house was snoring in its sleep.

Now I must get up and go while they are all quiet. Where are my things? Things have a will of their own in this place and hide where they like. Daylight will strike a sudden blow on the roof startling them all up to their feet; faces will beam asking, Where are you going, What are you doing, What are you thinking, How do you feel, Why do you say such things, What do you mean? No more sleep. Where are my boots and what horse shall I ride? Fiddler or Graylie or Miss Lucy with the long nose and wicked eye? How I have loved this house in the morning before we are all awake and tangled together like badly cast fishing lines. Too many people have been born here, and have wept too much here, and have laughed too much, and have been too angry and outrageous with each other here. Too many have died in this bed already. . . .

Here all three passages happen to deal with stoic forms of experience. The first, in spite of its flat austerity, carries a literary echo: the Flaubert of *Un coeur simple*. They all insist, almost as much as Mark Twain's lines, on an essential innocence of character. That innocence, matched in the language they use, has reverted again to straightforward narration, even when, as in the last passage, a state of half-conscious reverie is evoked. The tone of all three is documentary, but the sense of drama is minimized far more than it was in the Bierce and Crane paragraphs. Anything impulsive, spontaneous, energetic, has been subdued to the stoic instinct of fate (though the third passage conveys an impulse to resist it). Gertrude Stein, in the first quotation, is already on her way to the laboriously dispassionate notation of the elemental processes of life that was to reach epic proportions in *The Making of Americans*—the reduction of language to terms almost biologically elemental that was to make its impression on Sherwood Anderson, Hemingway, and a new age of American narrative. Hemingway, in the second quotation, generates a greater power by a more studied selection of words. A calculated candor or transparency appears, suggesting another of his formative influences, Turgenev. The laconic notation defines the instinct

of the individual will to face and survive the social or historical
forces that threaten it, and no pretense or subterfuge of emotion
is allowed to disguise what that struggle will entail.

In the third quotation, from Katherine Anne Porter's *Pale
Horse, Pale Rider,* subjective memory and emotion emerge, the
speaking voice of consciousness. But neither in these few sentences
nor in the story that follows will this emotion be rendered in terms
of the neurotic or poetic or imagistic fantasy that is likely to figure
in Katherine Mansfield or Virginia Woolf. The nagging crudity
of fact will insist. Grim truth-facing will prove inescapable. The
plain language (as in Hemingway) will, by its very guardedness,
its choice and selection, its conscious honesty, define the existence
of inhuman or antihuman forces, powers of evil and cruelty,
against which the human words must set their resistance. By this
means it will generate a dramatic and psychological force more
effective than a complex or a poetic style could arrive at.

Six brief quotations can show only a given trace or line of
style, and while these have not been arbitrarily selected, they
cannot cover the habits of sentimentality, the rhetoric or recklessness, the bluffer energies and derivative effects, the frequent
falseness or the learned ingenuities, that American writing will
reveal in other authors. But to identify the essence of a national
style is necessarily to sieve out the radical evidence, to define
something that approximates as closely as possible to a basic
drive or impulse in the culture that has produced it. The above
examples, then, may permit a few conclusions.

There is a basis of skepticism, of realistic rigor, in the best styles
that America has produced. Even when they are also visionary,
or romantic, or humorous, or sophisticated, they are on guard
against imported or unnatural mannerism. The earlier bent of
American expression toward piety, oratory, English imitation,
academic servility, verbal excess, has been curbed in favor of
plain-spoken naturalism. Its ramifying derivations have tended
increasingly to find a center in average communication. The
basis of that communication may be social (Cooper, Mark Twain,
James, Whitman); it may be personal to the point of eccentricity

(Melville, Emily Dickinson, Cummings); it may be complexly historical (James, Pound, Eliot); but it remains conscious of a standard of human sincerity and community. The old American drive for independence and moral isolation here links characteristically with an equivalent drive toward conformity and democratic averageness. Poets as far apart as Whitman, Dickinson, Cummings, and Marianne Moore will show these twin instincts as much as novelists as dissimilar as Hawthorne, James, and Dreiser. There is a persistent sense that to be learned, specialized, privileged, or antisocial is to exclude oneself from the rights and vitality of the community.

A poet as complex as Pound, Miss Moore, Cummings, or Wallace Stevens will thus break through his specialized personality by reverting to the elements of colloquial speech and diction. James himself breaks the spell of his intricacy by carefully calculated hints of vulgarism. Even if a writer does not train himself in the severely reduced, antiliterary language of the six here quoted, he is likely to know that a standard of realistic intercourse exists and that it provides a norm of equity and human intelligibility. He is drawn back to it as to an essential timbre or resonance of sincerity.

Such an inhibition can, of course, be a hindrance when a writer's resources and invention are weak. But it can also stimulate the curiosity, perverseness, or invention that inhibitions usually generate, which the mobile, fluctuating conditions of American life and language have particularly induced. The liabilities of such a condition have certainly been evident in American life, but the creative advantages of it have also gradually emerged. Conformity coupled with eccentricity; a multiracial, multilingual heritage joined with a passion for unity; the "emotion of multitude" linked with a passion for individuality and apartness—these antitheses struggle to find a common ground in the laws of reciprocity and moral solidarity. By doing so they seek a voice that will be understood, and that will express the necessities of human persistence and survival. The sound of that voice, in its best and sincerest utterance, is what talk of an American idiom or style usually reduces to: what Mr. Wilson meant when he deduced from cases as far apart as the "international style" of Henry James and the colloquial prose of "relatively uneducated writers" like Ring Lardner and Mark Twain the claim that "the American form of English has been rapidly coming into its empire—absorbing, for purposes of literature, more and more of the idiom of daily life, redeeming it from its comic and plebeian connotations, blending it with the language of books, and pouring it into well-molded form for work that may prove enduring." There is enough of such work already in evidence to make the claim reasonable and the existence of an American style as much a fact as the now generally admitted existence of an American literature.

The Passing of English Influence

NOT MANY years ago an American specialist in the history of the United States was introduced at an English university as a "professor of colonial history." The attitude implicit in the title conferred upon him by his English host is very familiar to historians of the literature of the United States. That literature, some English commentators have asserted, is essentially "colonial" and can claim no traditions or character of its own. Other critics have maintained that, even though American authors have written some books that no Englishman could or would have written, and that therefore may be "American," these works are without merit. In other words, the valuable literary products of the United States are to be thought of as English; the valueless are American. Such dicta have understandably infuriated American critics and historians and have provoked them to utter counterblasts, often absurd in their patriotic hyperbole. The American may be excused for his declarations of literary independence; his English opponents deserve forgiveness too, because there is some historical evidence for their views.

A great deal of American writing, since the beginnings in colonial Virginia, has been patently deferential to English conventions and standards. Even when its material was local and its ideas more characteristic of the Old World than of the New, its style was more often than not imitative of works that were, or had been, in vogue in London. There were exceptions, of course. In the years before the Revolution a few American authors showed both in matter and manner the influence of their environment sufficiently to entitle them to be called American. In the century after the establishment of the new nation Washington Irving in his comic *History of New York,* James Fenimore Cooper in his *Leatherstocking Tales,* James Russell Lowell in *The Biglow Papers,* Mark Twain, and, of course, Walt Whitman, convinced even foreign critics that their work was not wholly to be accounted for by English tradition. But the ordinary English reader of American books has found many in the past and a few even now that are in no essential way distinguishable from the work of his countrymen. Quite naturally he has been inclined to assume that all American literature is derivative and provincial.

It seems clear, however, that the relation between the best American writing and that of England has in the last two decades markedly changed. No dispassionate critic can now confidently repeat the old doctrines as to the domination of American letters by English influences. He may well find more to censure than to praise in recent American books, but there are many that he cannot dismiss as basically imitative. Just what has happened, and why, may be difficult to define; that something has happened is plain to anyone who reads at all widely—or wisely—in the American critics, poets, and storytellers of the last twenty years.

For one thing the wind has begun to blow, at least in occasional gusts, from the west rather than from the east. If one is to speak of literary influences at all one must acknowledge that some American fashions, especially those of the 1920's, have significantly affected a considerable number of writers outside the United States.

Another symptom of the new state of affairs is that the very language of some of the most widely celebrated American writers is no longer precisely the "standard English" of London or Oxford. It represents rather a slightly altered tongue, accepted, for better or for worse, in the speech, and often in the writing, of the greater part of the English-speaking world. Even the style, in the broadest sense of the word, of some of the most praised American artists is no longer fully in tune with central English tradition. Ernest Hemingway's prose and Robert Frost's verse quite clearly owe more to other sources than to prevailing English stylistic modes, past or present. American speech has developed a variety of flavors in various parts of the United States; more and more American writers have turned to it rather than to English books for their accents and rhythms, just as Mark Twain tried in *Huckleberry Finn* to reproduce the diction, tone, and pace of the kinds of American speech appropriate to his characters and his theme.

Another reason for the waning of English literary influence on American writers may be the fact that they have become increasingly conscious of the resources offered by the folklore, legends, and myths of their country. In these are expressions of American attitudes, now traditional, toward nature and man, and of traditional values cherished, consciously or unconsciously, by the people of the United States. Out of the experience of the colonists and the founders of the new nation, of the pioneers in the wilderness, of the farmers and the city-builders, of the greedy materialists and the ardent reformers, there has developed a kind of American mythology with its own characteristic heroes, real or imaginary. Mountains, lakes, rivers, and the sea, and, of course, animals, birds, and fish, because of their role in the colonists' contest with the wilderness and in their successors' conquest of a continental domain, have taken on mythological stature. From them have been derived metaphors, images, proverbs, and fables serviceable to the artist and rich in symbolic possibilities for his stories or poems.

The association of mountains and high land with decency and happiness in Hemingway's tales is surely not accidental. The same author's old fisherman belongs to a long line of primitive heroes, representing concretely a type of valor dear to Americans for many generations. The hero of Sinclair Lewis's novel *Arrow-smith* is a medical scientist, but also a traditional pioneer, a man pushing forward to extend old frontiers. The first pages of the novel indicate the parallel. William Faulkner's bear, trees, and swamps, and his Indians and Negroes, all become on occasion symbols of values, of moral conflicts, and of psychological states, notations for the otherwise intangible. The central figure of Arthur Miller's play *The Death of a Salesman* seemed to American audiences to be not merely a little man who failed, but a genuinely pathetic or even tragic figure, probably because his struggle to plant a garden among the bricks of the city, his reveries about the country and the West, and his admiration for his brother who had tasted life in the wilderness paralleled in familiar symbols the ambitions and frustrations of many who saw the play. The presence in a culture of myths and traditionally understood symbols does not, of course, necessarily engender good art, but it at least offers the artist resources that, rightly used, may free him from too great a reliance on material less immediately adapted to the expression of what he, as a representative of his culture, has to say.

The use of materials derived from the American past is not new in American writing; what is new is the increased emphasis put upon such materials by recent authors. There are many reasons, probably. Among them is certainly the attention given by modern psychologists and literary theorists, both in the United States and in Europe, to myth. Equally important, it may be, is the increased feeling of national self-consciousness stimulated in the 1930's by the realization on the part of many thoughtful Americans that threats of war, conflicts of ideologies, and crises in their economic and social system made re-examination of themselves and their habitual ways of thought acutely necessary. It was in the 1930's that John Dos Passos temporarily abandoned fiction and wrote *The Ground We Stand On,* a volume of historical and biographical essays on some of the pioneers in American democratic thought. It was in the 1930's that Van Wyck Brooks turned from the acerbities of *The Wine of the Puritans,* with its drastic criticism of American culture, and brought out *The Flowering of New England,* the first of a series of volumes on the literary history of the nineteenth-century United States in which his appraisal of his country's accomplishments leans so far toward eulogy that the effect is hardly critical at all.

The ten years after the First World War affected in quite a different way the passing of the English influence on American writing. The decade was one in which, in spite of its violent crudities and stupidities, a surprising number of valid literary successes were produced in the United States. It was also the decade of the "expatriates" who turned from America to Europe. Some of the writers who began their careers then or earlier are still major figures in the American literary scene—among them Frost, MacLeish, Marianne Moore, Edmund Wilson, Dos Passos, Hemingway, Thornton Wilder, and Faulkner—and of these writers of the 1920's a considerable number worked for a time abroad. The result was an increased cosmopolitanism. According to Carlos Baker, Hemingway in his apprentice years in Paris read closely Turgenev, Chekhov, Tolstoy, Dostoevsky, Stendhal, Balzac, Flaubert, W. H. Hudson, Mark Twain, Stephen Crane, Henry James, Thomas Mann, Joseph Conrad, and James Joyce. Many English writers were then in Paris, and Hemingway saw something of Ford Madox Ford, Wyndham Lewis, and a few others, but most of those whose conversation and writing he valued were not English. His case is typical of many of the "expatriates."

Today the influence of Mann, Joyce, Proust, Rainer Maria Rilke, Søren Kierkegaard, the existentialists, the nineteenth-century French realists, naturalists, and symbolists, and the Russian novelists, together with that of a few American writers, is far more easily traced in American literature than any lessons learned from a comparable number of English authors. This is not solely because of anything the "expatriates" discovered abroad: the consciousness that the United States was closer to Europe and more involved in its destiny than ever before had revived in many Americans a curiosity about European culture. This curiosity had often been manifested earlier, but the special circumstances of the 1920's and 1930's did much to intensify it.

Of course, the English literary influence on American writing has by no means wholly disappeared. Its "passing" is partial, not

complete, but it exists as only one of the many forces that have
molded the special character of the fiction, poetry, and criticism
now being written in the United States. It is a single element,
and no longer dominant, in a complex organism. To understand
whatever literary influences have affected the best of current
American literature it is important to remember the foreign masters
who have been already mentioned here and also Freud, Ezra
Pound, T. S. Eliot, and Emile Zola; and such Americans as
Ralph Waldo Emerson, Henry Thoreau, Herman Melville, and
Emily Dickinson, together with others more nearly contemporary.
How many English writers now have as much influence? Shakespeare and the translators of the Bible, it is to be hoped; Donne
and the metaphysical poets, probably; Dickens, Browning, Hardy,
and Hopkins, perhaps; Coleridge and Arnold, it may be—but
who else?

There is nothing in this to shake one's faith in the enduring
value of the English literary tradition. Whether or not the dilution
of their loyalty to it has benefited the writers of the United States
remains to be proved. The verdict must depend on one's judgment of current American letters. If one looks only at the "best
sellers" in New York, at the novels that are nothing but expanded
journalistic records, at the trite verse greeted as poetry, and at
the barbarously loose style of some American writers, one may
feel that England is fortunate in having no present responsibility
for American literature.

But the question is not whether bad writers, who abound in
every nation, are worse or better than they used to be in the
United States, but whether the American artists who are generally
esteemed as having merit have gained or lost by their partial re-
nunciation of English literary influences. Today the younger
writers in the United States have probably produced no masterpieces, but they are actively at work experimenting and trying
to fix valid critical standards. Their cosmopolitanism, to judge
by their best work, has not hindered their artistic development.
It is worth remembering that some of the great flowering periods
in English literature have been those in which men of letters have
been most hospitable to foreign literatures and most ready to

learn from Europe. In these periods English writers have been none the less English, however diligently they studied Dante or Molière. The growing tendency of American authors to extend their literary horizons eastward beyond London seems to have enriched American literature in its current phase, without impairing its specifically American character. If this is so, no one need mourn for the timeworn notion that it is "colonial," its lifeblood English, and its success or failure to be measured ultimately by its conformity to traditional English standards. If cosmopolitanism fertilizes American writing, there is reason to rejoice, since, in these days of increased potentialities for artistic communication between free nations, the gains of one may profit all the others.

Karl Shapiro, a young American poet, has said that "the aftermath of poetry should be love." Robert Frost has emphasized the need of never "letting go with the heart." William Faulkner declared in Stockholm that the novelist must deal with "the old verities and truths of the heart . . . love and honor and pity and pride and compassion and sacrifice." Nothing in these sayings is novel or peculiarly American. They may pass current wherever men still think and feel. What matters most in the world of letters today is the extent to which all nations, independent but united by a common devotion to the truths of art, can mint from the metal of experience, observation, and emotion a literary coinage that can nowhere be devalued.

The Southern Revival

A LAND AND ITS INTERPRETERS

FOR SOME years Americans have accepted the fact that much of the best literature produced in their country in our century is Southern. They are not sure that they understand why this is so.

Superficially there are many reasons why it should not have happened: the South suffered a crushing defeat in the Civil War; its lands and industries were depressed for several decades, its people impoverished; educational facilities were the lowest in the country; the universities, for some years after the war, existed almost in name only; tradition survived in a few places, but was shattered elsewhere. The sociologist might have said that from these conditions nothing of enduring value could survive, nothing could be born. Some sociologists said as much, and some spokesmen of Northern liberalism were happy to preach the funeral sermon over the grave of Southern culture.

Nevertheless the literature at least has solidly established itself as the most important, the most talented, interesting, and valuable in the United States. Since 1920 it has grown rich in its abundance of gifted works, and it has more and more compelled attention to its virtues. Mr. Faulkner does not stand alone as the Southern genius, though he is by all standards the most important. Throughout the years since 1920 there has been a remarkable growth of distinction in the literary arts. This phenomenon is almost wholly distinct in kind from the economic recovery of the South. The South has been rehabilitated; it is now perhaps more Northern than the North—more anxious to expand, to add factory to factory, mill to mill. At some time in its post-Civil War history it decided that the way to economic salvation was to imitate Northern industrialism, to become "American" in the sense of showing evidence of economic prosperity in superabundance. Industrially, the fate of the South is now linked inevitably with the modern destiny of commercial expansion, with progress as that word is currently and popularly understood.

The normal literary reaction to industrial progress in America is a literature of protest. The North has given us many writers whose work is nourished by the fund of satire, parody, irony, and plain realistic statement that such a situation provides. The South also has its measure of protest writers: T. S. Stribling, Erskine Caldwell, Lillian Smith among them. But this is not the main direction of Southern literature. The best writing goes deeper, sustains itself on other levels, exploits another vein.

The question has often been asked and debated, why should the region least favored by social and economic progress, suffering the worst damage to its institutions, prove to be the richest in literary gift, the most productive of works of more than passing interest? The answer is not easy to give. There is a complex of reasons, which may be generalized at some risk of inaccuracy. The Southerner began in a way of life different from that of the North. The South had, or pretended to, " a social tradition," and this tradition included a complement of ceremony, belief, and dynastic observance. This is to say, not that the Southerner was more fortunately born, but rather that he fancied he was, or that he exploited more fully than the Northerner the occasional slight evidence of a leisurely, aristocratic world to which he thought himself entitled at birth. The image of a society graced by ceremony and by an affectation of culture took hold of the Southern imagination early and was not easily given up.

The South was also—and more self-consciously than the North —a *land,* more easily identifiable as such than New England, for example, which was in essence an idea or a battleground of ideas. The image of a land on which its people lived in close physical and moral dependency was a popular one and persisted in spite of all evidences to the contrary in the South's economic history. From this image arose several convictions, firmly held and hotly argued by many of the best Southern writers: that the land is sacred, that the ideally moral life is one lived in close relationship to it, that the land should not be "violated" (*i.e.,* that Nature should neither be ignored, exploited, nor viewed abstractly), and that violation of the land is a major sin, for which there were major punishments. The land *was* violated repeatedly in the decades that followed the Civil War. It was grossly abused in many ways. Southern recovery depended upon an increasing pace of violation. In his frenzy of excitement over industrial progress (or his fear of economic ruin) the Southern business man hastened the process of despoliation. The defeat of the South in the Civil

War was followed by the destruction of its pretensions to an agrarian culture. Instead of encouraging its writers to a literature of optimism or of "boosting," this development merely forced them back to the memory, the image, of a land, a community of peoples living close to a land, respecting it, and paying ceremonial tribute to its symbolic value.

The formal, literary respect for the South was, therefore, a creation of the imagination. The literary record of the South's history since the Civil War is largely the history of a legend, the legend of a community and a way of life. The war threatened to destroy it, and in doing so made it more precious, more firmly a part of the aesthetic form that the legend retrospectively assumed. The economic history of the South fortified the legend, made the memory of it more precious than ever.

The great value of modern Southern literature is derived from two important virtues that help to establish and sustain the literary consciousness: a sense of the imagined whole, a sense of the concrete. Southern writers are gifted in both these senses. The "whole" that is in this connection imagined is not especially well associated with the real; it is for the most part the result of a work of refinement upon the crudest and rawest generalizations. The South has always been blessed and cursed by a fondness for public rhetoric. But this rhetoric is not merely one of public demonstration: it has become a style, a manner of making the language reveal its secrets elaborately, of torturing the syntax of human thought. The great rhetorical talent of the South's political history reappears in the qualities of style that we see in Mr. Faulkner and his contemporaries. To make a half-truth whole one must reveal its subrational nature, persist along the path to the source of its wholeness, reveal it in as many of its human and natural ambiguities and paradoxes as the language can hold.

This rhetoric is also the style of the folk tale, the story told and retold, filled out by hazard and by guess, in the long afternoons and evenings of the Southern home, store, public square. More than half of the literary forms that have excited modern readers have had their source in this folk improvisation. The tradition of the folk tale is almost as old as the South itself. It has become sophisticated, or at least has been made more complex, through generations of translation into literary form. In the great folk-inspired literature of the modern South (Mr. Faulkner's *The Hamlet,* Carson McCullers's "The Ballad of the Sad Café," for example) the permanent truths of the human condition are given in a rich context of folk superstition, folk humor, folk pathos. The best writers transcend folk materials without too obviously showing their transcendence; the writings of Faulkner, of Robert Penn Warren, Eudora Welty, Carson McCullers, Caroline Gordon, and others transmute the folk narrative into an examination of a universal moral circumstance.

Above all, Southern writing is noted for a sense of the concrete. The details that make the object "precious" (to use John Crowe Ransom's word), that save it from annihilation by the abstracting mind, have nowhere been so much respected, so well understood. The fire-eating Southern orator is the greatest murderer imaginable of simple truth; but the Southern writer rescues that truth in its intimate and realizable detail. The individual scene, the fugitive nuance, the quality and tone of speech have been preserved. Perhaps the Southern literary tradition has been the most active of all in adhering to the concrete fact. This is not the "realistic" fact or the scientific fact so much admired in most modern literature. It is the object, or the experience, observed with a most thorough and tender concern for preserving its essential nature. The revolution in critical attitudes generally referred to as the "New Criticism" is largely the work of two groups: an "expatriate" group including Mr. Eliot and Mr. Pound, who led an attack upon current literary standards from 1910 to 1920; and a number of Southern critics (conspicuously those at Vanderbilt University in the early 1920's and at the Louisiana State University in the late 1930's).

Quite apart from this argument for aesthetic and formal concreteness, modern Southern literature has preserved and utilized the natural folk love of concrete detail, in every aspect of public and domestic arrangement. Much of this detail is violent, grotesque,

the exaggeration made palpably real. It is also clearly allied with
the most obvious and the most frequently discussed moral issues—
the responsibility of self to nonself, the margin of error discernible
in legal interpretations of man, the difference between Sunday
display and weekday decorum in the religious life, the special
moral issues arising from differences of temperament and race,
the inherited responsibilities and fates in family histories. That
these (and other) situations have been described in the best of
the South's literature with the most painstaking respect for both
local circumstance and universal implication is almost a miracle
of literary history; given, that is, the Southern love of exaggeration, of rhetorical embellishment. In fact, the exaggeration and
the rhetoric have been made a part of the texture of the truth.

One may say that the South has had the most interesting and
the most valuable literary history in recent times because its writers
have had more to go on, or more to draw from. Literary excellence
in this case at least has had little or nothing to do directly with
economic opportunity or educational facilities. The South suffered severely in the Civil War; its economic depressions and its
political disgraces led to a long period of reflection over human
values, an examination of the ideas, imagined or real or both, that
had gone into its social and moral structure. The images of Southern
history and culture have become viable realities in themselves,
and they have been translated variously into works of literary
art. The pattern of the Southern imagination begins in a world
desirable but not quite real; proceeds to a bitter struggle in which
that world seems all but destroyed; becomes thereafter an ideal
design of life somehow vaguely located in a past (a pre-Civil
War past); and is finally made to serve as a starting point for
many arresting examinations of the modern spirit. In the South
there have been many Hamlets; and a Hamlet is indispensable to
the modern tragedy. Paul Valéry has said of this modern Hamlet:
"He reflects on the boredom of recommencing the past, on the
folly of always striving to be original. He wavers between one abyss
and the other, for two dangers still threaten the world: order and
disorder." The risks are presented as well in modern Southern

literature: the risk of a too rigidly fixed order discoverable in the past (the "stubborn back-looking ghosts" whom Mr. Faulkner's Compson fears), the risk of the apparent disorder of the present. Between the two dangers the hero of the Faulkner novel lives out his life and endures his fate.

These images, half borrowed from an historic past, half formed by the creative sense, of tradition, the land, and a way of life, are found in much of the literature; they were given a kind of "official" defense in the work of several Southerners (most of them academic men) in the late 1920's and in the 1930's. As Richard Weaver has said, "it was not until about 1925 that Southern intellectuals caught up with Lee and Jackson. The latter had shown in 1862 that the one chance for the South was to carry the fight to the enemy." A number of the most talented Southerners wrote not only poetry but also prose, biographies of Southern figures or discussions of matters vital to the Southern position: Tate's biographies of Stonewall Jackson (1928) and Jefferson Davis (1929); Warren's *John Brown* (1929), an unfavorable account; Ransom's *God Without Thunder* (1930).

The first decisive act in "carrying the fight" led to the publication in 1930 of *I'll Take My Stand,* by "Twelve Southerners." The statement of principles that introduced the volume specified the issue of "a Southern way of life against what may be called the American or prevailing way," or, otherwise phrased, "Agrarian versus Industrial." The primary object was to define the failures of an industrial (that is, a Northern) society. Religion, the arts, "the amenities of life" cannot flourish in such a society. Ransom's essay in the volume fully defined the Southern traditionalist, the "unreconstructed Southerner," who "persists in his regard to a certain terrain, a certain history, and a certain inherited way of living." This South, said Ransom (who, like his fellows, had experience of and reverence for the European tradition), "is unique on this continent for having founded and defended a culture which was according to the European principles of culture." Tate's essay pointed to the advantages of simplicity in the Southern culture. Only in the South was there still a sense of unified culture:

"The Southern mind was single, not top-heavy with learning it had no need of, unintellectual, and composed; it was personal and dramatic, rather than abstract and metaphysical; and it was sensuous because it lived close to a natural scene of great variety and interest." The Southerner must now take hold of his tradition "by violence." He has inherited an unfortunate history, and he cannot in present circumstances "fall back upon his religion." He finds it necessary to use the instrument of politics to restore his private, self-contained, and essentially spiritual life.

He must do this. But the agrarians were neither sanguine nor "violent." They felt deeply the loss of prestige suffered by the Southern tradition, and they knew that culturally the South was neither ready nor anxious for any radical reaction. The literature produced by these men was bitterly caustic at times, at other times concerned merely to portray the dilemma of the young Southerner as a modern dilemma, the predicament of the modern "solipsist" who cannot give himself to any heroic tradition or challenge.

Ransom and Tate both concerned themselves with the general theme of lost innocence, combining it with the "dynastic wound" of a defeated tradition. They were sensitive to the very complications of man's life that threatened to destroy that innocence. The only way to preserve the innocence was to continue it from one generation to the next. But people may lose a sense of the past when they yield to the persuasions of the present. Most important of all, the viability of tradition depends upon one's ability to sustain some quality of heroic emotion from past into present. Symbols, archetypes, do continue into the present, but if allegiance to them is weak, they become merely "quaint."

Ransom's poem "Antique Harvesters" is at once a recognition of the Southern present ("Declension looks from our land, it is old") and an appeal to retain what has become a symbolic memory of the Southern past. The "old men" of the poem meet to gather the harvest; they are reminded by their appearance ("dry, gray, spare") and by the place, of age and of the imminence of death;

they must save their lives by passing on the qualities of the past to the young. Their experience in maintaining the tradition, their equipage of ritual and observance, is all that they can give the new generation. In the image of the hunt Ransom offers the essential quality of this situation and of what it means. The hunters participate in a symbolic rite; the fox becomes a ritual figure, his act motivated by the need for ritual sacrifice:

> And the fox, lovely ritualist, in flight
> Offering his unearthly ghost to quarry;
> And the fields, themselves to harry.

The harvest is itself a memorial act; the yield, "full bronze," is gathered not for profit but in worship of "The Lady."

> Bare the arm, dainty youths, bend the knees
> Under a bronze burden. And by an autumn tone
> As by a gray, as by a green, you will have known
> Your famous Lady's image; . . .

The poet finally asks that the youth remain within the tradition. View your own lives, he says, *sub specie aeternitatis;* the young will become old,

> . . . and if one talk of death—
> Why, the ribs of the earth subsist frail as breath
> but God wearieth.

In this poem, in Tate's "Ode to the Confederate Dead," in novels of Robert Penn Warren, and in other places the haunting sense of need to keep whole the spirit of the past is expressed. These works are not concerned so much with tradition as with frustrating modern circumstance, the failure to reach beyond the self, to realize and believe in something of real substance. This is in essence a fable of the modern condition as Tate and the others saw it. The writing of the agrarians was almost entirely retrospective. The past as an ideal (and an idealized) unit of experience both remembered and imagined is one of the major images of modern literature. As such, as an idea made specific by reference to a history, a region, a folk, it remains one of the valuable contributions made by the South to the complex of modern American writing.

Rival Approaches to History

GENTLEMEN VERSUS PLAYERS

THE DISTINCTION between scientific and literary history is a deceptively simple one, for "scientific" is a word with many meanings. When it was applied to history in the closing decades of the nineteenth century it meant to some people nothing more than objectivity in the use of documents. To others it suggested a search for laws in the development of the historical process. It was a matter for further debate whether the most profitable analogies would be found in the social or in the natural and physical sciences. Nevertheless, in spite of these differences among themselves, scientific historians were agreed in rejecting the type of history written by the so-called "literary" historians of the nineteenth century. They were not opposed to literary values, but they considered narrative history written by the amateur man of letters as little more than storytelling. In their protest the historical profession was born, for the general result of the scientific movement was to turn the writing of history into a profession, with standards, methods, and values known only to the initiated. The majority of history books ceased to be read by the general public and became monographs to be studied by fellow professionals. No longer was the first criterion of an historical work its literary value or its popular sale.

This did not mean that the new professionals were incapable of writing works of literary merit; yet the nineteenth-century amateur historian is clearly distinguished from those historians of the present century who have been able to produce contributions to literature almost, it might be said, in spite of the handicaps of their profession. During the nineteenth century in America there were four outstanding historians: Motley, Prescott, Parkman, and Henry Adams. The last was a scientific historian: the first three were plainly literary ones, writing history in narrative form, telling a story with little attempt at analysis. All four men wrote works of great literary distinction, and their achievement seems to suggest that it was not so much the methods of their writing or their conception of history as the fact that they were pioneers in their field that brought success. They were the Gentlemen who could make their own rules, free from academic restraints; the Players who succeeded them were governed by established codes.

The Bostonian group of Motley, Prescott, and Parkman was homogeneous in many ways. All three men were educated at Harvard, all were wealthy, and all kept themselves aloof from the changing industrial society of a contemporary America with its rising tide of democratic politics. As gentlemen, as amateurs, they devoted their lives to the writing of narrative history. Motley went to Europe for his subject matter; Prescott followed the Spaniards to the New World; Parkman found his destiny in the American forest. Wealth combined with hard work to unearth the documents, and writing could then begin. Each of them followed the contemporary European method of writing history. Their themes had a unity, at once dramatic and romantic, that centered on leading personages. The arrangement of the facts was intentionally dramatized to capture the imagination and sympathy of the reader. For them, as for Carlyle, history was "heroic." Motley was the most partisan and flamboyant of the three. He frankly took sides, glorying in Protestantism and liberty and heaping insults on Roman Catholicism and despotism. His final verdict on Philip II is almost a parody in prejudice: "If there are vices— as possibly there are—from which he was exempt, it is because it is not permitted to human nature to be perfect in evil." This prejudice completely commanded his use of his materials, and no one would maintain today that *The Rise of the Dutch Republic* is serious history. Yet it is impossible not to be gripped by the passionate vitality of such descriptive set pieces as the siege of Leyden or the full-length portrait of William the Silent. Motley lent the magic of his pen and imagination to a rebellion, and in so doing made it an immortal legend. It is as firmly rooted in the popular mind as Parson Weems's view of George Washington.

To Prescott the story of Spanish expansion into Mexico and Peru offered a dramatic theme in which Cortés and Pizarro were the heroes. There was less opportunity here for prejudice, and indeed Prescott was generally more restrained in style and approach than Motley. He transports the reader into the past, and the narrative flows from episode to episode with skillful ease. The conquest of native peoples by a handful of conquistadores invited colorful narrative, and it is for that reason that Prescott's accounts in *The Conquest of Mexico* and *The Conquest of Peru* have suffered less historical criticism in the twentieth century than has Motley's work. The Netherlands revolt is the ideal subject for a searching analysis of causes, and its very complexity is a delight to the scientific historian. But with Prescott's topic, even if we do not agree that Cortés was "the instrument selected by Providence to scatter terror among the barbarian monarchs of the Western world, and lay their empires in the dust," yet there is little call for involved speculations about the conquest. Neither Motley nor Prescott was concerned with analysis. They had a story to tell, like the nineteenth-century novelist, in which clearly recognizable individuals played a part in a swiftly moving series of events leading to a clear and determined climax. Clarity, certainty, and color were the ingredients of their writing and gave them a reputation to rival the most successful novelist.

The third Bostonian, Francis Parkman, is the most distinguished of the three. Although he held similar views on the writing of history and called Scott, Cooper, and Byron his favorite authors, yet his choice of subject presented new problems. He was the first historian of the traditional theme in American history—the contrast of men and a continent. His aim was to tell the story of the American forest, where, in the eighteenth century, the two rival powers of England and France struggled for supremacy, condemning the Red Indian to destruction as a result. It is in the conflict of these two empires that Parkman finds the dramatic unity for his eleven volumes. "New France," he wrote, "battled against a fate which her own organic fault made inevitable. Her history is a great and significant drama enacted among untamed forests with a distant gleam of courtly splendors and the regal pomp of Versailles." It was this drama in the wilderness that haunted Parkman's life, driving him to visit the scenes of battles, to talk with Indians, guides, and old frontiersmen, and to explore a country that a hundred years had changed but little, since Montcalm and Wolfe had fought their heroic action. His mastery of written sources was as complete as his knowledge of the ground.

Like Motley and Prescott, he liked to have a central personality dominating a volume, whether it was Pontiac, Montcalm, Frontenac, Wolfe, or La Salle. Of the last he wrote that his "very pride which Coriolanus-like declared itself most sternly in the thickest press of foes has in it something to challenge admiration. Never under the impenetrable mail of paladin or crusader beat a heart of more intrepid mettle than within the stoic panoply that armed the breast of La Salle." Here was the type of character—stoical, medieval, manly—that Parkman admired. He avoided melodrama in his writing: skillfully, easily, and quietly he guides us through the forest, strangely silent but filled with the dramatic action that spells the doom of Frenchman and Indian alike. Like Macaulay, he could show sympathy for those with whom he had nothing in common, and indeed there is a striking similarity to Macaulay in Parkman's tribute to the Jesuits. "Casting from them every hope of earthly pleasure or earthly aggrandizement, the Jesuit fathers buried themselves in deserts, facing death with the courage of heroes and enduring torments with the constancy of martyrs. . . . They were the pioneers of Northern America." Parkman in fact could blend criticism with a sympathetic contemplation of the past. In many ways the virtues of absolutist France were more to his liking than the democratic excesses of contemporary America, and the result was a moderation in his judgments that makes *France and England in North America* outstanding in history as well as literature.

Motley, Prescott, and Parkman all looked upon their labors

as essentially literary. Henry Adams, more of a Boston Brahmin even than they were, approached history from a totally different direction. He repudiated the literary historians of his own day as mere storytellers: history "was a hundred years behind the experimental sciences. For all serious purposes it was less instructive than Walter Scott and Alexandre Dumas." Adams himself was a brilliant spoiled dilettante, born with a silver spoon in his mouth and throughout his life weighed down by his distinguished forebears who had placed it there. He was an amateur in all his pursuits, illuminating each one of them with his disappointed genius. As a scientific historian he wrote his nine-volume *History of the United States during the administrations of Thomas Jefferson and James Madison* before he became involved, as he did in his later life, in trying to fit history to laws from the physical sciences. This was fortunate, since, when he wrote, his scientific approach simply meant letting the facts speak for themselves. Facts were obtained by a careful scientific scrutiny of the documents, and in their natural arrangement the evolution of some broad idea or principle would emerge. The historian "cannot but become conscious of a silent pulsation that commands his respect, a steady movement that resembles in its mode of operation the mechanical action of nature itself." It is this consciousness that makes the historian more than a chronicler. There is therefore a certain inevitability in the historical process, and individuals are unimportant. Adams could write of Jefferson and Madison: "They appear like mere grasshoppers kicking and gesticulating on the middle of the Mississippi river. . . . They were carried along on a stream which floated them, after a fashion, without much regard to themselves."

The history of America from 1800 to 1817 was the story of the development of national unity, in spite of the bunglings of statesmen, the treason of the Federalists, the paucity of resources, and the hostility of England and France. Adams's account of these years is an intellectual one: he arranges the documents with consummate artistry, commenting where necessary, and avoiding any emphasis on dramatic or colorful incidents. He is interested in individuals as public figures, in their minds and consciences above all else. His Olympian detachment penetrated into the recesses of human thought, presenting the weaknesses of his characters with justice but no compassion. There could be neither heroes nor dramatic climaxes in such a work. The last volume ends on a note of doubt; though nationalism had emerged, the future held no certainty or hope.

It might seem that such a history, whatever its intellectual power, is hardly a work of great literature. But Adams was a brilliant stylist, clear, restrained, and serene, with a fine sense of balance and form. He invites comparison with Gibbon and, like the English historian, he is most impressive in the total effect of his work. The urbanity of his style can perhaps be seen in the description of Madison's inaugural speech. Adams quotes the *National Intelligencer* as describing the new President dressed in a full suit of cloth of American manufacture, and the historian continues:

> The suit of American clothes told more of Madison's tendencies than was to be learned from the language of the Inaugural Address, which he delivered in a tone of voice so low as not to be heard by the large audience gathered in the new and imposing representatives' hall. Indeed the Address suggested a doubt whether the new President wished to be understood.

The New England Federalists were summed up in the words:

> The obstinacy of the race was never better shown than when, with the sunlight of the nineteenth century bursting upon them, these resolute sons of granite and ice turned their faces from the sight, and smiled in their sardonic way at the folly or wickedness of men who could pretend to believe the world improved because henceforth the ignorant and vicious were to rule the United States and govern the churches and schools of New England.

Adams himself continually smiles in a sardonic way throughout his *History* as the documents reveal his characters in the most humiliating light. He does not avoid heightening the contrast of characters; Napoleon, "like Milton's Satan on his throne of state," had to be faced "and overawed by the gentle optimism of President Jefferson": Madison, "such a man as Jefferson who so much disliked contentious and self-asserting manners loved to keep by his side," was pitted against the sinister and enigmatical Talleyrand.

Adams could hardly be more different from Parkman in his approach, method, and style. He emphasizes documents against narrative, intellect against emotion, the inevitable flow of history against the individual hero. Yet both wrote history on the grand scale from Olympian peaks; both were amateurs working in fields where none had trespassed before. But even as they were writing, the historical profession was being born. Their successors were professionals trained in graduate schools with methods and standards more closely akin to those of the scientist than of the man of letters. The historian worked for his living as a teacher and wrote history, it might be said, for promotion. Yet history and literature even under a professional historical discipline are not incompatible. Turner and Beard, Becker and Morison have all written challenging books with a varying degree of literary distinction. Becker's *Heavenly City of the Eighteenth Century Philosophers* and *The Puritan Pronaos* of Morison are minor classics, and Morison's three-volume history of Harvard is a major work of great intellectual power and eloquence. Allan Nevins has set out in four large volumes to cover the era before the Civil War. He has undoubtedly written a work of major importance with infectious fluency, but there is perhaps a weakness in his philosophical approach that makes his achievement fall short of greatness.

There have been, too, recent historians still free from academic duties. James Truslow Adams and the late Douglas Southall Freeman and Bernard DeVoto have been the most popular. Adams as the historian of New England and DeVoto as the historian of the West both exhibited a vigor and imagination that made their books best sellers. They may secure a permanent position. But there can be no doubt that Freeman's life of Robert E. Lee, conceived on a grand scale in four long volumes, is a work of outstanding power and brilliance. Freeman lived "as it were for more than a decade in the company of a great gentleman," and he not only paints a living portrait of his hero, but by the novel device of allowing the reader no more knowledge than Lee had at the time of any particular battle or campaign he succeeds in a brilliant analysis of Lee's generalship. No work of the twentieth century can more unhesitatingly be called a classic.

These reflections on the writing of history in this century suggest that it is only in the spheres of biography and intellectual history that literary classics are likely to be written. In these spheres personal genius has an opportunity of creating a work of art. Elsewhere, however, the expert character of the historical profession has led to a separation, if not divorce, between literature and history. Almost every field of historical study has the footmarks of other travelers scattered upon it: no longer are the forests virgin as in the days when Parkman blazed his trail. Today the historian must follow the trail trodden by his predecessors, and his historical accuracy counts for more than his literary distinction. Of course, extremely readable history providing a synthesis of many monographs can still be written; J. T. Adams, Nevins, and DeVoto prove this. Nevertheless it is difficult to imagine in England or America that the literary giants of the nineteenth century will be followed by similar twentieth-century figures, since the professional approach to history has confined its literary freedom. The Gentlemen could make their own conventions: the Players must follow those of their profession.

Recollected in Tranquillity

SOME FORGOTTEN AMERICAN CLASSICS

THERE ARE advantages in seeing America at ocean's distance. (The disadvantages are too plain to be worth notice.) One can more easily focus a certain aspect or period and evade the bewilder-

ment of vastness. Matthew Arnold chose an even easier view-
point by assembling that vastness into a literary dependency: "I
see advertised *A Primer of American Literature*. Imagine the face
of Philip or Alexander at hearing of a Primer of Macedonian
Literature! We are all contributors to one great literature—English Literature." He had the omniscience of school inspection in
his marrow; yet omniscience holds an inevitable grain of truth.
Emerson, whom he hailed as "the friend and aider of those who
would live in the spirit," confessed it. "Our American literature
and spiritual history are still in the optative mood." The Boston
Brahmins were sharply aware of "a too long dependence on the
muse of England." English readers, less omniscient than Matthew
Arnold, have felt exciting differences in that unfinished and unexplored immensity called America, since they came upon *The
Scarlet Letter;* or Parkman's description of La Salle's descent of
the Mississippi until "the brackish water turned to brine and the
great Gulf opened on his sight, limitless, and voiceless, lonely, as
if born of chaos"; or Fenimore Cooper's saga of the wilderness
at the moment when Natty Bumppo and his companion stand on
a little hill that thrust up from the endless forest, and see about
them an ocean of treetops spreading to the horizon. Cooper, it
is to be remembered, after his first imitations of Scott, resolved
to write novels "that should be purely American." For the English reader American Literature was very obviously American.

The War Between the States, waged and won without counsel
or hindrance from Europe, hardened the difference. "Our obligation to the dead," said a university orator, "is henceforth . . .
not to write English but American. We have gotten our position,
we are now to have our own civilization, think our own thoughts,
rhyme our own measures": a more strident note than Boston gave
out. It may have been a little too strident even for that exalted
moment. A gentler expression of it was the nation-wide impulse
to write of the things of home. Most of the novels that came to
England at the turn of the century were of this "local color"
school. The defeated South found comfort in remembrance of
things past. "Moonlight was brighter before the war," said Mark

Twain; and chivalry was brighter—bright as a bared sword; and women more beautiful, in those pillared houses that grew up along the James River and were left desolate after it. The victorious North had more than nostalgia to uphold it. Boston, where legend pretended that "Lowell spoke only to Cabot and Cabot spoke only to God"; Boston, that for young Howells from Ohio and for Emily Dickinson at Amherst had a sanctity almost Paradisiac, lost its Athenian atmosphere when the Lowell mills began to be staffed by Irish immigrants. Literary leadership moved to New York, and New York, like all heirs apparent, made a mock of its elders, while New England itself, in the afterwar flood of patriotism, found material for the expression of American rather than Emersonian individuality in its small towns and villages.

It was a stark and lonely individuality, local color being generally black. Young men whom Lowell had supposed inspired by Emerson ("To him, more than to all others together, did the young martyrs of our civil war owe the sustaining strength of thoughtful heroism") had left uncounted women to wither into spinsterhood. Mary Wilkins's *A New England Nun* was the first of many novels to peer between neat drawn curtains and find immaculate cleanliness and hearts wrung dry. For her imitators, who lie unrecognized in old volumes of *Harper's,* spinsterhood was plentiful enough almost anywhere; always angular and nearly always bitter, but at the writers' bidding sentiment oozed from the sharpest corners. From spinsters to James Lane Allen's porcelain charm and mannered but lovely prose—it has the whispering sound of an Aeolian harp, the Aeolian harp that Emerson placed in his window at Concord—meant a startling change of intellectual climate, but it was still American. *A Kentucky Cardinal* gave forth "a breath of Eden" combined with the warmth of new-dug earth. George W. Cable's New Orleans enclosed a fantastic, wistaria-draped world of exotic beauty in decay, where Negroes kept some of their African splendor and white women their French grace. Present-day critics allow him to be "perceptive"; no more. The social order that he so perceptively saw was even then dying. But he was memorable, one thinks, when matched against other local colorists; memorable and—remembered. His novels, apart from New Orleans, are not even mentioned by most critics. *John March, Southerner* and *The Cavalier* had a slight Meredithian flavor. Again, memorable; an America that had nothing of the homespun. Cable lingered on, in this country at least, until the beginning of this century, but he was so far in oblivion by 1914 that a writer in a literary review spoke of him as "a Mr. G. W. Cable."

Virginia had its Mary Johnston, whose novels of Virginia's past were followed by solider, better documented, and rather duller fiction superimposed upon the war itself—her father was one of the Southern generals. Winston Churchill's *The Crisis* kept fiction more to the front and tried to be fair to both sides by having a Northern hero and a Southern heroine, thus making use of a plot that had served novelists since the War of Independence. Owen Wister's *The Virginian* fathered innumerable heroes "quick on the draw," but he remained *the* Virginian, even when Hollywood took charge. Ellen Glasgow is remembered for the astringent tone she brought into the pervading nostalgia. Her novels were something more than chaplets of remembrance. Her old ladies who believed that nothing had been changed, or need be, were brilliantly observed as they did their best to take the heart out of the present.

These writers of contemporary repute have withered, it seems. Growing America wanted a world's horizon. William Dean Howells did much to provide it; mindful of what was good for America, as well as good intrinsically. He never forgot the exhortation of one of his early employers in Ohio: "Never—*never* write anything that you could not read to a woman." He lived to see women writing what he thought they should be ashamed to read to men. A realist by conviction, but no showman, he, too, is dimmed, yet America should honor him for the encouragement he gave as both critic and editor to newer writers: and he, too, contributed his patch of local color in *Years of my Youth,* written when he was nearly eighty.

Mark Twain stood on his own feet. He hated with the bitter-

ness of the born last-ditcher the changing scene, the coming of
big business, the machine, the millionaire. He himself grew rich
by pleasing the crowd, not by grinding it in the Satanic mills. It
was of the older, rougher, uncouth America that he wrote, with
the passion of its free growth in his blood. He wrote not only of
it, but for it, by his own proclamation. "I can't stand George Eliot
and Hawthorne." He loathed Scott and detested Jane Austen. His
Americanism is so native and so strongly woven in his fiber that
no change of taste or fashion can break it. One may be repelled
by his dogged refusal of any finer judgment—he would be pleased
to hear it—but he brings a little pleasing profanity among the
immortals: the profanity that troubled his friend Howells, who
was one day to write *My Mark Twain*. The writer of *Huckleberry
Finn* (himself ingrained Huck) respected Howells's literary judgment. When Howells penciled in the margin of the manuscript of
Tom Sawyer, "Awfully good but a little dirty," against a bit of
too intimate description, Mark deleted it, mindful that the masses
for whom he wrote have their primmer moments. Nothing of the
sort could ever be scrawled in the margin of anything Howells
wrote. He has been labeled, by those who came after, "genteel,"
as harsh an epithet as any devised by Mencken, who did his duty
as a critic by "knocking someone on the head every day," pref-
erably "with a meat ax." Yet Howells did, at a measured step,
move with the times. His enthusiasm for Tolstoy was eager and
sincere, and his wish to Europeanize, as well as to Americanize,
American writing shows the range of his intelligence. After all
he had been American consul in Venice, was a friend of Henry
James (as well as of Mark Twain!), and had seen the great men
of New England in their prime.

It is almost time to remove the label of "genteel." His novels
speak of life: not the screech or the thud of our piston-driven
life, but the life that a writer of wide and humane understanding
saw near at hand. *The Rise of Silas Lapham* may not stand among
the ten or twelve chosen "world's greatest," but freed of its period blight and labels affixed by critics with an itch to collect
scalps it can be seen as intrinsically good work. There is no fum-

bling. Silas Lapham, receiving the journalist who wants the "story" of his success, is seen immediately in his integrity. The journalist, Bartley Hubbard, has but to sharpen his pencil and speak and his innate cheapness is known. Bartley Hubbard is drawn at full length in *A Modern Instance,* which most critics think Howells's best novel. The ordinary reader (if Howells has now any ordinary readers) may find it hard to displace Lapham. Howells's sureness in dialogue is infallible. The scene between Irene Lapham and Tom Corey in her father's half-built mansion is as bare of accessories as the house itself, but how excellent in its implications! How much that is unseen and unsaid is deftly conveyed!

Out of this new Americanizing hustle other names come to mind. Harriet Beecher Stowe ("Uncle Tom's" work being done) wrote vivid tales of New England that bred the finer work of Sarah Orne Jewett. (This in quite recent years has been thought worthy of republishing in England.) It adds a delicate shade or two to this transatlantic picture of a bygone but still habitable America; habitable, that is, by the sauntering mind. One could have lived alongside Mrs. Todd in *The Country of the Pointed Firs,* with the sound of the sea and the smell of Mrs. Todd's garden herbs to bring forgetfulness. "If I were asked to name three American books which have the possibility of a long, long life," wrote Willa Cather, "I would say at once *The Scarlet Letter, Huckleberry Finn,* and *The Country of the Pointed Firs.*" It may seem a singular conjunction of immortals, but, adding to it Willa Cather's own *Death Comes for the Archbishop,* they are not a bad throw for immortality.

As the nineteenth turned the corner into the twentieth century the vast foreign immigration of the mid-nineteenth and the city's victory over the farm must have broken the mold of Lowell's Hosea Biglow, even as it shatters our transatlantic dream picture. Yet Van Wyck Brooks in his autobiography, *Scenes and Portraits,* says that when he was at Harvard in 1905 "the days of the New England Renaissance were not too remote, and living survivors or epigoni were still to be seen." He names Thomas Wentworth Higginson and Charles Eliot Norton, the friend of Emerson, Carlyle,

Ruskin, and Lowell. One may suppose the old gods musing apart: for the America that Emerson foresaw and carried with him to the England of Thomas Carlyle plainly lies beyond the farthest stars. In this assertive, arrogant, and uncertain time George William Curtis kept alive the memory of it and of Thoreau's house that he himself had helped to build by Walden Pond, and of Brook Farm where he "preferred the wiping of dishes to the washing." He died within a year of Lowell. His faith in Emerson had never waned. Lowell, on the contrary, gives an impression of repenting his earlier enthusiasm. "As for Emerson's verse, though he has written some as exquisite as any in the language, I suppose we must give it up." There is a present dampness about Lowell that forbids hopeful approach. He had done his best work before the War, when his *Biglow Papers* were received with delight in England as the "real" America, the shrewd, drawling, irreverent, get-the-better-of-you America that English writers from Basil Hall and Mrs. Trollope to Charles Dickens had rather strangely endeared to us. We like our foreigners to be a little comic.

> But John P.
> Robinson he
> Sez they didn't know everythin' down in Judee.

and—"Seventy-six year cum next tater diggin' and there an't nowheres a kitling spryer'n I be." A *Life* of Lowell "by the Author of *Tom Brown's Schooldays*" places him "in the first rank by the side of the great political satirists of ancient and modern Europe . . . England [has] her Swift, her Thackeray, America her Lowell, France her Rabelais, her Voltaire"—a remarkable judgment, even for a bedazzled contemporary who allows Hawthorne "dramatic power of a high order though mixed with a certain morbidness and bad taste," and Emerson's "singular metallic glitter of style" to be "one of the best counterfeits of genius that has been seen for many a day."

Lowell had been a lecturer admired even in Van Wyck Brooks's

Harvard days. Rereading his Essays, one remembers a patronizing note in the Browning Letters to the effect that "Mr. Lowell" in writing about the English poets says what has been said by every critic before him: too tart and, perhaps, too true? They now give off a sort of library effluvium, save when he writes with the native warmth to be felt in such as the one that Tom Hughes calls "pretty." This begins with White of Selborne and strays delightfully (and delightedly) over Lowell's own garden. His pleasure in the caw of a rook "on a clear winter morning as it drops to you through five hundred fathoms of crisp blue air" has an engaging zest even now. Yet something hesitant and cautious in him repels, when one has cried an answer to the proud recklessness of Thoreau—whom Henry Seidel Canby presently set in his rightful place among "the small group of really great Americans" —or has heard Emerson's strange and silvery call from afar. Lowell is impatient if not contemptuous of Thoreau—"he squatted on another man's land, borrows an ax; his boards, his bricks, his mortar, his books, his lamp, his billhook" presuppose an artificial civilization "which rendered it possible that such a person as Henry Thoreau should exist at all." As the century came near its end, and he with it, Lowell may have remembered that "at any rate [Emerson] gave us life, which on the whole is no bad thing." That "on the whole" is typical of Lowell. A sentence that begins like a clarion ends with an aside. He is always afraid to lose hold of the traditional. Even when he first listened to Emerson "we could not say exactly what we gathered from his lecture. We only felt that something beautiful had passed by." "Passed by" is the revealing phrase.

Emerson and Thoreau—the forerunners, with giant Whitman to follow—lifted the darkness of Calvinism from the American mind. With dust already gathering upon them they met the destructive force of the twentieth century. Mencken, accoutered with his meat ax, calls Emerson "an importer of stale German tracts." Whitman, transcendentalist by his own choice, also had little honor in that disoriented day, nor had Melville. One historian of the expiring nineteenth century sees him walking about unnoticed in the New York streets. Both he and Whitman have since come into the company of the great, among whom Hawthorne was seated in spite of Mark Twain. Emily Dickinson, unknown, unseen when she died in 1886, shines forth now in their midst. She was brought forth timidly by Thomas Wentworth Higginson, who wrote of Whitman's *Leaves of Grass:* "It is no discredit to Walt Whitman that he wrote *Leaves of Grass,* only that he did not burn it afterwards and reserve himself for something better." As a "tutor" to Emily Dickinson—"tutor" was her suggestion—Higginson must often have been in sore straits. Dr. Oliver Wendell Holmes lived on, a not too withered "last leaf upon the tree." A cheerful octogenarian, he accepted change as it came, "the telephone, electric illumination, white and steady as the moonbeams, burning but unconsumed, the silent bicycle," strange successor to the One Horse Shay.

They are now safely niched as classics, subjects for college lectures. Will they ever return as gods? For the moment at least they lie embalmed in their fame—or may it be only becalmed, waiting for a freshening wind? In his life of Emerson Richard Garnett speaks of him as a Voice. Even his own contemporaries failed to hear it clearly. "Do you understand Mr. Emerson's lectures?" someone asked a well-known judge. "No, but my daughters do" was the answer, summing up the cloudiness of daughters' minds and prophets' preaching. A reader who knew Emerson only at distance of place and time copied many of his utterances into a notebook as provision for the journey of life. Our publishers were generous with small books of "Selections" and "Gleanings" in the first decade of this century, selection and gleaning being the first sign of having come to the classic stage of unreadability in the bulk. "A Voice?" Does it or can it carry as far as our uncharted age? A century ago, when thousands listened to its strange mesmeric unhurried tone, it was understood—at least by the judge's daughters. Emily Dickinson, now enskied by general acclaim (and understanding? hardly)—Emily Dickinson said:

"When I feel physically as if the top of my head were taken off I know that it is poetry." It is the acknowledgment a modern reader gives to her own "bolts of melody" that, like Emerson's teaching, pierce unknown skies. And often they have the Emersonian touch. "He gave us life," says Lowell, who could not take it from his hand. Yet even Lowell "felt that something beautiful had passed by." Passed beyond time's reach?

> Who gave thee, O Beauty
>   The keys of this breast—
> Too credulous Lover
>   Of blest and unblest?

Negro Writing

A LITERATURE OF PROTEST

IF THE Senegalese-born slave Phillis Wheatley ever guessed that she would one day be in anthologies of American Negro verse and that she herself would, with Jupiter Hammon, open the history of American Negro literature, her Augustan elegiacs give no sign of it. The Countess of Huntingdon, who entertained her, would no doubt have found the thought intriguing, if scarcely credible, for to her Miss Wheatley must have been a higher animal, a benighted savage who, by the grace of God and the favor of a tailor in Boston, had learned to turn an ode as well as any of the school of Pope. Miss Wheatley did not often write of her race or situation, but when she did it was to praise her deliverance from "the land of errors and Egyptian gloom." Only in one poem, addressed to the Earl of Dartmouth, does she venture to mention the feelings of the African; but the poem itself is, ironically, in praise of Freedom, and the reference is oblique:

Should you, my lord, while you pursue my song,
Wonder from whence my love of freedom sprung . . .
I, young in life, by seeming cruel fate
Was snatched from Afric's fancy'd happy state. . . .

Phillis Wheatley's *Poems on Various Subjects, Religious and Moral* was published in 1773, but it was not until 1829 that another book of poems by a Negro appeared. This was *The Hope of Liberty,* by George Moses Horton, who, like Miss Wheatley, was freed late in life. Only when he escaped to the North during the Civil War, however, was Horton really able to speak out against slavery. The northern Negroes, on the other hand, had been working and speaking actively for their cause ever since the foundation of the Negro newspaper *Freedom's Journal,* in 1818. James Whitfield's *America and other Poems,* which appeared in 1853, is a good example of this. "America," says Whitfield, in this book,

. . . it is to thee,
Thou boasted land of liberty—
It is to thee I raise my song,
Thou land of blood, and crime, and wrong.

Whitfield was an ardent worker for "colonization," that is, the various schemes for promoting emigration of Negroes to Liberia or Central America, which, the Negro scholar Miles Mark Fisher recently maintained in his *Negro Slave Songs in the United States,* was much more popular with Negroes than the idea of abolition. However much this may be illustrated in the slave songs, though, a desire to get away from the United States does not appear in Negro poetry. The various complaints and addresses are to freedom in the abstract, and the most positive demand is for a rhetorical "redressing of wrongs."

Their freedom granted, the Negro poets of the period after the Civil War were presented with something of a problem, which Professor Sterling Brown, in his excellent *Negro Caravan,* compares with the problem of Irish writers. The Irish, he says, either had to deny the "stage Irishman" of English literature or, using this stereotyped creature as a basis, endeavor to make him into a more rounded personality. There were Negro stereotypes enough after the Civil War, for Southern white writers, seeking to show how happy Negroes were in the Old South and how miserable and uprooted in the New, filled the stage with romanticized "uncles" and "aunties" contentedly living under Massa's wing on the Ole Plantation. Some poets, like Albery Whitman, therefore, tried to counteract the comic and romanticized picture of the Negro by presenting him in a heroic light, as Whitman does in *Twasinta's Seminoles: or, The Rape of Florida*. Others, of whom Paul Laurence Dunbar is an example, endeavored, in dialect poems like "The Party" and "At Candle-Lightin' Time," to put life into Tim and Mandy and Old Cripple Joe. It must be confessed that, however much Negroes today—because of their intense wish to see the Negro presented as a cultivated person—may dislike Dunbar's dialect verse, it is much better than the lifeless iambics of Albery Whitman, and it is perhaps significant that when Dunbar himself wrote poems in standard English they lacked the warmth and nearness of "When Malindy Sings" and "When de Co'n Pone's Hot." The latter are successful because he obviously felt them deeply. This is a comment that can be applied to almost the whole of Negro poetry since Dunbar. Where it strikes a pulsing rhythm and captures the inimitable tang of Negro speech, as in the blues of Langston Hughes and the ballads of Sterling Brown, it is moving and successful. Where it tries to reproduce the lyrical echoes of English poetry (which, of course, naturally draws upon the quite different rhythms of English speech), it never quite succeeds in striking an original note, but even at its best, as in the poetry of Claude McKay or Countee Cullen, reads like a very skillful imitation. W. S. Braithwaite, James Weldon Johnson, Georgia Douglass Johnson, Joseph Seamon Cotter, Jean Toomer, Frank Marshall Davis, Robert E. Hayden, Margaret Walker, Gwendolen Brooks: one sympathizes with the feeling that led all these poets to write and praises the skill that they have obviously devoted to writing; but one is forced to admit that none of them is really very good. Up to the present at least, something seems to have happened to the Negro poet who has tried to write in standard English. He has, as it were, put on his solemn poetry face and a veil has come down, taking the life out of the images and deadening the phrases. This is probably why anthologists, seeking to make a collection of the best American poetry, scarcely ever find it possible to put a Negro poet in. If they do, they put him in because he is a Negro.

Why should the American Negro not so far have been able to write striking and original English verse? One reason at least is fairly obvious. If we take American Negro society as a whole, he is still, in spite of his long sojourn in America, a different kind of person from the American white man. He is looser, freer, more vital, and more relaxed; song flows in his veins and he is untroubled by that instinct for self-deprivation that doth make Calvinists of us all and colors our happiest songs with sadness. Three hundred years in America have not yet obliterated the Negro's sense of life and timing, and yet Negroes appear to wish that it had. For all the brave statements of "New Negro" days, they still try to emulate a style that evolved over centuries in another place, in another climate, among a different kind of people. Why should the Negro not try to build on what he has, instead of trying to emulate the white man? Negroes might answer that all they have is the language of the white man. This is quite true, but in both song and speech they have stamped their own pattern on English, mirroring the Negro spirit. But like white Americans in the nineteenth century they have not yet got a poetic tradition of their own. When it develops it must, one feels, draw from what is innate in the Negro: his sense of life, his joy, his inspiring gift of song. But this point has not yet been reached. Apart from one or two poems, like James Weldon Johnson's "O Black and Unknown Bards" and Countee Cullen's "Heritage," in which the emotion lights up the clichés, Negro poetry is still mainly derivative, and this one feels even in the more recent poets like Margaret Walker. The only difference is that whereas, say, Countee Cullen reads like a Negro Edward Shanks, Miss Walker reads like a Negro Carl Sandburg. One hopes that future Negro poets (Miss

Gwendolen Brooks is perhaps a portent) will throw off sheer "literariness" and develop in a different mode, from the deepest springs of their being, the spirit that triumphs in Negro songs and ballads.

It is not the same with Negro prose. Prose, except at the very highest level, does not demand that delicate ingrained sensibility that can come only from a secure tradition. The standard of descriptive and naturalistic writing in the Negro short story and the Negro novel is therefore now quite high. Even the first novel published by a Negro, William Wells Brown's *Clotel, or the President's Daughter,* which came out in London in 1853, shows, in spite of the sentimentality of its characterization, a very promising skill of description and narration. Less can be said for Martin Delany's *Blake,* for Frances Harper's *Iola Leroy,* or for Paul Laurence Dunbar's four novels. But Charles W. Chesnutt developed a style of his own and dug deep into the life of the South. Chesnutt was a better writer than his time could support. His success as a short story writer in the *Atlantic Monthly* encouraged his publishers, but, in a climate of taste that demanded the insipid romanticism of Thomas Nelson Page his novels were unpopular and lost money. His *House Behind the Cedars* dealt with the relations between near-whites and Negroes, a subject that, as a near-white himself, Chesnutt could scarcely avoid. *The Marrow of Tradition,* published at the turn of the century, treated realistically of a race riot. *The Colonel's Dream* explored the gulf that lay between Southern racial prejudice and the utopia of complete equality.

Chesnutt was a better novelist than many of his successors, for the burden of injustice did not lie so heavily on him that he felt he had to use the novel to air the very real grievances of the Negro. He treated the novel, therefore, as the novel should be treated, for dramatizing human conflicts, hopes, and fears, where many of the Negro novelists of the twentieth century—among them James Weldon Johnson, Walter White, and W. E. B. Du Bois—have turned it into a vehicle for propaganda. Yet these later novels, whatever judgment one is forced to make on them aesthetically, at least reflect the actual speech and manners of the Negro. This was the product of a new spirit among Negroes, the spirit of the "New Negro." Langston Hughes gave this concept expression when he said: "We younger Negro artists now intend to express our individual dark-skinned selves without fear or shame." It is rather self-consciously put, but it is a sign that Negroes had begun to recognize that there lay little hope for Negro art in imitating the white man, and particularly in trying to make Negroes act and talk like white people. Since the "New Negro" movement, which is well described by Alain Locke in a book of that title published in 1928, Negro writers have tried not only to present their speech and people realistically, but also to explore Negro experience other than that which results from racial prejudice and conflict.

One of the best of these is Zora Neale Hurston, a short story writer and novelist of great skill whose books are set in Florida. She is particularly good at conveying a sense of atmosphere—as in the hurricane episode in her second book, *Their Eyes were Watching God*—and at capturing the authentic echo of conversation, white or black, as she does so well in her psychological novel *Seraph on the Suwanee*. Miss Hurston is one of the few Negro novelists who still write about the South. Another novelist who managed to free himself from the incubus of the "problem" was Claude McKay, whose *Home to Harlem* has the full-bodied flavor of life in Harlem in the speakeasy days. In *Banjo* Mr. McKay wrote of low life in Marseilles, and in *Banana Bottoms* and *Gingertown* of his native Jamaica. Other outstanding novels that, one feels, show more interest in life than in propaganda, are Langston Hughes's *Not Without Laughter,* Arna Bontemps's *God Sends Sunday,* the story of a Negro jockey, and Waters E. Turpin's *These Low Grounds,* which traces the life of a Negro family from the days of slavery to the present. Jean Toomer, who was both short story writer and poet, ought also to be mentioned here. His collection of short stories and poems entitled *Cane* received enthusiastic and well-deserved praise in the 1920's, and one finds in his work, perhaps more than in that of any other Negro writer, a sense of poetry and wonder; it comes out in such sketches as the one entitled "Avey."

Of recent novelists who have turned to what Carl Milton Hughes in a survey called "Common Denominator: Man," the best known and most prolific is Frank Yerby. Only a year after Mr. Yerby had won the O. Henry Memorial Award for an excellent short story, there appeared his historical novel, *The Foxes of Harrow,* and this has been followed by *The Golden Hawk, Floodtide, Pride's Castle,* and *The Vixens.* Mr. Yerby the young story writer of great promise and Mr. Yerby the writer of historical novels filmed by Hollywood seem to be two entirely different persons. The one had a quiet competence and a capacity to convey the pathos of a simple human situation. The other has sweep and color, but his characters are cardboard, his situations romanticized, and his language often melodramatic. Mr. Yerby is an object lesson. There is no one else in recent years who affords quite so dramatic an example of the rewards of writing badly. Even in Scott Fitzgerald, who, during a period of his life, succumbed to the lure of easy money, there is not such a contrast between the actual caliber of the writing in the good and the bad stories. Mr. Yerby is an object lesson because his situation is in a certain sense representative of our time. At a certain level of education and society, the level of the majority, the climate of prose—in the newspapers and magazines, perhaps more even than in the novels—encourages these clichés of language and situation that breed from loose thinking. By an extraordinary effort the young writer can extricate himself from the contamination of the material that is thrust upon him from the moment he begins to read. He can write well if he works hard. But there is always the temptation to fall back into the easy ways of writing and thinking that a debased taste encourages. In the midst of his labors he realizes how high is the premium on good writing and how unlikely it is that his work will appeal to more than a discriminating minority. This, we may conjecture, is what happened to Mr. Yerby, and the result was *The Foxes of Harrow* and its successors, in which a considerable talent can be studied going to very profitable waste.

Two other recent Negro novelists have also written about white people. The first is Willard Motley, whose *Knock on Any Door* appeared in 1947 and provoked comparisons with Theodore Dreiser's *American Tragedy* and James T. Farrell's *Studs Lonigan*. In spite of its fatalism, however, it is in fact nothing like Dreiser's novel. It is nearer to *Studs Lonigan,* if such a comparison is worth anything, not merely because it is set in a poor Chicago district and traces the history of an underprivileged boy who comes to a tragic end, but because it has a similar naturalistic style and a similar "philosophy," which places the blame for bad actions entirely on environment. Through lack of opportunity, bad companions, and a fatal handsomeness, Nick Romano goes to the electric chair, and all the efforts of his skillful and liberal lawyer (who closely resembles Clarence Darrow) cannot save him. Mr. Motley, however, does not have Mr. Farrell's capacity for evoking atmosphere, and although his novel is competent, compelling, and fast-moving, the reader feels that he has been carried with a rush into the outer suburbs and that all of a sudden the wind is dreadfully cold and there is no bus back. The suffering is passive and the tragedy therefore no tragedy at all. We do not even feel very sorry for Nick Romano; we are merely horribly fascinated by the lurid details of his downfall.

The second Negro novelist who has undertaken to write of white people is Miss Ann Petry, whose second novel, *Country Place,* is about the life she imagines under the placid surface of a New England town. It is a story of people who bring dissatisfaction to themselves and disaster to others through their insistence on pursuing their pleasure at all costs. The wife of a returned soldier abandons him for another man on the ground that the other man affords her more sexual pleasure. Her mother, who also lives merely for her own pleasure, marries the son of a rich old woman. Both mother and daughter are in the end confounded, the one by the death of her inamorato and the other by the death of her potential benefactor. The soldier achieves some sort of catharsis and goes off to New York—presumably to start life afresh. Miss Petry weakens her narrative by telling it through the person of the town chemist, but she writes well, using natural phenomena to heighten the sense of helplessness in the grip of circumstances, which is her theme. Whereas Mr. Motley in effect seems to be asking us not to blame Nick Romano because he could not help it, Miss Petry at least implies the blame attaching to the selfish mother and daughter.

These two novels, brave attempts as they are to get away from race relationships, leave one wondering why in pursuing "Common Denominator: Man" the Negro novelist should fly so far from the life he knows best. Why do so few Negro novelists seem inclined to deal with life among Negroes alone? Is it because when they think of themselves they cannot help thinking of the conflict of white and black, because whenever they attempt to get away from the same old theme they feel compelled to jump into a different world entirely? We may agree, first of all, that it is natural that the majority of Negro novels should be about the relationship between white and colored people, for this is the biggest single factor in the lives of most American Negroes. It is not the theme that matters, but the way it is treated. Even though we feel, after reading a number of these novels of race relationships, a certain dread at the prospect of yet another catalogue of injustices and petty cruelties, the fact that these novels play only one tune is not the real reason for our reaction. We do not, after all, when we pick up yet another play by William Shakespeare, say: "Oh, the same old thing again. Nothing but love and hate, love and hate." The tune can be arranged and played in a number of different ways, and it is the degree of insight and subtlety in the arrangement that gives us grounds for appraisal. One may take miscegenation and its complementary subject of "passing," as Negro novelists from Charles W. Chesnutt to Jessie Fauset and Nella Larsen have done, and one can explore this theme either in the form of a complaint or as material for a human drama, as Sinclair Lewis did in *Kingsblood Royal* and as William Faulkner did so much better in *Light in August*. But very few Negro novelists since Chesnutt have found it possible to do this.

For a time, in the 1920's and 1930's, things did seem as if

they were going to be different. A number of novelists turned to satire and even self-criticism. Miss Fauset's *Comedy, American Style* dealt with color prejudice among middle-class Negroes, a phenomenon that one feels to be as much an indictment of the middle class as of the evil of color prejudice itself. In *Black No More* George Schuyler satirized the color problem by writing about an electrical invention that turned black skin into white. Rudolph Fisher, in an amusing and well-written novel about life in Harlem, also showed the absurdity of color prejudice. His Miss Cramp is the embodiment of white bourgeois ignorance and hypocrisy, and his white Negro, Merit, the embodiment of educated enlightenment. Merit, in fact, makes rings round Miss Cramp, and this one feels is great fun. But the irony is too heavy. Miss Cramp is just a little too silly and Merit just a little too good to be true. The balance is being redressed too far. It is all very awkward, because no averagely sensitive white man can help feeling pity and sympathy for the injustices the American Negro has had to suffer. Even if there were some truth in Southern statements that Negroes were on the whole better off during the antebellum period than during Reconstruction and that it was not until the Northern states poked their noses in that pride and resentment took the form of discrimination against the Negro and "Jim Crowism" appeared—even if all this were true, there would still remain the simple fact that before the Civil War, in direct contravention of the solemn terms of the Declaration of Independence, the American Negro did not have the most precious thing a man can possess. One might expect American Negroes to write about the struggles and feelings of those days, and indeed they have done so—in the person of Mr. Arna Bontemps most nobly and movingly. One might also expect that there would have been for a considerable time novels protesting against persecution in the South and discriminatory practices in the North. But only for a time. There is a greater subject for the novel, the true subject of the "human heart in conflict with itself." There have indeed been one or two Negro novelists who have regarded the novel as a stage for a whole and rounded, even if tragic, picture of life, but the overwhelming majority continue to use the novel as a means of protest, and this is where the awkwardness comes in. The white critic, faced with an outspoken but (as novel) not very good piece of Negro writing, feels that he ought to show his friendliness, his sympathy, and his essential liberal-mindedness toward the Negro cause by suspending his normal standards of judgment. If he does not and, instead, attempts to judge by the highest aesthetic standards, he knows that—although the Negroes are rather less touchy in these matters than the Jews in America—he is likely to be accused of discriminatory practices. Mr. Hughes, in his otherwise objective *The Negro Novelist; 1940–50,* does in fact accuse white reviewers of discriminating against Negroes, a charge very hard to believe—at least of Northern reviewers and critics. There comes a point when it is doing no service either to the Negro or to literature to maintain a separate set of standards, and it seems likely that this point has now been reached.

Let us take the case of Richard Wright's *Native Son.* It is a book about a Negro boy from Mississippi who obtains a job with a wealthy white family in Chicago. The daughter of the house and her fiancé, both sentimental Communists or fellow travelers, treat the boy, Bigger Thomas, as an equal. One night Bigger drives Mary back from a meeting with her friend and realizes that she is drunk. He carries her up to her room and is just about to make love to her when the mother looks in. In his anxiety to keep the girl quiet Bigger accidentally suffocates her. In a panic he cuts up the body and burns it in the furnace. The rest of the book is concerned with the way he is discovered, his trial, and his defiant death. It is where Bigger cuts up the girl's body that the book begins to go wrong. The reader's first objection is that this is not what the Bigger Thomases of America are likely to do; he must be able to feel that the character he is asked to believe in is, if not exactly representative, at least plausible. It takes either a very callous or a very mentally ill man to cut up someone he has accidentally killed and to act as Bigger does after this event. And we are not moved by the story of a callous or mentally ill man unless he is presented to us as a human being with mixed motives, with that compound of love and hate, good and bad, that we feel within ourselves. Mr. Wright does not present Bigger Thomas as such a man. He has written a deliberately sensational book, and yet he asks for our pity and our compassion. We cannot give it, for we feel that Bigger Thomas has been exploited by his creator.

We feel much the same emotion when we read the equally naturalistic novels of William Attaway and Chester Himes. It is not that we object to raw details, but that we are not satisfied by these alone. There are no halftones and there is no catharsis. Are we expected (we ask) to believe that all white women are hypocritical sluts, like Madge in Mr. Himes's *If he Hollers Let Him Go,* or all white men as mean-natured as John Stoddard, the gambler in Mr. Attaway's *Blood on the Forge*? It is all, as it were, so black and white, and one cannot help thinking of William Faulkner's portrait of Lucas Beauchamp in *Intruder in the Dust*. That magnificent, proud, pigheaded Mississippi Negro is a long way from the stereotypes of Mr. Himes and Mr. Attaway. Through him we feel, perhaps for the first time in literature, the Negro as a human being, and that is more than one can yet say of most of the characters in Negro novels.

Although the limitations of our subject do not allow us to go into the treatment of the Negro by white writers to any great extent, it ought to be mentioned that there has been an immense improvement since the days of *Uncle Tom's Cabin* and the poems of Longfellow, Bryant, and Whittier. With Melville's Negroes and Mark Twain's Jim there begins an attempt to portray the Negro as an individual rather than as a stock character. The realistic novelists, Stephen Crane in *The Monster* and Theodore Dreiser in *Nigger Jeff,* told the truth as they saw it, and Ellen Glasgow's *Barren Ground* was the first indication that it was possible for a Southern novelist to do what William Faulkner later did with such understanding. Eugene O'Neill's *Emperor Jones,* Paul Green's *In Abraham's Bosom,* and Marc Connelly's *Green Pastures* brought the Negro into drama, and, in the South, novelists and short story writers like William March and Erskine Caldwell took up the

cudgels on behalf of the Negro. Since the 1930's, however, it has
become increasingly clear to white writers that the "Kneel to the
Rising Sun" and "Trouble in July" kind of story was not the
whole truth. Robert Penn Warren's story "Her Own People" is
a good illustration of the fact that not only the Southern writer
but the whole society of the South has been slowly changing. Mr.
Warren puts the dilemma of an intelligent but not especially saintly
couple in the face of a Negro servant who has "gone sour on
them" after they have moved from her home state. The girl leaves
her work on the eve of a party and deceives both the white couple
and the Negroes with whom she is lodging. But it is her meek,
resigned obstinacy that arouses in her white employers the combination of guilt, responsibility, and impotent fury with which they
leave her, lying, as she has been for three days, doggedly on her
bed. The story ends:

> "It's right pitiful," she finally said, "thinking of her lying up
> there."
> He slammed the gears into second for the grade.
> "I'm fed up," he said.
> "What do you think I am?" she said.

Mr. Warren's story gives some indication of the complexity of
the emotions that the Southern white man experiences in his dealings with Negroes. If the Northerner is continuing righteously indignant at the legality of segregation in the South, the Southerner
is hounded by his sense of guilt and responsibility. And all the
while the situation is changing.

Since the last years of the last war there have been great improvements, culminating in a Supreme Court decree that should,
in a very few years, complete the slow progress of the American
Negro towards social equality. Gunnar Myrdahl's survey, published in 1944, is now quite out of date. A Negro sociologist
lecturing in England recently reported that he had to correct many
misapprehensions among members of his audiences. These misapprehensions can be summed up in the remark of a lady attending

a course of lectures on "American Life and Letters" who asked: "Please tell us in the next lecture what we can do to help the poor blacks." It was not merely that she was still living in the atmosphere of Erskine Caldwell's short stories, or even that she was being unwittingly insulting to the American Negro, but more pointedly that she did not realize the extent to which the Negro, over three hundred years, has become assimilated into American society. He does not think of himself as anything other than an American, and his way of life and his ideals are little different from those of the average American in the part of the country in which he lives. He is every shade from black to white, very often considerably better to look at than some white people, and he feels no kinship with and in many cases looks nothing like his brother in Africa. The thirteen million Negroes in America earn among them almost as much as the national income of Canada. The illiteracy rate among the younger generation of Negroes is now, according to Dr. Eli Ginzberg, only 4.4 per cent compared with 32.4 per cent among those over sixty-five. The percentage of Negroes who go to the sixty-eight Negro colleges and universities is greater than that of white people who go to universities in England, and although the educational standards cannot be compared, these figures are not without meaning. One by one, too, the white universities of the South are receiving Negroes. Lynching is now a thing of the past. In the army alone there are 4,000 Negro officers, and the sort of treatment that George Schuyler described as being meted out to a Negro officer in the South during the 1914–18 war could not happen in these days. These are heartening facts, and it is only a matter of time before their effects are felt. As Miss Lillian Smith said earlier this year, "In the cities the pressure will be heavy from both liberal whites and Negroes and the change will come rapidly, I think."

The development of Negro literature may be compared with the development of American literature itself. In the nineteenth century American writers were suspended between desires to imitate the English and to draw from their own resources. When the break came the native literature was crude and its American-ness was overstressed. It was a literature of protest. Now, how-ever, a balance has been reached, and Americans can look back on their own tradition with pride and write in the secure knowl-edge that their literature reflects themselves and does not ape the styles and mannerisms of another people. Similarly, Negro writers were suspended between a desire to imitate the white man and a passionate feeling that they ought to write about and out of themselves. Cultivated Negroes, disliking the traditional comic stereotype of the Negro, reacted away from the vernacular to-wards "literary" English. Since the 1920's, writing naturalistically, they have developed their literature of protest. The next stage must surely be, as with the American white man, the emergence of a true Negro literature, born of a harmonious integration. And perhaps, in the final stage, the very term "American Negro Lit-erature" will be an anachronism, for, as Ralph Ellison has pointed out, the "image of the American," when it is finally defined, must inevitably be an amalgam of white and black. When that day comes, to write about "American Negro Literature" will be an occupation for historians rather than for critics.

Part 3. INTELLECTUAL OPINION

Authorized and Revised Versions

Contemporary Religious Studies

Philosophical Speculation

The Two Cities

Ivory Towers in the Market Place

Authorized and Revised Versions

THE MOVEMENT OF HISTORY IN THE UNITED STATES

THERE IS a sense in which England is a profoundly historically minded country. Its sense of tradition is very living. There is, in addition to a great deal of mixed and erroneous historical knowledge of the 1066-and-all-that school, a great demand for serious historical work. In most universities history is the most popular arts subject. But compared with the United States historiography in England is a minor matter, a hobby, a respectable activity but not big business, not one of the pillars of the State. We have no real equivalents of the state historical societies, no historical society of the antiquity and prestige of the Massachusetts Historical Society, no great scholarly enterprises (allowing for the *D.N.B.* and the *Complete Peerage* and the *Victoria County Histories*) on the scale of the Washington or Jefferson papers or the promised edition of Franklin's works.

It is natural that this should be so. The United States is, in a special sense, a creation of history. It has a legal birthday, a legal birth certificate, a legal proof of confirmation. History is here open and operative. Then, there are few if any dark spots in American history. There may be disputes about Folsom points or the light that carbon dating throws on the age of man in America, but for *real* American history the record is full. There are no ambiguous texts in Tacitus to support theories of the three-

field system or of the origins of Parliament; there is no need to
fall back on Stubbs's theory of occultation. All questions can be
answered.

The size of the country, the multiplicity of academic institutions, the worship of the PH.D. mean that an immense amount
of research is done and published. The English Saul cannot compete with the American David. The mere bulk of American production staggers the observer, and the American Historical Association is more like an English trade union, in size and functions,
than our modest Historical Association. Then, in a country of
such diverse racial origins, "history" is an historical necessity. It
is important to explain the role of Fort Snelling to Scandinavians
in Minnesota, if only to keep them from believing in the Kensington stone. Polish tobacco farmers in the Connecticut River
valley must be given by *history* a spiritual kinship with the East
Anglians who shook the dust of Massachusetts as well as of Lin-
colnshire from their feet.

It is not to be thought that American historiography is devoted
entirely to American history. The wealth of the country, the diverse racial origins, the ability to attract European scholars have
given American college faculties unrivaled opportunities since the
days of Francis Lieber; the occasional Gaillard Lapsley only un-
derlines the truth: westward the course of learning takes its way.
More than that, the great American universities are less convinced
than ours that training in history is and must be primarily a training in the history of one's own country. The American college
student is free to range from China to Peru. He may "major"
in history without knowing or caring who Millard Fillmore was,
not to speak of Daniel D. Tompkins. Nevertheless, the main effort
of American historiography, the main concentration of labor, of
money, and of interest is in the field of American history, and it
is in themes suggested by that history that modern American historical scholarship is seen at its best. It can be seen in admirable
biographies like Mr. Pusey's Life of Chief Justice Hughes, in very
learned, very lengthy, very combative constitutional histories like
the first two volumes of Professor Crosskey's vast work. It can

be seen in series like *The New American Nation.* It is, above all, in regarding its own past that American history is most varied and most impressive.

It is still true, as it has been for three generations, that the historical theme that excites the most popular interest at the higher level (and some of the most learned acrimony) is the Civil War. No American martial enterprise, not even the great naval and land campaigns in the Pacific between 1941 and 1945, has as yet replaced the epic of the War Between the States. It could be argued that this is because the most conspicuous memorials of that war are at home. The forts that once defended Washington against the threat from the Army of Northern Virginia still exist as place names and even as entrenchments, like Roman camps in Auvergne or Scotland. Frederick and Fredericksburg, Chickamauga and Chattanooga are present in a way that Okinawa, Bastogne, Cantigny are not. Even the heroes of that remote war are living in folk memory in a way that many of the living heroes of the late war might envy. Fairly obscure generals find new biographers; the exact words of Nathan Bedford Forrest are warmly debated, and a recent attempt has even been made to redress the balance that so long tilted against Lincoln's War Secretary, Stanton.

Superficially, all this does not differ much from the academic assessments and revisions to which we are accustomed. But it would be a superficial view that compared the continuous outpouring of writings, at all levels, on the course and conduct of the Civil War with English discussions of the consistency of Clarendon, the role of Cromwell's generals, or even the personal histories that lay behind the charge of the Light Brigade. Many of the American writers bring to their task not only learning, but a sound and simple scholarly desire to describe the thing "as it really happened." But there are more Macaulays and fewer Rankes in the American field, and if they fall beneath Macaulay in narrative power and in learning, they at least equal him in partisan zeal. The Civil War is a fighting theme; the very name is a fighting theme. The ashes are still hot at Gettysburg and at Fort Sumter, especially at Fort Sumter. In part, the continuing interest in the history of the Civil War is due to the special interest that the South takes in its own past and to the renewed self-confidence that has come both from the rapidly increasing wealth of the South and its revived political importance, a result of the long period of Democratic domination. It has also come from the exploitation of a general national malaise. As long as it was possible to see in the United States the "Triumphant Democracy" of Andrew Carnegie's paean, the case of the defenders of "the Lost Cause" was hard to put, outside the South itself. But as criticism, doubt, something like despair invaded all parts of the United States, although in different forms and with different degrees of intensity, the appeal of men who, for whatever motives, had not wanted the America of 1929 or 1939 or 1945, grew.

The simple "revision," to borrow a phrase from the discussion of German war guilt, was inevitable. It had been attempted from the end of the war, for Southern leaders at once rushed into print, like so many German generals, explaining the unnatural fact of their defeat and the righteousness of their cause. But apart from a mild success of curiosity, nobody outside the South noted these apologies and explanations. The sword had decided; the great twin brethren, Right and Might, had, as Augustine Birrell put it, been in this case on the same side. Gettysburg and Appomattox were not to be appealed against. The result, the abolition of slavery, the preservation of the Union for its visibly magnificent present and even more magnificent future, was too obviously an example of the march of historical providence for the protests of the vanquished to excite interest or even pity. Of course, the romantic side of the Southern resistance was, after the first years of peace and reconstruction, admired in a vaguely sentimental way. It provided themes for scores of novels and plays till it reached its apogee, if not its end, in *Gone with the Wind*. But the gallant officers in immaculate gray, not in drab butternut, the lovely belles, first of all in glorious white crinolines and then in equally fetching mourning, were, nevertheless, on the losing and the wrong side.

The Southern counteroffensive did not effectually begin until the more or less unconscious basis of the Northern sense of superiority was attacked. It was not enough, hardly even useful, to refute the thesis offered by Lincoln's official biographers, Nicolay and Hay, or by the most representative Northern historian, James Ford Rhodes. It *was* necessary to refute *Uncle Tom's Cabin*. And this, in brief, is what the dean of Southern historians, Ulrich B. Phillips, did for more than thirty years, his work culminating in popularity, if not in scholarly merit, in *Life and Labor in the Old South*. Slavery was seen as one of the main institutions of the old South but not its basic, peculiar institution. It was seen as an instrument of civilization, on its way to gradual, nearly painless and health-giving amelioration and extinction, when this beneficent process was stopped by Northern fanaticism and hypocritical avarice. Threatened in its very existence by this alliance of ignorance and greed, the South was driven to resistance, heroic if foredoomed, but certainly guiltless.

This thesis got support, if not complete support, from the North. For there the orthodox view that, in the causes if not necessarily in the conduct of the war or in the administration of the victory, the North was wholly right was one of the living political assets of the Republican Party. The enemies of the dominant party— and some were of its own household—seeing little resemblance between Lincoln and Nelson Aldrich or between the zealots of 1854 uniting to resist the "slave power" and the agents of big business uniting to defend the tariff and child labor, were very willing to reconsider the question and to look with a skeptical eye on the official historiography.

Then Northern historians, with nearly all passion spent—with the battles and leaders of the Civil War living in memory, indeed, but not exciting the passions of the years of James G. Blaine or even of John Hay—began to examine the causes and conduct of the war in a new spirit. Edward Channing, the last scholar to have the courage to attempt, singlehanded, a history of the United States on the heroic scale, was a Yankee of the Yankees. Harvard personified. But in his teaching, and in his writing, there was a marked change of emphasis; of course the right cause and the right men won, but not all the rightness or all the righteousness were on one side. Channing's correspondence with Albert J. Beveridge is most revealing, if only in the way it shows each of them rehabilitating Stephen Douglas, who, for the old historiography, never appeared as "less than archangel ruined." Douglas, they both concluded, was a great man. Of course, neither Channing nor Beveridge was strictly a pioneer. A group of middle Western historians had begun to rewrite the history of the origins of the Republican Party (and so of the war), to see in the Kansas-Nebraska Act not a mere deed of perfidy provoked by an unnatural lust for the presidency, but a not abnormal example of state and railway politics, and in the opposition to Douglas less a rallying of all the defenders of the rights of man and the spirit of the Constitution than a combination of politicians seeking in the wreck of the Whig and Know-Nothing parties a local habitation and a name.

Indeed, for two decades it was bold to see in the early Republican Party "the party of moral ideas." It was dangerous even to see in Lincoln the dedicated apostle of the antislavery cause awaiting the moment to strike once and strike no more. The classical Lincoln was best preserved in the Life by an Englishman, Lord Charnwood. The revision (and reduction) of Lincoln's role was significant of the temper of the professional historians, "the guildsmen" as the professional jargon put it. It affected the public very little—hardly more than that public was affected by the learned, acute, and unmalicious examination of the Washington legend by Bernard Knollenberg, who showed that more than the cherry tree was doubtful in the traditional hagiography. But the work of the Bollandists does, in the long run, affect popular devotion, and the critical work of the scholars began to percolate. More immediately effective was the work of the "debunkers," of whom Rupert Hughes was the most prominent, but their work was directed to showing the human weaknesses of the national heroes, their addiction to strong waters or weak ladies. It did not affect the majestic creation of the heroes, the United States itself.

What no scholars, what no best sellers could have done, was done by the depression; it shook the faith of the average American in America and so made him ready to consider more favorably the results of the critical historical scholarship of a generation. In the great crisis of faith from 1929 to 1933 more temples crumbled than the New York Stock Exchange, more gods proved to have feet of clay than Mr. Samuel Insull. It was easier, now, to consider the possibility that the Civil War was a racket, to see its representative figures in Simon Cameron or such noncombatant captains of industry as Rockefeller and Carnegie, to give half belief to the ingenious thesis that Lincoln was murdered not by Southern fanatics, but by the ruthless but farseeing leaders of the business wing of the Republican Party. The young men and women who had gone through college, the young men who, having graduated, found no jobs, were young men who had been exposed to such Jeffersonian revisions of American intellectual history as Parrington's *Main Currents in American Thought*. They had heard of Charles Beard's proof that the sacred Constitution itself was a counterrevolutionary document, designed to make the United States safe for Hamilton and his heirs, J. P. Morgan and Company and the National City Bank. In the years of breadlines and apple sellers at the corners of Wall Street or La Salle Street, history acquired a new and a more vivid meaning. The experience drove many, for longer or shorter periods, into the Communist Party or Marxism (the two were not identical). It drove others into various historical schools, all of which professed, explicitly or implicitly, to explain the plight in which the United States found itself.

This situation favored various and, indeed, contradictory historical schools. It favored the Southern revisionists, for had not the grim prophecies of the more extreme prophets of the Old South come true? Was Fitzhugh's *Cannibals All* so far wide of the mark? Was the slave, who was fed and housed and clothed, worse off than the white millions who stood idle in the marketplace because no one would hire them? The Southern agrarians, poets, novelists, critics who in the lush days of the Coolidge boom had preached the virtues of the old order, seemed to have been better prophets than the panglossian economists and business forecasters who had not so much predicted as seen the millennium. Republican history, like the Grand Old Party itself, was washed away in the flood of misery and resentment.

Naturally Marxism acquired a new importance. Here was the crisis, predicted so long. Marxism was old enough in America. Had not the dying First International been exported to New York to save it from anarchist body snatchers? In America the most complete English translations of Marx had been published, and in German and Yiddish there had been a continuous flow of Marxist propaganda and exegesis. In Jack London's *Iron Heel,* a simple but telling version of the Marxist view of history had attracted hundreds of thousands. Henry Adams knew of Marx and of his importance, and Theodore Roosevelt had at least read a refutation. Nevertheless Marxism had had a feeble life in America. It never fused with the native radical tradition. It remained in most cases a political religion preached in strange languages to immigrant groups. Nor did it display much interpretative power in face of the American scene. The writings on America of Marx and Engels are among the least impressive parts of their work, and the book on America written by Marx's son-in-law, Edward Aveling, has some claim to being the silliest serious book ever written on America. But what Daniel de Leon or his rivals could not do, the depression did. Marxism explained the depression completely, fitted it into the world picture as no less ambitious philosophy of history could do. It explained, for example, the failure of the frontier theory. This, as popularly interpreted, had explained the Americanism of America in the terms of a great area of empty land on which the American could draw. But that area (as Turner was erroneously believed to have said) had vanished by 1890. Where was the American to go now? Turner was aware of the dilemma; *if* the special American virtues were the result of the existence of free land, how could they survive its disappearance? Marxism could answer that question.

Marxian interpretations of American history were all the rage.

Economic interpretations of American history poured from the press. The age of the muckrakers returned, but the old, simple ethical condemnation of the era of Theodore Roosevelt was regarded as naive. The "Square Deal" of Theodore Roosevelt, like the "New Freedom" of Woodrow Wilson, was seen as pills to cure an earthquake. The robber barons could be fitted into a new historical context as *necessary* wicked men, or simply as personifications of the ineluctable movement of the dialectic. It was as absurd to condemn the elder Rockefeller as to express moral indignation at the distasteful activities of an earthquake or a mosquito. A great deal of this Marxism was very superficial. Charles Beard protested that he had learned that politics is about economic interests, not from Karl Marx, but from James Madison. A simple system of motivation that would have shocked Marx himself was briskly applied. The Civil War was seen, in face of all the evidence, as a deliberate conspiracy of the Northern business interests, bent on creating the conditions of a new plutocracy. Foreign Marxists joined in the fray armed with doctrinal zeal almost in inverse proportion to accurate knowledge. One very eminent American scholar found, to his intense irritation, that a learned book of his, setting out an economic interpretation of American history, had been coolly plagiarized and issued in short version by a Communist writer under a hearty Anglo-Saxon pseudonym.

Not all of the results of the Marxist *engouement* were bad. American economic history was rewritten in a less optimistic tone. More than that, the frontier hypothesis was revised, both in the sense of a return to what Turner had really written and in a reassessment of what living meaning the frontier had for modern America. The fact that the United States was more and more an urban society was beginning to be accepted; the problems of the growth of American urban society were studied, by historians as well as sociologists. The farmer was not vanishing like the Indian or like Billy the Kid or John Wesley Hardin, but it was a fiction that he was any longer the backbone of the Republic. His last frontier had been reached; from the *antiqua silva* of Pastorius to the almost too celebrated tree that grew in Brooklyn, was the movement of American history.

This realistic assessment of American life involved a reassessment of American history. The novelty of American life was not the "new man" of Crèvecoeur, erect, independent in the wilderness, but the business civilization that had transformed the log cabin into the skyscraper, had lined Midwest roads with California-style "ranch houses" where the white farmhouse had stood. In this spirit Louis Hacker called for a reassessment of the real movement of American history, and, greatly daring, Allan Nevins, far from deploring the great twentieth-century burst of business energy and domination, argued that America had had just enough business energy to win two wars that, but for the robber barons, she would have lost. It is probably around that question, the ethics and the results of the great capitalist enterprises of the century, that the controversies of the immediate future will rage.

The crisis that brought on the New Deal had results in other fields of historiography. In the 1920's the fashion among the more modern academic historians had been to exalt Jefferson against Hamilton. Beard's work could not but cast a shadow on the reputation of the greatest Secretary of the Treasury before Andrew Mellon. That was not Beard's intention; it was against his view of politics; but it was an inevitable result all the same. The revival of interest in Jefferson was a natural reaction in the age when, incompletely quoted, President Coolidge was credited with saying that "the business of the United States is business." But in the depression, in the first golden months of the New Deal, Jefferson the semianarchist, the agrarian, the contemner of cities, the skeptic of government, was a poor symbol for the young men in a hurry who proposed to remake American society by the power of the federal government. It was not accidental that Franklin D. Roosevelt's favorite predecessor was Andrew Jackson, that Roosevelt wore perpetually a relic of the great man; and in Arthur M. Schlesinger Jr.'s brilliant and acclaimed *Age of Jackson* the New Deal found its historical pedigree and was told that urban radical politics had a far longer ancestry than most people had thought.

The war brought about revision in many ways. Few could now be found to defend the wreckers of the League of Nations. Henry Cabot Lodge, living, had had few friends; dead, he had none. A new "Atlantic" school of diplomatic and military history came into being. The realities of geopolitics were now on every lip, and Professor Gipson's profoundly learned and sympathetic study of the problems of the eighteenth-century British Empire was more intelligently received than it would have been a decade before. The war produced an immense amount of memoirs, some of them actually written by their authors. It produced what posterity may well judge to be a masterpiece, Samuel Eliot Morison's history of the naval war in the Pacific. But it also bred a bad habit of using history as a weapon of political warfare. Scholars or semi-scholars had hardly adjusted themselves to seeing in Germany the *fons et origo mali* when they had to do the same job for Soviet Russia. Revision started again; some of the veterans of the campaign against the Treaty of Versailles returned to the fray, and the story of American entry into the second war was retold in the spirit that had animated the "bankers' ramp" theory of the 1920's. Of course, work of a very different quality was also done, as in the really magistral diplomatic history of Professor Langer. Even actually contemporary history could be treated in a scholarly fashion, as Herbert Feis showed in *The China Tangle*. In another field the revision of early New England intellectual and theological history by Professor Perry Miller showed how far American scholarship had moved from the simple pieties of the orthodox tradition or the mere reaction against it of the two Adams brothers, Charles Francis and Brooks, and of their namesake but not kinsman, James Truslow Adams.

As a business, as a field of academic endeavor, as a molder of the public mind, American history has never been more flourishing. But (and American historians are conscious of this) it is also, because of its prominence, in danger. It is called on, too often and too loudly, to perform specific patriotic tasks. It is assumed, too simply, that a study of American history must breed hope and faith, if not charity. That it can breed skepticism, that even if only American history is studied, that history will reveal to the unthinking that no nation is an island, that many heroes lived before George Washington, and that not all problems can be or should be solved in purely American terms, are possibly dangerous thoughts. But the traditions of American candid and objective scholarship are now too deeply rooted for even a demagogic senator to destroy them. The danger is other: the danger that the American people will seek in the past, not merely an explanation of the present, but a kind of Sibylline book in which ready and infallible answers will be found to problems some of which are so novel that no answer can be found in history, in an age when "the great globe itself and all that it inherit may dissolve."

Contemporary Religious Studies

ANY ATTEMPT to survey the more notable output of American religious studies within the last years encounters two major difficulties. First, it is not easy for anyone to be sure that things of importance have not been entirely missed from view. Secondly, the private English library and the private collector both suffer deeply from their inability to purchase American books and periodicals. The consequent gaps in English private collections are greatly to be lamented, and this lament might well echo not only through the corridors of the Treasury in Whitehall, but also through the Department of State in Washington. In any event the choice of works for so short a survey brings with it much heart-searching. There must of necessity be many a backward glance at notable omissions like the works of Professor Niebuhr and Monsignor Fulton Sheen, both well known in England.

Professor Latourette of Yale has specialized in the spread of Christianity in both ancient and modern times. His great work is devoted to this subject, but more recently he has given us, not a synopsis of the longer volumes, but a new *History of Christianity*. In every library there are to be found many different histories of the Church, of the earlier and later heresies, of Reformation leaders and movements, not to speak of periods, saints, and orders, but as a rule there is little by way of one grand conspectus of all Christian thought and endeavor. And the reason is obvious. Few adherents of one communion, Church, or obedience have the necessary patience and quiet of mind to consider with sovereign objectivity the work and beliefs of others. Whence the special histories, the swift refutations, the charges and countercharges, the controversy, and the thinly disguised disapproval or sometimes even hatred. All this is refreshingly absent from Professor Latourette's latest work. He has realized that an author may chronicle almost anything provided he avoids the swift judgment of value and the epithet of opprobrium. To cover anything like the whole ground of Christian history the author has been forced to take a bird's-eye view and to confine himself strictly to outlines. Even the outlines must be faint in many parts, more especially as he wishes to see Christianity at work within world history.

After his long survey Professor Latourette's conclusions are arresting. He sees Christianity struggling toward unity in the World Council of Churches in close association with many organic units and ecumenical movements. He sees the vast influence of Christ in many institutions and societies, like the Red Cross for instance, that owe "their existence at least in part to Christ." Often he sees the Christian standards and beliefs in action when he considers the devoted work for the sick and wounded, for refugees and exiles. More important than all the labor and skill devoted to these causes, the author observes that "the idea of self-denying service [is] derived from their Christian faith." Unfortunately, little of all this conscious or unconscious Christian influence is open to statistical survey, and like every good American the

author enjoys statistics. Even less open to inquiry is the effect
of the Gospel on millions of individuals all over the world. At the
close of his history Professor Latourette says of the change wrought
by the Gospel in the years since 1914: "To some it came with
dramatic suddenness. In others it was wrought more slowly.
Whether abruptly or slowly, it was marked by what Paul called
the fruits of the Spirit—love, joy, peace, long-suffering, kindness,
goodness, faithfulness, meekness, and self-control." This lengthy
work closes with words of restrained but vigorous hope. It is, in
fact, a survey for action, though readers who enjoy browsing in
books will find in it matter for urgent reflection and sustained interest.

To turn from religious history:

American authors have produced many studies in the philosophy that lies behind religion, by which is meant neither the
philosophy of religion, if indeed there be such a subject matter, nor
philosophy properly so called. Of these many American contributions, the recent lectures by Professor Paul Tillich on *Love, Power
and Justice* are noteworthy. Of German descent, their author is by
nature and disposition of mind at home in the metaphysical
world, which he scans with a keen, experienced eye, and in these
lectures he gives incisive, compact analyses of the three fundamental forces that move the world. His conclusions, after dense
reasoning in surprisingly few words, may be summed up in the
following quotations: "Love, power and justice are one in God.
But we must ask: what do love, power and justice do within an
estranged world?" Again:

> *Agape* cuts into the detached safety of a merely aesthetic *eros*. It
> does not deny the longing towards the good and the true and the
> divine source, but it prevents it from becoming an aesthetic enjoy-
> ment without ultimate seriousness. *Agape* makes the cultured *eros*
> responsible, and the mystical *eros* personal. . . . What *Agape* does
> to the ambiguities of love, Spiritual power does to the ambiguities
> of natural power. . . . *Agape* conquers the ambiguities of love,
> Spiritual power conquers the ambiguities of power, grace conquers
> the ambiguities of justice. . . .

Lastly:

> Fulfillment is bound to eternity and no imagination can reach the eternal. But fragmentary anticipations are possible. The Church itself is such a fragmentary anticipation. And there are groups and movements which although they do not belong to the manifest Church, represent something we may call a "latent" Church. But neither the manifest, nor the latent Church is the Kingdom of God.

It is not for nothing that these enthralling questions are handled by a German metaphysician of American citizenship. That he could condense so much into a few lectures and subsequently into 125 pages is an achievement.

Moreover, the probing of ultimates in religion is not confined in America to the Christians. Professors Nahm and Strauss recently published the *Philosophical Essays of Isaac Husik*. The biographical introduction, a model of power through brevity, tells all that the student needs to know of the learned and lovable Dr. Husik, who was secretary of the Jewish Publications Society in America. His studies led him to concentrate for years on the greater Jewish medieval philosophers, and at the end to declare that there neither is nor can be nowadays any distinctive Jewish philosophy. Philosophy concerns man as man, not Jew as Jew. Moreover Judaism is a religion, "a positive and historic faith." Some of the papers recently published, for instance those on Maimonides, on Joseph Albo, the last of the Jewish medieval philosophers, and on aspects of Aristotle's work, notably the Categories, show insight and power. After years devoted to philosophy Husik reveled—there is no other suitable word—in the study of justice, jurisprudence, and law. Some of the papers published are only half completed as he left them in manuscript. They nevertheless convey an authentic note of patient research. His papers on the legal philosophy of Stammler and Kelsen will make strong appeal to lawyers. Everyone, however, who reads this last volume of collected essays will recognize and salute in Husik a man who emancipated himself from the ghetto both in mind and spirit. In the America that he loved he felt free, and he opened his mind to all the winds that blow from East and West. His was a *fides quaerens intellectum;* his loss to American Jewry and their band of scholars must indeed be great.

There remain to be considered the many volumes published by the Franciscan Institute of New York under the learned editorship of Dr. Boehner, Dr. Wolter, and Dr. Buytaert. As the texts and studies now number nearly two dozen, it is not easy to do justice to this sustained effort of scholarship. We have grown accustomed to long series of studies in medieval philosophy and theology, both in French and German, but as a rule they appear slowly and at irregular intervals. Not so the Franciscan studies. In the short space of some ten years these Franciscan editors have produced a whole library of texts and studies, especially on Duns Scotus, St. Bonaventure, and William of Ockham. The volumes succeed one another with a truly American dash, and the program for future work is vast. Some of the texts are presented with a welcome unadorned translation, others reprinted without comment from the *editio princeps*. Some of the volumes will be of no little interest to modern logicians, and several on Ockham will be of importance not only to the historian of modern philosophy but also to the many who quote the *Venerabilis Inceptor* as a luminary in the world of meanings, concepts, and words. The whole of the nonpolitical works of Ockham are on the point of being published under the editorship of Dr. Boehner and others, with a number of collaborators. This critical edition will be a welcome addition to the text and study series. In general it may be suggested that these volumes cast a strong light on the faith of the great Franciscan masters and on their power to think metaphysically with a rare independence of judgment. To any unprejudiced reader it may seem that their faith was not so much a guide as a light to their reasoning powers and to their philosophical rigor of search. Nor will the medievalists be alone in their gratitude to the Franciscan Institute for this grand panorama of study.

Even so slight a survey may convey the impression that in the United States many people of diverse religious convictions, united however in belief in the one God, Creator and Lord of all, are actively studying not only their history but also the philosophy that lies behind their treasured beliefs. Moreover, there is not one that does not sound a note of high hope and of adventure, notes that perhaps may be deemed characteristic of American life and effort.

Philosophical Speculation

IF BERKELEY had succeeded in his American scheme, and if his had been the dominant philosophical influence in American thought, we might have observed the paradox of an unprecedented advance in material wealth accompanied by a belief in the insubstantiality of matter. In reality philosophy did not cross the Atlantic very rapidly. Accounts of the North American continent up to the middle of the nineteenth century communicate a tone of society scarcely congenial to pure speculation. America's first philosopher of international reputation and her first philosopher of real eminence arrived simultaneously in William James and Charles Sanders Peirce.

North American civilization developed in an age of experimental science. It is evidently possible, and it is verified for many modern men in every continent, that the conquests of science may come to make philosophical speculation seem unnecessary or impotent. When the ancient traditions of European philosophy have weakened in a positivist atmosphere, we should not be surprised that philosophy in America is rarely assigned the importance that philosophy used to claim, but that recent philosophy has scarcely deserved. Nevertheless, every civilization has implicit philosophical presuppositions, and the presuppositions of the

founders of the American republic have shown a strong capacity
for survival in the American mind.

The men of the Declaration of Independence were products
of the eighteenth century. They combined a confidence in the
natural man after the manner of Rousseau with a utilitarian
practical morality of the pursuit of happiness. At the same time
they retained much of their old Puritan tradition; they acknowledged a Creator, and their conception of natural rights was
anchored in the older theistic recognition of natural law. They and
their successors have been perhaps even less conscious than
British liberal progressives of the tension between the two sides
of their outlook, and have managed without too much embarrassment to unite a vigorous cult of man with a decent respect for his
Creator.

Hence it is not surprising that the first typically American movement in philosophy should have been pragmatism, and a pragmatism that was by no means a Machiavellian doctrine of ex-
pediency but an invitation to adopt ideals precisely because they
exercised the attraction of ideals and promised scope to what was
best in man. A philosophy that upholds the ideas that work in
practice might have been a highly cynical doctrine, but, if American pragmatism has often been naive, it has never been cynical.
Nevertheless, in spite of the continuing respect enjoyed by John
Dewey's instrumentalism, the ambiguities of pragmatism have
become more and more evident.

For what does it mean that an idea should prove itself in practice? The undetected murderer and the successful thief have
found one variety of pragmatic justification for their activities,
and indeed gangsterdom has established itself pragmatically as a
feature of American city life. The maxims that have received pragmatic force from the tycoons of finance are written in many pages
of unsavory economic history. No doubt this is not what William
James meant by pragmatic justification, but then what exactly did
he mean? What he was trying to do becomes intelligible when we
think that it is by no means a short or easy task to find an adequate
theoretical basis for our procedures of scientific investigation and

for our moral ideals, and that some short cut is desirable for the needs of practical life. Then, however, pragmatism stands revealed as an unphilosophical or prephilosophical approach rather than a philosophy.

It was no wonder that, when James had made pragmatism popular, Peirce, who had first preached it, decided that he was no longer a pragmatist but a pragmaticist. For Peirce did his best to give a rigorous meaning to his terms. Part of his pragmaticism was a reaction against Descartes and the persistent Cartesian influence. Modern philosophers had supposed themselves bound to disregard all their prephilosophical thinking and to begin again from the beginning in the construction of a philosophical system. This, according to Peirce, was both absurd and impossible. It was absurd because nothing could have a better initial claim to truth than the deliverances of experience; it was impossible because no one could really divest himself in a moment of the mental acquisitions of a lifetime. Criticism had to be tentative and piecemeal, gradually refining upon an acquired stock of ideas that had to be acknowledged before they were criticized. In this way pragmaticism was a negative kind of pragmatism; ideas had to be surrendered when they were discovered not to work, but it was only in a very general sense that what had hitherto survived criticism was assumed to be adequate to its purpose.

Another facet of Peirce's pragmaticism was that the meaning of terms resided in the practical difference made by thinking that they were verified. If something could be taken as true or as false without making any difference to the world of experience, it was meaningless. Peirce's affinity is obvious with the logical positivist principle of verification, but, since he was not a Humian and did not restrict experience to sensations and feelings, his empirical theory of meaning was not involved in the same difficulties as logical positivism. Although Peirce's occasional attempts at metaphysical synthesis are neither very clear nor very plausible, there can be no doubt that he thought that philosophy ought to culminate in a metaphysical synthesis.

The most fruitful purely American element in recent philosophy has probably been the gradual discovery of Peirce. His persistent concern with logic has joined with the stimulus of the Russell-Whitehead investigations into mathematical logic in provoking a vigorous development of logical studies. It is possible to question whether the adoption of nonverbal symbolism has been either such a revolution or such a reform of logic as it is sometimes supposed to be; it is equally possible to wonder whether an exclusive interest in the nature of symbolic systems has not occasionally made thinkers neglect the reality that such systems were devised to symbolize; but there can be no doubt that, whatever the real contribution of mathematical logic to knowledge has been, American logicians have been responsible for a considerable share in it.

Whitehead's residence in the United States during his later years not only reinforced interest in his earlier logical work but called attention to the systematic philosophy of his old age. On the eastern side of the Atlantic this work now excites a noticeably tepid interest. Not only is it desperately obscure, but it seems to belong to a class of thinking dependent on scientific fashion, which has condemned other such attempts at synthesis by Alexander, Lloyd Morgan, and the like to early oblivion. In America, on the other hand, there is a continual flow of thesis literature and of more solid comment on Whitehead.

(This is the point, perhaps, at which we might suggest without undue malice that far too much thesis literature is produced in the United States. If the rule that candidates for degrees had to publish were replaced by a rule that they would lose their degrees if they published their theses within ten years, the world would be very much the gainer. After ten years, if they still thought they had something worth publishing, they would be much more likely to be right, and the product would have profited in maturity and weight.)

What else is typically American in contemporary philosophy? It would be superficial to allude to what are merely American types of expression, like the mention of "the half-dozen top-ranking American philosophers" in an academic dissertation. More seriously again, America is remarkable for its preoccupation with the theory of value. This is, of course, a natural refuge for a philosopher in an age of science. If he doubts whether he can maintain as his own any part of the realm of fact, he can still stake a claim to the realm of ideals. Even so, his claim is somewhat precarious. For, unless he can rely on a metaphysic of being and so reassert his ultimate jurisdiction in the realm of fact, his ideals are liable to be expropriated by psychology in the name of the science of fact. Neither W. M. Urban nor Ralph Barton Perry, with his admission that value is simply a matter of human "interest," quite succeeds in making himself secure against the incursions of psychology. There are, however, many younger American philosophers to go on debating values with undiminished ardor.

Liberal Christianity has produced many versions of the philosophy of religion. These are often innocent of metaphysical rigor, and we become a little tired of progressive and well-intentioned deities who, like successful business men, manage for the most part to guide the universe in the right direction although they are subject from time to time to unforeseen and disastrous slumps. Such deities appear to be objects for respectful sympathy rather than for worship. Brightman's God is finite, temporal, and in conflict with a stubborn element in his own nature, while Boodin's God is engaged in a fluctuating warfare with matter. For other thinkers God is the sum or system of values, and any personal factor in the divine seems to disappear. The importation of democracy into religion makes a metaphysic of transcendence appear unduly arbitrary and remote. Yet all this metaphysical naïvety goes with a real vitality of the religious impulse, which has in the course of history been so often a source of philosophical speculation.

There is certainly life in American philosophy. Although no second thinker of the caliber of Peirce has yet made an appearance, there is no reason why one should not turn up at any time. The great problem of the immediate future, for American as for other philosophers, should be the problem of the possibility of restoring metaphysics. What are the metaphysical presuppositions of logic, of the theory of value, of the philosophy of religion? Until the need of dealing with these presuppositions is faced, philosophical speculation remains scrappy and mutilated. But the great problem that is already recognized by the age is the problem of what can be said or, if it cannot be said, can at least be shown. Do the metaphysical foundations of philosophy come among the statements of science in the broadest sense, the things that can be said, or do they belong to the region of mystery, the things that cannot be said but can be shown, or are they beyond all human saying and showing? This is the concern of every philosopher, to whichever side of the Atlantic he belongs.

The Two Cities

PROFESSOR NIEBUHR ON CHRISTIAN REALISM

THE RELATION between the Christian Church and the world in which it functions has always been a matter of complex discussion. What is the Church to think about the world from which it gathers converts but which for the most part remains aloof and regards its august claims with an attitude that may be completely indifferent, wistfully doubtful, or frankly hostile? Is it of the devil or of God? Is it a permanent condition of the Church's life, or will it at last be converted and the dream of the rule of the saints come true? Or again, what is the Church to think of the policies and systems of government that the world devises, and is there some one system of managing human affairs that can be pronounced Christian? Is there a Christian civilization, or do the world and the Church stand over against each other, two "cities" as Augustine called them, mutually exclusive, and yet each needing the other, the world doomed to perish unless the Church can save it, and the Church unable to save it unless by strength of government the world will provide the peace in which the Church can perform its saving task? And what comment is the Church to make on that peace? Is it a Christian thing, or is it, too, somehow evil? What is the Church to say to our distracted world about Communism, about Socialism, about democracy, about the idea of world government?

It is to questions of this kind that Professor Niebuhr addresses himself in his deeply interesting volume of essays, *Christian Realism and Political Problems.* He attempts his answers knowing, as he shows in his first essay, that the Faith does not "endow the believer with a superior wisdom which will enable him to escape errors, miscalculations, and faulty analyses of the common life of man," and that he is dealing with a world that regards him and his thought as an irrelevancy to its belief that by the more rigorous application of scientific thought man and his affairs can somehow be manipulated into security.

Even the terms of the problem are most difficult to define. What is meant by the "Church" or by the "world"? Each term is used very loosely in popular speech. Most people mean by the Church simply the particular local Christian community to which they belong, and they would escape from the problem raised by a wider use of the term by maintaining that the Church at large consists of all "true believers," and when they demand that the Church should take some action they rarely mean more than that some fairly representative person in authority should speak about the matter in question. Professor Niebuhr uses the term to signify the total congregation of Christian people, whatever may be their denominational allegiance, and, given the situation in which we do in fact find ourselves, any other course would be unreasonable and certainly profitless. But it is important in considering his essays to realize exactly how the term is being used, and important also to remember that those who would tighten the term by confining it to some particular organized Christian society are, for his purpose, engaged in an argument that is almost startlingly irrelevant. At the same time the "world" is a term with an even less precise connotation, and for this reason Professor Niebuhr's first essay must be read where he has placed it. The modern non-Christian Western world, though it may have no overt creed, does seem to be directed by thought that must be described as technicological, and it is that kind of world that he has in mind, the world that believes that with the application of thoroughly scientific thought all will be well.

That, as his whole book makes plain, is the fundamental heresy to which he addresses himself. Men, observing that their plans go awry, that each economic method leads to tyranny, that each form of government proves eventually intolerable, invariably ascribe the corrosive fault to the system. The economic thought was imperfect, the facts upon which it was based were incorrectly assessed, the appropriate balances were inaccurately adjusted; the form of government, the monarchy, the oligarchy, the democracy, proved inefficient because its constitution was too loosely or too rigidly contrived. The evil is in the system; it is Communism, monarchy, League of Nations, what you will, that is wrong. Given the correct scheme, all will soon be well, for man, educated properly, is perfectible, and so, therefore, are his societies. What is the matter with man is that he has been badly educated, and what is the matter with his societies is that they have been ill planned. "The method is to examine man as if he were no more than one of the many objects in Nature, which the scientific method will be able to comprehend fully, if only its tools are sufficiently precise and the scientist is sufficiently objective."

Thought of that kind is outrageously false. Cassius had, to be sure, a very human ambition in mind when he reminded Brutus that the fault was in themselves and not in their stars, but he had touched the heart of the human problem. The fault is not in the societies, but they are what they are because they are the expression of ourselves, and—a fact that Professor Niebuhr does not seem to have seen as clearly as he might—we disguise that truth from ourselves when we think about the world by habitually speaking of "man" rather than "men." We lose our way by discussing an abstraction that does not really exist, for there is no such thing as Man or Mankind. It is more than doubtful, that is to say, that the Church can have anything to say about "Communism" or "Capitalism," but it has to see them as methods by which men contrive their lives and persistently to warn them that they are sinful men needing the grace of God to live well in whatever society they contrive. The evil in human affairs is in people.

That is one side of the problem, and Professor Niebuhr deals with it extremely well, though there is one essay, "Why is Communism so Evil?" in which he comes dangerously near to finding the evil in the system rather than in the men. Communism in our time has expressed itself in a totalitarian State, and totalitarianism, whether it passes itself as a monarchy, an oligarchy, a dictatorship, or—and this is possible—as a democracy, does provide an almost perfect example of the temptation of power; but the Christian must not allow himself to be deceived into writing as though in some particular form of human government the temptation were irresistible. Communism, based in our day upon the philosophy of Karl Marx (which Professor Niebuhr deals with admirably), does tend to take small account of the common man; but the Christian must remember that the same attitude has been characteristic of polities that were very far from being communistic. Again, Communism as we know it is an aggressive doctrine, in so far as it is urged to extend its influence as a consequence of the dictum that it and capitalism cannot live peaceably in the same world; but the Christian must remember, when he is asked to comment, that imperialism has taken many forms and has been the policy of States of many different kinds, so that he is therefore unable to say that Communism is inevitably aggressive. The Christian thinker has always to be on his guard lest he make the mistake of finding evil somewhere else than in a man.

But the Christian in the modern world is in a very different position from that of the Christian when the apostolic mission first penetrated Europe. Then the relation between the Church and the world was comparatively simple. The Christians were gathered into compact communities instructed to be in everything that touched religion separate from the pagans, while as citizens they honored and obeyed the Emperor. They regarded the world, "this world," as evil, and saw themselves as people who had been called out of it, and they seem to have made no attempt either to denounce or to alter the world's institutions. It is noticeable that St. Paul takes slavery for granted, only advising slaves to be good ones and not to ask for release even from a pagan owner; nor does he make an adverse comment on the games and theaters that later on moved the Fathers to scathing denunciation; while— and this is very striking—there is nothing in the New Testament to suggest that there was any specifically Christian attitude to war. Nevertheless there was in Christian teaching all the material out of which a difficult situation could be made, for in almost every respect, and especially in its view of the nature of man, Christianity took a very different view of life from that current in the Empire; and it may well be that the real cause of the persecutions was that the imperial authorities saw in Christianity a movement dangerously critical of accepted social and political thought. Still, at the first the Church was separate from the world, and if anyone was demanding apostolic pronouncements upon contemporary policies we have no record of the result.

By the time Rome was captured by Alaric the whole situation was changing rapidly. The imperial world that had seemed so strong was failing, and the Church was about to become the residuary legatee of Rome. Augustine could not see that, but from what he saw taking place before him he worked out the extremely important thesis, contained in his monumental *De Civitate Dei,* of the "two cities," the one founded on love of self, the other on the love of God. Professor Niebuhr examines his doctrine very closely, and his criticism of the Augustinian conception of love deserves careful study; but he does not follow out the historical line, and the lack of an essay on Dante's *De Monarchia* is unfortunate, for it is from the developed medieval conception of society that our modern problem stems. In the medieval period there was no problem in the modern sense; the evil, persecuting "this world" of the Roman Empire had gone, and in the persons of the Pope and the emperor the ancient dream that the saints should rule the earth seemed to have come true.

The idea of the Holy Roman Empire may never have been successful in practice, and at times an individual ruler, like the King of England, who was outside the Empire, could be a very unwilling instrument of papal rule, but in general the idea of the Church-State was accepted, and the fundamental Law was the old Imperial Law Christianized and operative with a divine sanction. The problem of the Church and the world appeared to have been solved, for the Church was master of the situation and everyone, except the Jews in their ghettos, was a Christian. The Church now spoke in condemnation or approval to its own people, and if Bernard at Cluny sang *Tempora pessima,* he had not the activities of nonchurchmen in mind, and when he added *hora novissima* he knew that anyone who heard his hymn would understand him and at least conventionally accept the ideas that directed his thought.

The Christianization of the world did not perhaps go very deep, and it is possible to criticize the position by saying that the medieval Church was only the world in an ecclesiastical dress, but at any rate if the Pope condemned the actions of a king and excommunicated him or placed his country under an interdict, everyone knew what he was doing and understood the principles upon which he claimed to be acting. The charge against him could only be that he was acting unjustly or with an imperfect knowledge of the facts, not that he was *ultra vires.* That is important, for in this medieval conception of the Church-State are buried the roots of the modern problem.

The essence of that problem, and it deserves a closer analysis than Professor Niebuhr gives it, lies in the fact that owing to the complicated inheritance of this past it is still taken for granted, not only that the Church has something valid to say about the world's policies, but that it should do so, and it is further taken for granted that it can speak in terms that the world can understand. An obvious illustration is the hydrogen bomb. It is suggested that the Church, presumably through some combined pronouncement from the Pope, the Bishops, and the leaders of the free churches, should outright condemn its use. To do so would be popular and comparatively easy, for the bomb outrages the sense of humanity in everyone, but what the demand overlooks is that it would not be on that ground that the Church would condemn it. The Christian view of man, which sees each of us as a soul made by God for his eternal glory, is not one that is today accepted by people who are not Christians, in spite of our inheritance of what is still called Christian civilization. Or the Church is urged to act as a rallying point on behalf of Christian civilization against Russian or Chinese aggression, as though the issue were superbly simple—as simple as it was, for example, when Europe faced the Moorish invasion; but in fact the Church would find itself leading a crusade comparatively few of whose members accepted the principles upon which the idea of a Christian civilization is based.

It is of immense importance that, in considering the comment that the Church has to make upon the modern world, we should fully recognize that since the medieval period a really vast reorientation of thought has taken place. It is not merely that the organization of the Church has been broken, so that there is no single voice that can fully express the Christian point of view, nor is it merely that States have passed completely outside the control of the Church; it is rather that immense numbers of people have no sort of contact with any form of Christianity, no knowledge of its terms or modes of thought, and see no reason why it should play any part in their lives. Probably few of such people are actually atheistic, fewer still have qualified by sober thought to be called agnostic; most are simply people who, particularly in industrial areas, have grown up outside any kind of Church and are completely ignorant of the faith and of its history. Professor Niebuhr is inclined to assign to these people a kind of materialist creed, a belief that somehow through technics mankind can be perfected. That may be true of the leading men of the type, but most have probably no creed at all, live from day to day with a hope that does not extend far beyond the immediate future, and vote in an election on little more than the emotion of the moment.

In such circumstances it is difficult to know what meaning should be attached to the phrase "Christian civilization." Certainly the mark of Christianity is on the institutions of every country in the West, but it almost seems that in the past four hundred years the situation has been so changed that the position of the Church is not incomparable with what it was in the earlier stages of its invasion of Europe. It is again a minority, and its opinion, however venerable, a minority opinion, and those who ask it to make pronouncements or to take a side in a political struggle are really looking back to the medieval world. It is almost as though one of the Apostles were being asked for an opinion on an aspect of imperial policy. Almost, but not quite, for the modern Church is being asked to address a world that has once been Christian, a world whose public men at times still use Christian language. Meanwhile we observe that in Communist countries the Church has difficulty in maintaining its right to exist, and it may be that the difficulty is increased by its memory of its medieval position, so that it desires still to control the world unmindful of the fact that the world is not the medieval world. Its true course might be to revert to the apostolic concern with the evil in men and to be content to work in whatever institutions the world provides; but Russia was once "Holy Russia," and that memory, in the Church and in the people, complicates the problem.

The Christian realist cannot, of course, make the mistake of equating Nazism with Communism, but from his point of view they have at least this in common: that in Russia and Germany they have in our time taken the form of an attempt on a gigantic scale to manipulate Man. All the resources of scientifically designed educational propaganda have been used to produce something different, a different man, from what was there before the attempt was made. It is impossible to be sure what would have become of Hitler's experiment had it not collapsed in war, but while the Christian cannot help regarding the whole story as wildly wicked, he must also reflect that since it was based on an erroneous view of man's nature, it would certainly have petered out. The same kind of reflection must apply to what is taking place in Soviet Russia, and already there appear to be signs of change, for example in the divorce laws, in education, or in degrees of personal wealth, and a greater toleration seems now in some sort to be extended even to the Church. The attempts to manipulate society as though men could be made predictable and universally conformable with an accepted single type, while these attempts are by no means new, are so certain to fail that they perhaps occasion more alarm than they deserve. What has made these two experiments politically dangerous is the ruthless cruelty that has accompanied them and their determination to expand over neighboring countries. And it must be remembered that the false idea of man, the desire to mold him to a pattern, is not the product of a single ideology. Professor Niebuhr pertinently recalls the comment of Mr. Churchill (as he was then) at the anniversary convocation of the Massachusetts Institute of Technology: "The Dean of Humanities assured us this morning that the day would soon come when psychologists could control the very thoughts in our minds. I may well be content to be dead in that day." Sir Winston Churchill stood for a political conservatism that insists that, within obvious social limits, a man is a person in his own right and entitled to personal freedom—a soundly Christian attitude—and it is extraordinarily interesting that when attacking Hitler he called him "wicked," and in commenting on Russia spoke of "the evil men in the Kremlin." With such thoughts the Christian is very much at home.

While in this series of essays the reader follows Professor Niebuhr's discussion of the various modern dreams and ideologies he gradually gets the picture of a Church almost inextricably involved in a dance of death that it seems powerless to prevent or even to check, and the essay in which this point is particularly discussed, "The Christian Witness in the Social and National Order," deserves the most careful consideration. What happened was that in the process of time the Church, from being a compact and isolated, though missionary, society, gradually overran the world. It reached the point when it not only governed the world, but was the world. To object that Christendom was never a solid political fact, or that the Age of Faith was not always marked by something more than a superficial Christianity, is beside the point. The Church's writ ran everywhere, and men, in spite of racial or geographical concentrations, acknowledged an overriding allegiance to a way of life and to an authority whose ultimate sanction was otherworldly. When, with the passing of the Middle Ages, that came to an end, the Church, whether Catholic or Protestant, found itself in the strange position of being part of a nation, *cujus regio, ejus religio,* and being involved in policies, external or internal, which it had not itself devised, but which followed national lines. The illusion of world government had dissolved (and it is strange that in his essay on that subject Professor Niebuhr does not discuss the medieval forebear of the modern attempts), and its place had been taken by the ever-changing alliances of highly self-conscious national groups. In that nationalism or, it should be added, in that Easternism and Westernism, or whatever may be the political picture of the moment, the Church is tempted to become involved—nationalist, communist, democratic, according to the social and political complexion of its members.

> It allows the accents of national pride and of racial prejudice, the notes of self-esteem and complacency, to color its message, so that the whole business of religion in our day could seem to the cynical observer (even as it must appear to the righteous God) as a vast effort to lobby in the courts of the Almighty to gain a special advantage for our cause in the divine adjudication.

That is a most penetrating comment; it uncovers the nemesis that has overtaken the Church, which, at the advent of the modern world, was betrayed by the stresses and anxieties of the times into a policy of internecine warfare, defending itself against itself, Catholic against Protestant, and so descending from its ancient seat above the whirlwind. Its position is obviously difficult. There are, as has been noticed, Christian men and Christian elements in the institutions of all the Western nations, as there are in Russia; and even in China reliable missionary sources affirm that Christianity is still vigorously alive; but the danger is everywhere plain that the Church might allow itself to become merely a party to the struggle, and so stultify itself that it had nothing to say to the survivors.

The world today stands at what is clearly one of the great crises of history; possibly, since the peril of a vast and unpredictably terrible destruction is evident, at the greatest of all; and people looking this way and that for a lead out of the darkness tend very naturally to look most often to the Church. Very naturally, because whether its transcendental claims are admitted or not, it is an institution that has survived the world's storms for two thousand years. It has seen empires come and go; it has watched political and economic systems develop, flourish, and fade. To the Church Karl Marx is only the latest of very many leaders of revolt, and it will still be at work when Communism has either vanished or has purged its crimes and become respectable; and the Church has seen precisely that happen more than once. But how through its various organized communities is Christianity to answer the appeal? What should the Church do? Its temptation, certainly in the West, is to listen to the cry that Christian civilization is in danger and to lend its voice to the denunciation of Russia, and we may be sure that the same temptation is being presented to it on the other side of the Iron Curtain. We must hope that it will have the courage to refuse, for that is only the ancient temptation, "and showed him all the kingdoms of the world in a moment of time . . . all these things will I give thee if thou wilt fall down and worship me." Even for so great a prize as the allegiance of the West, or of the East, the Church cannot do that. What then? The common answer is that "the Church must be the Church," but, as Professor Niebuhr points out, that can very well be no more than an attempt to withdraw from the world, much as the anchorites once fled to the deserts. Here the context needs to be quoted in full:

If the slogan that the Church should be the Church is to have a meaning other than its withdrawal from the world, must it not mean that by prayer and fasting it has at least extricated itself in some degree from its embarrassing alliances with this or that class, race or nation so that it may speak the word of God more purely, and more forthrightly to each man and nation, but also to each generation according to the peculiar needs of the person and the hour?

Men want to be rescued from the fruit of their misdeeds and their fears of one another by some magic word, or they want an august blessing on their "side," and they are apt to be outraged when the Church refuses or, when it yields, to be disappointed at the meager results of the blessing. Christian realism as Professor Niebuhr sees it demands not only that the Christian view of man—a person made in the image of God and with an eternal destiny, but a person in whom the divine image has been damaged by evil—shall be fully accepted against the current view that since the evil is not in man himself he can be manipulated into perfection; but it demands also that the Christian shall refuse to look unrealistically at the world's policies. Disentangling itself from its mistaken commitments, the Church must refuse to be blinded by the excitement of the critical moment, which with racialism, nationalism, or even economics, conceals the pervading heresy.

But when the book is closed, and the reader has been made acutely aware of the complexity of the problems involved and of the urgent necessity that the Church should free itself from its commitments with the world, he is probably bound to feel that the discussion has ranged only over the collective aspect of his life. Certainly that side needs the most careful thought that he or anyone else can give it, and he will agree that the Church needs to be extraordinarily careful lest in the emotion of a political crisis it find itself blessing something that history will reveal in very tarnished splendor. It must permanently speak of the righteousness of God, of the exceeding sinfulness of sin, of the redemptive power of grace, and of the kingdom that does not derive its authority from this world. But the reader is also likely to want to remind Professor Niebuhr that he, the Christian individual, is caught in this terrifying dance of death and has judgments to form, decisions to make, actions to put in hand. There is no essay directly concerned with that deepest perplexity of all. Nevertheless the essays help toward its elucidation. While time lasts the Christian, like the Church, belongs inevitably to two worlds, the city of God and the city of earth, and he cannot separate himself from the latter. Patriotism will distress him as it will distress the Church, but he cannot avoid the dilemma by some specious form of contracting-out; he has his duty to Caesar, and perhaps the most that he can do when Caesar's actions are patently evil is, like the Church, to use what influence he has on the side of justice and love, but to remain a citizen. At the same time, we cannot ignore the fact, which has been made very clear in recent years, that circumstances can arise in which the Church and its members have to choose the concentration camp.

> If such a day should come we will remember that the mystery of God's sovereignty and mercy transcends the fate of empires and civilizations. He will be exalted though they perish. However, He does not desire their perdition but rather that they turn from their evil ways and live. From us He demands that we work while it is day, since the night cometh when no man can work.

Ivory Towers in the Market Place

THE MAJOR problem that confronts the teacher of literature in an American university is one common to the universities as a whole and perhaps inseparable from the idea of a university in America. It is essentially a simple numerical problem: too many students want too many courses. The root of the matter lies in the democratic, "popular" nature of the universities. With a few exceptions they belong to the people; they stand on land granted them by the federal government, and they are supported by state tax funds. They represent the American ideal of mass education carried to the highest academic level. This circumstance creates two demands not easily reconcilable: the demand for education in the humanities (for in spite of the current anti-intellectualism of American officialdom the American people retain their faith in the beneficent virtues of "culture"); and at the same time the insistence that a university education should provide practical training of ultimate economic value.

Faced with this dual demand, university faculties have responded with a multiplicity of courses, a something-for-everybody program that attempts to satisfy both the humanistic and the practical requirements of the students. This division of interests can readily be seen in the curriculum of a typical university department of English. The department will offer a variety of courses in English and American literature, from Anglo-Saxon grammar to the poetry of T. S. Eliot, but it is also compelled to provide instruction in the mechanics of reading and writing, and indeed such "tool" courses will absorb a large proportion of the total teaching effort. This "practical" portion of the curriculum will include such courses as Engineering English, in which engineering students are taught to write intelligible technical prose, remedial reading for students whose reading speeds are below freshman standards, and composition, a course in grammar and syntax required of all or nearly all freshman students.

All these "tool" courses are legitimate manifestations of the practical function of the university. For the department of English, however, they are a considerable burden. They require a comparatively high number of man-hours of work a course, and they divert qualified department members from what seems to most of them a more important concern—the teaching of literature. The task of teaching such courses is customarily assigned to junior members of the staff, who are trained to teach literature, not composition, and who regard composition as a drudgery imposed on them because of their humble station, and therefore to be resented. This situation is not likely to create an ideal classroom atmosphere, and composition students understandably come to share their instructors' boredom and irritation. The obvious solution would be a corps of instructors trained to teach writing, but the departments of English do not seem willing to give their practical function a status equal to that of literature, and it remains a backstairs occupation.

"Creative Writing," which most universities offer as a credit-earning course, is a link between the practical and literary aspects of the department curriculum, appealing partly to the desire to learn how to earn a living and partly to the American faith in the therapeutic value of self-expression. The character and quality of such courses vary widely. At worst they simply offer emotional undergraduates an opportunity to be emotional for credit. At best they provide students of ability with a chance to learn techniques of professional writing with professional guidance and criticism. Here again the difficulty lies in finding capable, experienced instructors; training in literary history does not necessarily equip an instructor to teach students how to write (though many departments of English assume that it does, as they assume that a graduate degree in literature is a license to teach grammar). There are, however, some teachers of creative writing who have proved themselves brilliantly effective—Martha Foley at Columbia, for example, and Hudson Strode at the University of Alabama.

The literary portion of the department curriculum composes a pyramid, with the broad "popular" survey courses at the base, and at the apex graduate seminars providing specialized training in a wide variety of literary studies, from Shakespeare and Milton to such arcana as "The Lyceum Movement in Nineteenth-Century American Literature" and *Finnegans Wake*. One year's exposure to literature is generally regarded as the minimum essential to a humane education, and first-year students are required to attend what is commonly called the Freshman Survey.

The typical survey covers English literature from *Beowulf* to the present day, pausing along the way at Chaucer, Shakespeare, Milton, Pope, etc. Such a course has its obvious weaknesses, but it is not indefensible. It provides students who may not take another course in literature with some idea of the chronology and development of English letters and at least a passing acquaintance with the English Worthies. On the other hand, it introduces students to English literature at its thorniest point, a poem in a strange language (or in an almost equally strange translation) out of a primitive past; the youthful sensibility may well be numbed before it advances to literature that can be enjoyed without a glossary. Some departments of English have tried to find a practical substitute. Swarthmore College offers its freshmen modern American literature, on the theory that this is at least familiar ground and that the interested student can then move backward in time toward the difficulties of Anglo-Saxon. But this in turn deprives the student of the benefit of a first quick trip over the field.

In any event the survey course is invariably a ministering to multitudes. A large university will have several hundred students enrolled in whatever freshman survey it offers, and even if the students are separated into several sections the lecturer may find himself addressing gatherings of fifty or a hundred students at a time. No sort of student-teacher relationship is possible in such circumstances, and the despairing instructor may easily settle into a communication of dates, titles, and the mechanics of scansion —literary history at its lowest possible level. It is not always so, but clearly the conditions work against effective education; for material that depends upon individual personal response cannot be successfully taught *en masse*.

One cut above the freshman survey are the second-year classes known in academic jargon as the "period courses," which divide English literature into pieces of roughly one hundred years each —Renaissance, seventeenth century, eighteenth century, Romantic, and Victorian are common units—for closer study. This system has been in general use in American universities for a long

time—long enough for these arbitrary divisions to become what
T. E. Hulme called "pseudo-categories." Generations of American students have come to see English literature as a series of
walled gardens—one formal, marked "eighteenth century," one
wild, marked "Romantic"—all quite distinct bits of literary real
estate, adjoining, but not connecting. The effect of such a system
on American critical habits of mind is not easily defined, but it
is discernible enough, most clearly, perhaps, in the average scholar's desire to cultivate his own garden exclusively. A department
of English will have its "Spenser man," its "Milton man," perhaps even its Scotch Chaucerian, and such specialists, unless they
are exceptional, will give little attention to developments in other
literary periods. The result for the department is likely to be a
staff of scholars who each teach one course superlatively well and
three courses badly.

The superlatively well-taught courses, because they are specialized, are ordinarily offered at an advanced level, and it is here
that the real merits of the American system lie. This is unfortunate if one considers the popular function of the university, for
the majority of students who enroll in English courses do so at
the lower level, and there are no specialists in surveys. However,
for the English "major," the student who is concentrating on the
study of English literature, the specialist structure provides a wide
choice of subjects, each taught by a man who has made it his
own. When the habit of dividing literature into conventional periods breaks down it does so at this higher level; many departments of English now offer advanced courses that cut across periods or are devoted to writers other than the traditional Big Three
—Chaucer, Shakespeare, and Milton. In recent years modern literature has become academically respectable, and at some universities one can take advanced courses in Joyce, Eliot, or even Dylan
Thomas. It is at the advanced level, too, that the unilingual limitation that has been a traditional weakness of American literary
study is occasionally overcome, and courses in comparative literature occasionally appear.

Even in advanced, specialized courses the problem of numbers exists. It is often only in graduate seminars that student enrollment is small enough to allow anything approaching a personal student-teacher relationship to develop, and in at least one large Eastern graduate school doctoral seminars in English literature commonly have fifteen or more members, with large waiting lists. This burden of students is an important factor in the form that American graduate education has taken. Universities such as Harvard and Columbia have more graduate than undergraduate students; Columbia in a recent year had more than seven hundred graduate students in English literature alone. In such circumstances the personal direction of individual graduate programs is patently impossible, and graduate study necessarily assumes the methods of the undergraduate program—survey lectures to audiences of several hundred students, overcrowded advanced courses and seminars, and a mass-production awarding of degrees.

Other universities have been compelled to set up graduate programs that are simply a matter of another year or two of classroom attendance beyond the baccalaureate degree. The graduate students write term papers and take regular examinations just as the undergraduates do, and often in the same classes. In some universities one can earn a master's degree without doing any work distinct from the undergraduate program—neither writing a dissertation nor demonstrating proficiency in a foreign language. As a consequence, the prestige attached to a master's degree has declined until it scarcely exists. The cause of this unfortunate state of affairs lies in the importance that graduate degrees have come to possess in professional circles. In university teaching the Doctor of Philosophy degree is commonly regarded as a "union card," and many state universities will not employ a teacher, even as an instructor (which is the lowest regular academic rank), without it. This forces persons who may be potentially valuable teachers, but are not scholars, to attempt scholarly work, and necessitates an adjustment of standards to make their work acceptable. The mass of scholarship produced as doctoral dissertations is consequently of a lower quality than it would be if the PH.D. were a degree reserved for students of genuine scholarly aptitudes. There has been in recent years much criticism of this system, on the ground that it penalizes both teachers and scholars by not distinguishing them. So far, however, there has been no noticeable effort by university authorities to re-examine the ways and means of graduate education.

The principal weakness of American scholarship lies in its volume. There is too much of it, and much that should be left to die a quiet, unpublished death somehow finds its way between boards. This is in part owing to the professional advantages of publication—*any* publication; the young scholar anxious to make his way in the academic world may be excused if he relaxes his critical standards to see his own work in print, when professional advancement may be the result. Some responsibility also rests with the university presses, which sometimes seem more zealous than discriminating in their publication programs. But at the same time one cannot ignore the substantial services to scholarship that American university presses have performed—Yale, for example, with its proposed publication of the Franklin papers, the Walpole letters, and the Gertrude Stein material, and the presses at Harvard, Princeton, Pennsylvania, Oklahoma, and Minnesota. As publishing costs rise in the United States the university presses are more and more essential to provide outlets for work that merits publication but is not commercially attractive.

If some of the worst American criticism being written today comes from the universities, so does the best. There is, in fact, scarcely one critic of any stature in the United States who is not a working university teacher (the significant exception being Edmund Wilson). One may hear American criticism and scholarship dismissed as "analytic jargon" (it was so described recently on the B.B.C.), but such a generalization can be supported only by a careful selection of bad texts. It is mere ignorance to define the present level of American scholarship by the worst work of the graduate students, as a distinguished English critic was apparently doing in a recent article when he condemned roundly the "Germanic manner" and "Latinized prose" of "pedantic or esoteric" American professors. Such a criticism scarcely seems to describe the writing of Messrs. R. P. Blackmur, Lionel Trilling, Robert Penn Warren, John Crowe Ransom, Cleanth Brooks, Yvor Winters, or Allen Tate, to mention only a few of the university professors who are also critics and scholars. Not only the best criticism but much of the best poetry and fiction comes out of the universities, and this is not, as the same English critic asserted, because the writers are "driven into academic life," but because American university life provides a fertile intellectual soil in which good writing can flourish. The universities are not little Siberias but rather communities of men and women who share a common faith in the persistence of humanistic values. Because the universities are "popular," they attract persons who are not essentially scholars. Poets, painters, novelists, and composers find the academic life productive as well as pleasant. And the presence of such artists in turn gives the American university community an unusual vitality and breadth of interest.

The teacher of literature, though he may not be himself a creative artist (many, of course, are), is touched by the creative atmosphere in which he works. He is also touched (and this, too, is not without benefit) by the mixture of intellectual and practical desires to which the American university, by its very nature, must cater. To make the ivory tower and the market place coexist is not an easy task, and the universities do not always strike a happy balance; but when that coexistence is achieved the result is an educational institution that is unique and, in a democracy, supremely valuable.

Part 4. THE CRAFT OF FICTION

A Search for the Conscience
of a People

To ANNOY James Fenimore Cooper it was enough to refer to him as the American Scott. The annoyance was understandable: by no stretch of the imagination was it conceivable that anyone should call Scott the North British Cooper. Though it might look like it, it was not a question of their respective talents. Each had the same aim as a novelist: to uncover his people's history to the world in order to show how that history had made it the people it was. Scott, however, had the whole past of a proud and antique nation to tap, a past expressed in written story, in laws, in architecture, in poetry, in folklore; you had only to read Scott to learn what Scotland and the Scots were like: the Waverley Novels defined them for you. What comparable could you take away from Cooper? There was the American, of course, and the country he lived in, the new man in the new country, and Cooper had a full sense of both. But the attributes that defined them—the largely empty land rolling for thousands of miles like the ocean, the nebulous frontier, the log cabin, the buffalo hunter, and the Redskins —these were surely altogether too sparse. Scottishness was a quality, a condition of being, the whole world could recognize: in what sense was Americanness, if indeed it existed, real at all?

At bottom, Cooper's annoyance was with the fate that made him an American at his particular time in history. As a novelist he did as well as he could with the material that existed; Scott himself could not have done much better. It was Cooper's fate as a writer that he was an American when the condition of being an American could still be defined only in terms of negatives. The negatives echo from writer to writer from the days of the War of Independence onward. There is Crèvecoeur, in his famous "What is an American?" well before the eighteenth century ended: "Here are no aristocratical families, no courts, no kings, no bishops, no ecclesiastical dominion, no invisible power giving to a few a very visible one; no great manufacturers employing thousands, no great refinements of luxury. We are," he said, "the most perfect society now existing in the world." Eighty years later Hawthorne faced the pleasing prospect rather more ruefully:

> No author can conceive of the difficulty of writing a romance about a country where there is no shadow, no antiquity, no mystery, no picturesque and gloomy wrong, nor anything but a commonplace prosperity, as is happily the case with my dear native land. It will be very long, I trust, before romance writers may find congenial and easily handled themes either in the annals of our stalwart republic, or in any characteristic and probable events of our individual lives.

Almost within a year of Hawthorne's writing those words the guns of the opposing armies in the War Between the States were already producing the ruins from which so much of the poetry and romance of later generations of Americans was to flower. Even so, to the young Henry James nineteen years later what America had to offer the novelist seemed even bleaker than it had seemed to Hawthorne. When he listed, in his study of Hawthorne in the English Men of Letters series, "the elements of high civilization, as it exists in other countries, which are absent from the texture of American life"—the passage is quoted on another page of this volume—he must surely have had consciously in mind the passage from Crèvecoeur quoted above. It was not that he either disliked or misunderstood the summoning together of vital particles that were later to be joined in a single Union. These particles were not, however, necessary to his purpose as a writer. A poverty of scene, a poverty of differentiation between man and man, this was James's view of his native land at the age of thirty-six. Yet the point of view was not constant; or rather, other elements came into it as he shifted his gaze from the spectacle of the United States as such to the contemplation of the individual American. The individual American was himself. "It's a complex fate, being an American, and one of the responsibilities it entails is fighting against a superstitious valuation of Europe."

James had made his classic pronouncement some years before he wrote his book on Hawthorne, and therein he had defined not only his own predicament as a man and a novelist but also the dominant theme in American fiction, the theme that, beginning with Cooper and continuing down to the youngest moderns, such as Saul Bellow, John Phillips, and Wright Morris, allows us to speak meaningfully of the tradition of the American novel.

There have, of course, been great writers outside it. The most conspicuous is Melville. What constitutes an American, what it means to be an American, was not Melville's theme; he was preoccupied by other things and could take the fact of being an American for granted. It was less easy for Hawthorne, whose finest work is, from one aspect at least, an analysis, in which criticism and imagination are beautifully merged, of the meaning of the New England spirit, of New England puritanism. With Hawthorne the exploration of Americanness, as something mysteriously different from any other national quality, is well under way. The search for a specific American identity has begun. Its existence conditions the whole of American literature, and nowhere more strongly than in the novel, where it produces a fiction distinct from any other. The Englishman takes his Englishness for granted; the Frenchman does not constantly have to be looking over his shoulder to see if his Frenchness is still there. The difference is simple: the quality and condition of being an American is not something to be inherited so much as something to be achieved. This is the complex fate; and the history of the United States has been such that for each succeeding generation it has meant a beginning again. Stephen Dedalus's great boast in *Portrait of the Artist,* "I go to encounter for the millionth time the reality of experience and to forge in the smithy of my soul the uncreated conscience of my race," might be the declaration of principle of innumerable American novelists. Some such concept of the novelist's function lies, for example, behind the myth of the Great American Novel, in which is expressed the belief that a people may be born of a literature.

James's own great contribution to the tradition of the American novel was a sharpening of the sense of American identity. He wrought this almost in terms of a crude contrast between Americans and Europeans, and this is seen at its most transparent in his treatment of the "American girl." It is easy to misunderstand her and James's treatment of her, at this late date when we are probably much more conscious of the affinities between Isabel Archer and Clara Middleton than of their dissimilarities. But Trollope, too, in his later novels has something to say of the American girl, and the contrast between Trollope and James is revealing. There is, for example, Mrs. Hurtle, in *The Way we Live Now*. Mrs. Hurtle is a free spirit, and the freedom she claims for herself is terrifying to Trollope: "She had shot a man through the head somewhere in Oregon." True, one does not see Isabel Archer shooting a man through the head somewhere in Oregon, but she has a similar largeness and freedom of spirit, she makes similar claims to lead her own life. Poor, she rejects a fortune; poor, she rejects aristocratic position. "She spent half her time thinking of beauty, and bravery, and magnanimity; she had a fixed determination to regard the world as a place of brightness, of free expansion, of irresistible action." There we have the true American note; and once Isabel sets foot in Europe, with her American dreams and aspirations, she is doomed and will be despoiled. Europe is infinitely old, infinitely calculating, infinitely corrupt: its atmosphere will instantly befog and befoul the bright simplicities of the American dream. It is a view of Europe that American politicians have traditionally held.

For all the fascination Europe exercised upon him, James's final attitude toward it, as expressed in his fiction, was not so very different from Huck Finn's in the presence of Aunt Sally: "I reckon I got to light out for the territory ahead of the rest, because Aunt Sally she's going to adopt me and sivilise me, and I can't stand it. I been there before."

The sense of space, the sense of a territory ahead, the sense of infinite possibility, whether material or spiritual: these are the constants of the American dream. James showed what happened when they ran head on against Europe; but in his tragic heroines they glow the more brightly because of the defeat. Mark Twain expressed them consummately in *Huckleberry Finn,* a boy's dream that mirrors the dream of a whole people, and in doing so he discovered the American voice and liberated American prose. The novelists of just before and just after 1900, Frank Norris and Jack London, expressed them more crudely and vulgarly in their pictures of the United States as the battleground of opposed amoral supermen. We catch echoes of their work and attitude in the novels and stories of Mr. Hemingway; and in *The Great Gatsby* F. Scott Fitzgerald showed us the pathos of the tycoon when his dream lies shattered about him.

For the dream, whether noble or vulgar, and however inspiring or intoxicating, is still a dream. What happens when the sleeper wakes, when the promises we are told by the poet America is, turn out to be dishonored? It is here that Dreiser is crucial in the tradition of American fiction. Dreiser's great significance is that he was the first major non-Anglo-Saxon American novelist: in him the voice of the cheated immigrant is heard for the first time. At first, in novels like *The Financier,* he appears merely as a superior Norris; the social and economic scene reflects the life of nature interpreted in terms of the crudest Darwinism. The spectacle, in these early novels, is even seen as exhilarating. In his best work, however, in *An American Tragedy,* he pierces beyond this. The huge materialistic promises that are one part of the dream are phony promises, and he arraigns by implication the society that makes them.

From Dreiser stems a whole race of novelists who have attacked and arraigned American civilization: Sinclair Lewis, in his earlier and better novels, John Dos Passos, James T. Farrell in his Studs Lonigan novels, John O'Hara, down to Norman Mailer and James Jones. "Nothing sacred" has been one of the American novelist's more successful mottoes, and no nation can have probed itself and exposed itself so mercilessly in its literature as the United States has done in the fiction of the last half century. But what is to be noted is this: the probings, the exposures, the muckraking have always been carried out in defense of the promises that have been falsified, perverted, or broken. They have been carried out in defense of the great promises made by the Founding Fathers. These novels, too, are expressions of the American dream, attempts to define the nature of American man, that nature which must always be incomplete because aspiration, the idea of a territory ahead, is fundamental to it. Novelists like Dreiser, Lewis, Dos Passos, Farrell, O'Hara, Mailer, and Jones have chastened because they loved.

American fiction, then, is nothing if not critical, critical of the scenes and people from which it draws its material as no older literature is. It is also a highly self-conscious fiction, because its underlying theme is so often what it means, or ought to mean, to be that mysterious thing, an American. The American scene at any given moment is being checked against the shaping dream, the ideal conception. The ideal conception may be vague enough; indeed, the vagueness we feel at the heart of Dreiser's view of America, or Mr. O'Hara's, is responsible for much of the weakness of American fiction. But it is always there, even if we often decide that it can, once again, be defined only by negatives.

It is most fruitful, of course, in the works of those novelists who are most conscious of their identity with a place and a historic past; in the much-neglected fiction of that fine novelist James Gould Cozzens, for example, and above all in the best fiction of the Old South. For Hawthorne's and Henry James's complaints about the United States as the source of material for the novelist's art are still more true than we often care to admit: the American urban scene, repeated in an eternal sameness from city to city and from state to state across a continent, is still a very thin soil for literature. A novelist like Mr. Faulkner, who can draw, as Hawthorne did, on a rich historic past, is fortunate. It would not even greatly matter if Mr. Faulkner's interpretation of the past of the South were wrong. It gives him a measuring rod with which to judge the present, a criterion more substantial than an immigrant's dream of America. Yoknapatawpha County exists in depth certainly because of Mr. Faulkner's genius, but also because it has had time enough to do so:

> For every Southern boy fourteen years old, not once but whenever he wants it, there is the instant when it's still not two o'clock on that July afternoon in 1863, the brigades are in position behind the rail fence, the guns are laid and ready in the woods and the furled flags are already loosened to break out and Pickett himself with his long oiled ringlets and his hat in one hand probably and his sword in the other looking up the hill waiting for Longstreet to give the word and it's all in the balance, it hasn't happened yet. . . .

The theme is still the complex fate of being an American, the even more complex fate, indeed, of being an American of the defeated South; but the nature of Mr. Faulkner's Americanness has been perfectly defined, for all that his sense of it follows him like his shadow everywhere.

American Fiction Since the First World War

THE BLESSED rage for order, as Wallace Stevens called it, is very characteristic of the academic mind, and particularly of the literary historian's mind. Learning could hardly exist without it, for we never feel quite comfortable with writers until the historical imagination has arranged them in some sort of chronological pattern and to their "age" ascribed a character that each well-behaved writer, we are made to feel, displays. It is, no doubt, easy to be ironic about the histories of literature, which conclude each chapter with a few paragraphs on writers "born out of their time" and solemnly describe Blake as "pre-Romantic" because something called "The Romantic Movement" is not allowed to begin officially until 1798. Nevertheless, this kind of historical ordering is invaluable: it fixes writers within a tradition for us, so that we do not have to reimagine the foundations of a whole culture every time we wish to contemplate a particular book.

Like most blessings, however, it is mixed. Its drawbacks are greatest when literature more or less contemporary is being considered, especially when that literature is fiction, of which so much is produced that sheer ignorance—if not of the best writers, then of the important second best—frequently distorts the history. One thing we can be sure of is that before the effects of temporary preoccupations have been eliminated from our history of "contemporary" literature, it will have been revised a good many times. We need to keep our history of contemporary fiction as fluid as possible, for what Mr. Eliot said of culture as a whole is even truer of this brief stretch of it: "for order to persist after the supervention of [a new work], the *whole* existing order must be, if ever so slightly, altered." Yet there is nothing the historical mind appears less comfortable with than change.

Not many years ago, the then young students of American literature conducted a vigorous guerrilla campaign to persuade their elders that the history of the novel did not end with Howells. Having won, they constructed their own history of the twentieth-century novel, handsomely equipped with periods and subdivisions and with a dramatic climax in which the English novel as a whole immolated itself on a pyre of classics in the Oxen of the Sun episode in *Ulysses*. As a result of this satisfying academic triumph their history of the twentieth-century novel got established and became resistant to change, so that they have persisted for a couple of decades now in acting as if Ernest Hemingway were still a dashing young man of considerable promise—in spite of his fifty-five years and some evidence that his best work is behind him. It reminds one of Miss Thorne's conviction that the Squire of Ullathorne was an enthusiastic young man hurried away into democratic tendencies.

It is possible to see how this distrust of change works out in Marcus Cunliffe's excellent Penguin history of *The Literature of the United States*. The writers discussed in Mr. Cunliffe's chapter on "Fiction Since World War I" are aging young men whose reputations were established in the 1920's (only two of them were born after 1900). Mr. Cunliffe is only following precedent here, and he is doing so with uncommon intelligence. The fact remains that he is writing about only one generation of the novelists of the past forty years, the oldest, and that he has selected from that generation a very small number of writers for reasons that are never made clear and perhaps could not be.

The purpose of these sketchy observations on literary history is twofold. We have, in the first place, reached a time when we can begin to modify the original tentative arrangement of the "contemporary" writers who were young men twenty-five years ago. We ought, in the second place, to recognize that there have been young men of talent since the 1920's.

Mr. Cunliffe deals with nine writers. Of these, four (Anderson, Lewis, Fitzgerald, and Wolfe) are dead and no longer elicit the hopeful hesitation of judgment that we reserve for even the most evidently exhausted living writer. Of the other five, several—possibly all five—show signs of having done all the good work they are going to do. At least, the recent work of Dos Passos (*Most Likely to Succeed* [1954]), Steinbeck (*East of Eden* [1952]), and Farrell (*The Face of Time* [1953]) is inferior—in some instances shockingly inferior—to their earlier work. Faulkner has always been an uneven writer, and the critical uneasiness over *Requiem for a Nun* (1951), while probably justified, may not prove much. As for Hemingway, the clamor against *Across the River and into the Trees* (1950) was certainly excessive; the American reviewers had intoxicated themselves with Hemingway in the 1940's, and *Across the River* was their morning after—as *The Old Man and the Sea* (1952) was a pick-me-up to which they responded with a vivid but temporary sense of well-being; it has about it the flavor of a writer remembering his best manner rather than re-creating it.

Mr. Cunliffe's choice of the "best" writers of the period is con-ventional and would probably be concurred in by most literary historians; and, though he has his enthusiasm for these writers well under control, his conception of their virtues would prob-ably also be generally shared. Yet, firmly established as this view is, it is obviously inadequate in the two respects mentioned above. It is a reiteration of a very tentative historical view that was es-tablished in the early 1930's, and it is a history, not of fiction since the First World War, but of fiction between about 1920 and 1940. As to the first point, our perspective has surely im-proved—or at least changed—since 1930, and if it would be dif-ficult to get perfect agreement on details there would none the less be widespread agreement on the general outlines of the modi-fication that this history needs; as to the second point, it is nearly as arbitrary to end our history of American fiction with Hem-ingway as it was for our elders to end theirs with Howells: Hem-ingway is, in the "50's," far from the latest interesting arrival on the scene.

Some of the likely revisions of the conventional historical view of the older novelists appear fairly obvious; the following exam-ples, if not universally acceptable, are certainly not unusual. As early as 1925, when Hemingway wrote his parody of Sherwood Anderson (*The Torrents of Spring*), there were serious doubts that Anderson was more than a very interesting minor writer. "I agree with Ernest," Fitzgerald wrote to Max Perkins, for ex-ample, "that Anderson's last two books . . . [are] cheap, obscu-rantic and awful." He and Hemingway were not alone in this feel-ing, even then. The attitude of Irving Howe's *Sherwood Anderson* and of the reviews of it suggest that this judgment is now wide-spread. Farrell, Steinbeck, and Dos Passos benefited greatly from the special interest in "proletarian" novels that existed when the conventional view of the period was established. It looks now as if Farrell will hardly survive this temporary prejudice in his favor except as an example of the way the emotionally charged ideas of the age distorted its literary judgments. Steinbeck's reputation —which he has been hard at work diminishing since about 1940 with a series of bad books—appears now to rest largely on books like *Tortilla Flat* (1935) and *The Long Valley* (1938) rather than on his somewhat uncertainly "proletarian" works like *In Dubious Battle* (1936). There is some feeling that Dos Passos's *U.S.A.* (1930–36) is admirable for an attitude—a melancholy or even despair—that is very different from the supposedly collectivist qualities of the trilogy, which were regarded as its chief merits in the 1930's. This feeling may be leading to a re-examination of *District of Columbia* (1939–49), which is usually ignored by literary historians—as it is by Mr. Cunliffe—but which has been highly praised by so good a critic as Alfred Kazin. There appears to be an increasing conviction that Sinclair Lewis will not bear serious rereading and that Thomas Wolfe's faults are more trying than they seemed at first.

On the other hand, the reputations of Faulkner, Fitzgerald, and Hemingway have risen considerably since the 1930's. In each case there has been a marked change in the conception of the purpose and meaning of the man's work and an increased inclination to regard him as a serious and responsible writer. This revaluation has probably gone furthest with Faulkner and is clearly evident in Malcolm Cowley's *Viking Portable Faulkner* and in Irving Howe's admirable *William Faulkner*. It is pretty generally agreed that Faulkner—not the Faulkner of *Sanctuary* (1931), but the Faulkner of *The Sound and the Fury* (1929), *As I Lay Dying* (1930), *Light in August* (1932), and *Go Down Moses* (1942)—is the greatest American novelist of the century. The opinion that Fitzgerald is something more than a charming "laureate of the Jazz Age" and Hemingway something more than an ominously anti-intellectual American tough has penetrated even to *Life*. The serious evidence for these changes in opinion constitutes something suspiciously like a boom in Fitzgerald's case; in Hemingway's it is well represented by books so different as Carlos Baker's earnestly scholarly study and Philip Young's critically brilliant one.

These illustrations are perhaps sufficient to indicate the extent to which critical opinion has been modified in the twenty-five years since the literary historian's view of "Fiction Since World War I" was more or less frozen. Obviously a history that reflects the critical judgment of the 1950's would modify considerably all the opinions usually expressed by the conventional historian and would drop some of his "best" writers altogether. It would also add some writers from a group of approximately the same age who were either slower to develop or were simply not much regarded in 1930. This group would certainly include James Gould Cozzens, John P. Marquand, and John O'Hara; it might conceivably include also Katherine Anne Porter, Glenway Wescott, Nathanael West, and Caroline Gordon. This is not to say that Mr. Cunliffe's chosen writers do not have their interest for the social historian or for the historian of ideas, or even for the historian of literature. It is merely to say that literary history written in 1954 is bound to differ from literary history written in 1930.

The conventional historian's inclination to ignore nearly all the writers who have appeared since the 1920's is even more disturbing than his habit of assuming that the critical judgment of 1930 or thereabouts is immortal. If we are to talk about contemporary fiction, we ought not to ignore *contemporary* fiction, whatever else we may choose to omit from consideration; and if we are interested in the novel as a living art, genuinely engaged with the actual world, we ought to be especially alert for young writers of promise: they have a hard enough time as it is without being further handicapped by our disregard. To be sure, commitments about such writers are dangerous and may easily make us look foolish a couple of decades hence. But this kind of risk is our responsibility. In a few cases at least this risk is not really very great; not many people would question the importance of Robert

Penn Warren, for instance—as indeed Mr. Cunliffe does not in the brief paragraph he allots to Warren. It is certainly more risky to suggest that some attention be given to Warren's contemporary, Andrew Lytle, whose first novel, *The Long Night* (1936), appeared three years before Warren's *Night Rider*. These two writers are the last representatives of the Southern group that called itself the Fugitives. About the time they appeared a number of writers of a different kind began to make what ought to have been an impression. Most of them have since become associated, to their financial advantage, with the *New Yorker* as short story writers, but none of them began that way. This group includes Irwin Shaw, Edward Newhouse, Mary McCarthy, and, later, J. D. Salinger and Vladimir Nabokov, a Russian who writes in English with great brilliance and charm. Of their books the least known, considering their merits, are Salinger's *For Esmé* (1953) and Newhouse's *Many Are Called* (1951), both collections of *New Yorker* short stories, and Nabokov's *Bend Sinister* (1947).

The American novelists who have written about the Second World War, such as Mailer, Burns, and Jones, are well known and, on the whole, disappointing. But they are certainly worth reading, as are some of the writers of about the same age who cannot be so easily—and possibly superficially—categorized, such as Budd Schulberg and Saul Bellow, both of whom have suffered recently at the hands of the serious critics because of their popular success.

The writers who have emerged during the decade since the war divide into three not very clear groups. There are the self-consciously brilliant and decadent writers like Truman Capote, Paul Bowles, William Styron, and William Goyen, several of whom come from the South and seem to have been influenced by Faulkner in an unfortunate way. There is a second, less extravagant and less known group of Southern writers, of whom the most interesting are Peter Taylor (*A Woman of Means,* 1950) and Shelby Foote (*Shiloh,* 1952). Perhaps the most interesting group of young writers, however, are the Northern novelists of manners.

Though they differ considerably in certain respects, they are all concerned with the life of the American upper middle class and interested in it in a way that has not appeared among able American writers—parts of Cozzens's and Marquand's work excepted —since before the First World War. The most productive of these writers is Louis Auchincloss (*Sybil,* 1951), who is so perceptive and skillful in his quiet way as nearly to justify the blurb-writer's comparison of his work with Edith Wharton's, a comparison that he himself must find thoroughly embarrassing. Another interesting novelist of this kind is Wright Morris (*The Deep Sleep,* 1953). But the strength of this group is best suggested by the number of good first novels that came out of it in a single year or so— for example, Brendan Gill's *The Trouble of One House* (1950), John Phillips's *The Second Happiest Day* (1953), and Charles Flood's *Love is a Bridge* (1953). (Mr. Flood was only twenty-three when he wrote this novel.)

Finally, there is a group of writers who probably constitute a really dangerous gamble for the historian, the group that has sometimes been called the New York Wits. They are not quite fiction writers, and, dependent as they are on magazines for a living, most of them have written too much. But they are a persistent element in American literature throughout the period since the First World War, and the best work of Benchley, Thurber, White, and Perelman may well survive the work of a good many more solemn writers. It would be impertinent to propose anything like an official history of writers like these, but it is an even greater mistake to act as if they did not exist or have not far more to do with the nature of American fiction in the 1950's than have middle-aged gentlemen like Hemingway and Dos Passos, however estimable one may think them, or however highly one may rate their current work. It is probably too much to expect that historical arrangements will not become fixed and frozen assets in the minds of literary historians; the notion of a history of fiction as fluid and alert as our basic need for order will permit is doubtless a utopian ideal, as ill realized in these remarks as in other efforts to write literary history. But it is only by trying to approach such an ideal that we make our histories more helpful than harmful.

The World of the Detective Story

THE DETECTIVE story started in America—and in the world—with the publication of *The Murders in the Rue Morgue* by Edgar Allan Poe in 1841. After Poe's brilliant beginning the craft remained in the doldrums in America (though there were developments in England and in France) until the appearance in 1878 of *The Leavenworth Case* by Anna Katharine Green. She was followed by a long procession: Jacques Futrelle (*The Thinking Machine*), who used Poe's shorter form rather than the full-length style of Anna Katharine Green; Mary Roberts Rinehart, who combined mystery and romance in rather sentimental stories; Melville Davison Post ("Uncle Abner"); Arthur B. Reeve, creator of Craig Kennedy; and a number of less-known writers, most of whom—with the exception of Mary Roberts Rinehart—are now forgotten.

The 1920's was a period of brilliant achievement in American fiction; but the American detective story showed no originality for most of that period. It lagged behind the British detective story. The works of Willard Huntington Wright (as "S. S. Van Dine") brought the virtues of greater literacy and plausibility, but left the form and general type of the *genre* unchanged.

The great change—and probably the most important and influential development—in the American detective story came with Dashiell Hammett at the end of the 1920's. Hammett's best-known books are *The Glass Key* (his own favorite), *The Thin Man,* and the classic *The Maltese Falcon*. They are fast-moving, often brutal stories, told in terse, Hemingwaylike prose. Hammett's own experiences—he was a private (Pinkerton) detective in California and worked on the Nicky Arnstein and Fatty Arbuckle cases—no doubt account for the realism of his backgrounds. His great success started the hard-boiled school of American detective fiction that still flourishes, inspires Hollywood, and now has so many British imitators.

Hammett's private detective in *The Maltese Falcon* is Sam Spade. Spade, tough, dynamic, and fearless, looks "rather pleasantly like a blond satan." He is a lone wolf, used to fighting not only his enemies but the police—"It's a long while since I burst out crying because policemen didn't like me." He is attractive to women, and he has a strong, though very individual, sense of personal integrity. He is, in short, a highly romanticized figure, and a startlingly good example of the American hero—chiefly in his role as a lone fighter who uses unorthodox methods for ends thought to be good. Spade has proved a model for hundreds of imitators.

Only a few of Hammett's successors have reached his standard. The best is the highly popular Raymond Chandler (*The Big Sleep, Farewell my Lovely,* etc.), whose first four books alone sold three million copies. Chandler's private detective, Philip Marlowe, is more intelligent than Spade, better educated, and even more attractive to women. But he is genuinely Spade's descendant—laconic, fearless, a fighter, with highly individual standards. He has more social awareness than Spade, who accepts his social environment but does not judge it.

There is some question whether the best-selling Mickey Spillane (his books have, to date, sold eleven million copies in English and have been translated into six languages) can properly be said to belong to this tradition. It has been claimed that his fast-moving, sex-charged, highly sadistic stories are the logical culmination of the hard-boiled school. But in the best works of this type, from Hammett onwards, brutality, though always present, is usually a logical element in the story and not there for its own sake alone. With Spillane, the brutality appears to be an end in itself; all else is secondary. To that extent, he should probably be considered outside the Hammett tradition.

The hard-boiled school is only one, though in some ways the most representative, type of American detective fiction. But many American detective writers do not follow this tradition. In 1929, the year of *The Maltese Falcon,* "Ellery Queen" (actually two men, cousins) began to publish the first of a long series of puzzles for the literate, the latest of them with strong psychological overtones. J. P. Marquand, better known for his regular novels, began to write about his Japanese detective, Mr. Moto; and Earl Derr Biggers was producing the "Charlie Chan" stories.

The 1930's saw a further improvement in the quality of American detective stories. The standards of writing and of characterization were better; backgrounds became more varied and plausible; and there was a tendency to mix humor, or even farce, with murder. These trends have continued to the present day. An important figure in this "liberalization" of the American detective story was Rex Stout. But there were many others, including a large number of women.

In America, as in England, women writers have been prominent in the field of detective fiction. But whereas in England many women writers have been the innovators and developers of new techniques in the detective story—particularly for the literary and cultivated reader—in America they have tended to stay on conventional paths. Some have specialized in the straight detective tale, often with humorous overtones. But more have followed the Mary Roberts Rinehart tradition of mystery, romance, and (frequently) oversentimentality. England has, in fact, produced many writers, both men and women, whose detective stories closely approximate to novels. This trend has been less marked in America, and readers who prefer what might be called "detective novels" have relied chiefly on English writers, just as English readers who favor the hard-boiled school have relied, until recently at least, mainly on American writers to provide them.

The detective story in America is, as in Britain, one of the

most popular types of fiction. Accurate statistics are hard to obtain; but according to rough estimates twenty per cent of all fiction published in any one year in America is of this type. (This
is a very rough figure, since it would include not only the "straight"
detective story but also such related types as the "action thriller,"
the spy story, the psychological crime novel, etc.) Total reader-
ship has been estimated at 250 million a year, which would mean
that every American adult reads between two and three such
books a year.

Some people say that detective stories are read not for new
experiences but to repeat an experience one has enjoyed and
would like again. In one sense, certainly, there can be nothing
new about a detective story, whatever variations are introduced.
However modified and "literate" the form has become, or may
become in the future, it remains highly conventionalized. Some
writers may produce lively, clever puzzles, like "Q. Patrick."
Others may introduce highly specialized backgrounds, as Elizabeth Daly with her bibliophilia. The humor may, like Elliot Paul's,
verge on the farcical. Tension and suspense may be brought to
an almost unbearable pitch, as with Mabel Seeley. Characterization may be at the high level of Helen McCloy. The stories may
be fast-moving detective adventures with legal fireworks, a lawyer
hero, and an apparently interminable romance, as provided by
Erle Stanley Gardner (who was the best-selling author in the
field in the 1940's). But whatever the variations, the true detective story must unfold within a set framework. There is a crime,
nearly always murder. Various persons are found, or known be-
forehand, to have motives and in turn come under suspicion. The
crime is eventually solved—by a policeman, a private detective,
or an amateur. The criminal is punished, though not necessarily
by the law. Generally, though not invariably, the lives of most
other characters become more satisfactory as a result of the death
of the victim. These are the basic elements of the detective story
and, whatever else may be added, are nearly always present.

The popularity of the detective story in America, again as in
Britain, cuts across all economic, social, and intellectual lines—

though among the better educated the "literate" or light-hearted mystery may be preferred to the products of the hard-boiled school. But two things are more clearly evident in American detective fiction, which go far to explain the universal popularity in modern industrial society of this type of writing. The first is the obvious desire for fantasy-gratification; and the second is the fact that, at the deepest levels, the elements that satisfy these fantasy-wishes are the same for virtually all Americans. These two things are everywhere true of the cult of detective fiction.

American detective stories in particular exemplify the well-known American liking for violence and often reveal a sadistic or masochistic streak. (It may be that they provide a harmless release for violent or aggressive tendencies that might seek expression otherwise.) They show, too, the complacence with which Americans view their own lack of respect for laws and their enforcement and the extent to which Americans take for granted the existence of corruption in high places. This in a sense excuses lawlessness and justifies the hero (detective) who takes the law into his own hands to see that right ultimately triumphs over wrong.

But this is not all. At a deeper level the public that eagerly devours detective stories of all types seems to be looking for a secure, safe world. This may sound strange, in view of the violence, viciousness, and mayhem in the stories. But in a strict sense the world of the detective story *is* secure. The good are rewarded, the bad punished; every man has his deserts; and justice is done.

In the second place, the world of the detective story is simple. People act for understandable, and often single rather than mixed, motives. More than most others, Americans tend to like the plain analysis and the simple solution. Both are increasingly difficult to find—except in the world of detective fantasy.

Finally, detective stories provide a meaningful world, where things "make sense" and the individual is important. The solution of the detective story must always "make sense." The tangle is unraveled and all the seemingly unrelated pieces of the puzzle fall into their proper places. But that is the surface view. Things also "make sense" below the surface because life is here, at last, and at least, seen to have some point. Murder is dramatic. It gives urgency to ordinary lives. This may be enhanced by having the characters important people in their own right—rich, socially prominent, distinguished, or powerful. And the ordinary reader is free to identify himself with the man who solves the crime, the hero—determined, unorthodox, but a fighter for the right, usually against odds and at great personal risk. Above all, the detective hero is *himself,* an outstanding individual in a mass culture and a mass society. Americans have always admired individuals who go their own way, whether or not these ways were socially admirable—and in the detective story they can almost always be seen to be so. If it be said that much of all this is true of other peoples besides Americans who cultivate detective fiction, the answer must surely be that in this—as in many another context of modern, urban, industrial mass culture—America has been the matrix and microcosm, the forcing bed and laboratory, in which so many of us can see our own trends and tendencies carried to more striking extremes.

The Art of the Short Story

PRINCIPLES AND PRACTICE IN THE UNITED STATES

H. E. BATES, in his excellent book *The Modern Short Story,* records that it was not until some years after buying Series I and II of *Selected English Short Stories,* published in the World's Classics Series, that he noticed that more than a third of the stories in Series I and exactly half the stories in Series II were written by Americans. "It was this discovery," says Mr. Bates, "that first gave me a clue to the poverty of the short story in nineteenth-century England, and an abiding respect for the short story in America." Remembering Scott, Stevenson, Conrad, Hardy, Kipling, Conan Doyle, W. W. Jacobs, and the early Wells, we may feel that "poverty" is perhaps too strong a word. But Mr. Bates is right to praise the American contribution to the short story in the last century. If we cannot exactly agree with some American critics that the short story was an American invention, we can at least say that, even before the Civil War, it was practiced in that country with an assiduousness and considered with a seriousness for which it had to wait half a century in England. Washington Irving, Hawthorne, Poe, and Melville were pioneers of the American story, and after the Civil War William Dean Howells, Bret Harte, Ambrose Bierce, Sarah Orne Jewett, Frank Stockton, Stephen Crane, Jack London, Hamlin Garland, "O. Henry," Henry James, and Edith Wharton placed it firmly on the map.

William Dean Howells suggested that this extraordinary development and interest were fostered by the magazines. The most famous of these were *Godey's Lady's Book,* in which Poe published "The Cask of Amontillado"; *The Dollar Magazine,* in which Hawthorne first published "Ethan Brand"; *The Gentleman's Magazine,* the *Broadway Journal, Scribner's Monthly* and *Scribner's Magazine,* and the long-lived *Harper's* and *Atlantic.* And no doubt the presence of so many flourishing magazines itself had something to do with the spread of popular education in America, the absence of class barriers, and the increased pace of life in a society becoming very rapidly industrialized—all of which conditions, as we know from our own experience in the present century, lead, among other things, to the demand for entertaining and portable reading matter. Authors were not loath to supply the demand, for, as Somerset Maugham once pointed out, "writers quite naturally feel themselves impelled to write the sort of things for which there is a demand." Another reason for the early development of the short story in America lay, it has been suggested, in the absence of satisfactory copyright laws, which meant that English novels were pirated and American writers were driven by this competition into the short story market, where the native product was preferred. Both these explanations are plausible, but they leave us with the feeling that this does not fully account for the seriousness with which, for example, Poe considered the form. It was Poe, after all, who, in his review of Hawthorne's *Twice-Told Tales,* gave us the first working definition of the short story. "If wise," said Poe,

> [the skillful literary artist] has not fashioned his thoughts to accommodate his incidents; but having conceived, with deliberate care, a certain unique or single *effect* to be wrought out, he then invents such incidents—he then combines such events as may best aid him in establishing this preconceived effect. If his very initial sentence tend not to the outbringing of this effect, then he has failed in his first step. In the whole composition there should be no word written, of which the tendency, direct or indirect, is not to the one pre-established design.

This is our first critical intimation of the birth of a new literary form, which, Poe said, belonged "to the highest region of Art." It places emphasis upon structure, upon a careful ordering of thought and effect, which we now see to be fundamental. Whereas the *Gesta Romanorum,* the *Decameron,* and the short tales that Dickens inserted into his novels are alike in that they are no different in kind from the longer narratives of their time, the modern short story is quite distinct, in intention and effect, from the modern long narrative or novel. It is, Elizabeth Bowen has said, "in its use of action . . . nearer to the drama than to the novel." Its effects are gained through implication and suggestion rather than through detailed description or delineation of character. It is essentially literary, the product of much careful craftsmanship, and this is perhaps what chiefly distinguishes it from the "told" tales of the past. And if in some instances it is nearer to the drama than to the novel, in others it is nearer to the poem. And this perhaps may give us a clue to the peculiar interest that the form held for Americans in the nineteenth century.

American society was unsettled. The state of the new nation, the growth and movement of population, the physical and mental challenge of a vast continent had the effect of stirring up writers' minds. These are conditions that might have inspired the poets, but the poets of America, with the exception of Whitman, were not to be stirred up. Perhaps because they sensed their alienation from a vital but crude and unformed society, they clung to a narrow circle and to narrow and superficial subjects. And so, to a certain extent, the short story became a vehicle for those speculations and explorations that may largely be termed "poetic." We can see how near Poe comes to defining the intention of a poem in his demand for the ordering of the short story and the attainment of a "single effect," and, as Dr. and Mrs. Leavis have at different times pointed out, Hawthorne's method can also be called "poetic." But American society in the nineteenth century, like our own in the twentieth, was prose-conscious, and through a prose form the literary artist in America played a poet's part.

The Civil War marks the beginning of a critical phase in the American story. In the hands of Bret Harte, William Dean Howells, and Ambrose Bierce it became realistic, and in Stephen Crane, Hamlin Garland, and Jack London (no doubt influenced by Zola) naturalistic, reflecting the conditions of American society. "By God! I told them the Truth," said Frank Norris a few years later. "They liked it or they didn't like it. What had that to do with me? I told them the Truth, I knew it for the Truth then, and I know it for the Truth now." Even Henry James thought he was being realistic. We, remembering Stephen Crane or Sherwood Anderson, protest that that was the last thing James was. But it was in fact the first thing he was. In the sense that he used "real" situations and "real" people, in the sense that his work conveys the atmosphere of a scene or situation, he was being realistic, and this may be seen quite clearly by comparing his work with that of Poe and Hawthorne. Henry James was as much affected by his age as Hamlin Garland or Stephen Crane, but he chose to convey more than the sensuous vitality of everyday existence. Apart from an interest in symbolism that led him to praise Hawthorne's "allegorical glimpses . . . of the whole deep mystery of man's soul and conscience" his main preoccupation was the moral and psychological implication of various human situations.

It is odd, this praise of Hawthorne, for although in his best novels Hawthorne has a certain power that compels us to read on in spite of the tediousness of the prose, he was in his shorter pieces about as much of a short story writer as Cotton Mather. We may suppose that it was Hawthorne's preoccupations that interested James, for, as stories, those amateurish, didactic attempts to "open an intercourse with the world" must surely have grated upon James's fine sensibility, so few of them have that level of interest and competence that must be present before we are inclined to swallow the real excuse for the story, the allegorical message. Even if we confine ourselves to the very best of the stories, lovingly chronicled and kept in circulation by American literary historians and preservers of Americana, there is only one, *Young Goodman Brown,* that makes some sort of impact. Most of them read like faintly disguised sermons, the efforts of a country parson who has just discovered Bunyan. In *Young Goodman Brown* and *The Scarlet Letter* there are indications that Hawthorne really wanted to write symbolically, but something seems to have prevented him, with the result that the majority of his stories are neither allegory nor symbolism, but a very unsatisfactory confusion of both. Poe, on the other hand, can be seen to be the father of the art of the short story in America. As Mr. Bates points out in the book already quoted, Poe has "atmosphere, hypnotics, mathematical exactitude," and "of those it is interesting to note that at least two, the first and the last, are qualities of whose essential importance nearly every short story writer of quality has given proof." Although his writing is mannered and his characters hardly realistic, it is in his power of conveying atmosphere, which in turn arises from power of personality, that Poe shows himself to be the forerunner of modern short story writers, and that is why his stories are still read and enjoyed today.

If Poe is the father of the American short story, then Henry

James is its favorite son, but a son whose luster so outshines the father's that comparison is not merely invidious but impossible. In the hands of Henry James the American story came to an early maturity. In his stories, perhaps more than in his novels, he "sees into the heart of things" and conveys a moment of truth. This, surely, is Poe's "single effect," a definition that critics have denounced because it has not seemed to them to convey the heightened awareness, the multiple consciousness of many facets of life with which the very best stories leave us. But the term "single effect" does not preclude artistic ambiguities. The "single effect" that James aims at in "The Real Thing" is the establishment of the idea that art is art and life is life. The two people who are really genteel do not look the real thing; the fakes do. And so the artist chooses the fakes because he is not concerned with moral standards but with art, and art consists in creating the right effect. One might say the same of the short story writer's art. It lies in creating the right effect, and all the honesty, sincerity, and experience in the world will be of no avail if the writer has not the requisite insight and skill to translate his vision into the right words in the right order.

The days are gone when Van Wyck Brooks's strictures on Henry James had positive meaning for young American writers. In those days Sherwood Anderson was felt to be more truly American, more "truthful." But either directly or indirectly—through such polished writers as Miss Katherine Anne Porter—Henry James has had great influence on a sizable section of the youngest generation of American writers. They see, once they have got over their distaste for the effeteness of Henry James's characters and their distrust of the elegant society in which they moved, that the artistic preoccupations of Henry James, in spite of his alienation from the main stream of American life, were no less serious and no farther from the heart of things than those of William Faulkner or Ernest Hemingway. The English reader will think this perhaps a very odd thing to say, since it is to him self-evident. But one must not make the mistake of imagining good American taste to be exactly the same as good European taste. In some circles, in New England especially, it is very little different; but the majority of intelligent American readers have a different set of conditions which they "feel as facts": the land itself, whether it be the endless plains of Nebraska or the lush glades of Louisiana; the sense of native life and atmosphere that comes out of idiomatic American speech and a quite different set of habits and customs; the general predilection for the large, the loose, the carefree, the good-natured, and the easygoing. Against such backgrounds Henry James can seem very alien, just as some of the stories that arise from the caldron of American society can seem very alien to us. It is not a question of their being unable to see the wood for the trees; it is simply that the wood, the trees, and the whole landscape are seen from a different angle.

But which of their other short story writers in the nineteenth century, apart from Henry James, do Americans now value? Only Stephen Crane seems to be really in favor. (One speaks, of course, of writers who genuinely appeal and not of writers who merely provide fuel for the American academic machine.) Crane, it is felt, was in the same line of country as Ernest Hemingway. The prevailing mood of American taste being for naturalism, his stories have an appeal and a flavor that the mannered constructions of Poe and Hawthorne do not. He is sharper on the tongue, carrying conviction through details that the modern reader can feel to be true. Beside him, Americans seem to feel, Bret Harte and Ambrose Bierce give the impression of artificiality, and Hamlin Garland and Jack London are lesser figures as artists. With these judgments we might not entirely differ except perhaps to put in a plea for Edith Wharton, who is a great artist in her own right and not merely a lesser Henry James, as many appear to think. We might also feel—not being quite so satisfied with the techniques of the naturalists as are the Americans—that Ambrose Bierce is receiving less than his due. He had the misfortune to be born before the age in which the raw details of life had only to be set starkly upon the page. He was, therefore, a clear, sure craftsman. O. Henry, too, is for most English people more than just another magazine writer with a click. He is a very skillful practitioner of the short story who, in his best work, manages to convey not only a sense of American life but also some significant, if small, truth about life itself. And, finally, if Frank Stockton is deservedly neglected, Sarah Orne Jewett is less deservedly so. Her world, as Mr. Bates says, "like Jane Austen's, was small, but, like Jane Austen, if she had chosen it herself she could hardly have been born into a world more aptly suited to her gift of interpretation."

To leave the world of the American short story in the nineteenth century and enter that of the twentieth century is to come from a headlighted country road into the blaze of Main Street on a Saturday night. The concerted glare is confusing, and the apparent brightness of individual lights can vary with the point of view. When the picture is projected across the Atlantic some strange distortions occur, and if one takes an amateur Gallup poll to discover what modern American short story writers are well known to the intelligent reading public in England, the results reveal a narrow and surprisingly unbalanced range of acquaintance. Almost everyone has, of course, at one time or another, read Ernest Hemingway, William Saroyan, Damon Runyon, James Thurber, and John Steinbeck, although not everyone has read William Faulkner, Erskine Caldwell, James T. Farrell, or Eudora Welty. Fewer among the younger generation have read Sherwood Anderson, Dorothy Parker, Stephen Vincent Benét, F. Scott Fitzgerald, Thomas Wolfe, or Kay Boyle. Almost no one seems to have read, and some have never even heard of, the stories of Ring Lardner, Ellen Glasgow, Ruth Suckow, Conrad Aiken, Glenway Wescott, William Carlos Williams, Katherine Anne Porter (even though her two volumes have been published in England), William March, Caroline Gordon, or J. P. Marquand. Of the youngest generation of writers only the names of John O'Hara, Mary MacCarthy, Carson McCullers, Truman Capote, Irwin Shaw, Jerome Weidman, Ray Bradbury, Paul Bowles, and J. P. Salinger seem to be at all well known. But there are a great many more who are almost as good, among them Edward Newhouse, Allan Seager, Nelson Algren, Mark Schorer, Wallace Stegner, Walter Van Tilburg Clark, Frances Gray Patton, J. F. Powers, Shirley

Jackson, Jessamyn West, Jean Stafford, Hortense Calisher, John Cheever, Robie Macauley, William Goyen, Robert Lowry, Wright Morris, Delmore Schwartz, Louis Auchincloss, Shelby Foote, Flannery O'Connor, and Peter Taylor.

This raises some interesting reflections. Let us take the first writer on our list, Ernest Hemingway. Mr. Hemingway, most people would agree, is outstanding, but it is significant that he should be the only serious American short story writer that almost everyone has read. If the curious inquirer pushes his researches farther he finds that Mr. Hemingway is regarded as "typically American." Two things seem to be responsible for this assumption: his terseness and his toughness, for a considerable number of non-Americans not only have a preconceived idea of how an American should look and act but also, apparently, of how he should write, and Mr. Hemingway almost fills the bill. Erskine Caldwell and John Steinbeck add to the picture, William Saroyan and Damon Runyon round it off, and, presto, we have the complete American short story writer—tough like Hemingway, naturalistic like Caldwell, irresponsible like Saroyan, loquacious like Runyon, and sentimental like Steinbeck at his worst. These writers at their best are, of course, superb and deservedly famous—Hemingway in "The Short Happy Life of Francis Macomber" or "The Snows of Kilimanjaro," Caldwell in "Kneel to the Rising Sun," Saroyan in "The Pomegranate Tree," and Steinbeck in "The Leader of the People." But they are not so often at their best that we could wish them the only representatives of the American short story. There are others less well known, among the names already cited, whom one would certainly wish to have in any representative collection of modern American stories.

Perhaps the most neglected of these, in England, is Ring Lardner, a Middle Western journalist who began writing the sketches he called "You Know Me, Al" when he was sports writer for the Chicago *Tribune*. Lardner was a ruthless, although not a bitter, satirist, whose best stories, like "Haircut," "Champion," and "Some Like them Cold," are written in a vernacular that makes Damon Runyon's seem like that of a stage American. William

Carlos Williams is another whose collections, *The Knife of the Times, Life Along the Passaic River,* and *Beer and Cold Cuts,* have an authentic flavor of American life. Dr. Williams's stories, like his poems, give, at first sight, the impression of random jottings, but they are in fact far from being just that, as consideration of such stories as "The Knife of the Times," "The Use of Force," and "The Girl with the Pimply Face" reveal. They are instinct with humanity, and their casual tone and offhand manner are in fact the fruit of a long involvement in the lives of poor immigrants and Negroes in the New Jersey industrial towns the author has lived in all his life.

Mr. William March and Miss Caroline Gordon are both Southerners, but whereas Mr. March is a master of the short poignant episode, Miss Gordon's stories, like her novels, are long and finely wrought. Her world is the world of Virginia and fox hunting and classical values (as befits the wife of Mr. Allen Tate). Like so many American short story writers—among them Conrad Aiken, Katherine Anne Porter, Kay Boyle, Wallace Stegner, and Shirley Jackson—Miss Gordon is fond of symbolism. Perhaps her best story is "Old Red," the story of the indolent, scholarly Mister Maury, of which Mr. Robert Penn Warren has said: "[It is a story] about a basic conflict in our civilization—the conflict between a man's desire for a harmonious development of all his faculties and a set of social conditions which tend to compartmentalize life."

Conrad Aiken has been preoccupied with the land that lies between sleeping and waking. His "Silent Snow, Secret Snow" is a masterpiece of its kind. Of the other writers who are interested in symbolism perhaps the best (as well as the oldest) is Miss Porter, a highly intelligent and highly polished writer, whose "Flowering Judas" might perhaps be placed beside William Saroyan's "Sixty Thousand Assyrians" as an example of the inhibited and the uninhibited in the American story. Mr. Stegner, who is better known over here as the author of *The Big Rock Candy Mountain* and other novels, is, like Miss Porter and a good many other practitioners of the short story these days, closely associated with various writing centers. Whereas Mr. Stegner is a permanent member of that peripheral world that lies between the academy and the great world outside, however, Miss Porter is only an occasional professor.

Mr. Stegner is a good example of the very satisfactory compromise that the short story writer in America can make with the academy. In England the short story writer must either become a lighthouse keeper or look for a job with the B.B.C. The university will have nothing to do with him because he is not a dedicated academic, and there are no liberal arts colleges. In America, however, the writer can fairly easily obtain a job at any one of the hundreds of universities and liberal arts colleges that have creative writing courses and can divide his time between writing his own stories and discussing those of his students. Randall Jarrell, in his recent "comedy," *Pictures from an Institution,* described the life of a writer who, as a temporary teacher of writing at an advanced college for girls, apparently, making no bones about it, spent as little time as possible on her students. It is, after all, she might have argued, the influence rather than any actual instruction that is beneficial. Permanent professors of creative writing are, through conscience or necessity or both, usually more conscientious.

It is fashionable in England to talk with a kind of pious horror of this professionalism, for we have a deep suspicion of anything not strictly amateur. But at the very least one can say that it does not seem to have affected the standard of short story writing in the United States. Mr. Stegner himself, in a volume of original short stories gathered in 1954 in a paperback edition from the Bread Loaf writing conference, puts it more positively.

> I have learned the most important part of my professional skill there [he says of Bread Loaf] by argument, analysis, lecture, conversation and osmosis, from the serious, intensive, responsible, nonarty, noncommercial, nontendential, patient and informed discussion of their craft by the people I taught with.

One has only to compare the stories in the British and American literary magazines, or the former British *Penguin New Writing* with the present American *New World Writing,* to be struck by the difference in quality. The American stories are not only more skillful but in some indefinable way more "alive." The life of a situation, the tang and feeling of it, is presented accurately and vividly. A story in *New World Writing 5,* "Who Lives Alas Away," by Miss Clare McGrath Butler, provides a good illustration of this. Miss Butler seems, as William Dean Howells said of Stephen Crane, to have "sprung into life fully armed." Her story, although it is a first publication, is both moving and vital, and this example, which may be multiplied from other numbers of the same publication and from the American smaller magazines, from the *Atlantic* and *Harper's* to *Epoch, Accent,* and the *New Mexico Quarterly,* contrasts vividly with the amateurish pieces of reportage that used to appear in *Penguin New Writing* and the genteel and mannered vignettes that set the tone of the *London Magazine.* Does it arise from the difference between English and American life at the present time? Perhaps partly so, but equally it arises from the serious attention paid to the short story in America.

Every young man and woman in America seems to have a short story in his pocket. American undergraduates write them as English ones tend to write poems, not for this or that glossy magazine with its glittering prizes but as expressions of intense personal feeling; the stories have their birth and sole reason for existence in this fact. This, perhaps, more than anything, contributes to the feeling of meaningfulness one gets from the American story. As one looks through Martha Foley's annual volume or the yearly O. Henry collection one feels that these stories vitally mattered to their authors, and this sense they convey to us. It is the legacy of Stephen Crane, Sherwood Anderson, Erskine Caldwell, William Carlos Williams, and Robert Penn Warren. It is a heartfelt activity, with that desperate honesty of intention that characterizes Sherwood Anderson's "I Want to Know Why." But although these stories are born of deep feeling they could not be what they are without the aid of skillful technique, and it is here that one can see that the lesson of Henry James has been well learned. Of course, not every short story writer has dealings with creative writing courses, either as teacher or student. Some, like Miss Mary McCarthy, are very suspicious of them. But, while it is certainly true that not everyone comes up to the high standard already described, the spirit of the great majority of them could not be better, and it is this that matters. The creative writing course is a product rather than a cause, engendered by a state of mind that encourages both personal expression and concern with craftsmanship, which is essential for true art.

Perhaps the best example of the polished craftsman among the younger writers is Eudora Welty. Not that Miss Welty is exactly a "young writer"; but by "younger writers" one refers to those who have made their names during and since the last war. Miss Welty's first book was published in 1941, and it immediately established her reputation. In so far as she began with natural speech rhythms and developed her craft from this Miss Welty is in the main tradition of American short story writers—in that of Hemingway and Caldwell and Steinbeck, not of Miss Katherine Anne Porter, who is polished in a more Jamesian way. Miss Welty has turned to writing longer and longer stories, the last one, "The Ponder Heart," filling a whole issue of the *New Yorker*. The stories immediately previous to this are collected in a volume called *The Golden Apples,* which shows that the quality of Miss Welty's writing is growing steadily finer. The later stories are atmospheric. The air quivers with sounds. One is acutely aware of breathing, smells; feeling is finely caught. It is a much more exciting kind of writing than that of the stories collected in *A Curtain of Green,* yet one must admit that no one story quite stands up by itself like "A Piece of News," "The Petrified Man," or "Lily Daw and the Three Ladies." It is novels Miss Welty should be writing now, and yet she does not seem to be able to make the transition. Even *Delta Wedding,* long as it was, was not a novel; nor was it a short story.

Another Southerner, Peter Taylor, is at present the most admired of the very youngest short story writers. His first volume, *A Long Fourth,* appearing in 1948, contained seven stories published during the previous seven years. Mr. Taylor, like other good young writers, appears regularly in the *New Yorker*. Much has been said about the tendency of this excellent magazine to standardize the short story in America. The famous blue pencil is supposed to turn every piece, however individual, into a "typical *New Yorker* story." Since the reader cannot know what actually goes on in the *New Yorker* offices, he must judge by what he reads in the magazine, and from this the accusations do not appear to have much truth. If the *New Yorker* edits, it edits wisely, preserving the spirit and tone of the story. If one *New Yorker* story is at all like another it is because the *New Yorker* prefers a certain kind of writer. It prefers those with the classical virtues, and its effect on the standard and polish of the short story in America has been considerable. One feels that the recent spate of nasty remarks about the *New Yorker* on both sides of the Atlantic must have come from disgruntled would-be contributors, for the magazine is highly selective and there is fierce competition for its space. Other writers who appear in the *New Yorker,* apart from Miss Welty and Mr. Taylor, are John Cheever, J. D. Salinger, Frances Gray Patton, and Edward Newhouse. Looking at Mr. Taylor's own stories one senses immediately why the *New Yorker* took to him. He is a leisurely, careful craftsman, not quite so obviously polished as Katherine Anne Porter and with less interest in symbolism. He reminds one most nearly of the later Eudora Welty, exploring as he does the minutiae of life in small Southern towns; but he has less of Eudora Welty's sense of the physical life of the place. One of the most successful stories in his last volume is called "Cookie," in which the weekly visit of a doctor to the wife from whom he has apparently been separated is described with careful detachment and understatement. What Mr. Taylor is particularly good at is the pointed last line, which usually directs the reader, with the same apparent detachment, to the heart of the story.

The South is strong in young short story writers. As with the established Southern writers, William Faulkner, Katherine Anne Porter, Robert Penn Warren, Caroline Gordon, Eudora Welty, and Carson McCullers, they make excellent use of the life of the region. The best of them, apart from Mr. Taylor, are probably Truman Capote, Flannery O'Connor, and William Goyen.

One cannot call these writers "regional," because their work transcends the life of the region. A strictly regional writer usually has only a regional significance. But, as Miss Welty insists, you cannot write a good modern short story without conveying an intense sense of place and atmosphere. Walter Van Tilburg Clark, another of the outstanding names among the youngest generation of writers, uses the background of Nevada and Utah. Wallace Stegner's stories cover the Rocky Mountain region; they range from Iowa to California. Jessamyn West's stories are set among the Quakers of Indiana. Irwin Shaw and Jerome Weidman write of New York, Nelson Algren of Chicago. It is possible, as Miss Martha Foley has done, to make a collection of short stories that illustrates not only the excellence of the American story but also the divergence of regional background. A great deal is talked about the standardization of life in the United States by commentators who have at best traveled through various regions and noted that the same goods are on sale and the same cars fill the streets. But the standardization of goods does not necessarily imply standardization of life. One has only to live in the United States to realize how different life is even within state boundaries. Cairo, Illinois, for example, is in a different world from Chicago, Illinois, and the same can be said of northern and southern Ohio. Between Wyoming and Maine and Wisconsin and Louisiana there are more than miles.

It is this divergence within the vast area of the United States that is responsible for the sense that young writers have of the multifariousness of life. To reduce life to a story on paper is one way of subduing and ordering, and at the same time of preserving, one's experience. And perhaps it is this, as much as anything, that is responsible for the urge young Americans have to write stories out of themselves. But then they learn, the best of them, that, as Stanford Whitmore says in *American Accent,* the recent collection of stories from Bread Loaf, writing is "an honor and a severe responsibility." Like the poet, the short story writer must submit his work to a tireless process of analysis and polishing, until every word counts and every sentence is balanced. But first he must possess within himself the spring that sets men writing. He must have not only a desire to communicate the vision of his experience, but also a kind of fundamental innocence and integrity. And this the best young American short story writers have.

Part 5. MODES OF FEELING

Castles and Culture

AMERICA AND THE GOTHIC TRADITION

GOETHE, IN a poetic greeting to the United States, congratulated her on possessing no ruined castles. America was better off than Europe, as he went on to explain, because the new world lacked such useless reminders of feudal strife. Consequently he voiced the hope that, when a breed of native poets arose, they would be able to dispense with ghost stories and legends of robber barons. Most Europeans of good will and enlightenment have in some measure shared this American dream. The map of an uncharted hemisphere betokened a fresh page of history, an escape from the confining institutions of what Tom Paine characterized as an "old world overrun with oppression." And if democratic revolution tended to shut off the past, Alexis de Tocqueville pointed out, it opened up the future to poetry. The European imagination, from Chateaubriand to Kafka, has looked toward the western horizon whenever it turned from the citadels of constraint and artifice back to nature or forward to Utopia.

Meanwhile the American imagination seems to have been embarrassed and somewhat obsessed by the idyllic virginity of the terrain, the very blankness of the *tabula rasa*. "Natural scenery" needed the embellishment of "poetic association," according to Washington Irving, the first American to gain a secure position in English letters—a modest but comfortable niche between Goldsmith and Dickens. Hence Irving's career became a sentimental journey in search of the picturesque and the retrospective, a realization of the longing expressed in his *Sketch-Book* "to tread in the footsteps of antiquity, to loiter about the ruined castle. . . ."

One of his landmarks was a castle in Spain, the Alhambra; another, closer to home, was Bracebridge Hall. When he returned
to the local color of his native region he celebrated New York
as an old Dutch colony. His characteristic spokesman, Rip Van
Winkle, sleeps through the present, dreams of yesteryear, and
awakes a bearded and bewildered wanderer in an epoch that has
passed him by.

From the other side European curiosity, whenever it dwells
upon American literature, is naturally attracted by the indigenous. Here the pioneer, in spite of himself, was James Fenimore
Cooper. As it happened, Cooper was a country squire who devoted some of his less popular novels to the rights of the landed
gentry. He spent some years in England and on the Continent,
attempting to challenge Scott and Dumas upon their own ground.
But the transatlantic popularity of his frontiersman hero led him
to revisit the pathless forest and to round out his five-volume
Leatherstocking cycle. Cooper's redskins had an even greater impact: predatory rivals rather than noble savages, they reappear
only thinly disguised in Balzac. Yet their creator, in a book dis-
creetly addressed to English readers and entitled *Notions of the
Americans,* lamented that his country had no peasantry to write
about. "No annals for the historian," his lament continued, "no
manners for the dramatist, and no obscure fictions for writers of
romance."

This attitude, struck repeatedly by American writers through
the nineteenth century, is formulated in a famous passage from
the *Life of Nathaniel Hawthorne,* contributed by Henry James to
the "English Men of Letters" series. James was preparing his own
career as an English man of letters when he catalogued those
"items of high civilization" so essential to the novelist and so absent from the American scene: no castles, of course, or cathedrals, no thatched cottages or ivied ruins, neither the parapher-
nalia of a court nor the monuments of an aristocracy—nor, indeed, to be devastatingly specific, any Oxford, Eton, Epsom, or
Ascot. But James was also exemplifying the romantic logic that
had set Hawthorne's final novel in Italy because, as the preface

to *The Transformation* attested, "romance and poetry, ivy and lichen and wallflowers, need ruin to make them grow." Whereas among his own compatriots, even then commencing their Civil War, Hawthorne incuriously could perceive "no shadow, no antiquity, no mystery, no picturesque and gloomy wrong."

But contemporary realism was for twentieth-century novelists; Hawthorne expressly considered himself a romancer. His contribution was the development of a sense of the past, the rediscovery of Gothic New England. His legendary sketches, *Mosses from an Old Manse,* were home-grown in the Concord habitation that had previously sheltered Emerson's cosmic optimism. Hawthorne treated the Puritan background at length in *The Scarlet Letter;* he was to deal with transcendentalist speculation in *The Blithedale Romance.* The middle novel in this trilogy, *The House of the Seven Gables,* records the tension between those two spheres. The decaying house with its ancestral curse, its secret panel, mysterious portrait, and buried treasure—what is this but Hawthorne's ruined castle? The seventeenth-century dwelling still shown to visitors in Salem today was for him "an emblem of aristocratic pomp amid democratic institutions." In describing a flight from its shadows into the sunlight via the newly constructed railroad he seems to describe his own hesitations between tradition and modernity.

Hawthorne's lifelong preoccupation with domiciles is reflected in the titles of his books—not least in that book of English impressions which he called, with mixed emotions, *Our Old Home.* He was confirmed as an unregenerate Yankee by his later years as consul at Liverpool; yet he was haunted by the recurrent fantasy of an American returning to England and seeking the estate of his ancestors. This is the subject of several unfinished romances; it represents a kind of legacy from Hawthorne to James. The latter starts in *Roderick Hudson* where *The Transformation* left off: with the fascinations and corruptions of Rome for the young American artist. These are embodied in the sinister smile of Gloriani the sculptor, a Bohemian and presumably a charlatan. It is not until the ripeness of *The Ambassadors,* and the recognition scene in Gloriani's garden, that the meaning of "the terrible life behind the smile" is revealed—the secret of art lived, life felt, and feeling mastered.

"The splendour falls on castle walls. . . ." Tennyson's trumpet call, faintly reverberating in Northampton, Massachusetts, summons Roderick Hudson from innocence towards experience. Daisy Miller begins by visiting the Castle of Chillon and ends by dying —like an early Christian martyr—of overexposure in the Colosseum. James's heroines, from Isabel Archer to Milly Theale, gradually learn that Europe is more than an aesthetic spectacle; it is a moral involvement in which they become the tragic protagonists, inheriting riches and victimized by intrigues. Education, culture, civilization itself is no grand tour of an endless art gallery, but a pursuit of the knowledge that good and evil are not respectively aligned on the western and eastern sides of the Atlantic. Thus, between Mr. Newman in *The American* and Prince Amerigo in *The Golden Bowl,* the hemispheric values are transposed. What is wrong with the United States, it follows, is not the lack of ivy or thatch, but the thinness and flatness of the psychological landscape.

James deplored those unimpeded vistas that Goethe had welcomed. European poets might complain of coming late into a world too old. James, reversing the plaint, had come too early into a world too young. Lacking "the tone of time," the richness of tradition itemized in his list of hallowed symbols, what was left for the writer of fiction? Simply the whole of life, retorted William Dean Howells. In giving up the foreign service to chronicle the small beer of American domestic life, Howells had abandoned the ruined castle—as it were—for the parvenu town house put up on the wrong side of Beacon Street by his Boston business man, Silas Lapham. And James could approve, perhaps envy, the course that his friend had taken. One of his own earliest stories, *A Passionate Pilgrim,* involves a sickly American who wants to see Oxford and die. Literally achieving his ambition, he dies amid the spires and quadrangles, but not before his last words have looked homeward:

There's a certain grandeur in the lack of decorations, a certain heroic strain in that young imagination of ours which finds nothing made to its hands, which has to invent its own traditions and raise high into our morning air—with a ringing hammer and nails —the castles in which we dwell.

This affirmation is less typical of the expatriate James than of his fellow Americans. For a full answer to his critique, an invidious comparison between American progress and the housing conditions of an antiquated and unsanitary Europe, we should have to turn to *The Innocents Abroad* or *A Connecticut Yankee at King Arthur's Court*. But Mark Twain had no conversance with Epsom or Ascot, though he had gambled with miners during the California gold rush; though he had not studied at Eton or Oxford, he had been educated at the pilot's wheel of a river boat; and in his account of that liberal education, *Life on the Mississippi,* he dedicates a chapter to this problem under the suggestive heading of "Castles and Culture." Passing by the state capitol of Louisiana, he is provoked by the gingerbread medievalism of its architecture, which bears so little organic relationship to the community or the period. (The skyscraper that has since replaced this edifice, built under Governor Huey Long, has provided a setting for recent novels by John Dos Passos and Robert Penn Warren.)

Here Mark Twain attacks a favorite target, the debilitating influence of Sir Walter Scott's romances upon the mores of the South and, more broadly speaking, the spurious cultural pretensions of the Southern plantation. Under the guise of fiction he goes farther; the self-styled "King" and "Duke," who are exposed as a bad actor and a cheap gambler in *The Adventures of Huckleberry Finn,* constitute a satire on royalty and nobility as measured by Mark Twain's faith in the common man. On the other hand, in *The American Claimant,* a young lord demonstrates his basic manhood by becoming a cowboy. There may well be a sense in which every writer is either a Don Quixote or a Sancho Panza: either a knightly idealist who insists that each inn is a castle, or a realistic squire who treats any castle as if it were an inn. In this respect, as in so many others, the relation between Henry James and Mark Twain is complementary.

Huckleberry Finn's confessions terminate in his resolve to "light out" before Aunt Polly can catch him and civilize him. Huck's declaration of independence, however, is tempered by an acknowledgment of continuity: "I've been there before." It is hard to say which conflicting impulse, wanderlust or nostalgia, dominates the American temperament. Hawthorne manifests a homing instinct, whereas Herman Melville seems embarked upon an outward journey; yet the paths of both men crossed in midcareer. On his first voyage Melville, too, had sought castles and cathedrals; but the British ports displayed slums and warehouses; and henceforth he pursued a more distant quest in the other direction. Among his "wooden-walled citadels of the deep" Benito Cereno's slave ship is compared with a chateau, and the mutinous *Town-Ho* with the Bastille. On such a stage, against a timeless backdrop, man in the open air, reliant upon his own efforts and unaccommodated by heraldic trappings, is both a national hero and an epic theme.

The English novel, from *Waverley* to *Brideshead Revisited,* revolves around great houses and conjures with the perquisites of a settled order. For these America, always on the move, has few equivalents; her log cabins are the milestones of exploration, her homesteads the expedients of subsistence, her skyscrapers the inventions of science. Her schoolboys, memorizing an earnest poem by Dr. Holmes, exhort each other to leave the "low-vaulted past" and build "more stately mansions." Accordingly, her millionaires have reared their crenelated battlements at Newport or reconstructed abbeys in Hollywood—reconstructions hardly substantial enough to resist the volleys of Aldous Huxley or Evelyn Waugh. A far cry, all this, from the hut that Henry Thoreau built near Walden Pond, or from the advice he offered to other American builders: first create your castle in the air, then put a foundation under it. The rate and scale of later developments made it increasingly difficult to preserve such an accord between the speculative and the practical.

Ralph Waldo Emerson had propounded a manifesto for original genius when he asserted that beauty and truth were quite as indigenous to Massachusetts as to Tuscany or the isles of Greece. But Walt Whitman was more ambiguous when he invited the Muses to migrate in person from Greece and Ionia to the isle of Manhattan, and especially to the Philadelphia Exposition of 1876. When he demanded that the sign "To Let" be hung on German, French, and Spanish castles and Italian collections it is not clear whether he regarded American culture as a competition with or an importation from "the elder world." Their successors, at all events, have continued to face the same dilemma. Typically, the late Sinclair Lewis took his Dodsworth abroad and poised that well-meaning motor car manufacturer between two equally insistent muses. One of them tells him: "American life is so thin, so without tradition." And the other says: "Create something native . . . dismiss the imitation château." But as the distance between hemispheres is shortened the difference between alternatives is neutralized. American criticism has cultivated a taste for such elaborate products of European literature as Edmund Wilson exhibits in *Axel's Castle*. The younger generation of Americans now writes such plaintive testaments as Robert Lowell has deposed in *Lord Weary's Castle*. Anglo-American poetry moves freely "between two worlds become much like each other"—and who, if not T. S. Eliot, has the authority to modernize the well-worn expression of Matthew Arnold? A more surprising witness is Ernest Hemingway, than whom no writer has ever seemed more intransigently American. Yet most of his fiction takes place in other lands: the West Indies, Africa, Italy, France, and particularly Spain. It is as if Huck Finn, after having lit out, grown up at last, and long been expatriated, discovered that the bells of Europe were tolling—and that, Mr. Eliot would add, the towers of civilization were falling—for him.

By this time the United States has accumulated, for better or worse, her own store of ruins and ghosts. Her darkest memory, in spite of Mark Twain, is what has made the South such fertile ground for writers today. So far as the ruined castle stands for the pride and guilt of authentic tragedy, its specifications are met by that gloomy mansion which Colonel Sutpen built on slave labor in *Absalom, Absalom!* But William Faulkner, as he declared in accepting the Nobel Prize a few years ago, is less concerned with regional traits than with universal passions. In this he resembles his fellow Southerner Edgar Allan Poe, whose ruined castle was the haunted palace of the mind itself, so terrifyingly disintegrated in *The Fall of the House of Usher*. Such terrors, Poe confessed, were "not of Germany but of the soul." How, then, could Goethe ever have foreseen that this brave new world would soon bring forth the most Gothic of all romancers?

Three Visions

THE TRADITIONS OF INNOCENCE AND HORROR

THE AMERICAN writer is a human being before he is an American, and he writes out of his own congenital temperament. The too simple formulation of what is or is not an American expression or attitude has first to explain away the variety in human temperament. Yet he does write inside the American milieu, and that milieu influences what he feels and believes. The now standard history of American literature, the *Literary History of the United States* (1948), says in effect that happy and forward-looking literature has been produced by a happy and forward-looking people:

> It has been a literature profoundly influenced by ideals and by practices developed in democratic living. It has been intensely conscious of the aspirations of the individual in such a democracy as we have known here. It has been humanitarian. It has been, on the whole, an optimistic literature, made virile by criticism of the actual in comparison with the ideal.

It is true that America has formed a vision of herself as the land of new opportunities and great expectations. As a nation America has been optimistic. It does not follow that the bulk of American literature has been optimistic. Whether intentionally or not, the editors of the *Literary History* have imposed a tendentiousness on American literature that it does not, except in small part, actually have. And the reason why they have done so is clear: they desire a literature in the service of democracy. Most literature, however, is written out of the author's vision of the nature of things, a vision that is much larger and more inclusive than a political system. He may, like Melville, Hawthorne, or Faulkner, create a vision of horror and yet be a democrat. Perhaps most good writers would feel a little uneasy with the label "optimistic," and with some justice they might say that a better word for this state of mind is innocence, the state to which optimism aspires. It is the better word too because it suggests ironic overtones. They could say that many American writers have discovered the tension inherent in the doctrine of innocence and, furthermore, that many of the best writers have been anything but optimistic.

Charles Brockden Brown, the first American novelist, wrote tales of Gothic horror. Edgar Allan Poe was obsessed by a universe haunted, malevolent, and in decay. Hawthorne believed in the doctrine of original sin, and he discovered his primary subject in the iron righteousness of the New England conscience. Herman Melville, his contemporary, possessed a profound sense of the human mind as the carrier of long-forgotten terrors and violences, and he inclined to be contemptuous of writers who had little or no sense of man's still living in the presence of roaring Niagaras. Twentieth-century literature in America looks backward to Poe, to Hawthorne, to Melville, as much as to Emerson and to Whitman. There is a Hawthorne aspect, as well as a Henry James aspect, to T. S. Eliot's poetry (if he may still be regarded as American). There is a Hawthorne aspect to William Faulkner's *Light in August* and, in part, to *Absalom, Absalom!* There is a Melville aspect to the "Hemingway world" and to the fiction of Robert Penn Warren. In other words, there is a continuity to pieces of American literature that are concerned with worlds of terror or horror.

Poe had sufficient reason for imagining a world shrouded in darkness and threatening disaster. But his decaying castles, slimy tarns, and "clammy virgins" are not merely the projection of a sick mind: they are a version of the world. And it is this—that they are a version of the world—that has caused Allen Tate to speak of "Our Cousin, Mr. Poe." Ambrose Bierce and perhaps Fitz-James O'Brien are the only significant nineteenth-century American writers who seem very close to Poe, probably because it is unnatural constantly to conceive the world as mad. But there are awarenesses in Poe's fiction of the world as mad or haunted or malevolent that find their echoes in twentieth-century literature, American as well as European. In *Morella* the nature of human identity is discussed very explicitly, and it is clear that Poe was not satisfied with Plato's doctrine of the soul as "one everlastingly, and single." W. B. Yeats in the introduction to the *Oxford Book of Modern Verse* said that modern poets are haunted by the idea of the human mind as flux. Instances might be quoted from Mr. Pound's *Cantos* or from any number of poems by Conrad Aiken. Again, Poe's generation did not have such terms as sadism, masochism, or the death wish, but Poe understood the phenomena. Gertrude Stein's Melanctha, Faulkner's Miss Emily, and Warren's Lilburne Lewis are all cousins to Mr. Poe.

Nathaniel Hawthorne continued the Gothic tradition in something like direct descent from Mrs. Radcliffe and Charles Brockden Brown. Wizards and witches hold their horrible seances in dark forests, portraits have mysterious powers, a curse hangs heavily in a family line, the wind and even flowers can be malevolent. But Hawthorne was not pre-eminently a teller of eerie tales. His plots were frequently an embarrassment to him. His interest was the psychology of evil, especially as he knew it, historically and contemporaneously, in New England. He believed profoundly in man's capacity for evil, and he was amused by, or contemptuous of, the doctrines of innocence proposed by his transcendental friends. He admired moral fiber, but he was fascinated by the iron morality of the Puritans and the righteous persecution to which it gave rise.

William Faulkner is also preoccupied with rigidity of spirit, which he suggests by the phrase "iron New England dark" and which he develops at great length in his anti-Calvinist novel, *Light in August*. None of Hawthorne's iron men is more intent on righteous persecution than Simon McEachern, foster father of Joe Christmas, and probably no other modern novel so clearly demonstrates the evil lurking in the righteous mind. *Absalom, Absalom!* also deals with rigidity of spirit, but this time Mr. Faulkner, a master of violence, uses a Gothic form: father and brother talking on dim battlefields, brother shooting brother, the decapitation of Sutpen, the "demon," with a scythe, a once great house roaring in flames, a slack-jawed idiot seeming to hover half disembodied in the night. Yet another form of horror is in his *Sanctuary,* with amoral creatures on a cooling ball in space pursuing their meaningless lusts of flesh and spirit and coming to violent deaths or vacuous ennui. Novel after novel, until rather late in Mr. Faulkner's career, says, and in a variety of ways, that life is a condition of violence and of horror.

In Mr. Faulkner's work a vision of innocence or the desire for innocence has gradually taken the place of a vision of horror. In Ernest Hemingway the two visions coexist, contributing to the dramatic tension and ironic tone of his fiction. The world of childhood is used to evoke a sense of innocence, but set against it are the images of evil, of Africa, Kilimanjaro, the hyenas, the sea, the bullfight, war. There is also something that might be called the Huck Finn aspect; that is, the Hemingway hero will have nothing to do with ordinary civilization, and, like Huck, he takes off for the territory. But—and this is Mr. Hemingway's double vision—the evil is there, too. If finally the truth is *Nada,* it is a truth heard by innocent ears, and the hearer is horror-struck.

One reason behind the renewed interest in Melville and the acceptance of Robert Penn Warren as an important novelist is that both writers have created visions of horror that in some inevitable sense seem true. Both are haunted by the earthy corridors of time, in which violences and terror beyond enduring have happened and were forgotten. There is, for example, a strong similarity between Melville's *Pierre; or, the Ambiguities* and Warren's *World Enough and Time*. The similarities seem not a matter of influence but a matter of a common view of the human condition. Between them in time but like them in philosophy is Joseph Conrad, whose Lord Jim, Stein, Captain Marlowe, Decoud, and the rest belong to the same company as Ishmael, Captain Ahab, and Pierre Glendinning, and as Jack Burden, Jeremiah Beaumont, and Wilkie Barron. The novel of violence, as it is called, is not peculiarly of the twentieth century, or, if it is, there are clear lines of descent from earlier American literature, from the Gothic novel, from Poe, from Hawthorne, and from Melville. Each of these forms has participated in or contributed to a vision of horror.

All American writers are influenced by their country's dream of innocence. The horrors of Poe or Bierce, or those in the novel of violence, may be darker than they might have been if the authors were not American. Hawthorne and Melville wrote with the ironic awareness that the received doctrine was that man is innocent. Grotesqueries as they appear in Stephen Crane, Sherwood Anderson, Nathanael West, Carson McCullers, Truman Capote, Tennessee Williams (there is a School of the Grotesque) have lent to them a quality of pathos and shock by their American *mise en scène*. America was not supposed to be like this, to let such things happen! Their grotesqueries are like the corrupted young or the wicked act of the dedicated idealist, doubly a betrayal, doubly evil. Presumably each of these and other writers would not be what they are were it not that innocence is a part of the landscape, a part of the topographical reaches of the American mind. The desire for innocence, aside from the question of the ways in which it influences American conduct, is a part of the national character.

In Henry Adams's novel *Democracy* (1880) one Baron Jacobi

complains bitterly about the American's vision of himself as a citizen of a nation of purity and innocence:

> You Americans believe yourself to be excepted from the operation of general laws. You care not for experience. I have lived seventy-five years, and all that time in the midst of corruption. I am corrupt myself, only I do have the courage to proclaim it, and you others have not. Rome, Paris, Vienna, Petersburg, London, all are corrupt, only Washington is pure!

He goes on to say that many business men and local legislators are corrupt—and why should not Americans acknowledge that evil flourishes among them as much as it does anywhere else? A half century and more later one finds Leslie Fiedler, in the symposium *America and the Intellectuals* (1953), writing a dramatically exclamatory paragraph on the American's horrified reaction when he discovers that not all is innocent:

> Among us, nothing is winked at or shrugged away; we are being eternally horrified at dope addiction or bribery or war, at things accepted in older civilizations as the facts of life, scarcely worth a tired joke. Even tax evasion dismays us! We are forever feeling our own pulses, collecting statistics to demonstrate the plight of the Negro, the prevalence of divorce, . . . the decline of family Bible reading, because we feel, we *know* that a little while ago it was in our power, new men in a new world (and even now there is hope), to make all perfect.

The student of the American temperament could collect innumerable quotations apposite in some way to America's desire for innocence. There is no doubt that the Jeffersonian heritage, among others, has helped to convince many Americans that they are not merely freer from prejudice than Europeans, but also infinitely freer from political tyranny. Any number of writers, regardless of nationality, have questioned these assumptions. The assumptions remain. The shocked surprise, to take a single example, provoked by exposé volumes—almost an industry in itself—suggests how deeply Americans, in intention, assent to the Jeffersonian doctrines.

The West, the frontiersman, and the cowboy have, of course, played a considerable part in the American's image of himself. The "horse opera" and books about the cowboy, most of them third- or fourth-rate or worse, are to the twentieth century what pastoral poetry was to Renaissance Europe. Perhaps no small number of Americans are a little uneasy with Stephen Crane's *The Blue Hotel* or Mr. Steinbeck's *Of Mice and Men* because they seem, by the sheer fact of being set in the West, a questioning of the reassurance and hope for which the West as symbol stands. James Fenimore Cooper's Leatherstocking, especially in *The Prairie,* affords an interesting introduction to the plainsman and to the West as symbols of American innocence. When Leatherstocking inhabits the settled land of New York State, Cooper feels obliged to give him a relatively low place in the social order—his love affairs, if they may be called that, were kept free from development by the impropriety of a woodsman's courting a genteel, that is upper-class, heroine. But in *The Prairie* the social structure of the East is not greatly in evidence, and Leatherstocking is seen against the backdrop of nature. Susan Cooper said that her father wished he had not introduced Captain Middleton and Inez de Certavallos, genteel aristocrats, and his reason is clear: the social hierarchies of civilization interfere with Leatherstocking's freedom and with his being apotheosized as a symbol of natural wisdom. Ironically, a weakness in stories of this sort is that the tensions of civilization are left behind and the resulting peacefulness, though enchanting, seems unengaging because undramatic.

William Faulkner's *The Bear* may well be the greatest paean to innocence in all American literature. It belongs, of course, to the latter part of the Faulkner canon, beginning with *Go Down Moses,* of which it is a section, when he turns toward a vision of innocence and hope. Ike McCaslin is a kind of Leatherstocking. He contemplates Nature as bountiful, peaceful, and moral. Civilization, with its lusts and axes and dirt, has destroyed it. Ike dreams a kind of Midsummer Night's Dream of innocence and of America as it might have been. The dream of innocence has also contributed to certain reputations, most notably those of Mark Twain and Walt Whitman. Their subject matter is the West and innocence, and it follows (by association if not by logic) that they are the most American writers. Twain wrote a number of declarations of independence from the Old World. He glorified the common man. He took the tall tale, an indigenous form, and gave it literary eminence. Twain himself came from Missouri, the very heart of America, and he lived near and worked on America's mythical river, the Mississippi. He was a home product, at once comic, shrewd, and innocent. The pathetic irony of his role is that (it is the conflict of visions again) he ended his life terribly disillusioned and pessimistic.

Whitman also was a celebrant of the West as natural innocence, and it is instructive that most propaganda poetry and most "war poetry" have been written in the Whitman idiom. Karl Shapiro in *Essay on Rime* says of epics or would-be epics written by his contemporaries:

> The bulk of these fall from the sanguine pens
> Of Emersonian and Whitmanian bards.

Innocence, of course, was Emerson's message: sorrow is "superficial" and varieties of evil are "the soul's mumps and measles." The Sage of Concord does not speak in tones that sound very compelling to twentieth-century ears, but most certainly he was the dominant figure in his own era, and if he did not begin the Genteel Tradition he was its prophet and lawgiver. Almost the whole history of late nineteenth- and early twentieth-century fiction in America is caught by saying it was in reaction against that tradition. When Sinclair Lewis made his acceptance speech in receiving the Nobel Award in 1930 he announced the final defeat of the Genteel Tradition.

But the tradition of innocence did not die with the rise of realism. One finds it in a variety of fiction—in Sherwood Anderson's search for the American soul and a return to some blessedness that has disappeared, in Thomas Wolfe's romantic search and his anguished cry that he cannot go home again, and in William

Saroyan's discovery that people are zany and yet somehow wonderful. Perhaps the weakness in these writers is that each felt he could find or rest in a state of innocence. America's vision of innocence has not invariably passed into literature in forms that seem mature or able to resist a skeptical gaze. On the other hand, some of the best of her writers have been preoccupied with it and have found therein a play of forces, moral and intellectual, that has engaged them significantly and seriously.

To say that literature is experience may, if it does not appear merely fatuous, seem merely another way of saying that literature is "knowledge" or "power" or a "criticism of life." But the term is useful: sometimes experience uses a vision of innocence to encourage hope, and sometimes to criticize excesses of hope; it says, with Lambert Strether, "Live all you can, it's a mistake not to," discovering refinements of mind, imagination, and senses; it helps to define the nature of life as quotidian.

American poets, from Anne Bradstreet to Marianne Moore, present a view of the unusual in the commonplace. In Emily Dickinson, who employed a most homely diction, New England had a poet who domesticated the Old Calvinist vision. In Robert Frost and John Crowe Ransom romantic innocence and romantic horrors are disciplined and restrained. Mr. Frost has written, "The fact is the sweetest dream that labor knows," and Mr. Ransom, "I am shaken, but not as a leaf." In E. E. Cummings, Kenneth Fearing, and Karl Shapiro contemporary poetry has critics of the Babbitt type of innocence.

Henry James had a whole gallery of American innocents— Christopher Newman, Isabel Archer, Milly Theale, Daisy Miller, Lambert Strether. Perhaps Newman, of *The American* (1877), is the prototype of them all.

A surprising number of modern fiction writers in America have found one of their major themes in causing characters to pursue romantic dreams and absolutes and come to terms with or be destroyed by the consequences. The beginnings seem to be with Henry James, but those who follow are legion: Edith Wharton, Willa Cather, Scott Fitzgerald, Glenway Wescott, Caroline Gordon, Katherine Anne Porter, James Gould Cozzens, and Lionel Trilling. Each is concerned with the phenomenon that Allen Tate called "positive Platonism"; that is, a "cheerful confidence in the limitless powers of man."

Edith Wharton, commonly seen as the most distinguished of the immediate followers of James, may be said to have found her major theme in explaining the need for compromise. That certainly is the theme of her *The Age of Innocence*. Mrs. Wharton ordinarily is not especially witty or humorous, but in *The Other Two* she has written a finely humorous story. It concerns the slow and ironic recognition on the part of husband number three that his wife owes her undoubted charms to having lived with her two earlier husbands; from the first, who was lower middle class in taste, she learned to appreciate delicacy, and from the other, who had had "advantages" but was a little on the libertine side, she learned to respect fidelity and loyalty. Husband number three comes finally to his discovery one afternoon when circumstances have caused all of them to be present in his drawing room. The men are embarrassed, but she, who has faced and surmounted difficulties before, is her charming self. He finds his discovery painful, but accept it he does, wryly appreciative.

Willa Cather, who also learned a good deal from James, is, though less ironic, like Edith Wharton in understanding muted joys. She understands the strangeness, pain, and pleasure of "obscure destinies" and the deep satisfaction in simple, unostentatious, and even hard conditions of life. Miss Cather's knowledge of frontier, village, and farm life may have given her an ever fuller understanding of the pretentious and the meretricious. Professor St. Peter, in her fine novel *The Professor's House,* tries to understand what had brought him to the edge of suicide, and he says to himself: " 'Perhaps the mistake was merely an attitude of mind.' He had never learned how to live without delight."

Scott Fitzgerald, when writing at his best, provides classic instances of romantic innocence defeated. Jay Gatsby is presented as a prototype of American innocence and hopefulness: defeat is impossible to him and even time can be brought to a standstill, or life can be relived and mistakes refined into nonexistence. Each of his protagonists, like the one in *Babylon Revisited,* is asked to recognize that the snow is "real snow." Each is subjected to a series of tests that, at long last, force him to face the consequences of living with sentiments that were ill understood, of having confused illusion and reality. Similar statements, modified to suit their special preoccupations and subject matter, might be made about the fiction of Glenway Wescott, Caroline Gordon, Katherine Anne Porter, James Gould Cozzens—and about still other writers who, consciously or not, write in the tradition of Henry James. However individualized their subject matter and tone, qualities they have in common are the surprise that attends failure and the pathos that attends making friends with death, time, and necessity.

Place and Time

THE SOUTHERN WRITER'S INHERITANCE

IN THE present surge of writers coming out of the South, William Faulkner is the Man—pride and joy and show piece. Even so, Edmund Wilson has put himself on record as wondering why on earth Mr. Faulkner doesn't quit all this local stuff and come out of the South to write in civilization. He asks how writing like that can possibly come out of some little town in Mississippi. The marvelous thing is that such writing comes. Let Mr. Wilson try calling for some in another direction, and see how long it takes. Such writing does not happen often, anywhere.

In America, Southerners are always being asked to account for themselves in general; it's a national habit. If they hold themselves too proud, or let themselves go too quickly, to give a reasonable answer, it does not really matter—at least it does not matter to the Southerners. Now that the "Southern Renaissance" is a frequent term, and they are being asked to account for that, some try, and others just go on writing. In one little Mississippi town on the river, seventeen authors are in the national print and a Pulitzer Prize winner edits the paper. It is also true that nobody is *buying* books in that town, or generally in the South. It seems that when it comes to books they are reading the old ones and writing the new ones. Southerners are, indeed, apart from and in addition to the giant Faulkner, writing a substantial part of the seriously considered novels, stories, and poems of the day in America and the most interesting criticism. One might just think that they are good at writing and let it go at that.

There has always been a generous flow of writing to come out of the South. One can begin with Poe and come up through George Washington Cable, Joel Chandler Harris, James Branch Cabell, Julia Peterkin, Willa Cather, Ellen Glasgow, Stark Young, William Alexander Percy, and so on—there are many more. Before the famous *Southern Review* of the thirties there were two previous *Southern Reviews,* the first published more than a hundred years earlier in Charleston. There was the *Southern Literary Messenger,* to which Poe contributed, and there was, and still is, the *South Atlantic Quarterly,* which has been going on in Durham, North Carolina, for the last fifty years, with many creditable pieces in it, as W. B. Hamilton's recently published collection from it has made plain. There has been a high standard of journalism in the South, not everywhere, but continuously somewhere; one thinks of it as a tradition out of which came historians and critics like Herbert Agar, who edited the Louisville *Courier Journal* before coming to England, or Virginius Dabney in Richmond, or Hodding Carter in Greenville, Mississippi, the aforementioned Pulitzer prize winner.

It is nothing new or startling that Southerners do write—probably they *must* write. It is the way they are: born readers and reciters, great document holders, diary keepers, letter exchangers and savers, history tracers—and, outstaying the rest, great talkers. Emphasis in talk is on the narrative form and the verbatim conversation, for which time is needed. Children who grow up listening through rewarding stretches of unhurried time, reading in big lonely rooms, dwelling in the confidence of slowly changing places, are naturally more prone than other children to be entertained from the first by life and to feel free, encouraged, and then in no time compelled to pass their pleasure on. They cannot help being impressed by a world around them in which history has happened in the yard or come into the house, in which all around the countryside big things happened and monuments stand to the memory of fiery deeds still to be heard from the lips of grandparents—the columns in the field or the familiar cedar avenue leading uphill to nothing, where such-and-such a house once stood. At least one version of an inextinguishable history of everybody and his grandfather is a community possession, not for a moment to be forgotten—just added to, with due care, mostly. The individual is much too cherished as such for his importance ever to grow *diminished* in a story. The rarity in a man is what is appreciated and encouraged.

All through their lives Southerners are thus brought up, without any occasion to give it wonder, to be intimate with, and observant of, the telling detail in a life that is changing ever so slowly—like a garden in a season—and is reluctant to be changing at all. Without the conscious surmise of how they may have come to find it out, they do habitually find out how to be curious and aware, and perhaps compassionate and certainly prejudiced, about the stories that can be watched in the happening, all the way—lifelong and generation-long stories. They are stories watched and participated in, if not by one member of the family, then without a break by another, allowing the continuous recital to be passed along in its full course—memory and event and the comprehension of it and being part of it scarcely marked off from one another in the present glow of hearing it again, telling it, feeling it, knowing it. Some day somebody is likely to write it, although nobody is quite so likely to read it. The main thing Southern writers learn is that the story, whatever it is, is not incredible. Of course, that is what they wind up being charged with—stark incredibility. Faulkner is all true—he is poetically the most accurate man alive, he has looked straight into the heart of the matter and got it down for good.

One thing Yoknapatawpha County has demonstrated is that deeper down than people, farther back than history, there is the Place. All Southerners must have felt that they were born somewhere in its story, and they can see themselves in line. The South was beautiful as a place, things have happened to it, and it is beautiful still—sometimes to the eye, often to the memory; and beyond any doubt it has a tearing beauty for the vision of the Southern writer, in whose work Place is seen with Time walking on it—dramatically, portentously, mourningly, in ravishment, in remembrance, as the case may be—though without the humor that this writing is full of, where would it be? It is a rural land, not industrialized yet—so that William Faulkner can still go out and get his deer—but threatened with industry now; and some towns are much bigger and are filling with strangers, though many, perhaps most, are still small, poor, self-contained, individual. only beginning to change around the edges. The South is in no way homogeneous, and even in one state there will be five or six different regions, with different sets of notions, different turns of speech. And yet most of the South's body of memories and lore and states of mind are basically Anglo-Saxon or Celtic—with a small dash of Huguenot French here and there—all of it, most likely, having passed through Virginia at some time or other. In the eighteenth or nineteenth century everybody who was coming to the South came, and mostly they stayed. The Civil War and industry have brought its only visitors. And the writing, in a way, communicates out of this larger and older body of understanding, the inheritance that is more felt than seen, more evident and reliable in thought and dream than in present life, in all the racket of the highways with the trucks and the transports bearing down. Quiet places are still left, if you know where to find them; and inwardly family life, customs, the way of looking at life, have hardly changed at all, and never will, it is safe to say, at the heart —pride and poverty and maybe a general pernicketiness prevailing. The essential landscape remains one to induce the kind of meditation from which real writing springs.

Place must have something to do with this fury of writing with which the South is charged. If one thing stands out in these writers, all quite different from one another, it is that each feels passionately about Place. And not merely in the historical and prideful meaning of the word, but in the sensory meaning, the breathing world of sight and smell and sound, in its earth and water and sky, its time and its seasons. In being so moved, the Southerners—one could almost indisputably say—are unique in America today. One would have to look to those other writers of remote parts, the Irish and the Welsh, to find the same thing.

Literature does belong in essential ways to place, and always invokes place to speak in its fullest voice. To Southerners that assumption is so accepted, lies so deep in the bones, as never to have needed stating among themselves. It belongs to the privacies of writing. The movement of the twenties that was called, to begin with, the Fugitive might never have quickened and burned so bright except out of defiance—that defiance that habitually springs up in Southerners in the face of what the North wants out of them. The ravishment of their countryside, industrialization, standardization, exploitation, and the general vulgarization of life have ever, reasonably or not, been seen as one Northern thing to the individualist mind of the South. This new defiance was the kind of emotion that called up a self-conscious power; and the group of poets and essayists clustered around Vanderbilt University in Nashville, Tennessee, in those days put all that into an eloquent statement, into the symbol of poetry, into a systematized ethical idea eventually to be christened Agrarianism. What they did was simply to see the South as an entity—historical, geographic, economic, aesthetic—and to take their stand to treat it as such, do or die. Strangely enough, they *did*. Perhaps there was something romantic and heroic about agrarianism, which history has trampled on; but their cause was not lost, for their ideas about writing, perhaps the heart of it all, persevered and triumphed. Their little group flourished and reached out, for the reason that they were, first of all, a group of creative minds, charged to bursting point with the poetic impulse. This was too much to defeat.

Their original organ was the little magazine called *The Fugitive,* green in the mind today for its poetry and criticism. The contributors have almost without exception been published ever since, all over the world; they were the original Southern galaxy of Robert Penn Warren, Allen Tate, John Crowe Ransom, Herbert Agar, Donald Davidson. The writers who came after them, whose early work was nearly all recognized by, and only by, the Agrarian group in its next established quarterly, *The Southern Review,* were not so consciously taking a stand; perhaps now it was not necessary. They wrote out of the same world and the same instincts, inescapably so, but in their own way, echoing only by the coincidences of strong place feeling these earlier writers. It is likely that the new crop, paying all respect and honor to what had been done before them, would have written their stories and poems just the same without the Agrarians: they simply would never have got published. *The Southern Review,* edited in Baton Rouge, Louisiana, by Robert Penn Warren and Cleanth Brooks and Albert Erskine—with Katherine Anne Porter, John Crowe Ransom, Allen Tate, and others acting in close editorial connection, while some of their finest work was appearing there— was of inestimable help to these new writers in giving them publication in austerely good company, under the blessing of discriminating editing, without ever seeking to alter or absorb them. This was to the good of everybody: the idea was, after all, to keep alight the individual vitality of the region. Eudora Welty is an example of the writers who owe publication of their earliest stories to acceptance by *The Southern Review.* Peter Taylor is another, published there and in a sister quarterly, the *Sewanee.* Of course there were up-and-coming Southern writers *not* appearing in *The Southern Review* or *Sewanee*—Carson McCullers, for instance, came out in Boston in a novel. But there were always enough writers to go around. For years *The Southern Review* did in fact bring out most of the best work of the time, by Warren, Tate,

Ransom, Katherine Anne Porter, Caroline Gordon, and others, in an array seldom matched in the files of American magazines. Though *The Southern Review* is gone, *Kenyon* came, and it and the *Sewanee* have carried on the early ideas, though more critical than creative work is filling their pages these days.

A number of these writers have been published recently in England. *Brother to Dragons,* the brilliant long poem of Robert Penn Warren, is an example of that act of Mr. Warren's imagination of drawing up together in one astonishing handful a hundred threads, of passions, deeds, convictions, curiosities and facts, symbols and searchings, holy and unholy, and shaking out before our eyes a resultant poem that is a wonder of dazzling pertinence and beauty. Always vigorous and magnetic, alive with thought and feeling, deeply probing, poetic, scholarly, proud and gay, bitter and affectionate, his work—poems, novels, stories, criticism —continues through the years to circle around the South, old and new, and illuminate it in new aspects and ways.

In *The Days Before* Katherine Anne Porter gives us a notable collection of essays. It is to be hoped, though, that her famous stories, too, will soon be available in new English editions. Born in Texas, a descendant, it is said, of Daniel Boone—who, as pictured in a United States advertisement of something, did his writing with a knife on the bark of a tree ("D. Boon kilt a bar here") —Miss Porter has perhaps the greatest purity and elegance of style of all living American writers. In thirty years of writing her output has not been large, and at home she has been asked to account for that, but has serenely continued to put forth perfect things in judicious amounts, just as it suits her. Reproaching her for little output is as illogical as trying to take down the performance of the moon because it is not out every night. Miss Porter's prose has lucidity and radiance, but one would not say it is lunar, for it is neither unearthly nor dreamlike nor particularly feminine. It has the rather more masculine power of mental and moral strength. She deals with states of mind, moral journeyings, with good and evil. She is not especially identified with place, or rather with one place, with her South: Miss Porter is a cosmopolitan in

the good and the literal sense, both. Within a range of three books
of stories she has written of Mexico, Colorado, Germany, Texas,
New Orleans, and the remembered South as handed down (with
great strength of mind and no vapors) from her grandmother. In
retrospect her writing seems to have the most sparingly allotted
sensory images of any Southern prose one can think of, but those
it has (the "Flowering Judas," the "Pale Horse, Pale Rider")
are all the more extraordinarily powerful and compelling; in their
role of symbols they control whole stories with the force of magic.
It is to be hoped that all three books of stories will shortly be put
within the easy reach of English readers; that they are not now
is surprising.

Peter Taylor is another writer whom one wishes better known
in England. He is not only a good writer and a young one but
the authentic voice of a part of the South too seldom heard from
out of the thick of the rumors and alarms of Caldwell and Cain
—that of the "nice people." *A Woman of Means, A Long
Fourth and Other Stories,* and the recent collection called *The
Widows of Thornton* will all be known in England, it is to be
hoped, before long. Eudora Welty is represented in England by
The Ponder Heart, a long story of comic design set in a small
town in Mississippi. One of Elizabeth Spencer's two novels, *This
Crooked Way,* is published in England; the unpublished one, *Fire
in the Morning,* is just as good. The author is a young and richly
talented teacher in the University of Mississippi. Other strongly
recommended recent novels out of the South are *A Good Man,*
by Jefferson Young, a sensitive study of race relations in a quiet,
authentic, and tender voice; and *The Chain in the Heart,* by
Hubert Creekmore, an historical novel of race, dealing with three
generations of Negroes in the deep South and notable for its
sincerity.

The Dominant Theme of Violence

MAN VERSUS NATURE AND SOCIETY

"WE ARE a violent people." That half proud, half apologetic statement by Americans recurs in all discussions of their politics,
manners, law, games, and literature through five generations. It
is frequently heard today; but it can be found in the earliest
travelers' tales, in a very different America, a century and a half
ago, long before American society had become mainly urban and
industrial and long before it began to be a melting pot of diverse
and often ill-assorted national and racial stocks. The critic,
analyst, and assessor of American literature—including that of the
stage, screen, and radio—can easily trace from its beginnings
a violent streak in subject matter and style, in plot and motive.
He can evaluate the role of violence itself, in all its forms, in
that literature. He can point, at every stage in the remarkable
development of a remarkable people and their institutions, to
particular manifestations in their literature of particular aspects
of violence; for violence in all its forms is one of the most obtrusive
of American folk patterns.

But while doing all this he will find *malgré lui* that his own
function broadens. Far more than the American creative artists
whose work he studies, he will be driven into the middle mists
between a society and its culture, where his bearings as a critic
are lost. And if he is a man of the Old World striving to comprehend the nature and comparative significance of the literature
produced by a man of the New World, he will probably find
himself even more fogbound. The reason is not the absence of

violence as a theme in the literatures of the Old World; far from it. The reason is rather that in American literature aspects of violence assume a role so different from, and so much more important than, that accorded to them elsewhere. Nor are those aspects in American literature, throughout its course, so restricted as in the literatures of the Old World to human violence. In American literature, as in the development of the peculiar society that it reflects, violence appears as a regular protagonist on the scene, and on something like an epic scale. It is always there, in view or in the wings. The human characters must always take account of it. Now they league with it; now they wrestle with it, as if with a *diabolus ex machina*. But in American literature violence is never there merely as the furies, never as an occasional element in the lot of Man, never as an accidental nuisance. It is there rather as Fate, as a brooding presence incidental to the unfolding alike of American history, politics, drama, poetry, fiction, life itself. Violence in American literature is not merely the violence of Man; it is that of Nature, of "the general chaos of the world," of the ineluctable order of things, of the whole creation. Thus the particular aspects of human violence—more recently so popular in American "comics," on the television or film screens, or in detective fiction—are but latterday manifestations of that presence which has brooded over American life and letters from their beginning. It is worth while to look at that beginning and trace the violent streak through the unfolding pattern.

Psychologists are wary of Puritans. The straitlacing of human nature—which remains, as we now know to our cost, as "red in tooth and claw" as nature itself—wreaks as much psychological havoc on the lacers as on the laced. The origins of American society and of its social patterns lie in a unique bedrock of circumstances: a singularly compact, small, self-conscious elite, in revolt from older ways of life, deposited in a New World, equipped with little more than their faith and hands, and confronting nature in an arena in which both her resources and her powers were—and still are—overwhelming. Perhaps the most striking example

of the persistence of human attitudes long after the original reasons for them have passed away is the legacy bequeathed to the
American character by Puritans, pioneers, and settlers. It is a
mistake to think of it as the Puritan tradition properly so called,
or as "New England." The patterns of thought, social attitudes,
and values bequeathed to modern America by pioneers and
settlers, seamen and traders, were by no means all "puritanical,"
nor were they only from New Englanders (the Southerners, for
example, first opened up the Middle West). But the outlines of
Americanism, its social pattern and values, its hard and hardy
dependence on individualism (paradoxically mixed with gregar-
iousness), its heavy emphasis on community and "the little pla-
toon," its sturdy insistence on absolute personal rights, private
property, conformity, and self-help—these steadily persistent
American characteristics were already being fused in colonial
society before the War of the Revolution. The pattern they formed
was woven into the first article of modern Americans' faith, the
Constitution.

The first European travelers' tales about American manners
and morals or "the American way of life" express, then, varying
degrees of shock at finding so uniform, so compact, so patterned
a society in a bewilderingly diverse environment. When Gladstone
made his famous eulogy of the American Constitution, it is much
to be doubted if, with all his integrity and moral fervor, he saw
that document as the attempt of a small, largely Puritan pioneering
elite to legislate into existence for all time their own conception of
a perfectible, if not already perfect, pattern of society and social
values. He surely did not see it as a blueprint for a society
wherein man could subdue nature. Yet that was the pattern to
which, by institutions of local scope, the biggest immigration in
human history within a hundred years, of widely diverse origins,
was made to conform. In that hundred years, between the War
of 1812 and the Great War, the Old America passed away, with
its roots in the soil, shipping, and small-town or state life. In its
place came the New America of big cities, industry, Lincoln's
"internal development," the tariff, and new nation-wide move-

ments tugging against the older local loyalties. The new Americans were largely foreign-born. They went mainly into cities. The farmers—heirs of the Old America—began to go to the wall before the nineteenth century ended. Bryan's famous "cross of gold" speech was but the opening shot in a struggle still going on about subsidies from the urban population to maintain the rural incomes. And today the tensions so evident within American society can clearly be traced to constraints imposed on persons, communities, and groupings under a social, legal, and administrative system conceived by, in, and for another order of society.

What any sensible parent or psychologist can foretell for adolescents has long been racking American society. A nation born in rebellion, bent on fixing its own social patterns (so far as possible) for perpetuity, has, on the one hand, long been breaking those patterns and weaving others; on the other, it has always tried to restrain rebels in its midst, to force conformity on nonconformists, to clothe its "way of life" with the force of law at all points of impact with its citizens. "Multiply the laws and you multiply crimes and criminals," said the Roman jurist; "a corrupt State has many laws." Not lawlessness, but overfrequent and persistent lawmaking, and therefore lawbreaking, characterize American society for a hundred and fifty years, as the original faith in legislation of morality, of the good life, and of the perfect order of society was challenged by inevitable and unforeseen convulsions. This, and this alone, is all that can justifiably be meant by the phrase "the Puritan tradition": an a priori concept of what society should be. Never was this inherent cause of violence in American society made so obvious as in the tragic "noble experiment" of prohibition in the Eighteenth Amendment to the Constitution; and all the world knows what American society still suffers from it.

One original and continuing cause of violence as a theme in American literature has been, then, the perennial struggle of the individual against social compulsions: against the local community, against its law, against its manners and morals. Since these constraints have always been more rigid in American life—by force of institutional education, of law, or of conformist opinion —and less a matter of voluntary acceptance (as they are in the Old World), the individual's rebellion against them has a greater content of violence. On the other hand—the hand of the strait-lacers and conformists—the will to impose and enforce these same constraints also arouses more violent emotions and manifesta-tions. The long social history of the Old World peoples has produced individuals less prone (until our own day) to violent rebellion against established ways of life. But the emigrants to America went away from the Old World's patterns of life in a mood of ambition, rebellion, disgust, or disgruntlement; and in their new environment they had, for all their disparities, greater opportunities to clash, mold, rebel, and express themselves, within a necessarily fluid society. That society could make to its rapidly growing masses little appeal through tradition or history; there was little of either. Hence the appeal to laws not primarily framed for such masses. Hence, too, the ferments of the melting pot and what Galsworthy called the Americans' "sublime dis-regard for the law." What the older nations of western Europe have only run into in recent years—widespread lawbreaking, vio-lence, and rebellion against traditional constraints—has always marked American society. That society has been more fluid than any other, but within a more rigid formal framework.

All this is limited to the man-made social framework. Outside that framework—as in the earlier era of pioneering and seafaring —or within it, there has always been the brooding presence of a vaster nature. Only those who have lived and moved much in America can appreciate the immensity, rather than the beauty (though beauty there is), of nature in the New World. In Amer-ica nature herself is violent; extremes of heat and cold, of fire and flood, of failure and abundance, of calms and storms, blizzard and blight, mountain and meadow, desert and prairie, field and forest. Americans have subdued all this to their uses—and made not the biggest agrarian but the biggest urban, industrial nation of the world—in little more than a hundred years. It could not be done so quickly without violence of many kinds: of men in the face of nature, of nature in the face of men, and of human nature against human nature. The cost was high. Oddly enough, Americans themselves have either never counted that cost or else have forgotten it. It would perhaps be more accurate to say that this knowledge exists among the mass of Americans only below the threshold of consciousness. It forms part of their folk memory. It is embodied in their formal education, their social rites, the small change of their conversation. But the nearness of it all in time to their everyday thought, emotional patterns, and behavior is obscured and ignored. Now and then, here and there, in one context or another, it bobs to the surface: as over the great central dust bowl of the plains, or in the waste of oil and iron ore and coal, or in the latterday social problems of urbanization and the drain of youth from the threatened rural regions. But throughout the same century and a half the theme of violence in social affairs has been reinforced by the sense of violence done to, and by, nature; and the two themes mix.

Revolt is the mainspring of violence in American literature. At once we sense a paradox. One would expect violence as the expression of revolt—against the obduracy of nature and the social compulsions of man—more among the more settled, more rigid societies of the Old World. It may be that we of the Old World societies are now facing precisely that: the delayed convulsions that the most rapid social and economic changes in human history produced much earlier in America (because they were consciously made to do so), and which Soviet Russian society may yet produce for the same reason. On a major scale only America and Soviet Russia have consciously set out to refashion "according to plan" both human society and the traditional relationship between man and nature. That the "plan" was, and still is, so different in each of those vast territorial and social systems must not blind us to the sameness of the underlying inspiration: the a priori concept of the perfect or perfectible human society, the forcible reduction of nature to man's uses, and inevitably the concomitant restraints (of different kinds) against which individuals revolt. Is it accidental that the imaginative literature of Soviet Russia reveals, here and there, remarkable similarities to that of America past and present—and more of a cleavage from the old line of Russian literature? Is it accidental, too, that American literature has had its significant influence upon that of Western Europe only in this century, since Western European society itself underwent convulsions due to revolts, growing pains, and radical transformations?

There is more similarity than dissimilarity between the public heart-searchings of Western European and American artists on the one hand and the equally public "purges" of their fellows in Soviet Russia on the other during the last thirty years. Both exercises are self-conscious analyses of the role of the artist in a society self-consciously transforming itself. Society in Western Europe was not doing so until the First World War broke it up. Nor was Russian society. But American society came into existence by so doing, and has been doing it ever since. The revolts against that American process—or incidental to its tensions—have not always, have perhaps seldom, been due to the individual's or the group's disagreement with, or dislike of, the process itself or the means employed to achieve its ends. In America revolt, expressed in recurrent violence, has been the necessary ingredient, the inescapable cost, one of the means themselves. Take, for example, the ruthless striving for money and power that figures in the American novel and drama from their beginnings in the youth of American society. In a society reared on paradox it is scarcely surprising that such ruthless striving for such an end should command both approbation and rejection: the one accorded for social reasons (reckoned necessary to the realization of the perfectible society), the other accorded from human sympathy and ethical, religious, or other motives.

Where ambivalence lies, where inner tugs-of-war occur between two sets of values held with equal fervor by the same person, tensions are bound to arise. So, too, with conflicts in any society between publicly avowed principles and practices that—equally publicly—do not conform with principles or cannot carry them out. These tugs-of-war were bound to become more violent in a society growing, in size and wealth and power, more rapidly than any other has ever grown in human history: a society in which that growing population was, for a century, most rapidly recruited with adults from disparate racial, national, and social backgrounds; a society in which, as it grew, a big proportion of each generation found itself tugged into a predetermined social order and tugging against the values of its immigrant parents. Here was matter enough for conflicts, tensions, and ambivalence. In so rapid a development of so fluid a society the wonder is not that the streak of violence in its literature is so persistent, not that it is so much more marked than in the literature of other lands, but that it has been mainly a streak in a background. Viewed in another way, the wonder is not that American literature for so long showed so many affinities with that of Europe, but that its distinctive elements—including the particular role of violence—remained subordinate for so long.

It is possible, in this analysis, to see the malaise of Emerson and others in the early period, of Henry James and others in the middle period, and of many American writers in the twentieth century as a symptom of this perpetual ambivalence, this struggle between "culture and anarchy" that shows up in the unfolding pattern of American life and letters. Not until Europe itself dissolved in social flux and anarchy did American literature really find itself and stand on its own feet. It is surely significant that, when it did, the streak of violence—called "realism" as long ago as in the middle era of Howells—became, in our own day, almost the predominant theme and prevailing pattern in both American and European literature. It is perhaps equally significant that our contemporary European writers, composers, and critics have discovered, with "the shock of recognition," the themes of Melville and of so many more American authors and their relevance in our own time of human troubles. Only superficial observers of the modern scene—particularly politicians, journalists, and the unreflective mass of their followers—will rest content with such "explanations" as "the Americanization of Europe," the deliberate permeation of other cultures by "the American way of life," and so on. The true explanation is that what American life and letters have always been elaborating, in a setting of social tensions and many kinds of violence, has also been working out in the past forty years in Europe and Soviet Russia—and now in lands and peoples remote from both. We are all now in social flux. We are all now face to face with vast natural and human forces and with many forms of violence springing from many forms of tension. What was once the epic age of an American microcosm has become an age of cosmic epic. It is exciting. It makes us live dangerously. But it is not kind and comfortable. Ages of great achievement seldom, if ever, are. The advantage for Americans—whether as artists or as "ordinary men"—is that they have always lived in such an age, even if few of them were aware of it. The advantage for the rest of us is that we can learn much, for both our life and our letters, from their laboratory.

In so learning we should do well to distinguish, in American letters, the various struggles and tensions—the causes of violence—from the various forms of violence itself, the effects and manifestations of those tensions. For example, William Faulkner and Erskine Caldwell do not show the poor, the destitute, and the Negroes as "idealized"—the error alike of the eighteenth-century Enlightenment, of romantics, and of social reformers everywhere. They show the face of violence between poor and poor, Negro and Negro, as well as between poor and rich, Negro and white. This is realism; whereas, violent as was much of *Uncle Tom's Cabin,* it was (as we now know) far from realistic. Again, the seamy side of big city life—portrayed by so many American authors, from Norris and Dreiser to James T. Farrell and Willard Motley —is not shown as part of a social reform campaign. The violence in it has little to do with "class," more to do with Everyman. Indeed, Farrell himself in the aftermath of the depression (1936) stoutly defended his realism and violence, then widely criticized in America as obscene, but equally stoutly opposed the Marxist concept of the role of literature. He limited that role, among many others in society, to one providing "understanding, sympathy, pleasure"; not what should be, but what is, so that men might recognize themselves. The formula is that of Dreiser, Fitzgerald, Sinclair Lewis, Hemingway, and Steinbeck; of O'Neill and the dramatists; and of the wartime and postwar realists. It lies behind Wilder's symbolism of little men and women in conflict with vast natural forces; for *The Bridge of San Luis Rey* is as symbolic as *Moby Dick*. The Russians may utilize American literature to prove their own social purposes or make propaganda for them; but in American realism in social matters, with all its violence, social and political purposes are conspicuous by ther absence. One has to go back to the self-conscious writing of the muckraking era at the turn of the century to find social purpose, idealism, and class consciousness in American literature. And that is what one would expect; for preoccupation with the poor, the Negro, and the underprivileged, with criminals and violence, with public and private tensions, has persisted throughout American life and letters from their beginnings.

The Russians, when they portray American life, show a society and a culture in decadence and cite American literature in proof; but there is much to be said for the contrary view that the flux of the melting pot is precipitating, that an anarchic-seeming welter of struggles and tensions has been taking shape this century, and that what seemed for so long—particularly in literary terms—without form and void is now suffering the pangs of formulation. Violence in all human relationships—with nature, between man and man, between man and woman—is still strikingly plain in the unfolding American pattern. But there are signs that American authors, critics, and readers may rebel against it as the dominant theme. If they do, it may be the biggest revolt in American life and letters.

Prophets Without Honor?

THE PUBLIC STATUS OF AMERICAN WRITERS

WRITERS OCCUPY a peculiar position in the class structure of American society: they compose what sociologists would call an out-group, or rather a collection of such groups. From the economic point of view they belong to the professional segment of the middle classes, and as a rule they have no inherited capital except that invested in their education. Their incomes are smaller on the average than those of doctors and attorneys, larger than those of clergymen, and roughly equal to those of college professors. Socially they do not fit into the middle class pattern, and their behavior is in some ways like that of the rich, in other ways like that of the urban poor. Their marginal position is typified by their choice of residence. In cities they often live in districts abandoned by the rich and taken over by the poor—like Greenwich Village—or else on the dividing line between rich and poor neighborhoods, as in the far East Seventies of Manhattan, the near North Side of Chicago, and in Boston on the wrong slope of Beacon Hill. When they move out of cities they go beyond the middle-class suburbs into areas where small farms are interspersed with gentlemen's estates.

Their profession gives them freedom of movement—and of conduct, too—but it confers no luster on its individual members, as medicine does to a greater extent than architecture and engineering. People do not say "He's a writer" with the undertone of wonder and distrust that creeps into their voices when they say "He's a scientist"; the distrust is there, but not often the admiration. Such luster—or prestige or mana—as individual writers possess is usually owed, not to the quality of their work, but to its public acceptance. The quality of the work is praised or condemned by their professional colleagues, but not by the public at large, which is interested chiefly in hearing that the author's last book had a very large sale and earned a great deal of money; in that case he may be admired in the same fashion as the politician who was elected by a very large majority. Alexis de Tocqueville thought that this sort of tribute to publicly selected individuals was to be expected in any democratic society. "At periods of equality," he says in the second volume of *Democracy in America,* "men have no faith in one another, by reason of their common resemblance; but this very resemblance gives them almost unbounded confidence in the judgment of the public; for it would seem probable that, as they are all endowed with equal means of judging, the greater truth should go with the greater number."

The novelist whose books have sold in millions and the dramatist whose last play was rewritten into a successful film after running two years on Broadway may both be minor writers, but they are great men by virtue of their public positions; in a democracy the consumer's dollars are ballots, and these authors have received millions of votes. Such an author is besieged by the public as if he possessed a mana that could be transmitted to others not only by personal contact, or by ownership of a book or program that the great man has autographed, but also by a pilgrimage to the house in which the book was written. Betty MacDonald's *The Egg and I* described her misadventures on a chicken ranch in a rather unfrequented section of the Olympic Peninsula. After her book had sold one million copies the new owners of the ranch were so plagued with visitors that they put signs on the road and charged an admission fee. *Anthony Adverse,* a great success of the early 1930's, was written by the late Hervey Allen in a Bermuda house called Felicity Hall. The house was later occupied by friends of James Thurber, who reports that for a year or two "there was a constant stream of sightseers. They offered fabulous amounts for a harp gate that Allen himself had built and for a large sewing chair he had made for his wife. And they offered as much as a pound or five dollars for any pencil he had used."

The mana of a famous author can be commercialized by others, but the author himself is unable to convert it into cash. If his income is to remain in keeping with his position in the world, he has to write new books as popular as those with which he earned the position, and sometimes the mana itself makes the books harder to write; either he cannot spare time from his public appearances or else the hero-worshipers have given him a false picture of his talent. Victor Hugo suffered from delusions of greatness; "He thought he was Victor Hugo," a younger author said. Entranced by his reputation as an historical romancer, Hervey Allen told an interviewer that he could hear his ancestors talking among themselves. If their conversation was what he set down in his later, less popular novels, it was stilted and makes dull reading.

Few writers have to face this problem of dealing with mobs of admiring or merely curious strangers. The others, if they do good work, are plagued with requests for assistance from younger persons in their own profession, but they have no public position to maintain. They are subject, however, to the mass pressures of a democracy; that is, they are constantly being admonished, by looks or gossip, to vote the right ticket, have the right furniture and kitchen appliances, drive the right sort of car, and shape their books to the right pattern. Lately some American critics have taken to scolding authors for feeling alienated from society. It would seem that conformity, not alienation, is the danger to which most authors are likely to succumb. At the very least they are tempted to prove their standing in society by spending and earning more money and thereby sacrificing the quiet and watchful indolence that a talent needs if it is to flower. Tocqueville said of the country in 1831, and might say of it today:

Everyone is in motion, some in quest of power, others of gain. In the midst of this universal tumult, this incessant conflict of jarring interests, this continual striving of men after fortune, where is that calm to be found which is necessary for the deeper combinations of the intellect?

Recent observers have noted a feeling of vague hostility that seems to divide writers and intellectuals from the mass of the American population. Although the feeling appears to be stronger today, it has a long history behind it. For each new generation it started in grade school, where most of the future intellectuals were poor boys who made high marks. If they were not poor, they had some other social handicap, like being Jews or the children of college professors, and of course the high marks were a handicap in themselves. The future writers were children of a somewhat different type and were more likely to come from middle class families with books in the house. Many were lonely boys and girls with plenty of ability, so the teachers said, but with mixed academic records: they made A's in their favorite subjects, but, unlike the future intellectuals, they often did badly in mathematics or science. Most of them were not very good at sports, were shy or boisterous in company, and were not invited to all the parties. It was the same in high school and later in college: the bright boys were resentful at not being asked to join clubs or fraternities in which they would probably have been unhappy, while the athletes and class politicians had an uneasy feeling that they were not being sufficiently admired. Still later in life the division that began by being one of temperament would take the form of opposing caste loyalties, though individuals might move from one caste to another. A few of the boys who belonged to the literary crowd in college might afterward become successful men of business or corporation lawyers, but their success might give them a sense of disloyalty to an earlier ideal. Very few of them would go into politics. Although the United States has had some literary Presidents, notably the first Roosevelt, it is seldom, and as if by accident, that a writer has been elected to Congress.

Politicians as a class are not friendly to writers, and that helps to explain why the American government has not made an impressive record for itself as a patron of literature. Except in the years of the Federal Arts Projects (1936–43), the republic has done less for its writers, even quantitatively, than some of the smaller European kingdoms, including Belgium, Denmark, and Sweden. It has no ministry or bureau or governmentally sponsored council of the fine arts. It offers no prizes, medals, or honors of any sort and no financial rewards in the shape of stipends, pensions, or sinecures to writers, artists, or musicians. In the civil service, with about two million employees, there is only one post that is reserved for a man of letters: it is the privately endowed chair of poetry at the Library of Congress. A succession of fairly distinguished poets had been appointed to the chair for one-year terms. In 1954, however, it had been empty for about two years because the last poet nominated for the position had failed to receive a security clearance.

The picture is not quite so negative as this account has made it seem. In an indirect fashion the government has offered not a little help to the arts in America. Notably its taxation policy has favored the establishment of great endowed institutions like the Ford, Rockefeller, Guggenheim, and Bollingen foundations, which in turn have subsidized a number of scholarly projects and a smaller number of literary projects; together the foundations serve almost the same purpose as a European ministry of culture. Besides granting them tax exemption the government has taken a few measures of its own to encourage the literary trades. It helps to arrange for the exportation of books to countries with foreign-exchange problems. It maintains the Library of Congress, the largest in the country, which offers many services to other libraries. The Army and the Navy have purchased books in quantities for camp and shipboard reading. The United States Information Service has purchased others for distribution abroad and has maintained overseas libraries. A few writers have been granted government fellowships, known as Fulbrights, after receiving security clearances, and others have been sent abroad on cultural missions by the Department of State.

On the other hand, there are some respects in which writers, as compared with members of other professions, are penalized by federal laws or administrative practices. To mention a few of these, some old, some new:

Until recent legislation there was the inadequate copyright law, which not only offered little protection to American authors, but was also unjust to foreign writers and full of traps for the careless and unwary. For years the Authors' League and the publishing industry have been trying to bring it up to date; modern copyright bills were introduced at sessions of Congress but repeatedly failed of passage; usually they did not even reach the floor.

There are unfair provisions of the income tax. Over a five-year period an author is likely to pay more in taxes than members of other professions whose total incomes were larger than his, but more regular. He may have spent the five years in writing two books, only one of which was a financial success. In that event most of his income has been received in one or two of the years and has been taxed at a much higher rate than he would have paid on his average income for the whole period.

There is the postal regulation that any parcel containing as much as two or three lines of handwritten or typewritten material must pay postage at the letter rate. The manuscript of a novel is a "letter" that may weigh pounds, and it is doubly expensive to post because the author has to enclose stamps for its return. In many countries manuscripts and corrected proofs can be posted as "commercial papers" at a lower rate; a Canadian author can submit a manuscript to a New York publisher for about one third of what it would cost in postage if he lived in Connecticut.

Finally, there are the restrictions on travel abroad and on employment by the government that have been imposed as a result of the cold war. In theory the restrictions should not bear more heavily on the writing profession than on any other. In theory they are intended to prevent Americans from acting as Communist couriers in Europe or Asia and to keep untrustworthy persons from being appointed to posts in which they might betray government secrets. In practice the restrictions have extended to a much wider field, and many public, private, or endowed institutions—including some of the radio and television chains—have begun to require a modified form of security clearance for work that bears no relation to national security. Appalled by the prospect that a congressional committee might accuse them of giving money to homosexuals or subversives, some universities and some foundations have hired professional investigators to look for "derogatory information" about applicants for posts or fellowships.

In practice derogatory information about writers is easy to find, or to fabricate or imagine, if only because of the gossip that circulates at cocktail parties. A writer conducts his education in public, expresses his opinions, and leaves a printed record of his mistakes. Any talented writer likes to associate with other men of talent, who may not always be men of discretion. Trying to be honest, he is certain to offend some people; he is lucky if he makes two friends without making at least one enemy. If an investigator wants to find derogatory information about a book reviewer, for example, he has only to interview the authors whose books the reviewer did not like. One or two of them are pretty certain to believe sincerely that the reviewer is either a fascist or a paid agent of the Cominform: how else could he have failed to acknowledge the deep cogency of what they had written?

Investigators are trained as policemen, not as literary critics or evaluators of literary gossip, and they live in a world with different traditions from those of writers. Sometimes their reports contain items of derogatory information, soberly repeated, that sound fantastic to a writer's ears. One well-known poet who had often been scolded in the 1930's for his lack of interest in radical movements was refused a security clearance in 1952 on suspicion of having been a radical. Among the items of derogatory information that weighed against him were (1) that he had once, long ago, written an obscure and ambiguous poem in which the word "Communist" was used with what appeared to be a favorable connotation, though one could not be certain, and (2) that he had contributed to *Partisan Review*. The investigator had not read *Partisan Review* and did not know that it was anti-Communist. Another poet, who might be called X, was granted a Fulbright fellowship but also failed to receive his clearance. One derogatory item was that he and his wife had attended a cock-tail party given by Y, a distinguished author who was suspected of being homosexual. Afterwards Y applied for a Fulbright and received his clearance; the suspicion had not been confirmed. Z is a novelist who wanted to spend a year in Europe. He was re-fused a passport, not because he belonged to any organization held to be subversive by the Attorney General, but presumably because he had written and published a statement that the pass-port bureau did not like. One is forced to say "presumably" be-cause the bureau does not give a specific reason for such actions. It merely cites the McCarran Act, which it interprets in a broad fashion, and the victim, if he is a writer, usually keeps quiet for fear of being branded as a subversive character. There are many denials of passports that do not get into the newspapers.

As for positions with the government, very few writers applied for them after 1950, word having been passed around that any-one who had published a book was likely to get into trouble with Congress. Roy M. Cohn, formerly chief counsel for Senator Mc-Carthy's investigating subcommittee, might have been speaking for many congressmen when, asked about the choice of speakers for a television program, he said, "Any author is out."

Any author was open to political attack, because authors as a class had little or no political power. What some of them wrote might influence voters in ten or twenty years, but they were sel-dom able to help their candidates in a given election. It is even a serious question whether their almost unanimous support of Mr. Stevenson in 1952 added to or subtracted from his total vote; other groups may have decided to vote against anyone who aroused such enthusiasm among the "eggheads." There is one congres-sional district out of 435 in which persons in the literary pro-fessions—including writers, editors, publishers, agents, and book designers—have settled in such numbers that they might conceiv-ably hold the balance of power in a close election. The district is the Fourth Connecticut, and at one time, exceptionally, it was represented by a writer, Clare Boothe Luce. Her successor was John Davis Lodge, now Governor of Connecticut, who is the son of a fairly gifted minor poet. By 1954 the district was being represented by a citizen of Danbury who, if he had ever read books, spoken to authors, or defended authors' interests in Congress, had managed to conceal the derelictions.

The Common Reader's Choice

THE FIRST thing to be said about the American common reader is that he is not common enough. His number, in ratio to the 160 million people in the continental United States, is small indeed. Speaking before a New York audience on "Leisure for what?" Mr. George Gallup gave a preliminary report on what he was finding in a two-year study of American reading habits, conducted by his method of questioning a large sample of adults in every level and every section of the population. He made several startling assertions: Fewer people buy and read books in the United States than in any other modern democracy. The typical Englishman reads nearly three times as many books as the typical American citizen. In the entire country there are only about 1,450 bookshops carrying a fairly complete line of books; if the United States had as many bookshops per capita as Denmark, there would be 23,000. Lest Americans take comfort in the thought of their public library system, their 7,500 public libraries would have to be 77,000 if Americans were to be as generously supplied per capita as Sweden. Of a questionnaire sent to the alumni of a class graduated from a Middle Western university twenty-five years ago Mr. Gallup reported that more than half of those replying admitted that they had not read any book in recent months.

It is true, therefore, that American book buying is not commensurate with widely diffused prosperity and a generally high level of formal education. The reasons are many. Geography is against the United States publishing houses, and consequently the chief media for reviewing and advertising remain clustered on the eastern seaboard. A pioneer society did not develop a bookstore system. A large part of the population still lives in towns of fewer than 10,000 people and in vast rural areas, where adequate bookstores are not economically possible. The lack of them is both effect and cause of nonreading. The furious tempo of business life and the nonintellectual tone of the country club set are not conducive to habits of thoughtful reading among businessmen. The wage earner who can afford a radio, a television set, and a motor car turns to less intellectually strenuous forms of entertainment than books. In considering the nonreading habits of college graduates Mr. Gallup was probably right in attributing them partly to the use of assembled textbooks rather than true books in college teaching. He might have gone farther and suggested that one of the chief corrupting forces has been the misapplication by educationists, from kindergarten through college, of John Dewey's doctrine that education is preparation for life situations and not training of the intellect.

Nevertheless, though qualified "common readers" are relatively few, the number of those who read and buy books is absolutely large. Last year commercial publishers risked their capital on about 12,000 titles. In recent years not a few individual books, some of them good ones, had sales figures in the millions. What sort of person, then, reads what? What influences work upon readers in their choice of books? What are the routes from the publisher's office to the reader's hand? A few generalizations may be ventured, bolstered by some statistics from more authoritative reports. In general the channels through which books move to readers in America are not greatly different from those in England. Of new books in hard covers, not counting textbooks and technical books, about three fourths go from trade publishers to bookstores, either directly or through wholesalers; about one fourth are distributed by the book clubs to their members; comparatively few are sold by direct mailing from publisher to reader, though millions of potential readers do not live near a bookstore. Readers have adequate notice, through reviews and advertisements, of books of general interest. The book sections in the Sunday editions of the *New York Times* and the *New York Herald Tribune* reach a wide audience, even in regions far from New York. Hundreds of other newspapers carry at least a book page. Weekly papers, monthly magazines, academic quarterlies all carry reviews. Advertising is extensive and, because the chief media have large circulations, expensive.

Not to be ignored, if we are to think of the reader of limited purse, are the 250 million copies a year of paper-bound books, chiefly reprints. Mass-produced and distributed through the system already set up by the magazines, they are displayed on self-selling racks in 100,000 retail places—newsstands, drugstores, cigar stores, and so forth. They are bought because they are inexpensive and ubiquitous. Mr. Gallup would discount their cultural importance, on the grounds that the great majority of them —detective stories, Westerns, and exploitations of sex, titillating or raw—are entertainment of a low grade, that three fourths of them are bought by ten per cent of the population, and that sixty per cent of the adults whom he questioned had never bought a copy. Certainly it is significant that, according to Freeman Lewis, the most popular authors in paper-bound books at the end of 1951 were Erle Stanley Gardner, Erskine Caldwell, Thorne Smith, Ellery Queen, and Mickey Spillane, and that Erskine Caldwell's *God's Little Acre* had passed six million copies. Yet even if we allow that seventy per cent of these reprints are negligible, the remainder means a large number of good books bought and read. As Mr. Lewis said, "in fiction the record is superb. A list of novels now published in paper bindings would contain nearly all the great names in literature of the last seventy-five years, as well as the names of many of our young writers of promise and a generous sprinkling of the classics." Observation suggests that paper-bound books have, increasingly in the last few years, encouraged the habit of buying and reading good books among college undergraduates. They read fiction, biography, history, philosophy, anthropology—almost everything.

One way of getting a partial answer to the question "Who reads what and why?" is to look at any typical list of best sellers compiled from current reports of sales in leading bookstores throughout the country. A list dated July 25, 1954, divides titles into "Fiction" and "General." First place under "General" is occupied by *The Power of Positive Thinking,* by Norman Vincent Peale, a book that had then been on the list for ninety weeks, much of that time at the top or near it. Many thousands of readers bought this "inspirational" book—not particularly intellectual people, but decent, kindly churchgoing folk aware of their shortcomings and persuaded that its humane, sincere, and skillful author could help them to become not only more successful members of society but better human beings. Such books have a wide appeal generally.

Second on the list was *But We Were Born Free,* by Elmer Davis. This vigorous, high-minded plea for the preservation of a free mind in a free society deserved all the success it had. The reviews were enthusiastic, and Mr. Davis had written good books before. Yet it is no detraction to guess that he won many of his readers chiefly because he had been among the most effective commentators on radio and television. The presence on the list for twenty-five weeks of E. B. White's *The Second Tree from the Corner* was and is encouraging to those who care for good writing. Mr. White owes his popularity to the "passionate few" who discovered in the pages of the *New Yorker* the grace of style, the brightness of wit, the lightness of touch, and the underlying fundamental seriousness of one of the best of American prose writers, and who passed along their enthusiasm by word of mouth. Reviews were good, of course, but they probably had the most effect upon those who were favorably disposed. Another author whose book had been on the list for eighteen weeks, Emily Kimbrough, probably owed part of her popularity to the fact that her gay, funny, and unpretentious *Forty Plus and Fancy Free* appeared partly in *The New Yorker*. Three years before, a very different kind of book, Rachel L. Carson's *The Sea Around Us,* became a best seller after parts of it had appeared in the same magazine.

One or two examples in fiction must suffice. Leading the same list of best sellers, after being on the list for twenty-seven weeks, was Morton Thompson's *Not as a Stranger*. It was issued as a book club selection, and other sales accrued until now there are 148,000 copies in print. Except for established novelists with a following, widely read novels come, generally speaking, from the book clubs. Their first readers are, for the most part, stay-at-home wives. Then, if the books take hold, other things happen. Herman Wouk's *The Caine Mutiny,* for instance, published in 1951 both by a book club and through the trade, soon appeared also in paper covers and was adapted for a stage play and a motion picture. In the first fifteen months 1,500,000 readers had bought the book. After initial critical success the chief force that makes more readers for a novel is personal recommendation from one reader to another. There is a good reading public for novels in America. Not only the novel of the month but also the best novels of the century continue to be read. For example, many undergraduates catch up on Hemingway and Faulkner while they wait for a new novelist to emerge.

We need not be surprised that poetry does not appear on lists of best sellers. Much contemporary poetry, by its very nature, requires disciplined readers, who are comparatively few. The publishing of poetry, except for the work of a few poets such as Mr. Frost and Mr. Eliot, is not a profitable enterprise. Yet publishers with a sense of responsibility can be found for poetry that they believe in, even in the face of fairly certain financial loss. The readers are not many, but they are an important element in society, and there is reason to believe that their number is increasing. A keen and growing interest in contemporary poetry among the most alert of the young leads to the hope that the next twenty years will see a better reading public for poetry than has been known in this century.

Of scholarly books in history and the humanities, it may be said that the actuality of a reading public is not up to the potentiality. Neither trade publishers nor the reviewing media of general circulation assume the existence of any considerable educated lay public who will be readers of scholarly books. The result is that such books are largely published by generously subsidized university presses, reviewed in professional journals, and read by people in academic places. The Association of University Presses prepares a list of publications and sends it periodically to the 1,425 college and university libraries, 550 junior college libraries, and members of the faculties. There is also a good deal of direct mail advertising. Yet press managers agree that they can generally count upon a sale of about three hundred copies to libraries; that is, only about one fifth of the college and university libraries regularly attempt to keep abreast of scholarship. Professor W. Stull Holt, in an article on "Who reads the best histories?" in a recent number of the *Mississippi Valley Historical Review,* comes to "the disturbing conclusion that most of our scholarly history, including the best, is not by specialists for specialists but is by specialists for a small fraction of the specialists." It might be suggested to some of the Foundations, generous as they are in their aid to educational institutions, that one of the surest ways to improve the intellectual tone of the academic world would be to grant to the smaller colleges funds specifically marked for the addition of scholarly books to the libraries.

College libraries, in a country in which a large proportion of the population spends the years from eighteen to twenty-two in college, are important. College and university libraries buy almost as many books as the 7,500 public libraries in the country. Many of the books, particularly those of general historical interest, will find numerous readers. For instance, a guess is permissible about a book seen lately on a shelf of recent acquisitions, Mr. John Bowle's *Politics and Opinion in the Nineteenth Century,* recommended for purchase by a professor of political science. It is possibly the only copy in a county of 100,000 souls. During the next few months probably eight or ten of the teaching faculty will read it; if it lives up to their expectations, two or three may purchase it for a personal library, one or two will order duplicate copies for reserve shelves, and most of the others will recommend it to their students. The total number of readers will be considerable.

There are as many kinds of readers as there are kinds of books. What they have in common, if reading has become an essential part of their way of life, is the belief that the truly civilized life is not possible without books. Pessimistic fears have been expressed in some quarters that, with television sets in half the homes of the country, the reading habit will almost disappear, or that mass-produced paper-bound books will make economic ruin of the kind of publishing that has given us good books. Such fears would seem to be baseless. As the novelty wears off and people tire of the eyestrain and inanity of television programs, they will return to the more rewarding delight of books. If a master work arrives, it will find a publisher and fit readers. There is some safety in numbers. We may dislike the condescending tone in Matthew Arnold, but there is comfort in what he said to us seventy years ago: "Even supposing that by the necessity of things your majority must in the present stage of the world probably be unsound, what a remnant, I say—what an incomparable, all-transforming remnant—you may fairly hope with your numbers, if things go well, to have!"

Part 6. LITERARY METHODS

The Serious Literary Review

Book Reviewing for Middle-brows

Publishing Problems and Responsibilities

Paperback Publishing

Religious Book Publishing

Printing and Production

Science as Friend of the Printer

The Serious Literary Review

LITERARY REVIEWS abound in the United States. When, however, as here, the adjective "serious" is added to the title of an article dealing with them, their numbers are notably reduced. Many, though, remain—too many for mention in a brief comment—that are close to that uncertain dividing line separating "serious" from "popular."

Of those that, issue after issue, justify both the terms "serious" and "literary," each has, at least in the eyes of its sponsors, its individual character and reason for existence. Nearly all, however, share certain conditions, have certain characteristics in common. One of these is that the serious review in the United States is almost invariably a quarterly; another that—also almost invariably —the title of the quarterly proclaims attachment to a given region or institution. And where the title does not make the announcement, copyright line does, as, for example, with *The American Scholar,* which is the organ of the Phi Beta Kappa Society. Except, however, for those published south of the Mason and Dixon line, that always self-conscious region, this localization is carried little farther than the cover. Most, whatever their beginnings, aim at national, not regional, influence. *The Yale Review,* for one, adds to its main title a supplementary line, "A National Quarterly"; *The Virginia Quarterly Review,* "A National Journal of Literature and Discussion"; and so with others.

In spite of these qualifications the use of the local name continues, new journals following the example of the older ones. It must do so; it is a condition of survival. In the United States no serious review is wholly self-supporting. Even when for a year or two income rises, it can be counted on with dismal certainty to fall again. Subscribers, taken all together as a class, form a group numerically insignificant when contrasted with those of any of the larger weeklies. And advertising, that main prop of publication, conforms to the subscription list. Subsidization from somewhere, then, is a necessity. The "somewhere" resolves itself almost without exception into one of two sources: the large foundations and the universities. The foundations (the Rockefeller Foundation in particular) have been consistently generous in providing for the expenses attendant on the beginning of publication and have helped out along the way; the required yearly support comes usually from universities and colleges. *The Virginia Quarterly Review* depends not on the State of Virginia but on the University of Virginia, an organ of that state; *The Sewanee Review* on the University of the South. *The Pacific Spectator* here stands a little apart from the rest in that it draws, not on one institution, but on twenty scattered the length of the three Pacific Coast states.

Another likeness, this time not financial, among the serious literary quarterlies is the large space given by most of them to the formal book review—a space so large as to raise in a reader's mind the question why these sections are relegated to the back pages and why they are set ordinarily in type smaller, less easy of reading, than that of the articles preceding them. Is there tradition only here? Or economy? If it is economy, it is furthered by another custom common to all—one forced on them, indeed, by the rapidity with which new books tumble from the presses. Half a dozen biographies, half a dozen novels or books of verse are made the subject of a single consideration, a paragraph or two for each. The book that is permitted to stand alone must be one that the editors of the quarterly concerned regard as of outstanding importance. Which books are so chosen, what treatment is accorded to them and to the others under review marks a chief cleavage between one group of American serious reviews and another. It is the cleavage between those editors who define "literary" as applying solely to the arts and almost wholly to the printed word—*The Sewanee Review, The Hudson Review, The Kenyon Review*—and those who give the term a broader meaning and include in their columns discussions of national and international politics or economics—*The Yale Review, The Virginia Quarterly Review, The Pacific Spectator, The American Scholar.* The last named has passed so far over from the arts to public affairs that in the spring issue of 1954 only one article, and that doubtfully, could be named "literary," though "philosophical" might be applied, also doubtfully, to several.

Whatever their differences, there is one article of faith remaining that all members of both groups hold in common: all give importance to poetry. All publish freely from the work of living poets, offer abundant comment on that work and evaluations of it. Beyond this, difference in definition, reinforced by a no less great difference in tone, affects the entire content of each quarterly in either group. Nowhere is this effect more readily assessed than in the voluminous book sections already mentioned. *The Yale Review*—not the oldest of American literary reviews, but one that, under Helen MacAfee's editorship, became a kind of doyen among them—may stand as an example on the one side; *The Hudson Review,* which in a brief life has spread its influence widely, on the other.

Reviews in *The Yale Review* tend to be moderate in tone, to give evidence of the reviewer's erudition, to be written oftener than not by persons already eminent in the field covered by the works with which they deal. Mr. Alvin Johnson, a notable present-day liberal, reviews a biography of Robert LaFollette, a notable liberal of a day just past; a pair of books on the English Parliament are reviewed by Miss Mildred Campbell, author of *The English Yeoman* and chairman of the Department of History at Vassar College. These are typical. The position of the reviewer, the fact that he will be held accountable by his professional fellows for the fairness and penetration of his comment—these make for sober estimate, tend towards qualified judgment and away from black-or-white pronouncements.

Reviewers for *The Hudson Review,* on the other hand, write usually in provocative fashion, deal in unstinted denunciation, in unstinted praise, and as a result take to themselves—or seem to take—an authority that can be exemplified only by quotation. One example must serve—the review of a novel, *The Disguises of Love,* by Robie Macaulay. The book was given the distinction of an entire review to itself, was favorably presented by the reviewer, who explained it to readers as a narrative ". . . in which . . . accounts of homosexual relations are disguised as accounts of heterosexual relations," since, owing to American prudishness, ". . . our authors have no choice but to metamorphose gender." Therefore the heroine's name, Frances, the reviewer points out, is to be altered to Francis by any discerning reader. In the following issue of the quarterly the author of *The Disguises of Love* denounces at length this misinterpretation of his story, rejecting it *in toto.* Frances *is* Frances, none else. No homosexuality is involved or suggested, the reviewer's "disclosures are fake." This indignant disclaimer might perhaps be expected to disconcert the reviewer? Not at all. The protesting author, he answers, "is not the first novelist to have builded better than he knew or will admit." He, the reviewer, is "not to be scared out of a critical reading of a novel by the author's waspish insistence that it is not *his* reading." All this makes lively reading. What nourishment it provides for readers is open to question, but there is no doubt about what it reveals of the reviewer's self-confidence, of his sense of final authority. Many of the reviewers, as also many contributors of the articles appearing in this group of quarterlies, exhibit something of the same authoritative attitude, one ballasted often by a weight of Freudian doctrine and guided by a profound absorption in the symbol. The example just given is an extreme one, but it by no means stands alone in its elevation of the reviewer's opinion over the writer's.

The differences dividing review from review inside a group are subtler than those that separate the one group from the other—subtler and more subject to swift alteration. They are largely the result of individual editorial attitudes, the tone and even the substance of the publication tending to change with a change of editors. There are, though, a few distinguishing marks to be found. *The American Scholar* has instituted an "American Scholars' Forum," which brings together several persons, more or less prominent, for informal discussion of a previously suggested topic, the discussion being recorded—perhaps a little to the damage of its informality—for later appearance in the magazine. This quarterly differentiates itself, too, by having reduced many of its references to new publications to brief notices; in one issue there were twenty-eight of these as against five reviews. *The Pacific Spectator,* published almost within sound of the greatest ocean, carries a department, "Asian Literature," containing articles and stories translated from the work of contemporary Japanese, Iranian, Indian, and Filipino writers. It has no formal review section, but instead publishes in the body of the magazine articles dealing with aspects of contemporary writing. *The Virginia Quarterly Review* makes a skillful admixture of the sectional with the international.

A visiting Englishman, Ian Wilson, writing lately of his impressions of the United States, complains that he finds earnestness everywhere, a tendency everywhere among Americans to what he calls a "hand-on-heart" attitude. It is an odd characteristic to be attributed to a people traditionally humorous, but a survey of the reviews in either group goes some way to confirm him. If it does not reveal quite what was discovered by Mr. Wilson's transatlantic glimpse, it does show a certain sense of mission and of the emotional intensity that accompanies such a sense. What is accomplished by that sense of mission and the resultant emotional pressure—what is the worth of the serious review—is open to varying judgments. Whatever the basis of judgment, however, the judgment must, like any concerned with publication, fall into two parts: one dealing with immediate accomplishment, the other with ultimate influence.

Immediate accomplishment—or the lack of it—can be measured with some accuracy. Judged commercially, the reviews are negligible; no one of them can live without subsidy. Judged by numbers of subscribers, they are negligible, too, though here with two qualifications to be stated presently. In the field of their main interest, however, they are important in some ways not easily disregarded. One of these is the present aid that they give to imaginative writing; to the building up of the writer not yet established or to the one whose talent is such that he will never have more than a small public. All the reviews publish some stories as well as much verse. Lacking the outlets that they provide, the exceptional, the unconventional poet or story writer, who, as it is, meets difficulty and delay enough in getting a hearing, would find the attainment of that hearing harder still. The "little magazines" help, but it is largely through the reviews that the generally unacceptable work of one decade becomes the acceptable of the next and that a new unacceptable talent appears to be supported.

Those reviews that include discussion of public questions perform for these the same service. And, doing so, they have an advantage over their more prosperous contemporaries. Where there is no expectation of profit there need be no timidity. And, fortunately for the nation as well as for the individual publication, neither patron university nor patron foundation has shown an inclination toward censorship. It was noted in an earlier paragraph that, with the serious reviews, judgments based on size of subscription list were more than usually subject to error. For this there are two reasons. Free libraries, whether public or collegiate, usually have one or two or more of the reviews in question on their shelves. And since quarterlies call for a larger expenditure per copy than do magazines of more frequent appearance, their library use is increased proportionately. And, secondly, such subscribers as quarterlies have are likely to be strategically placed for the influencing of opinion. Ministers, college professors, zealots in behalf of one or another literary cause—remove these, and what remains is negligible indeed.

It was an American scholar of the earlier years of this century who said: "When I look at history in the terms of fifty years, I

despair; when I look at it in the terms of five hundred, I do not."
In a lesser time measurement, but in the same terms, the serious
literary quarterly looks forward to making its final impress on the
civilization within which it has developed.

Book Reviewing for
Middle-brows

THE MIDDLE-BROW book review in the United States appears in
some 250 newspapers that devote regular attention to books, as
well as in half a dozen magazines for the general reader. In all
the newspapers, and in such magazines as *Time* and *Newsweek*,
new books are considered as news and treated as such. Genuine
criticism—the examination of the corpus of a writer's work, the
relation of a new book to other books or to ideas, or a re-examination of some past work—is so rare in the middle-brow reviews
as to be virtually nonexistent. What the middle-brow review offers its readers in place of criticism is a brief summary of the
plot, accompanied occasionally by the reviewer's opinion of the
work in hand. As in British newspapers, brevity is generally the
keynote in reviews, and a review of more than two or three paragraphs is exceptional, although the British practice of grouping together several unrelated books in a single review is not followed.
Most reviews are favorable, since the average book editor prefers
to use his limited space to give news of good books rather than
to warn readers against bad ones. An exception, of course, is the
occasional fall from grace of a Hemingway or some writer of
similar stature. Most book reviewers and book editors are news-
papermen (many of them older men retired from the news sections, editorial pages, and even the sports columns to the less

arduous duties of the book page); others are librarians or university professors. Comparatively rare in the United States is the professional writer who does regular book reviewing.

Standing above all other publications in its treatment of books is the *New York Times*. In the excellence of its editing, the thoroughness of its coverage, and the quality of its reviews it has no rival. Although published in New York City and distributed as part of the regular Sunday edition of the newspaper, the *New York Times Book Review* has an enormous influence among the reading public of the East Coast, from New England south to North Carolina, and an impressive circulation throughout the rest of the country. In addition to its Sunday section, the newspaper has, under separate editorial control, a daily book review column conducted by Mr. Orville Prescott and Mr. Charles Poore. Mr. Prescott is probably the country's most influential book reviewer. In spite of his dislike for naturalistic books and his reluctance to review controversial ones, he brings his readers a cultivated taste (including a special fondness for good English historical novels) enhanced by a quality that he alone among his colleagues seems to possess: the capacity for enthusiasm. There was a time in American reviewing when a single reviewer—an Alexander Woollcott or an Edmund Wilson—could make a book a best seller. That sort of influence is lacking today, but Mr. Prescott sends more readers into bookshops and libraries than any other reviewer.

Second in influence to the *New York Times* is the *New York Herald Tribune,* one of the three newspapers with a separate book section. Like the *Times,* the *Herald Tribune* is read throughout the country. With a smaller corps of reviewers and less space than the *Times,* the *Herald Tribune* covers fewer books and makes less effort to publish its reviews in good time. The daily reviewing is done by Lewis Gannett, the "dean of American book reviewers," whose interest in American history and in nature books has won him a loyal following over the years. His coreviewer is John K. Hutchens, a comparative newcomer to the task of daily reviewing, but an experienced book editor and commentator on books whose deft and lighthearted reviews are increasing in popularity. And it is safe to say that no one in the United States seriously interested in books—writers, librarians, and other book editors—fails to read, if not both the *New York Times* and the *New York Herald Tribune,* at least one of the two.

The third separate book section is the Chicago *Tribune's* "Magazine of Books," the mid-continent's most influential book medium. The Chicago *Tribune* publishes a great many brief reviews and devotes much of its space to its staff of literary columnists. The *Tribune* is an articulate champion of Middle Western culture and a sturdy opponent of what it considers an East Coast plot to foist *avant-garde* literature and overrealistic writing on an unsuspecting public.

Ranking fourth in national importance is the San Francisco *Chronicle,* thanks largely to its late book editor, Joseph Henry Jackson, who guided literary taste on the Pacific Coast for almost twenty-five years. In addition to editing a book section of approximately eight pages, for which he wrote a column of literary news every Sunday, Mr. Jackson also conducted "The Bookman's Notebook," a review column that appeared five times a week in the San Francisco *Chronicle* and the Los Angeles *Times,* two of the Coast's most important newspapers. Mr. Jackson had an inevitable predilection for books dealing with California and other parts of the West; but his judgment was respected and his influence great.

Apart from these four papers, there are no others carrying daily book reviews of their own or with weekly book sections of more than one or two pages in size. Two papers may be instanced as typical of the reviewing that appears elsewhere in the nation. First of these is the Dallas *News.* The book editor of this Texas paper is Lon Tinkle, a professor of romance languages at Southern Methodist University. As Mr. Jackson was on the Coast, Mr. Tinkle is the literary arbiter of Texas, and his activities are by no means confined to the book page. Books by Texas authors have first claim to attention on his page, but he is a man of wit and urbanity, and it is his continual championing of good writing that has helped to make reading more fashionable in Texas than it is in most of the forty-eight states. The second important book page is that of the Providence (Rhode Island) *Journal*. Under the editorship of the poet Winfield T. Scott and his successor, Maurice Dolbier, this page has become the first in New England and is considered by many to be the best in the country. Mr. Dolbier has brought together a staff of good reviewers, and his page offers demonstrable proof that, under a good editor, a group of excellent local reviewers can be assembled and, as it were, rubbing against each other, produce consistently fine reviews. It is in the pages of the Providence *Journal* that middle-brow reviewing makes its closest approach to criticism.

No discussion of book reviewing in the United States would be complete without mention of Carl Victor Little, the *enfant terrible* of the Houston (Texas) *Press*. Now in poor health and no longer reviewing regularly, Mr. Little boasts that he is the only book reviewer in the world willing to back up his reviews. A reader who buys a book on Mr. Little's recommendation and finds it less than it was represented to be may return the book to the reviewer and receive in its place another volume of equal cost. Mr. Little also combats space restrictions by offering to give telephone reviews of any books not treated at length in his weekly column. In addition to those already mentioned the best newspaper book pages are to be found in the following newspapers: Birmingham *News*, Cleveland *Press*, Columbus *Dispatch*, Dayton *News*, Louisville *Courier-Journal*, Miami *Herald*, Milwaukee *Journal*, Minneapolis *Tribune*, Norfolk *Virginian-Pilot* (the only paper to run a regular column of poetry on its book page), Omaha *World-Herald*, Richmond *News-Leader*, St. Louis *Post-Dispatch*, and Winston-Salem *Journal and Sentinel*.

Many local book editors, as well as some newspapers without book editors of their own, make use of one or more nationally syndicated book review services. The most widely used of these is "The Literary Guidepost," a column conducted for the Associated Press by William G. Rogers. Mr. Rogers reviews five books a week and also covers every important New York event in the fields of art, music, and ballet. In spite of this seemingly impossible undertaking, Mr. Rogers manages to produce some of the country's best reviewing, and he is known for the sympathetic attention that he gives to younger writers. His column is available to more than 1,700 papers, but is ordinarily used by fewer than fifty of them—a figure that indicates the apathy of the average newspaper editor to book news when there is not a local book editor to prod him into providing space for it. Of the other syndicates the most important is the Saturday Review Syndicate, run by *The Saturday Review* magazine, but with its own reviews, done usually by John Barkham. About thirty-five papers in the United States and Canada make use of this service. Smaller in the number of papers using them are the Sterling North Weekly Book Review Service; "The Literary Journal," distributed by Classic Features; and the column of Van Allen Bradley, a reviewer for the Chicago *Daily News,* whose reviews appear in various other newspapers in the Middle West and upper South. The United Press, the leading competitor of the Associated Press, sends four or five short reviews weekly to many newspapers, and the King Features Syndicate supplies a weekly review column written by Clark Kinnaird and used in the Hearst newspapers.

Hundreds of magazines, ranging from *America* (a Jesuit weekly) to *The Rotarian,* from *Glamour* (a magazine for young women) to *The Combat Forces Journal,* give regular attention to books of interest to their readers, but six magazines that appeal to the general reader of books rank above the rest in influence, if not always in the quality of their reviews. The two news magazines, *Time* and *Newsweek,* cover, in the country's only unsigned reviews, from three to six new books each week. In spite of a fondness for the detailed description of a book, which represents the ultimate in noncriticism, *Time's* reviews are widely respected and can be markedly influential. *Time,* seeking to elevate its readers' tastes rather than to cater to them, is generally impatient with the popular best seller and hospitable to poetry, criticism, and other works of narrower but deeper interest. *Newsweek* has in the past staked out as its particular area of interest Americana, especially books dealing with regional history.

There are two monthly magazines, *Harper's* and the *Atlantic Monthly,* with small but literate circulations. Appealing to the upper middle-brows, both avoid in their book sections any taint of the high-brow. In the *Atlantic* its editor, Edward Weeks, writes a personal essay that occasionally deals with specific books; his colleague Charles Rolo writes short reviews of the month's important titles. In *Harper's* the reviewing has been done by Gilbert Highet, a professor of classical languages at Columbia University.

Another important home of middle-brow reviewing is the *New Yorker,* which has declined considerably in prestige and influence since the days when its reviews were being done by Edmund Wilson and Clifton Fadiman. Occasional *New Yorker* reviews are done by Brendan Gill, who, in spite of his infrequent appearances as a reviewer, is considered by many to be the most able critic in the field. Synonymous with middle-brow book reviewing in the United States is *The Saturday Review,* a transatlantic counterpart of *John o' London's Weekly.* The magazine only recently, and significantly, dropped the word "literature" from its title. Concerned with international affairs, records, and drama as well as with books, *The Saturday Review* retains a large and loyal audience composed in no small part of librarians and teachers, who depend upon it as their chief source of news of books.

An important aspect of middle-brow book discussion is the "book news" column, a variation of which appears on almost every book page and the most popular of which are those written by Harvey Breit of the *New York Times Book Review,* John K. Hutchens of the *New York Herald Tribune,* and Bennett Cerf in *The Saturday Review.* These columns, composed in part of interviews, in part of literary gossip, reflect a national curiosity about the personalities behind the news in any field. Another indispensable adjunct of the average book page is the best seller list. The most influential of these are the two in the *New York Times Book Review* and the *New York Herald Tribune* and the one prepared by the trade publication, *Publishers' Weekly,* and widely reprinted throughout the country.

In general, middle-brow book reviewing in the United States is a labor of love. Except for the larger sections, most newspapers do not pay their reviewers, and some do not even permit them to keep the books they have reviewed. Unlike his high-brow counterpart, the middle-brow reviewer gains from his work no academic preferment or chance for advance publication of work in progress. His reward is usually the satisfaction of seeing his review in print. But the integrity of these reviewers *as* reviewers cannot be impugned, and their reviews, while perhaps lacking in critical quality, rank high as journalism, which is all that most of them ever attempt to be.

Publishing Problems and Responsibilities

THE FUNDAMENTAL similarities between British and American publishing, like those between British and American speech, are so great that the differences are exaggerated by their unexpectedness. The publishing of books in the United States, as in the United Kingdom, is carried on by a great many independent firms, small as corporations go, and of the widest diversity as to their ownership, the volume and character of their business. All the forms of distribution—bookstore sale, school and library purchase, book clubs, direct mail sale, export, newsstand sale of paper-bound editions—found in the one country are present in the other, though varying materially in their relative individual importance. British concern over mounting manufacturing costs, diminishing profit margins, inadequate trade outlets, subsidiary rights, and censorship makes familiar reading to American publishers facing the same problems.

Certain conditions, however, produce important differences in the structure of book publishing and distribution. One is the difference between British and American laws on monopoly. The very rigid American antitrust statutes make anything even remotely approximating the Net Book Agreement out of the question. Organized discussions among publishers or between publishers and authors or publishers and booksellers may not deal with prices, royalties, discounts, or terms of trade. In consequence the book trade has none of the formally organized pattern that governs it in Britain, and it lacks the accompanying stability. It is, on the other hand, perhaps freer to experiment with new patterns and to utilize varied and nontraditional channels of distribution. As one result, the American Book Publishers Council, in contrast with the Publishers Association, devotes its attention to external problems affecting the industry as a whole rather than to the trade relations among publishers or between publishers and booksellers.

The nearly universal school attendance through the high school level (that is, to the age of eighteen), the rapid increase in the school age population, and the startling increase in college enrollment in the postwar years, coupled with the provision of government funds for the purchase of textbooks, have enormously increased the importance of textbook publishing. Sales of texts are now in the order of $150,000,000 a year, and in addition to the firms publishing only in this field many of the largest general publishers rely on textbooks as their principal source of profit. The educational market, including reference books and school libraries, is now several times as large as the market afforded by the retail book trade. A number of circumstances, indeed, have combined to limit the effectiveness of the retail bookstore as an instrument for book distribution. The American population, for all its relatively high formal education and its relatively abundant means, neither reads nor buys books with the frequency of the British. Surveys in 1949 and 1950 found only 21 per cent of Americans who said that they were reading any books at the time they were questioned, compared with 51 per cent in Great Britain in 1949 and 55 per cent in 1950.

Moreover, this already thin market is further attenuated by being spread over a much wider geographic area. Only a minority of the American population lives in a community large enough to support even one adequate bookstore. In consequence, other channels of distribution have shown a greater relative development in the United States than in the United Kingdom. Book clubs, for example, have proliferated. The Book-of-the-Month Club is the prototype. It distributes monthly selections to a large membership, usually at list price, and gives a free book for each second book sold. An even larger public is reached by the Literary Guild, which uses reduced prices rather than dividends as its primary incentive. Largest of all is the Reader's Digest Book Club, which publishes quarterly volumes, each containing abridgments of four or five popular books, and selling at about two dollars. Dozens of other book clubs cater for specialized tastes and particular interests. Altogether, some eighty clubs distribute about fifty million books a year and provide a means of reaching hundreds of thousands of buyers with no other ready means of book purchase. The larger book clubs lease plates from the original publisher and manufacture the edition they use, paying royalties, with a guaranteed minimum, to the original publisher. The small clubs, which may have only a few thousand members, purchase their stocks from the original publisher.

The startling postwar growth of the inexpensive paper-bound book is treated elsewhere; it has been a much discussed area of publishing. An interesting recent development is the establishment of paper-bound reprint lines of more durable physical quality and higher price ($0.75 to $1.25), including titles of high quality but more restricted interest, and printed in editions of 20,000 to 40,000 primarily for bookstore sale.

Direct postal sales by the publisher are also important, especially for professional and technical books and others having a clearly defined market that can be reached through specialized mailing lists.

The public library has perhaps been somewhat more extensively developed in the United States than in the United Kingdom. It provides some of the social services in terms of the continuing availability of serious books that are provided elsewhere by the bookstore, and it provides also for the publisher a helpful market for books of high quality but too limited a demand to enter the mass channels of book clubs or reprints.

The development of alternative channels of book distribution in response to the relative inadequacy of retail bookstores has in turn doubtless had a negative influence on the growth of book-stores in number and size, thus further aggravating the problem. There are only some 4,500 bookstores in the United States to serve a total population of some 160 million, and of these fewer than 1500 can be thought of as adequate in size. Margins of profit even to these remain slender, and there is an insufficient economic stimulus for expansion. A consequence of this distribution pattern, which gives extra rewards to the books achieving a mass audience and affords few outlets for those with only a small market, is pressure on the publisher to avoid the more speculative book—the first novel, the volume of poetry, the advanced work of research or criticism—and to restrict his list to fewer titles of more certain sale either by mass appeal or by command of a clearly defined specialized market. This pressure may in part account for the fact that American publishers produce in the aggregate only some two thirds as many titles as the British. However, the 12,000 or so titles produced annually in the United States would seem to be enough to offer the opportunity of publication to nearly all works of merit. Perhaps the most serious problem is the publication of novels by authors not yet established. This has become an increasingly less profitable—or rather an unprofitable—business, and here there can be no question that the competition with cheap or free entertainment through magazines, inexpensive reprints, films, and television is keenly felt.

For other types of books of limited market an outlet is often afforded by the numerous and lively university presses, of which some forty-one are members of the Association of American University Presses. Though none is so large or so catholic as the Oxford University Press, the presses of many universities play a distinguished role in the publication of works of scholarship, frequently of wide interest, producing among them about 950 titles a year. Small presses with low overhead costs, and devoted to publishing programs that reflect the personal tastes of their owners, come and go, but a considerable number are in existence at any given time, and together they afford a means of publishing many works of specialized literary and aesthetic significance.

The market for English-language books outside the United Kingdom and the United States is largely served by British rather than American publishers, partly because traditional marketing agreements reserve to the British editions of books published in both countries the other principal English-using areas, save Canada and the Philippines, partly because British editions are less expensive. Hence the export market has never been anything like so important to American as to British publishers. In spite of dollar shortages, however, there has been a very rapid growth in sales abroad in the postwar years, especially of textbooks and of scientific and technical books not appearing in British editions and of inexpensive reprints. Total foreign sales are now about $35,000,000, or 6 per cent of total sales, as compared with about 2 per cent in 1939.

American publishers, like British, have been caught between the pressure of rapidly increasing manufacturing costs and the opposing pressure of competition from other means of information or entertainment, which has limited the possibility of increases in book prices. The answer has been sought in many ways —in part by developing economies in manufacture through investment in research, the development of new printing equipment, and other means; in part by seeking ways of cutting distribution costs—quite successful so far in utilizing magazine and book club distribution methods, but of very limited success so far as the regular book trade is concerned—and by expanding the potential market. The last of these objectives has engaged the special attention of the American Book Publishers Council through its Committee on Reading Development. At a conference on reading development sponsored by the Council in 1950, sociologists, psychologists, and social scientists concerned with the problem pooled their knowledge of reading habits in the United States, of the influences forming those habits, and of obstacles to their development. The report of this conference (Lester Asheim: *Report on the Conference on Reading Development,* New York, 1951. American Book Publishers Council) has been a guide to subsequent research and effort. A similar conference in 1951 focused attention on rural reading, the stimulation of reading interests in rural areas, and the development of means to provide a more nearly adequate book supply in those areas. Another conference in June 1954 brought together leading figures in the field of public secondary education (13–18 years) to consider the most effective means of inculcating lifetime reading habits in pupils of that age. All these conferences have been followed by publications and by various steps to give effect to their conclusions. Similarly, publishers have worked closely with librarians, acting through a joint committee of leaders from both professions that meets for a full day half-yearly, to strengthen libraries in the United States and particularly the tax support of public libraries.

The organized efforts of publishers have been devoted to preserving the freedom as well as to enlarging the role of books. In the political realm the pressures toward conformity of expression in the United States have never been anything like so serious as those unfamiliar with the characteristic hyperbole of American political declamation may have feared from the rantings of Senator McCarthy. Books of every conceivable political hue are freely published and sold. Such pressures as have been applied have been directed not at publishing itself but at selection of textbooks for schools and purchases for public libraries, and they have met with a most vigorous response. This response was perhaps most effectively stated in the "Freedom to Read" declaration adopted in June 1953 by the American Library Association and the American Book Publishers Council and reproduced in millions of copies in newspapers and other journals throughout the country. (The text appeared in *The Bookseller,* July 11, 1953.) This document helped to bring to an almost complete halt the attacks on libraries, which had been growing in severity.

As in Great Britain, censorship on grounds of alleged obscenity has been rapidly increasing in the United States. It has been confined almost entirely to inexpensive editions sold on newsstands, which have provoked resistance by bringing to a larger and less sophisticated audience the frankness that had come to be accepted in the contemporary novel. Clothbound editions of the same works are generally sold without restriction. The narrower definitions of obscenity in American law and the greater constitutional protection of the freedom of the Press, however, have largely prevented successful prosecutions, of the sort now encountered in Great Britain, of legitimate publishers and booksellers, and such censorship as does occur largely takes the form of pressure on newsstand proprietors by church or civic committees. Publishers have been quite ready to resist, even in the highest appellate courts, any censorship of seriously intended literary work, and they have done so with success in several recent cases.

American publishers had long been most active in seeking ratification of the Universal Copyright Convention, approved in June 1954 by a 65-to-3 vote of the Senate, and the enactment of related legislation to remove, with respect to citizens of other adherents to the convention, the requirement that their books in English be manufactured in the United States to obtain copyright there. Legislation implementing the Copyright Convention was passed by the Senate in August 1954.

This brief summary has indicated a number of ways in which the British and the American publishing industries differ. Perusal of the reviews and other articles in this volume will suggest, however, that in the face of the economic and other difficulties that confront them both, the American publishing industry resembles its British prototype in serving as the channel for a full, diverse, and potent flow of books that extend the scope of knowledge, sustain a vigorous cultural life, and afford a varied and unfrightened commentary on public affairs.

Paperback Publishing

AMONG THE many American profusions that startle the visitor is the profusion of paperbacked books—not of our British Penguins, though these are to be found in larger cities and in college towns, but paperbacks of the native variety. They are in the bookshops, where you would expect to see them. And they are in the drugstores, crammed in their racks and wire towers, gleaming out among the extraordinary miscellany of clinical or cute things that the drugstore proffers you. You encounter them on newsstands—in fact, at almost any place where you might pause a moment to buy some cigarettes.

But after noting their abundance, what further reaction does the European traveler feel? Superficially, he may be horrified, amused, impressed—or all three in mixed proportions. He may be horrified by the quantity of trash displayed in garish pictorial covers, many of them showing a woman of sultry aspect in scanty clothing: or by the absurd and misleading blurbs (on *Candide*, for instance: "He chased a virtuous maiden through Europe's most bawdy age"). The European may be amused by what he considers the simpleness of American taste (as revealed by the figure of four million copies sold in paper covers of *How to Win Friends and Influence People*), or by an eclecticism that accepts the Koran side by side on the drugstore rack with *Kiss Me, Deadly*. The European, on the other hand, may well be impressed when he sees how many excellent books accompany the execrable ones, and when he understands that, for instance, more than half a million people have bought paperback editions of *Dialogues of Plato* or of *The Confessions of St. Augustine.*

Whatever the reaction, the phenomenon remains. A little inquiry will reveal that it is not altogether a new phenomenon in publishing history. But the novelty of the current phase lies in the application of mass-production techniques to manufacture and distribution. The large rubber plate presses now in operation can in one hour turn out 12,000 copies of a 192-page book. Binding machines can attach glued covers at the same rate of 12,000 copies an hour. A first printing of 225,000 has been the average figure for a 25-cent fiction reprint; and such a book is quite likely to sell half a million copies or more. *God's Little Acre,* by Erskine Caldwell, has sold more than six million copies, and Mickey Spillane's *The Big Kill* has been not much less in vogue. Distribution has had to be organized on the same enormous scale, with paperbacks going to 100,000 "outlets" in the United States and Canada. Here, we may say emphatically, books have been merchandised.

However, a little further investigation will make the traveler realize that for some paperback publishers the boom is over. One reason is that the barrel of material suitable for reprinting has been scraped. In 1953 alone more than 1,000 titles were added to these publishers' lists. At this rate, and in so fiercely competitive a field, the supply of books has become almost exhausted. No fewer than twenty-five titles by Somerset Maugham (to take one example) have been issued as paperback reprints; and these have been shared among six different publishers. Nor is the number of fresh books that are worth reprinting large enough; and yet the demand is so great that the works of popular writers tend to appear in cheaper format almost simultaneously with their publication in trade editions. A still more serious problem is that of satisfactory distribution. Mass sales have been achieved by treating books in the same way as periodicals. But the life of periodicals is designedly brief; each new issue supplants the previous one, and whatever copies of the old issue remain unsold can be returned to the distributor. With books, clearly, it is otherwise. New releases have come pouring in upon the bewildered retailer until his racks can no longer hold his stock. He has been returning the surplus in alarming quantities. In some cases publishers have even had to reckon with "premature returns" (bundles of new books still in their original packages) and have had to destroy their stock, with resultant heavy losses. Some are going out of business; one considerable firm, Permabooks, has been absorbed by Pocket Books. For those that survive, some retrenchment is inevitable. Fewer new titles will be issued, and first printings may be smaller.

Learning all this, our European traveler might be led to conclude that paperback publishing faces a disastrous future in America and is merely an extreme symptom of the plight of all American publishing, as well as of the orthodox bookshops. To some extent he might be right. Yet it would be wrong to blame paperback publishing in general for what is happening. Abundance has undoubtedly led to a glut; a great deal of rubbish has undeniably found its way into print. Still, the reader has not suffered; whatever his tastes, he has been confronted by a vast selection of inexpensive literature. As for the publisher, he can feel confident that there is a sizable market for such books and reasonably certain that he can survive provided that the industry does not overreach itself. He will still be tempted to equip his books with gaudy covers and alluring blurbs (*e.g.,* to misrepresent George Orwell's *Burmese Days* as "A Saga of Jungle Hate and Lust"), so as to arrest the fleeting attention of his drugstore customer. But the more reputable publishers have always been reluctant to have such crude devices on their conscience.

On the whole, and from the point of view of the more fastidious reader, paperback publishers *deserve* to survive. Though the industry has revealed certain megalomaniac tendencies, it has already had some remarkable successes to its credit, all of which point to the healthy aspects of the current situation. Thus, in 1952 the New American Library began to issue a periodical named *New World Writing,* presumably modeled upon Mr. John Lehmann's *Penguin New Writing.* The first issue, at a cost of fifty cents, sold 110,000 copies—all that had been printed. Four subsequent numbers justified printings of 150,000. Though in terms of its circulation *New World Writing* could be called a popular periodical, it is in other respects a publication that attempts to reflect the best new work of all countries. And though *New World Writing* is still the best American periodical of this kind, it has been imitated by other paperback publishers with reasonable effectiveness. *New Voices* came from Permabooks, *Discovery* from Pocket Books; and like *New World Writing,* these printed original work. Ballantine Books, which publish in hard cover and paperback editions simultaneously, have also printed original work in *New Short Novels* (a collection of four *nouvelles* by American authors) and in *New Poems by American Authors.* Avon Publications have brought out two collections of short stories drawn from *Partisan Review.* Other no less earnest endeavors could be mentioned.

Two aspects of paperback publishing may be stressed a little further, both in order to indicate the virtues of the industry and in order to show the ways in which it can become soundly established. Both are involved in the recognition that, at any rate for many titles, it is wise not to seek too large a market, but rather to determine one in which distribution and sales are firmly based. The first aspect is the appearance of a line of paperbacks deliberately aimed at a small and relatively erudite audience. This is the Anchor Books series, published by Doubleday at prices ranging from 65 cents to $1.25. The series began in 1952; by the end of 1954 it had more than forty titles. These were chosen with great care and taste and given most handsome formats. They included Bergson's *Two Sources of Morality and Religion,* A. E. Taylor's *Socrates,* Alain-Fournier's *The Wanderer* (*Le Grand Meaulnes*), Basil Willey's *Seventeenth-Century Background,* D. H. Lawrence's *Studies in Classic American Literature,* G. M. Young's *Victorian England,* and Geoffrey Scott's *Architecture of Humanism.* It would be hard to imagine a more attractive series of books. Encouraged by the well-merited success of Anchor Books (which have first printings of fewer than 40,000 and a limited distribution), the firm of Alfred A. Knopf is inaugurating Vintage Books, a series chosen from the Knopf back list. The first nine titles (which will all be sold at ninety-five cents) include Gide's *The Immoralist,* Albert Camus's *The Stranger,* E. M. Forster's *Howards End,* and a very good two-volume edition of Tocqueville's *Democracy in America.* A third publisher, the Noonday Press, has a comparable series in preparation.

The second aspect to be noted is a new tendency of American paperback publishers to commission works directly instead of relying upon older titles. In part this is, of course, an effort to remedy the existing shortage of desirable titles. But its consequences will no doubt be to improve the general level by inducing paperback publishers to concentrate more upon serious works of nonfiction, and possibly also to become patrons of the novelist and the poet—as they have done in some of the collections already mentioned. Thus, the New American Library has planned a group of original volumes to cover the history of philosophy, under the general editorship of Isaiah Berlin and Stuart Hampshire. It is also extending its religious titles to incorporate an anthology of Confucianism, a selection from the Talmud, and so on.

What final impression is our European traveler to carry away with him? A confused and perhaps contradictory one, of an industry in the doldrums, yet full of new programs; of cutthroat commercialism, yet of *avant-garde* severity: of the best and the worst, in a grand medley. But the traveler would be ungenerous if he did not think that, on balance, paperback publishing has been a boon to the American public and seems likely to provide many more pleasures for the reader who will put aside a dollar now and then for the purchase of a book.

Religious Book Publishing

A TOTAL of 814 religious books, including new editions, were published in the United States in one year, 1953—an increase of twenty over the preceding year. Religious books accounted for slightly under seven per cent of the total output of new books and new editions. As a classification they stood third, ranking below fiction and juvenile and just above biography. More striking from a statistical point of view was the 1953 record made by religious books on the best seller list. Of the ten best-selling fiction titles the two most in demand were books with religious themes: *The Robe,* by Lloyd C. Douglas, and *The Silver Chalice,* by Thomas B. Costain. The Douglas book played a return engagement on this stage of best sellers because of a popularly priced movie edition. During its first three years of publication *The Robe* took curtain calls, first in popularity in 1942 and second in 1943 and 1944.

In the nonfiction category seven out of the ten best-selling titles were religious titles. For the second successive year the Revised Standard Version of the Bible was at the top of the bill. When Nelson's added up the total sales of this new Bible from its publication in September 1952 to June 30, 1954, the figure was 2,816,720 copies. Second, and also there for a second year, was *The Power of Positive Thinking,* by Norman Vincent Peale. Other religious books noteworthy because of sales pre-eminence were *Angel Unaware,* by Dale E. Rogers, *This I Believe,* edited by Edward R. Murrow, *Life is Worth Living,* by Fulton J. Sheen, *A Man Called Peter,* by Catherine Marshall, and *The Greatest Faith*

Ever Known, by Fulton Oursler. Of these last three titles the books by Bishop Sheen and Mr. Oursler appealed primarily to Roman Catholic readers, a fact also worthy of further comment. Mrs. Marshall's biography of her husband found a wide reading among the several hundred thousand who had previously read his posthumously published volume of sermons, *Mr. Jones, Meet the Master.*

This phenomenon of best-selling religious books has led many to ask whether America is undergoing a religious revival. Yes, if you judge by best sellers. Doubtful, if you use such other criteria as church attendance, converts, or the opinion of the "man in the street." Of course, church attendance and new members are on the increase according to the reports of ecclesiastical bodies—but so is the over-all population. Furthermore Americans do not, as a people, seem more pious or activated by a greater zeal for good works than they were a decade or so ago. It is certainly true that the intellectual climate for religious thinking and the social climate for religious living are much more congenial than they were in the twenties and thirties. Two world wars and a widespread depression have directed the attention of countless persons to the claims of religion, both as a possible explanation of tragic outer circumstances and as a likely source of inner strength. Furthermore, science is no longer hostile to the claims of religion; in fact, modern physics sometimes plays friendly cricket with metaphysics, and psychology has been seen cheering from the sidelines for the religious team. Finally, there is an impressive list of writers, known both in England and America for their literary output, who have made no secret of their religious convictions. When such established authors as Dorothy Sayers, Aldous Huxley, Evelyn Waugh, C. S. Lewis, T. S. Eliot, Christopher Isherwood, and Elizabeth Gray Vining also write on spiritual themes, readers everywhere are interested in this testimony. They may not get any nearer a church than the bookstore around the corner, but there they can browse without embarrassment and can buy a religious book without making a public confession of faith.

Another gauge of religious interest is the increasing demand for devotional books. A Library of Christian Classics is being published jointly by the Student Christian Movement Press, London, and the Westminster Press, Philadelphia. Faber and Faber in England and Harper in America sponsor a series of mystical books initially edited by the late E. Allison Peers. A popularly priced series called "World Devotional Classics" has just issued *The Journal of John Woolman* and *Christian Perfection,* by John Wesley. Dr. E. Stanley Jones is more widely read in America, perhaps, than any other writer of devotional books. *Growing Spiritually* is the title of his latest book of readings for each day of the year.

The close relationship between psychology and religion is shown not only by a spate of books that deal seriously with the theme, but also by several that hit the best-seller lists by popularizing this current interest. *The Power of Positive Thinking* is the chief among this group. Dr. Norman Vincent Peale, minister of a Fifth Avenue church, believes that pastoral care should include guidance given by expert psychologists, and he has one or more always on his staff. So far, so good, but when he writes about the manifold problems that harass people's minds and souls, this New York pastor and successful author makes the solution to these problems too simple and easy. To be sure, we all want to be happy, but we ought not to be fooled into thinking that happiness comes in easily swallowed capsules.

Saner advice comes from books that are written with more scholarship and discernment. One of the best is a symposium edited by Paul B. Maves entitled *The Church and Mental Health.* Two other recent books of significance are *Psychology and Pastoral Care,* by Paul E. Johnson, of Boston University School of Theology, and *Psychotherapy and the Christian Message,* by Albert C. Outler, who teaches in the Perkins School of Theology, Dallas. Enough books in this area are published to justify one of the eighteen book clubs that currently bid for American readers—the Pastoral Psychology Book Club.

An interesting commentary on this phase of religious publishing is that the really significant book on the psychology of religion remains to be written. Nothing in the field yet comes up to William James's *The Varieties of Religious Experience*. The theologians, however, are evincing some interest. Paul Tillich, who has accepted an appointment at Harvard—but in Theology, not in the Department of Philosophy that James knew—recently published a book with psychological overtones, *The Courage to Be*. His theological writing shows this concern, as was noted by the Macmillan symposium on Tillich's theology published a year or two ago. An excellent guide to theological writers and their contribution is Daniel Williams's *What Present Day Theologians Are Thinking* (published in London with the title *Interpreting Theology: 1918–1951*). America's best-known theologian, Reinhold Niebuhr, shows a concern for contemporary ethical and political problems in his *Christian Realism and Political Problems*.

Though theologians go on psychological and political excursions occasionally, they keep to their age-old concerns when they convene. For example, the second Assembly of the World Council of Churches, at Evanston, Illinois, in the summer of 1951, brought together a bevy of first-rank men to discuss "The Christian Hope." Much was made of eschatology at Evanston, but two theologians whose writings show how much they could have contributed to the discussion were not there. Albert Schweitzer was presumably in Gunsbach and Karl Barth in Zurich near by. A third theologian who was missed there—he is still universally mourned—was the late William Temple. One of his chief concerns was the growth of the ecumenical movement. The number of books written in this area is noteworthy, and their value is unquestioned. Nevertheless booksellers are apt to groan when they hear the word. Neither the clergy nor the laity seem to want to pay money for books on Church unity.

Bishop G. Bromley Oxnam is one of the presidents of the World Council of Churches. His *I Protest* was published during the height of the McCarthy hearings. What the bishop protested against was the tendency of the House Un-American Activities Committee to intimidate rather than to interrogate. He wrote of his experiences before this committee in the summer of 1953. The publication of his story nine months later was one of the few events that brightened up the dark days of the Senator McCarthy hearings. The Oxnam book dealt with a House Committee's work, but the principles involved were not dissimilar.

The relation of religious expression to governmental restriction is a subject sure to be treated perennially. The best book of 1954 was *Church, State and Freedom,* a volume in the Beacon Studies in Church and State by Leo Pfeffer. A book written to show what the Roman Catholic faith has contributed to our way of life is *The Catholic Church and the American Idea,* by Theodore Maynard. Jewish writers took note that 1955 marked the three hundredth anniversary of Jewish settlement in the United States, and *The Jews in America: A History* was published in the autumn of 1954. The same year was also an anniversary for a leading firm of Jewish publishers: the Bloch Publishing Company became one hundred years old.

Mr. Maynard's book illustrates a growing consciousness among Roman Catholics of their place in the book business. Harold C. Gardiner, S.J., wrote recently in *Publishers' Weekly* that "Catholic culture in the United States is showing every year more unmistakable signs of flowing over into creative literature." Eminent among writers is Bishop Fulton J. Sheen, a Catholic counterpart of the Protestant Mr. Peale on the best-seller lists and in his endeavor to show the way to happiness. In fact, he and his publishers chose *The Way to Happiness* as a title for one of his books, and one of the reprint houses brought out a low-priced edition backed by a high advertising expenditure. Sheen's popularity is partially accounted for by his success on television. Perhaps all good preachers are also good actors. Good looks help, too.

Two converts to Rome, one an American and one an Englishman, have added to the cause of Roman Catholic literature. Thomas Merton's books have been autobiographical, devotional, and poetical; those of Monsignor Ronald Knox have been scholarly as well as popular. His translation of the New Testament is being widely read, and Sheed and Ward issued *Off the Record,* a book containing letters of spiritual counsel. The canonization of Pius X inspired more than one publisher to get out a biography. The one most in demand is Giordani's *Pius X, a Country Priest*. Two archbishops have been the subject of biographies: *The Life of James Cardinal Gibbons, Archbishop of Baltimore*, by Ellis; and *The Life of Archbishop John Ireland*, by Moynihan. Both were included in the American Library Association's 1953 list of fifty outstanding religious books.

Good biographies of religious leaders are always in demand. Professor Roland Bainton of Yale, whose biography of Luther, *Here I Stand*, was widely read a few years ago, later wrote the life of Michael Servetus, a devout medieval scholar, "whose burning at the stake is a perpetual warning of the dangers of bigotry." Canon Alec R. Vidler, of Windsor Castle, wrote a biography of Abbé de Lammenais, which was well reviewed. Pantheon Press published a new biography of Kierkegaard, the nineteenth-century Danish thinker who has so greatly influenced Neo-Orthodoxy and Existentialism in this century. Good autobiography is also being published. In *As I Remember* Edgar J. Goodspeed tells the story of the controversy that followed the publication of his modern speech translation of the New Testament more than thirty years ago. Father John La Farge, also in a volume of mellow reminiscence, *The Manner is Ordinary*, shows how the two worlds of cultural privilege and racial segregation can meet.

During the past decade book condensations have been growing in popularity, and some have prophesied the demise of weighty tomes. But the success of such large books as *A History of Christianity*, by Professor Kenneth S. Latourette, a volume of 700,000 words, and of the large volumes being published by Abingdon in their *Interpreter's Bible*, eventually a twelve-volume series, goes to show that not all Americans have the *Reader's Digest* habit or mentality.

Books of sermons are of perennial interest. Scores are issued each year, even though most of them do not get much read outside a clergyman's church and denomination. Yet a few of merit always reach beyond the confines of a parish or sect. When Harry Emerson Fosdick was preaching at Riverside Church, New York, his sermons were not only broadcast from week to week, but also widely read in book form. His Scottish successor, Robert J. Mc-Cracken, published a first volume of sermons, *Questions People Ask,* and planned to follow it with a book on preaching. Another New York preacher, whose sermons are also published in England, is Ralph W. Sockman. A former Canadian, John Sutherland Bonnell, preaches in the fashionable Fifth Avenue Presbyterian Church; a recent book of his is *The Practice and Power of Prayer*.

Leslie D. Weatherhead of the City Temple, London, spent three months preaching and lecturing in the United States, where, according to his publisher's advertising, 350,000 copies of his books had been sold. The popularity of his visit and the timely issue of *That Immortal Sea* sent many people to bookstores asking for more. Another British author whose religious books are widely read is J. B. Phillips. The American edition of *Letters to Young Churches* has sold more than 125,000 copies; it was followed by *Plain Christianity*.

Thus English writers are contributing to the growing popularity in America of books with religious themes. British publishers have also helped. Sometimes a small importation of sheets has led to big printings later, after the book became known. The only reason why not everyone is happy is that many British books are exported to American schools, churches, libraries, and individuals in competition with American editions. No publisher is at fault, and jobbers say that they cannot take time to check export rights on thousands of titles handled daily. Nevertheless, in the interest of increasing co-operation between American and British authors and publishers this problem needs to be seriously studied and a solution found.

Printing and Production

"BOOKS, I'M sorry to say, are unimportant, or comparatively unimportant, in their influence on the graphic arts today. Look at the newspapers, the magazines, the advertising material—those are the pieces of printing, the products of the graphic arts, with which the American public is really familiar." Donald Klopfer's casual footnote to an article of his published in 1949 is as true statistically on one side of the Atlantic as on the other. What makes it sound American is not only the profoundly democratic implication that the artist is or should be influenced by the size of his audience. Beyond that is the fact that when we do look at the three "pieces of printing" he mentions we see in each something in the way of display style or dress that was invented in America and proceeded by conquest to establish itself as international style. The news headline that stampedes across two or more columns is no longer thought of as the star-spangled banner of the New Journalism, and few art editors of popular illustrated magazines anywhere in the world realize what they owe to Will Bradley's bold departure, in Hearst's *Cosmopolitan* of 1916, from the then conventional *"Strand Magazine"* style. Nor is it any longer a specifically American notion that advertisers are too important to be forced to follow the small-type classified style of announcement in the newspaper press. Yet these three large classes of printed matter were in fact revolutionized in style by American ingenuity.

But when we turn to that older and more august "piece of printing," the bound book, we find no innovation that can be recognized as specifically American. On the contrary, there has been a stylistic invasion there from central Europe, which, without amounting to a general conquest, has nevertheless made it more difficult than ever before to recognize any particular approach to book design as characteristically transatlantic. Exponents of the Bauhaus style, taking refuge in America before and after the Second World War, did their best to establish the basic proposition that the printed book was "shackled" by its typographic traditions—or, as some would say, by its recognizability as a book—and stood in need of stylistic reform and bold experiment. Every argument advanced by the newcomers was echoed and supplemented by a number of enthusiastic Americans—sometimes with a verbal opulence worthy to rank with Mr. Curdle's definition, for Nicholas Nickleby's benefit, of the dramatic unities. "We are moving," said Mr. György Kepes, "toward broader idioms of simultaneity, of transparency, of interpenetration." Such gorgeousness of language is too commonplace today in discussions of pictorial art to be particularly funny, save when it has to introduce some theory connected with the multiplication of texts by the convention of alphabetical forms; and even in that connection it can be, and by many writers was, made to sound remarkably plausible. The unshackled book was to represent everything dynamic, rhythmic, and otherwise admirable in present-day civilization; it was to become a vehicle for the graphic artist's creative urge; its new look might even, though this was seldom mentioned, stimulate sales.

The symposium *Graphic Forms: the Arts as Related to the Book,* published by the Harvard University Press in 1949, from which both Mr. Klopfer's footnote and Mr. Kepes's dictum are quoted, represents the high-water mark of this tide of typographic eloquence in the United States. There are signs now that revolutionism has talked itself out. It was never at any time seriously concerned with the problem of raising physical standards, *e.g.* of presswork, and although its purely destructive, shackle-breaking effect upon style should have opened up an opportunity for some second Will Bradley to evolve an American-looking book, it apparently has not done so. The tight-lipped, wry, here's-your-machine-age effect of Bauhaus typography has not proved congenial to American designers. Cheerfulness keeps breaking through, generally with disastrous effects upon the grim earnestness that is the hallmark of the genuine article.

Is it because the printed book is, to the American public at large, only one comparatively unimportant "piece of printing" among many, that the would-be innovators have failed to set their seal upon it? Or is it because the book, of its nature, is less susceptible to the kind of treatment that succeeded in Americanizing newspaper, magazine, and advertising style? In each of those three conquests there were two common factors. They were all three primarily concerned with "display"—the flashing of a relatively brief verbal or decorative message over some distance; and, in each, vertical lines of division gave way to a horizontal thrust. The "screamer" headline and the displayed advertisement both crashed through the conventional column rule; Bradley's magazine title heads bestrode two facing pages with their large roman-and-italic type. American books, or such of them as show special care in design, have not been unaffected by those same predispositions. In no other country can one find so many examples of the title treated as a double-page unit of space; nowhere else does the cheap or trade book so often incorporate "display stunts"—titles and chapter heads in sans-serif and so on —as in the United States.

The class of book that has most profited from the experimental movement is the textbook. Spurred on by the American Institute of Graphic Arts, the Society of Typographic Arts in Chicago, and a number of well organized "book clinics" in different parts of the United States, its designers have put their greater freedom to good use. A medical or mathematical treatise may now look as if someone had exulted at the opportunity of putting it into print and then binding it. Vivacity and ingenuity mark the treatment of cloth bindings in general, particularly in the field of the cheap reprint "two-dollar book." The comic book on newsprint, an American invention, continues to hold out its enormous opportunities to the first graphic artist and calligrapher who can persuade any publisher to take it seriously as a new proletarian art form.

Science as Friend of the Printer

SOME NEW PRODUCTION METHODS IN PUBLISHING

IN A message sealed in a time capsule at the new University of Iowa Communications Center Ralph Shannon, publisher of the *Washington* (Iowa) *Evening Journal,* prophesied:

> The citizen of 2053 . . . will still be receiving his entertainment from the air waves but he will be looking for his information from the pages of his favorite paper. There will be remarkable changes in the printing processes, of course. . . . Electronics and photography will join hands to simplify and improve the printing methods. Machinery that now grinds and clatters usefully in thousands of newspaper plants over the country will be transformed and rebuilt, and, in the transformation, it will likely lose much clatter. . . .

In these predictions of a newspaper publisher (and no doubt this is common to magazine and book publishers as well) one may detect an understandable concern for the future of the very life of the *printed* word in the face of the growing use of the *spoken* word in radio and television. Evidences of this concern, and proof that those whose livelihood depends on the symbols of the alphabet and the halftone dot have lost much of their complacency, are the activities of many newly created graphic arts research groups.

Competition and the drive to turn out more copies for less money have caused individual printers, their own inventiveness exhausted, to turn to their trade organizations and independent research groups for help. Investigations into paper, ink, presses, make-ready, typesetting, adhesives, book cloths, printing plates, and binding equipment have been accelerated in a feverish attempt to combat rising costs of materials and wages. Presses are being speeded up; inks made to dry faster; devices are sought to reduce make-ready time; photography has been introduced to by-pass the use of metal in typesetting; and much experimentation goes on with new materials that will improve on copper and zinc, now most commonly used in platemaking. The Screen Process Printing Association, Gravure Research Inc., Lithographers' National Association, Technical Association of the Graphic Arts, International Association of Printing House Craftsmen, Advertising Typographers' Association, Research and Engineering Council of the Graphic Arts Industry, National Printing Ink Research Institute, and the Battelle Memorial Institute are but a few of the organizations offering counsel and recommendations that will effect cost control and at the same time hold to standards of volume printing.

These shy overtures on the part of printing, this courtship of science—spurned in the past as having little place in an "art craft"—have resulted in a marriage. Engineering—lusty, brash, and a little overconfident (as befits the groom)—has taken to wife the prideful, complacent Graphic Arts, and within the limits of this space is an account of their offspring. It seems best to give fuller descriptions of a few of the more advanced youngsters and touch more briefly on those still in the crawling and bawling stage. New developments in the graphic arts consist mainly of improvements in raw materials and existing machines that, in turn, make for improved processes and methods of producing books, newspapers, and magazines. Of the three major printing processes—relief printing, planographic printing, and intaglio printing (taking them in the order of their widest use)—relief printing has altered the least. Presses run faster, and color controls have been applied, but there is little else. In the field of plate-making the introduction of plastic plates and of the newest comer, magnesium, is the big news. As for planographic printing, presses, plates, and paper used for offset printing have advanced mightily. Intaglio printing—off to a fast start—has somehow lagged behind, with but small improvements in platemaking. Typesetting has shown possibly the most revolutionary changes, with "cold" composition or photographic typesetting methods. Newspapers, inks, adhesives, and book cloths are fast emerging from the experimental stages and are being subjected daily to trial and subsequent rejection or acceptance by the still wary printing and book manufacturer.

The lifting in February 1953 of all price controls from printed products and services, paper, and pulp by the Office of Price Stabilization, and the removal of restrictions on the use of copper, aluminum, zinc, chromium, and nickel imposed in 1951 by National Production Authority Order M-65, gave impetus to the many developments here described.

Bimetal (copper-aluminum) offset plates developed through the combined efforts of Lithographic Technical Foundation and Printing Developments Inc. (a subsidiary of Time Inc.). These are described as grainless negative film plates. They are, however, more costly than zinc or aluminum, a drawback that stands in the way of their being still more widely used.

After some eight years of development magnesium has emerged to head the list of meritorious graphic arts materials. A metal known by the trade name of Zomag and produced by the Dow Chemical Company possesses unique chemical and metallurgical characteristics and offers photoengravers the chance to make printing plates more rapidly, of greater durability, and eventually, it is hoped, at lower cost than that of the current commonly used photoengravers' metals, zinc and copper. Zomag is 90.98 per cent magnesium metal, 6 per cent aluminum, 3 per cent zinc, and 2 per cent manganese. The supply of magnesium is practically unlimited, for it is extracted from sea water—about five ounces to a barrel. It is one fifth as heavy as copper and one fourth as heavy as zinc, a definite advantage in shipping and storing, and when used in curved plates on rotary presses it gives the pressman better control over his color registry. Its stamina, if all reports are true, is fantastic; there are tales of one million impressions from a plate before wear is shown. Add to this its unique characteristic of acquiring additional hardness under the repeated pressures of long use, and one can see why even skeptical book printers, newspaper publishers, and label and carton printers find this new metal more interesting. It is now being used for line engravings and solid tints of color. Halftone screens as fine as 200-line screen have been produced in laboratory tests, demonstrating Zomag's fine grain size, but halftone etching has not yet met the industry's standards for depth. Some pioneering newspapers in the West have by-passed the making of mats and stereotypes and are printing directly from curved photoengraved magnesium plates.

Switzer Brothers Inc. of Cleveland have developed a daylight fluorescent ink called Day-Glo. By the use of a new pigment formula a sixth color, rocket red, was recently produced. The others are neon red, arc yellow, fire orange, saturn yellow, and signal green. The first major magazine to use fluorescent inks was *Popular Science Monthly,* in its May 1953 issue. Comparison in daylight shows these inks to be four times as bright as the brightest of ordinary colors. When protected from direct sunlight they retain their brilliance for many months and can be stored indefinitely under cover without color change. In Lockport, Louisiana, the Valentine Pulp and Paper Company evolved a new method of manufacturing newsprint from bagasse (the residue of sugar cane as it comes from the mill), thus helping to maintain the precarious balance between newsprint production and growing demand. (The Newspaper Publishers' Association reports that a study is progressing on the problem of deinking old newspapers for re-use.) DuPont Finishes Division released a synthetic resin, "hot melt," an adhesive to replace animal glue in bookbinding. "Flexico" is a new adhesive that permits pages of magazines, telephone directories, and the like to be held to a cover without thread or wire; it permits inserts to be held in a publication without tipping, regardless of weight or variety of paper stock.

Of the many revolutionary typesetting methods the following three have shown the greatest promise:

(1) Variously known during its development stages as Lithomat, the Higgonet-Meyroud Process, and Lumitype, and now called the "Photon," this new typesetting method employs a photoelectric process. The developer is the Graphic Arts Research Foundation of Cambridge, Massachusetts, who devised the principle of operation from an electric typewriter keyboard that is hooked up to a series of electronic circuits. A disc eight inches in diameter, carrying sixteen different fonts of type, is rotated at twenty revolutions per second. A "memory" device causes a stroboscopic flash of light to pick the desired character from the disc for photographing on film. Sizes from 5- to 36-point can be set from the master disc. It has just been announced that the first of eight of these machines to be leased will be in operation this autumn.

(2) The Fotosetter, manufactured by the Intertype Corporation, Brooklyn, is a photographic line composing machine (much like its "hot metal" machine, except that it has changed its casting device for a photographic unit) that produced justified composition in galley form on film or photographic paper. The machine sets type from 4 to 36 points inclusive in lines up to 42 picas long. Fotosetter type on film is suitable for making albumin and deep etch offset plates, letterpress engravings, gravure plates and cylinders, and stencils for screen process work. One of its important advantages is that it provides emulsion-to-emulsion contact film for the platemaking operation (type side of film rather than the acetate base side is next to the plate coating during the exposure operation), thus assuring sharpness and fidelity in printing the type down on the plate. Enlarged Fotosetter type up to 144-point size and above can be had. This machine sets type photographically on film or photographic paper in one direct operation. The typesetting process is very similar to that used on the standard line casting machine. The operator assembles the required matrices by standard keyboard methods, the letters are

automatically exposed on film or photographic paper, then the matrices are returned to the magazine for use in succeeding lines. Following exposure the film or photographic paper is developed in a darkroom, with standard developing and fixing procedures, after which it is ready for platemaking. The sharpness of reproduction is a result of several factors. The matrices are photographic copies of the designer's letter. During exposure of each character the matrix is held stationary, and the result is reproduction proofs with no ink spread or smears, pitted letters, shadows around type, or loss of detail. The product of the Fotosetter is a negative ready for photoprinting. An Intertype desk model Fotosetter operates in the same manner as the normal Fotosetter machine with the exception that assembly and distribution of matrices are manual operations.

(3) In April 1954 the long-awaited demonstration of Mergenthaler Linotype's "Linofilm" took place. Immediately afterward it was withdrawn from exhibition for further development. It is classed as the "static character projection" approach to the problem of photo typesetting. Linofilm is a two-unit machine consisting of a keyboard unit (occupying the space of a typewriter desk) and a photographic unit (which contains a reader unit, an optical system, and a film magazine). The keyboard produces, in one operation, regular typewritten copy and perforated tape. The tape is fed into the separate photographic unit, which operates automatically to set type on film in response to the tape. The justification of the line is computed mechanically and punched into the type automatically. The optical system of the Linofilm consists of a light source and a vertical turntable that carries five small glass plates on which type characters are arrayed in a grid formation. Each glass plate contains a font complement of type characters. The turntable is controlled automatically from the tape and presents the desired font to the optical system for photography. The basic characteristics of the present Linotype faces are retained on Linofilm, not letter by letter but in over-all appearance. The film itself may be corrected by a splicing device or, if an error is detected at the keyboard, by use of a line erase key.

A number of new machines and processes that reduce plate-making costs and speed up the operation have been made available. Fairchild Camera and Instrument Corporation offers to weekly newspapers the Scan-a-Graver Cadet, a table-top machine that makes an 85 screen, four-column plastic halftone in twenty-four minutes. Eastman Kodak Company released their Kodak Ektagraph process, which reproduces continuous tone effects, making it possible to produce silkscreen halftones in four colors. Hailed as a device for lending realism to an illustration, three-dimensional printing came and went in a flurry of hullabaloo.

Xerography is a dry electrical copying process using no chemicals or film. The Haloid Company of Rochester, New York, has used a new principle of electrically transferring an image to paper. Although it is still regarded as an office copying method, its possibilities have interested those who feel that it can serve printing users in the future. The surface of a specially coated plate is charged with positive electricity as it passes under wires. Copy is then projected through the lens of a camera. A negatively charged powder is made to adhere to the positively charged image. A sheet of paper placed over the plate receives the positive charge. The positively charged paper attracts powder from the plate, and a direct positive image is formed. Print is then heated for a few seconds to fuse the powder and form a permanent print.

Both the gravure and offset printing processes have been plagued by troubles. Offset, in particular, which depends upon chemical and physical actions and reactions for its results, has the handicap of using water to repel ink and ink to repel water. Forty years of research and experimentation have not succeeded in eliminating this cause of trouble. It is commonly accepted that were it possible to eliminate water from offset printing, it would be a greatly improved printing method. This knowledge prompted the American Typefounders Inc. to build a dry offset press in which printing from a relief plate on to a blanket and transferring the image from the blanket to paper would remove the troublesome element of water. A comparative newcomer in the field, dry offset involves a thin flexible plate on which the image is photoengraved to positive relief. The depth of the etch is determined by the thickness of the basic plate and the relative open area of the copy. Plates of this type can be used on conventional offset presses by undercutting the plate cylinder and removing the damping assembly. The new process combines many of the advantages of offset and letterpress printing. Water is eliminated from the plate, and, together with the use of positive relief printing, better tonal reproduction is achieved. Magnesium can be used for making dry offset plates. It is interesting to note that dry offset as a specialty has been used for many years by the United States Bureau of Engraving and Printing in Washington in printing millions of excise tax labels.

A survey report of the Educational Council of Graphic Arts Industry and International Graphic Arts Education Association estimates that there are 77,000 students enrolled in graphic arts courses. (There are 130,000 workers in the book and job printing shops.) Of the 1,109 educational institutions offering courses, the majority report that these courses are given on a nonvocational level, not specifically training the students for jobs in industry. Further evidence of the heightened interest in the graphic arts is the fact that the Rochester Institute of Technology and Columbia University, following the lead of the Carnegie Institute of Technology, are now offering degrees in printing. Columbia University, with its 30,000 graphic arts books and 100,000 items, is laying its plans for a graphic arts center.

Typographers and production workers are admittedly at a loss to keep up with all the new developments, which in some instances alter overnight the procedures of book and publication making that have been in effect since their apprenticeship. The inflexible, the scoffers, the die-hards among them will surely give way to the new graphic artisan of tomorrow who will accept and use these new methods; and, like Publisher Shannon's printing plants of 2053, they will be transformed and rebuilt and in the transformation will lose much clatter.

Part 7. COMMUNICATIONS

Obstacles to the Free Flow of Books

OF THE obstacles to the free flow of books between Britain and America the largest is the Atlantic Ocean. This obvious fact needs to be stated, simply because it is sometimes disregarded by those members of the reading public who complain that not all books of all publishers are available to them at a day's notice and at the same price in the importing country as in the country of origin. The elementary factor of transportation makes it at least likely that the imported book will be published later by an interval running from a week or so up to a season, which in publishing may be six months. This same factor necessarily contributes to the higher price that must generally be paid for a book when it is sold in a distant country.

In addition to the natural geographical factor there are other considerations that interfere with the transatlantic exchange of books. There is one outstanding obstacle to any substantial increase in the distribution of American books in England: the Import License quota, by which no British importer may obtain in any year more than his limited allowance, which is fixed at twice the value of the books he imported in 1939. This emergency control measure was undoubtedly necessary at a time when Britain had to avoid every possible dollar expenditure. Today, when sterling is in so much stronger a position, it is time to suggest that the dollar saving effected, microscopic compared with the amount spent on tobacco, is wholly incommensurate with the serious interference with the spread of understanding, learning, and scholarship between the two countries.

For it is books of scholarship that are the most seriously affected by the continuance of the Import License quota. American novels, thrillers, books of humor, and other works of general interest have a sufficient market in Britain to be produced in British-made editions, and hundreds of such editions are in fact produced each year. An American work of learning, on the other hand, will generally command a market of fewer than a thousand copies, and a separate British edition is therefore impracticable. The quota, then, is at present working most seriously to the detriment of the American university presses, which have made impressive progress in the past twenty years, both in the quality and the quantity of their output. The quota limitation means that the stocks of American university press books held in Britain by the Oxford and Cambridge University Presses, who represent them, must be supplemented by the dispatch of countless parcels of single books by post, these single copies being allowed to come in outside the quota. Such a system is cumbersome and involves long delay.

Another factor that will continue to hinder the distribution of American books in Britain, even after the quota restrictions have been lifted, is the high price at which so many of them are published. A book that might cost 12s. 6d. if published originally in Britain is likely to be $3.00 when originally published in America. When this three-dollar book is imported into Britain it may have to be offered at about 25s., or twice the price that the British reader might expect to pay. The reason for the higher original American price is simply the higher material standard of living in the United States, under a system in which everyone concerned with the production and distribution of a book is paid at a rate very much higher than his British counterpart.

If the flow of American books into Britain is to some extent dammed by the Import License quota, the flow of British books in the other direction is hindered a little by an anachronistic tariff originally imposed to protect the infant American printing industry. American printers are today fully capable of taking care of themselves, but the duty levied on British books continues. The amount accruing to the United States Treasury is small, but all of it has to come out of the pockets of readers in America, many of whom are students and scholars who can ill afford it.

The two most frequent complaints in America about British books are, first, that they are difficult to get, and secondly, that they are expensive. Both of these complaints are based on misconceptions. British books are no harder to get in America than British marmalade, British soap, or British bicycles. These three products enjoy a wide sale in America, but even the best American grocer will probably be unwilling to order a couple of jars of marmalade if he does not carry it in stock. Most bookstores, on the other hand, put service ahead of dollars and are quite ready to order a single copy of any book in print. Unfortunately, many of those who have difficulty in obtaining a British book have failed to try the simple method of going into a bookstore and ordering it.

There are, unhappily, fewer good bookstores in the United States than there used to be. The booksellers themselves must bear part of the blame for this, as many of them have allowed the slick and transient best seller to oust from their shelves and from their consciousness books of more permanent value. In going after a quick and easy profit they have played into the hands of department stores, book clubs, and discount houses, who are naturally equipped to compete with them in best sellers. Publishers also, with less excuse, have made the position worse by competing with their retail outlets instead of supporting them, and even by offering substantial discounts to teachers, college instructors, and libraries, all properly a logical market for the bookseller. Even so, in spite of all discouragements, there remain alive plenty of booksellers in the United States who are perfectly willing to order a British book for a customer.

The complaint about price is more complex and must be examined in detail. In broad terms the British book is priced lower than its American counterpart. But books of large circulation can be priced lower than books of small circulation. British books of large circulation include those most likely to be manufactured also in American editions; those that are imported will obviously include a high proportion of books on special subjects with a limited market. A high price, then, will often be due to the very nature of the book, and not to the fact that it is British. An answer to a complaint of this kind may well be that if that particular book had been produced in America it would have cost even more.

Another form of the complaint about the price of British books is a comparison between the British price and the American price. It has already been stated that the mere geographical facts prevent a book's being sold abroad for the same price as at home. British bicycles and marmalade are sold in America at nearly twice the home price; a tablet of soap that is sold for tenpence in London is sold for thirty-five cents in Chicago; a crocus that is offered at 7s. 6d. a hundred in Cornwall is advertised at $7.50 a hundred in Philadelphia. In other words, the American consumer is asked to pay forty-two cents for a shilling's worth of soap, and a dollar for a shilling's worth of bulbs. The markup in books is much more modest, and although instances will be found of a ratio of twenty-five cents to the shilling, or even more, as a general rule a ratio of about twenty cents to the shilling is considered reasonable.

One form of obstacle, national prejudice, now appears virtually nonexistent. Even as recently as a generation ago the British book in America had a less friendly reception than it finds today, and the American book too often met with condescension or insularity among British critics. If evidence is needed of the great improvement in that respect, it can surely be found in the reviews of American books during the past decade in the pages of *The Times Literary Supplement*.

Radio, Television, and the Writer

IN RECENT public and parliamentary debates in Britain on the proposal that use of the air owned by the people be licensed to commercial companies owned by the few, those in favor and those in fear professed one common ground of agreement. The pattern of American radio and television must not be re-created in Britain. For the moment the debate has concluded, and legislation has been inscribed in the statute book. The new design, it is hoped by all, will be different.

While awaiting the emergent outlines of the shape of things to come, full-time, part-time, or occasional writers for British radio and television may find it profitable to re-examine a few of the perspectives and paradoxes of the American industry. The forces and pressures that it exerts upon their colleagues across the sea may, after all, have more than academic relevance to the future practice of their profession in the British Isles. During two decades as a dominant medium, American radio did create new, vital literary forms and techniques. An industry controlled by advertisers, consciously presenting programs that appealed to the broadest, therefore the lowest, tastes of the listening audience, somehow created a Corwin, aired a MacLeish, established a workshop in which writers could experiment with new patterns of words and sounds and fashion fresh moods and novel frames—without imposing upon them the lethal intrusion of "commercials" or the criterion of mass popularity. As a matter of fact, American radio always offered around its edges a small gift of experimental writing, off-beat drama, and superb actuality that were never intended to "move merchandise." For Americans who took the trouble to find it, there was always available a scattered "Third Program."

Under American law the air is assumed to belong to the people, and the Federal Communications Commission grants broadcasting licenses without fee to privately owned companies on the theory that they will transmit programs as a public service, catering for the cultural needs of the entire population without necessarily elevating them. Though revocation of license is a very rare occurrence, there has always been enough outcry against the damaging effects of most commercial programs (as cultivators of crime, cupidity, and violence) to make the networks seek to soothe the objectors by offering them small but well publicized rations of higher culture. The opportunities and financial support given to a Corwin and his kind—none of whom ever got a "rating" (large enough audience) to attract an ordinary advertiser—were carefully planned attempts, at comparatively small expense to networks, to make the exception seem more like the rule.

When American radio influenced or inspired British writers and producers, what was borrowed and improved upon came from this "fringe area" of American broadcasting. Norman Corwin listening to *Under Milk Wood* would have every right to be inwardly happy about clearing a path along which Dylan Thomas could advance to a last great triumph in sound. In the best of B.B.C. programing today one cannot escape hearing the echoes of the enthusiastic, exuberant adventures of the outsiders who made America's "Third." They matured in the age of Roosevelt and shared that refreshed faith in a democratic America that found chaotic but lively expression in the W.P.A. Arts Projects, the flowering of Orson Welles, and the new ballad styles of Earl Robinson, John Latouche, and Millard Lampell. Like Corwin, everyone who toiled in those marginal vineyards of American radio turned outward to look at the changing dynamic world around him, and they founded literary radio forms worthy of the beauty, truth, and excitement that they had discovered anew in their countrymen, their history, and their hopes. They were always tinkering with new effects and blending trial ingredients of words, music, and sound. Out of their experiments they shaped expression in sound that was a new literature. These outsiders, who wrote and produced with the insolent freshness of pioneers, may have existed precariously on the periphery of network schedules—as the window dressing—but when the cards were down they turned out to be much closer than that to the heart of America. When war came, it was they —Corwin, Robson, Shayon, McDougall, Lomax, Laurents, Berger, Sloane, Perl, to name a few—who were best equipped to sound the struggle's highest emotions and sharpest reality and finally to proclaim the victory.

The history of postwar radio is decline and fall. With so much of the national audience seduced and held by television, the old established structure is no longer profitable. Radio networks are beginning to wither away; their program budgets have been cut to the bone. Individual radio stations will have to find specialized means of survival; many will concentrate on recorded music, both classical and popular; others will devote themselves primarily to news and community services; some may even sink to the level of the few Latin-American stations that provide nothing but time announcements every minute on the minute with advertisements sandwiched between the ticktocks of eternity. American radio as a continuing market for new creative writing will soon have disappeared.

There has been another opening of another show: television. Its impact and its potential have been described in a profusion of clichés that reach from coast to coast without benefit of microwave relays. The least quoted of the truths is that never before has an infant of fabulous promise been nourished on such thin milk. It is sad enough that American television is doomed to develop in the rigid, constrictive commercial framework that devitalized so much of radio. The greater tragedy may be that the first crucial years of development will have been experienced during the deepest political reaction America has ever known.

The British writer who wishes to imagine himself transplanted to the workshops of American television faces a very wide range of possible experience. If he has ever been a Communist; if he was once a Communist but is not one now; if he has never been a Communist but lent his name to public movements in support of Republican Spain, or racial equality, or One World; if he never lent his name but associated with people who did; if he never associated with such people but married a girl who did; if —; if —, the chances are fair that he is blacklisted, that there is not a network, station, agency, or producer that will knowingly openly employ him as a writer. He may then decide to try his luck on the black market in television writing by finding a respectable acceptable author to "front" for him. If he cannot find another writer, he can use anybody presentable—a relation, the delivery man from the delicatessen, or even the house porter; it is a delicate and precarious plan, because he has to give up a sizable portion of his writing fee to his alter ego, and when a producer calls for a script conference his troubles can be overwhelming. He may occasionally earn a double fee by accident. A producer has purchased his script through his front man. It needs revision. The producer says to himself: "I know just the man for revisions; he's on a list, but I think I can make a deal with him quietly for cash." Thus the blacklisted writer finds himself rewriting his own script for an added fee. He may have nightmares about the fantastic chain of events, but the extra dollars are useful. Life for the blacklisted writer, until he makes a new adjustment within or without his profession, is a jungle; he needs cool nerves and a collected temper to survive sane.

If our transplanted author is respectable and a competent craftsman, he has another decision to face: whether the compromises imposed upon his writing by the inflexible formulae of most commercial programing are worth the imposing financial rewards that can accrue to him and his family (as much as $3,000 for a topflight original, an average of $500 for almost any adaptation). The great majority of written television programs are crime shows, Westerns, so-called situation comedies, and soap operas, presented in series once weekly, either live or filmed, within a time period of twenty-nine minutes and thirty seconds, including "commercials." This leaves the writer twenty-five minutes or less—with

"curtains" carefully planned within this frame for advertising in-
terruptions—in which he can develop his characters and propel
them through a meaningful plot. Writing with these limitations
may bear a striking resemblance to work in a sausage factory;
but this is the biggest market for commissioned writing in television, and the author will have to decide, by his own standards
and aims, whether he wishes to trade in it.

If he is respectable but many notches above the competent
craftsman, he may find an outlet in the four or five one-hour
dramatic programs now sponsored on the television networks, all
of which share to some extent the "institutional" flavor that once
flourished in radio. Though still writing in the strait jacket of
limited time with intervals of commercial intrusion, he would now
be collaborating with the handful of producers who have been
permitted to exercise their superior taste. He might then, like a
Paddy Chayefsky or a Horton Foote or a David Davidson, writing for producers like Fred Coe or Alex Segal, give television
some hope of linkage with literature.

Since networks still try desperately to create the illusion of association with higher culture, if the author has the fame, integrity, and curiosity of a Robert E. Sherwood he may receive a
commission from one of them to write drama, comedy, or fantasy
for television as he chooses, in a length of his convenience, and
with the promise that no advertising will be permitted to break
his moods. He will then have time to study the medium, to experiment in his own mind, to set his own deadlines for complet-
ing his work, and he will not be depressed or disappointed when
his first effort seems—to the public and the critics—to fall flat.
He will know that he is pioneering and that thousands of his colleagues in the salt mines below are cheering for his success.

If the author is famous but strange (like a poet), he may get
an occasional production of his work in a series like "Omnibus,"
produced by the Ford Foundation and supported by "institutional"
sponsors. His writing will be presented to viewers plainly labeled
as culture, and they will be told that culture is good for them
and that they would be better people if they exposed themselves

to more of it. He could be an author who considers himself not a writer but a journalist, and if he were Ed Murrow or Eric Sevareid he would probably be shocked to be told that the essays he writes in haste on the unfolding world are often the best and most moving use of words on American television.

Just as one cannot completely condemn American radio in its heyday on grounds of literary sterility, so one must not at this early stage predict that American television promises nothing better than national illiteracy. As long as there exists on the edge of its massive structure that "fringe area" of programing that once distinguished radio, there is reason to believe that there will come to television such a fine fruition as Thomas brought to sound.

Americans who write for television today, if they have high hopes for their craft and for this medium, cannot fail to perceive the tragedy of the empty spaces beside them, the stupidity of the vacant places in their brave new world that can be so significantly filled by their colleagues who have been driven from their chosen profession. Nor can they fail to understand that the climate of fear that has barred their friends and fellow authors strips their own work of so much reality and truth as to make them literary cripples. They and the banished can share the common wish that those among them who care will not always have to come to the market place to sell their wares to tradesmen barking at the stalls.

The American Press

I. HOW IT HAS COME INTO BEING

No ONE who has even attempted to hold—let alone read—an American newspaper can pretend that there is anything like it anywhere else in the world. Its immense bulk and size compared with European newspapers is not, of course, what really sets it apart, but this physical contrast is a convenient symbol. The fact that French menus are infinitely longer and more complex than English ones does not explain the difference between French and English cooking, but at least it suggests that the French take the subject more seriously. A comparison between the sixty-odd pages of the *New York Times* and the smaller size of the average English paper fulfills a similar purpose, and although newsprint rationing may be cited as an explanation, the real differences, as much in journalism as in cuisine, must be sought at a deeper level.

Tocqueville, writing in the middle of the last century, refused to accept the plausible explanation then current of why American newspaper circulations were so much higher than those in England or France. The argument that the heavy taxation on the press at that time reduced British circulations, he wrote, is a "very exaggerated estimate. Newspapers increase in numbers not according to their cheapness but according to the more or less frequent want that a great number of men may feel for inter-communication and combination." Today, although the contrast between American and British journalism is certainly to some extent caused by differing newsprint situations, the fundamental cause is that journalism, for a number of social and historical reasons, has come to play a larger role in the United States than in Europe.

Macaulay thought he was paying the press a great and revolutionary compliment when he described it as the "fourth estate of the realm." To Tocqueville, writing of the American press about the same time, it appeared as "the power which impels the circulation and political life through all the districts of that vast territory"—not the fourth estate but almost the first. Macaulay was viewing the British press against an historical pattern in which journalism played at best only a marginal part. Monarchy, Lords, Commons, and Clergy—these were the influences that had shaped British history. Journalism can claim no part in English legends. But in the United States it filled a crucial role right from the outset of American history. Without newspapers, for example, Washington's armies might never have enjoyed that sense of common purpose that gave them such powerful cohesion and direction. More significantly perhaps, the authors of *The Federalist,* seeking to explain and justify their blueprints for the Constitution, published them as articles in the *Daily Advertiser* and in the *Independent Journal* some time before they were issued as a book. Journalism can justifiably claim, therefore, not only presence at the birth of the American nation, but also a real degree of parenthood. The United States has, in truth, printer's ink in its very veins.

American attitudes generally are, of course, immensely influenced by the fact that national legends date almost from within living memory, instead of having to travel down the centuries from the misty twilight of prehistory. If King Alfred had burned the cakes because he had been preoccupied with the *Times* crossword puzzle, British journalism might not have had to wait for Macaulay's blessing before earning a high place in the country's admiration. In America, however, newspapers *are* a part of national legend, and journalists right from the earliest days move across the pages of American history as regularly—and in many cases as glamorously—as do in English history the great names of the ancient noble families. It is not simply that American growth as a nation happened to coincide with a particular development in the field of technology that made newspapers relatively easy and cheap to produce. The development of the United States and the development of American journalism are not parallel growths that happen, through the accident of history, to have coincided. The truth is that American progress down the paths of equalitarianism toward a classless and democratic society would have been scarcely conceivable without newspapers.

"Newspapers become more necessary in proportion as men become more equal," Tocqueville perceptively affirmed. "To suppose that they only serve to protect freedom would be to diminish their importance: they maintain civilization." Such a declaration would, of course, have been absurd in France and England when Tocqueville was writing, and even today, when social and political equality have made such progress, English and French civilization is certainly not maintained by the press, even if certain newspapers do exercise a civilizing influence. So long as the social structure remains stratified into classes—as in England it still does—people take their views and manners, and model their behavior very largely, from the views, manners, and behavior of the rung in the ladder immediately above their own. The fact that this is not so in politics is the exception that proves the rule, as in England it is in the field of government that equality has the most substance. Socially, intellectually, culturally the aristocratic tradition is still very strong. The influence of universities, of the public schools, of the cultural elite—in short of the top layers in any given field—is not resisted to any effective extent.

"When the members of an aristocratic community adopt a new opinion or conceive a new sentiment, they give it a station, as it were, beside themselves, upon the lofty platform where they stand; and opinions or sentiments so conspicuous to the eyes of the multitude are easily introduced into the minds and hearts of all around." But if habit and tradition in Europe still give this aristocratic process sufficient momentum to outlast the element of power upon which it was based, in the United States all the weight of the equalitarian and revolutionary tradition militates in the opposite direction, and it has enabled American society to resist influence from above long after the physical possibilities of such influence were in fact established.

American opinions, sentiments, fears, aspirations, and even fashions do not percolate from the rich down the income scale or from the universities down the intellectual scale, or from the summit of any profession or association down to its base. They seem to hit everyone at the same time, and the only difference money, for example, makes is the speed with which an inclination can be realized. This extraordinary process of horizontal communication is not encompassed by advertising, which only exploited and did not create the all-embracing American receptivity.

How, it must be asked, can this almost daily exercise of what can only be called the "general will" take place in a country of continental magnitude and among a people as diverse in ethnic

origins as those who failed to build the tower of Babel? To put
the question from another angle, how have the forces of democracy
and individualism, which tend by their very nature to isolate the
citizen in a way unthinkable in a hierarchic society—how have
they been so transmuted that all Americans, irrespectively of race,
function, income, or location, can experience the same feelings
at the same time? The need to achieve this miracle was the central
problem facing the United States at its outset. It was a totally new
problem, because the United States was the first country to cohere
in the age of individualism without the assistance of—indeed in
defiance of—the very cements by which previous societies had
been held together, at least during their early stages when the inevitable disruptive forces are at their strongest. To abandon, as the
United States did, the organic conception of society not only
raised the problem of leadership and of government—the eighteenth century was full of ideas for solving this aspect of the problem—but, more baffling and novel, it also raised in an acute form
the problems of communication and association between all the
free, equal, and independent individuals comprising the new
Republic.

The reciprocal influences of men upon each other are clearly
far less potent in a society of equals than in a graded hierarchy
where each man expects to look up to his superior for guidance
and instruction. But the United States was determined to revolu-
tionize the law of gravity by which ideas moved from the top of
society downwards, and to make them function horizontally instead. It is true that this determination was considerably qualified
in the early days of the Union, when the old traditions of European society still exerted considerable influence. But as the Western
movement expanded and new communities were formed where
"colonial" attitudes counted for nothing and the impact of Jack-
sonian democracy gave reality to the American legend, the discovery of some new method of intercommunication between individual Americans became perhaps the principal condition of the
successful development of a national consciousness. An all-power-
ful central government might have been strong enough to pump

blood into the extended limbs of the new body politic. But this solution was violently rejected. Instead the American people developed the newspaper.

American journalism today represents a fantastic complex of mass communication as a result of which every gradation of American life is constantly made aware of every other gradation. To an extent still unthinkable even by the most assiduous and uninhibited newspaper magnate in England, Americans of all grades and functions—from the President down to the Negro bootblack—of all incomes, professions, habits, indulgences, trades, and almost anything else one can think of, enjoy—or suffer—such a degree of intimacy with one another through the countless publications that daily and almost hourly hold up each tiny segment of the American people to the curious gaze of each other tiny segment, that everyone knows—or has the opportunity of knowing—everything about everyone else.

What is astonishing, wrote Harold Laski in *The American Democracy,* "is the speed with which newspapers multiplied [in the first half of the nineteenth century] and the self-confidence of their owners in making their growth almost parallel the expansion of the Western movement." What, however, would have been far more astonishing would have been if the fabulous expansion of the Union, both in area and population in the nineteenth century, had taken place without the multiplication of newspapers. Without newspapers to maintain contact between Washington and the new communities, explaining and interpreting both the center and the circumference to each other; without newspapers to relate the new communities to one another and, most important of all, without newspapers to assist in the formation of all the myriad associations—professional, commercial, cultural, sport, and so on—on which a free society is inevitably based, the task of forming a cohesive and dynamic nation out of such disparate elements could have been accomplished only over centuries of slow growth or by undemocratic methods.

The peculiar historical and social origins of the United States made it inevitable that newspapers should enjoy a prestige and perform a function incomparably greater than their counterparts in other countries. Clearly the more deeply an individual citizen feels the shape and coloring of his community, at the local as well as at the national level, to be determined by his personal judgment and opinions—and in America this conviction extends to all fields and activities—so much more will he demand the advice and information that only newspapers can supply. Equally, the more widely power and responsibility are distributed, so much more will the ordinary citizen require that daily sense of communication with other members of his community, almost a kind of unspoken conversation, which only a highly detailed journalistic complex can fully supply—but without which the onus of decision would appear impossibly burdensome. The classless society created a vacuum in human relations that newspapers have come to fill. It is, therefore, no coincidence that the United States, as the country that has established the widest degree of genuine equalitarianism—Americans genuinely feel equal within themselves even if they do not look it to the outsider—should enjoy a press more powerful, more highly organized, more respected than that of any other country in the world.

If American journalism got off to a flying start because of the nature of American society, other circumstances, some of them fortuitous, have served subsequently to buttress its position and add to its stature. First of all, the importance of the profession, which is well illustrated by the fact that universities have set up special journalistic faculties, has attracted recruits of an exceptionally high caliber. The editor in any given community is a leading figure and enjoys a prestige and an income far higher than those of the doctor, civil servant, or lawyer. (The American, incidentally, often writes to his editor about his problems before approaching a lawyer.) A comparison of relationships between reporters and officials in London and in Washington illustrates their very different status. In Washington the reporter patronizes the official—even the President himself—whereas in Whitehall the reverse tends to be the true case. All too often the British reporter approaches the civil servant from a position of educational and social inferiority, with the official safely ensconced behind the public school barriers of accent, clothes, and manner. Quite the opposite is true in America, where the reporter is usually the equal, if not the superior, in education and polish of the man whose brains he is supposedly trying to pick. American newspapers are also enormously assisted by the peculiar balance of the American Constitution, which, by setting off the legislative against the executive, makes it inevitable that each part of this governmental equation should woo the press. Equally, by excluding the members of the Cabinet from Congress, heads of departments cannot address the people by addressing representatives of the people and instead have been forced to initiate the institution of the press conference. The press conference has virtually established the reporter in the role of interpreter of government actions and views, as by his questions and by his sense of priorities the pattern of government is carried to the American people.

Of the innumerable other factors of American society that have assisted American newspapers to their high pinnacle, the least tangible, but by no means the least important, has been the tendency for American writers of talent to make their home in journalism. The habit cannot be explained by the enormously high monetary temptations that journalism can offer. It was formed long before journalism broke into high finance, and like so much else about American journalism it can be understood only by reference to the American origins. Because of a natural desire on the part of American writers to establish a definite national literature and at the same time their equally natural realization of the almost overpowering impact of European letters, all but the strongest of them escaped the problem by taking to journalistic, historical, or critical work rather than creative writing.

American newspapers are not, of course, without their faults, some of which have infected the whole profession of journalism throughout the world. They have done as much to debase as to raise standards and as much to spread ignorance as to foster truth. All great national institutions are inevitably compounded of good and evil. What, however, cannot be denied is that American journalism represents a unique and continuing social response to a continuing historical challenge. It should not be surprising, therefore, if the first newspaper a visitor to the United States picks up in New York seems extremely overpowering. We are, after all, scarcely surprised when Americans visiting England seem overpowered at their first glimpse of our ancient monuments and institutions, which, like the American newspaper, collect and sustain the course of history.

II. HOW IT STRIKES A VISITOR

One of the first things about the American press that might strike a visitor to the United States is the abundant evidence of the very high status that the American press corps enjoys. The regular press conferences held by the President at the White House—until President Eisenhower was inaugurated they took place nearly every week—are usually the main political and sometimes diplomatic event of the week. The President, followed by his retinue of advisers, walks into the ornate room in which two hundred or more reporters and columnists have assembled to meet him, much as some medieval monarch might enter to hold court with his barons.

The high status of the American press is partly due to its own, and to the public's, appreciation of the role that the press plays in the working of the American democracy. In a State in which each man is supposed to be equipped with enough information to enable him to approve or disapprove the actions of his government, the role played by the press in conveying that information is of fundamental political importance. Its contribution to the working of the political system has been understood and appreciated from the beginnings of the Republic. Unlike the press of other democratic countries, it has a power and a prestige that are not a comparatively modern expression of the country's political freedom, but original contributors to it.

A particularly important support of the power of the American press is its role as an unofficial day-to-day check upon the actions of the Executive. Though Congress's power of the purse can ultimately bring down a President who flies in the face of its wishes, and though reports of dissatisfaction with his behavior in Congress may deter a President from pursuing a certain policy, the separation of the legislative from the executive arm of government makes it difficult to maintain day-to-day relations between the two bodies. In Britain this function is performed by question time in the House of Commons. In the United States the nearest equivalent to this is the regular conference that the President, as chief executive, holds with the press.

What the press achieves in its relations with the President directly is only a part of what it achieves as a whole. The Presidential press conference is the apex of a great pyramid of press relations. Every department of the executive has its own built-in press and public relations departments, similar to, but much more influential than, its counterpart in other countries. The facilities made available to the press in terms of handouts, conferences, guidance, and accommodation are far more elaborate than anything to be found abroad. In them a visitor can read the measure of the importance of the American press, and the American journalist can see as in a mirror the reflection of his own importance.

American journalists would not have developed the potential power of the role of the press in the American democracy if circumstances had not combined to give the Washington press corps an unusual solidarity. It is in Washington that the most influential political and diplomatic journalists live. Washington is an artificial capital expressly created out of an otherwise useless and unattractive swampland to house the organs of the federal government. Inhabited only by politicians, diplomatists, civil servants, and tradesmen who serve them, it is a small city in which men easily meet. The journalists see a great deal of each other in the well-appointed press rooms with which each department of government is equipped and meet again at the clubs and parties that, in a city too much given over to the business of government to be much interested in cultural entertainment, take the place that the theater, music, and the arts occupy in the life of a city like Paris, London, or Rome. Since he lives away from his own town, away from his own newspaper headquarters and colleagues, each newspaperman in Washington is to some extent a foreign correspondent. His natural companions are the representatives of other newspapers interested in much the same subjects and living in the same peculiar atmosphere as himself. It is with them that he discusses the news and its implications. This accounts for the remarkable unity of press opinion in the United States, both when it is correct and when it is in error, as it was, for example, in 1948 when it was almost unanimous in predicting that Mr. Truman would be heavily defeated in the presidential election.

The temper of the American press is critical. The American journalist is conscious of his position in the capital as the representative of a people whose main historic concern has been to see that it never becomes a victim of its own government's powers. There is little deference to be noticed, consequently, in the manner of a newspaperman at a press conference, even when he is addressing his questions to the President himself. The summer heat and humidity of Washington and the tension of a city full of ambitious politicians and lobbyists uncushioned by culture or relaxed by recreation—these increase the propensity of the press to asperity. Moreover, the Washington journalist works at a much faster pace than his counterpart in Europe. The nature of the American democracy is such that the politicians and the lobbyists have much wider opportunities and rewards than they enjoy in any comparable country, and ambitious men work harder and longer and more competitively. These exertions and the strain that they cause are reflected in the press. And the journalist is conscious that it is a cardinal principle of the American democracy that the meanest citizen of the farthest state must be told in detail about all that is going on in the capital and that atmosphere or will or event must be reported.

This further develops the journalist's feeling that he is a member of an elite. He sees himself and a few hundred other journalists as the eyes and ears of the American democracy, continually watching and listening to the working of the selfish forces that, if left unreported, might undermine it. He looks on himself to some extent as the conscience of the United States, not so much because he thinks his profession shows higher moral discernment than any other as because he has daily experience of the force that the Washington press corps, by reason of its solidarity and its nearness to the seat of power, can exert upon the government. No real intelligentsia has developed in the United States. America's intellectuals are scattered throughout dozens of universities and cities, and these, thanks to the size and regionalization of the United States, have comparatively little contact with one another. In its absence part of the role of an intelligentsia is played by the American press corps. The work of the press at Presidential press conferences has done more to correct the vagaries of American foreign policy and to check the abuses of McCarthyism since the inauguration of President Eisenhower than any other agency.

If the American press corps' sense of its importance as a working part of the American democracy has made a firm imprint on the manners and bearing of its members, it has been no less influential in determining the techniques of American journalism. A reporter who believes that his vocation is not merely to report, but in his reporting to supply the information upon which the citizen is to make his decisions, will want to express himself in a manner sufficiently clear, vital, and cogent to engage the interest of the lowest level of intelligence. It is this fundamental striving to attract the attention of, as well as to inform, the normally indifferent citizen that gives modern American journalism some of its most striking characteristics. Notably, it is the cause of its tendency to oversimplify political and diplomatic situations and developments to the point of distortion; to heighten personalities and the part played by personalities in processes whose economic and social aspects are given inadequate attention; to dramatize and foreshorten the development of events; to describe complex events in vivid, breathless, exciting prose so that the regular reader must live with a perpetual sense of crisis or develop a deliberate indifference as a protection against it. The dangers and evils of the kind of journalism developed by the weekly magazines like *Life, Time,* and *Newsweek,* whose circulations run into several millions, are obvious. Without this kind of journalism, however, it is very doubtful if the revolution by which the United States was converted from an isolationist into an interventionist nation within half a generation could have been achieved.

The "scoop" type of newspaper story is to be found in all countries where the press is free and competitive. But the American press excels in regularly producing a special kind of "scoop" story—the exposé or revelation. In the sphere of international affairs Americans have been brought up to believe that the only trustworthy diplomacy is open diplomacy, a point of view held by even so learned and sophisticated a person as Woodrow Wilson. Very few American journalists, therefore, have the same view as their counterparts in Britain of what is responsible diplomatic journalism. Their basic feeling is that whatever a government wishes to conceal is contrary to the interests of the people, and that to withhold such a story if it comes to their knowledge is not responsible but irresponsible. Their attitude is shared by the very officials and politicians whose policies their revelations most damage; there is no other explanation of the tolerance that they display towards the journalists who have laid bare their designs. If they do not indeed believe that a democratic press should be continually revealing to the people every confidence that comes into its ken, they clearly feel that it is politic to pretend that they do.

Sometimes, however, politicians and officials exploit their intimacy with the press and plant true or false stories with them, denying or confirming them when they have seen what the public reaction has been. American officials talk much more to the press than do British officials, but they are less likely to be telling them what is true. While on the whole the American journalist is more powerful, more independent, and more truculent than his British counterpart, he is more likely to be made from time to time to serve ulterior purposes.

The most heroic period of American journalism was the muck-raking epoch. Great political and social progress was made in the early years of the century as a result of the publication of a series of revelations of administrative and political scandals. This kind of journalism strengthened the citizen's belief that one of the main duties of a newspaper must be to tell him what otherwise would be kept from him. It also had the effect of establishing the superiority of the reportorial piece over the editorial piece or leader as the molder of public opinion, a superiority that had always been implicit in the nature of the American democracy, which assumes that, all men being equal, any man is capable of seeing what course should be taken if only the facts of the matter are put before him. That the power of the editorial is limited was illustrated by the outcome of the Presidential elections from 1932 to 1948. Five times the bulk of the press—estimated at about 95 per cent—urged the nation to return a Republican candidate, and five times the nation voted for a Democrat.

In Britain the most influential journalists are usually those who edit newspapers or write leading articles. In the United States the most influential journalists are the reporters on the paper's staff, or the columnists, who, though their pieces are often not straight reporting, avoid hortatory or propagandist styles and appear to be, even if sometimes they are not, reporting situations or facts. In Britain influence is best exerted through well-thought-out leading articles. In the United States it is best exerted by being aimed, in the form of repetitive factual stories expressed in simple, urgent terms through the reportorial columns, at the ordinary reader. One of the most noticeable effects of this is that there is not as in Britain a clear difference between the "quality" press on the one hand and the "popular" press on the other. There are great differences between the most thoughtful and the least thoughtful of the American newspapers, but they are differences of degree, not of intellectual class. And if their best newspapers do not reach the level of the best in Britain, their worst are considerably superior to Britain's worst.

The Comic Strip in American Life

THE AMERICANS are the most earnest of peoples, and they have a fervent faith in the respectability of folklore. Thus they tend to clothe in misty feyness anything from Apache war dances to boogie-woogie, and any derelict Kentucky hillman humming to himself as he shears the goats is likely to find himself hailed as an authentic Elizabethan relic. Any popular manifestation can achieve respectability by the metamorphosis to a "native culture." A prime and pleasant example of the attitude is to be found at the farming village of Crystal City in southern Texas: for there in the middle of the square, painted in gay colors, surrounded by well-trimmed lawns, honored by all, stands a life-sized figure of Popeye the Sailorman, one of the most venerable personalities of the American cartoon.

The comic strip of the American daily press long ago achieved the status of a folk movement, and it is perfectly acceptable, in almost any company, to admit that you follow the fortunes of Dick Tracy or Steve Canyon. Indeed, the strips do have honorable popular origins. They first appeared in more or less their present form in the 1860's, when a tremendous flow of immigrants was arriving from Europe, and for many poor strangers who spoke no English they served as an introduction to American ways of thought and life. (They also, incidentally, ended the great era of Amer- ical political cartooning—the era of Keppler and *Puck;* for as the "funnies" gained ever wider popularity, more and more of the most skillful newspaper artists turned to their production. To this day the standard of skill of the comic strip is generally higher than that of the political cartoon.)

The early strips thus reflected many facets of American living, and it is perhaps not fanciful to suggest that they still express, often unconsciously, many of the chief characteristics of the nation— or at least that part of it approximating most closely to the urban Middle West, which has come to be accepted as standard America. The diversity of the United States is still immense, in custom as in contour; but that unpleasant alleged "norm" called the American Way of Life—drugstores and dating, profit motives and women's clubs—is spreading relentlessly, and it has about it a deadening and intolerant sameness. We may trace its traits and prejudices closely in the world of the strip cartoon.

For example, the visitor to a Middle West manufacturing town is almost sure to notice the predominance of women. This is a powerfully matriarchal society. In the home the self-possessed, well-read, relatively leisured housewife has innumerable advantages over her generally plodding husband; in civic affairs the women's organizations, from opera societies to church clubs, are always potent; and in politics such groups as the League of Women Voters have much influence. In any family party dining out a woman is likely to pay the restaurant bill. In economic affairs the purchasing power of the housewife is all-important, and the whole structure of American commercial life is designed largely to satisfy the demands of women.

This maternalism is accurately portrayed (without bitterness) in the strip cartoons. A favorite situation is that of Dad and Junior slipping away from the women for a weekend's fishing, pursued by admonitions about warm underwear. Dagwood, in Chic Young's admirable cartoon *Blondie,* is always getting into trouble with his wife for stealing a sandwich from the kitchen or muddying the hall floor. "We are going visiting today," announces the dictatorial wife in *Bringing Up Father:* and Father puts his hat on. Women are often ignorant in the strip cartoons, often drive their cars foolishly or make inane remarks; but they are always in command.

Many such episodes concern a wife's desire for a mink coat, the supreme American symbol of opulence; for the American has never lost his respect for wealth, however acquired, and still passionately enjoys the office-boy-to-millionaire saga. A man is judged by the make of his car, and there is scarcely a club or a hotel in the nation that will exclude any rich man from its custom. If you have money, you are consequently esteemed (only in certain parts of the country, outside the cartoon standard, does birth assume an equally absurd importance). Christine Jorgensen achieved celebrity a few years ago by a change of sex. Presently she was notable for earning $5,000 a week in the night clubs. Almost anything is respectable if it makes money.

Sometimes the awe of wealth assumes a positively mystical quality, and this is best expressed in the strip cartoons by the figure of the tycoon in *Little Orphan Annie*. He is a shadowy, ethereal figure, surrounded by servants of vaguely Oriental origin, at once exhausted and uplifted by the endless struggles of international finance; the telephones on his desk muffled-looking, his yacht always moored in quiet backwaters, his language always kindly, his associates loyal to the death. His is a godlike image, benevolent and aloof, like a thousand-dollar bill. But Mr. Warbucks (for such is his unlikely name) belongs exclusively to the world of Rockefeller Centers and J. P. Morgans. Extreme wealth of a more homely kind is represented in the cartoons by another personality: the sort of millionaire who prints a nickname on his visiting card. He is popular for a variety of *noblesse oblige* that requires him to slap inferiors on the back and call his juniors by their Christian names. He is cheerfully, if not garishly, dressed (one such man who recently appeared in *Dick Tracy* was wearing a yellow suit). He is the kind of millionaire most Americans would like to be; still a regular fellow, in spite of it all, and still a real scream at the Elks.

They are scarcely caricatures, these portraits, for it is undeniable that under the pressures of the system most standard Americans, within their respective sections of society, are very much alike. Even in the Far West the hardy eccentrics are disappearing, and the chambers of commerce are taking over. Few of the old crusading editors are still complaining, and the Mississippi pilots work by radar. Indeed, the strip cartoons generally decline to admit that there is any America at all outside their chosen "norm." There has rarely appeared in a cartoon narrative a poor white's cabin from the Southern states, squalid and crumbling and ridden with cockroaches; nor, for that matter, a trim little Maryland farm with its jolly housewife hanging out the washing. The American home of the strip cartoon is that of Dixie Dugan and her family in a famous series: it is a weatherboard house with a small garden running down to the street, with a mailbox by the gate, a hammock for Dad to swing in by the porch, and indubitably a refrigerator and a television set inside. For the comic strip, as for the Voice of America, this is the U.S.A.

When somebody appears who is not a complete American by these rigid standards, he is generally regarded as a figure of fun. More than one cartoon deals with hillbilly folk, the men heavily covered with tangled beards, the women wearing poke bonnets and smoking pipes. They talk in the quaintest of dialects and live in mountain shacks. One strip deals with an immigrant family still not totally Americanized and demonstrates their origins by spelling English words in the German manner. When Englishmen turn up (often as a subject of ambition for socially conscious mothers) they speak with a wildly exaggerated drawl and generally wear dinner jackets.

Perhaps allied with its maternalism, perhaps stemming from the heritage of the frontier, is America's overwhelming love of children. It is a pleasant experience to walk with a small boy along an American street and to find both men and women enthralled and delighted by the very presence of a child. American children must be the most violently loved on earth. As a result, some of the happiest and best of the comic strips are those that deal with children. Generally, in art as in life, the protagonists in these adventures are freckled, tousled, slightly spoiled boys or small girls of precocious tendencies. It is an odd fact that American children, in spite of their pioneering background, are closely home-bound in their enterprises. Sail along the Mississippi for a month and you will scarcely see a Huck Finn playing along its banks (if you do, he is in rags and lives in a shanty boat; he may even be a half-breed and therefore outside the cartoon pale). Young Americans will play daringly and imaginatively in their own backyard, but they seldom venture into the woods. So, in the strips, Mom is never far away, and the place is warm with security. Two situations often recur. Boys are depicted selling soft drinks for cash, thus displaying an early and commendable instinct for profit. Girls are forever interrupting their elder sisters' moments of courtship with remarks that sometimes seem to show an astonishingly early onset of puberty.

An agreeable American trait is a ceaseless greed for knowledge and experience, even vicarious experience. In the United States lecturers are often thanked with the words, "Thank you for sharing this experience with us": wording that sometimes softens the impact of an apparently totally insensible audience. Anything that will increase knowledge of any kind, any new sensation or point of view or reaction, is eagerly accepted. Discussion groups prosper, and newspapers are read more thoroughly, in general, than they are in England. The importance of keeping up with current events, even through somebody else's distorted vision, is demonstrated by the terrifying success of commentators and news digests.

To satisfy these worthy yearnings, strip cartoons often assume what might be called a documentary character, associating a fictional episode with a genuine background. A character in the cartoon *Joe Palooka,* for instance, has recently been climbing the mountain K2 (described, on unnamed authority, as being "probably higher than Mount Everest"); a choice of setting that happily coincides with a sudden American interest in alpinism. Dick Tracy's adventures are often accompanied by authentic "tips for crime-busters." The doings of the space rockets, while they appeal to a decidedly space-conscious American youth, also interest those many thousands of adult Americans who view the cosmos with a certain dark foreboding. One cartoon of highly educational leanings is likely to devote a whole day's pictures (without fair warning) to the habits of the red-crested quail. It is commendable for a cartoon, like a box of bricks, to be "educational." So it should be if (as one of the greatest of Americans said) education is the highest duty of government. It is easy to be too glib about the American strip cartoon, to scoff too unkindly at its naïvety, to correlate it only with the failings that are obviously prominent in American society. Today, in almost every field of American activity, the spread of numbing conformity is being challenged by men of taste, talent, and integrity. If there can be said to be one distinct class of Americans different from others, yet scattered throughout the continent, it is that body of people dubbed by its enemies "the intellectuals"; people of every political conviction, of every shade of background, but educated, honest, and (above all) reasonable. To this growing section of the population most commercial offerings must now make some appeal; and there are signs that even the strip cartoon is maturing.

For years the genius of Walt Disney has been exerted in the comic strips, both through Disney characters like Donald Duck and Goofy and through the efforts of many plagiarists. His own cartoons are nearly always good and gay. In another kind, Walt Kelly has devised an animal character named Pogo, an opossum living in the Florida Everglades, whose activities often give rise to a witty strain of political satire, besides involving some enchanting animal friends. Dennis the Menace is an agreeably annoying small boy whose parents are distinctly outside the Women's Club mold. Even in the strip cartoons, symbols of enveloping Americanism, there are signs that the United States will never be entirely standardized.

Nor, indeed, within the presently accepted pattern, are the vices of the newspaper strip cartoon really very vicious. The so-called "comic books," sold separately and irregularly, often contain material of nauseating fancy, but the press cartoons are usually innocuous enough. Now and again there is an unpleasantly violent scene, now and again a little too much sex (and the extreme comedy of sexual relations is accepted even by the *New Yorker*); but all in all they deal in fairly straightforward adventure and the lives of fairly decent people. And the cops generally win.

Inasmuch as the comic strips reflect materialism, contempt for the individualist, cloying sentiment, and parochialism, they do no more than express general American tendencies; and however much the foreigner may dislike such trends, whatever pride he may take in his own national superiorities, he must in fairness admit that the American Way of Life, like the American comic strip, brings happiness to many and no great evil. In any case, as the Chicago bartender said to his disgruntled customer, "If ya don't like the saloon, why doncha go fishing?"

Part 8. OPINIONS AT THE TIME

The following pages contain
in whole or in part
what was said in
The Times Literary Supplement
on the first appearance
of some selected
American books

JOAQUIN MILLER

OF LATE years the many-colored and exuberant verse of Cincin-
natus Hiner Miller has been generally neglected even among those
of his compatriots who know the life of the "Great Southwest,"
the scorched and luminous territory that marches with the Mexican borderland up to the glittering peaks of the shadowy sierras,
of all earthly mountains the most manifestly comparable with the
"blue hills of Time." A younger generation of poets, cleverer and
more careful painters of the vast airscapes of the Far South, has
entered into the old melodramatic singer's realm to possess it, and
their work has been accepted as the authentic "poetry of the
Sierras" by the critics of that city of literary purists, Puritans in
words if not in works any longer, of which it may still be said
in transatlantic Latin—

Dies erit praegelida,
Sinistra quum Bostonia.

The new poets of the Southwest seem to English critics, it must
be confessed, to be very nearly related to the laborious makers
of the "versicles and icicles of song" who have been, and still
are, one of the curses of American poetry. But none of these
younger men has seen the Southern borderland as Joaquin Miller
(who was born in the halfway State of Indiana) saw it fifty years
ago when it was the heritage of a race of mounted pioneers, the
free and independent *vaqueros* who had the dark, alert faces and
lean lissom figures and the quaint richly decorated riding gear (including the man-at-arms' fortress of a saddle) of the gay, reck-
less riders in a medieval picture of hunting in Italy. He knew that
land without law courts or overlords before the sheep farmer
crawled in with his flock of "hooved locusts," eating the pastur-

ages to the bone and contaminating them, and was shot at sight
as an accursed and unclean pest by the cattlemen. He was there
long before the small homesteader crept in to cover the well wa-
tered localities with a far-flung entanglement of fences and kill
the ancient industry of ranching on a grand style. He had seen
so much that will never be seen again that much of his verse is
a kind of history and comparable as such with Bret Harte's pictures of the Californian placer miners or Mark Twain's epics of
the Mississippi river life.

It is with a certain largeness of gesture that this maker of ornate ballads draws aside the curtain of the later days. As when
he says:

> And where is my city, sweet blossom-sown town?
> And what is her glory, and what has she done?
> By the Mexican seas in the path of the sun
> Sit ye down; in the crescent of seas, sit ye down.

All his poems are melodramas for recitation; to appreciate their
simple vigorous music they must be read aloud. Of all his pieces
the most popular among his own people was "Kit Carson's Ride,"
in which the heroic cattleman (one of the centaurs who conquered
the Southwest, where the unit of civilization's warfare was a man-
and-his-horse) loses first his friend and then his Indian bride—

> Her bosom wine-red and pressed never by one,

in the swift tide of a prairie fire with its heavy surf of "black
buffalo," the whole Southern herd—a million strong, fifty years
ago—stampeding for the Brazos, the nearest sanctuary from the
swift conflagration. The Western contempt for the "calculating"
morality of the East burns brightly in these and other sunlit open-
air verses. In such moralizing stanzas as

> It seems to me a selfish thing
>   To pray forever for one's self;
>   It seems to me like heaping pelf
> In heaven by hard reckoning.

he tramples on the Puritanism of the East with a Puritanism of his own—after the manner of the real, not the realistic, Westerner. There are times, however, when he wishes that he had lived his life in the West; so that his dead selves might have been buried within the compass of a single acre, so to speak, and each *hic jacet* might have been accessible in his old age.

> Better abide, though skies be dim,
> And the waters espoused of the ice and snow;
> Better abide, though the thistles grow,
> And the city of smoke be obscured of the sun,
> Than to seek red poppies and the sweet dreamland—
> Than to wander the world as I have today,
> Breaking the heart into little bits of clay
> And leaving it scattered upon every hand.

That is a thought that comes to every Westerner sooner or later; for you have only to scratch any American deep enough and you find the New Englander. Joaquin Miller, for all his hot blood and subtropical fancies and hatred of the habitual virtues, was never more nor less than a half pagan. As for his technique, he stands alone among the older American poets; so much so that his verse sometimes has the rhythmic iterations of Swinburne's:

> Her hands were clasped downward and doubled,
> Her head was held down and depressed,
> Her bosom, like white billows troubled,
> Fell fitful and rose in unrest.

The similarity is never so insistent as it is in the Australian verse of Adam Lindsay Gordon, when he sings of—

> . . . Lands, where bright blossoms are scentless
>   And songless bright birds
> Where, with fire and fierce drought on her tresses
> Insatiable summer oppresses
> Sore woodlands and sad wildernesses,
>   And faint flocks and herds,

but it is impossible to ignore it.

Joaquin Miller is perhaps best defined as the Gordon of America, which helps one to understand why he was—perhaps still is —more popular in Australia than any other American poet. In either case the poet is a centaur; in either case the swift galloping of hooves—

Quadrupedante putrem sonitu quatit ungula campum

is an underlying rhythm in the direct onrush of the first bright words that come in a hurry. These two poets were set on horseback, and they rode up the slopes of Parnassus until the loftier steeps cast them back.

(Reprinted from *The Times Literary Supplement*
of February 20, 1913.)

SPOON RIVER ANTHOLOGY

MR. MASTERS, an American writer we have never heard of before, has done a difficult thing that was worth doing. He has made a new form which is perfectly suited to his matter. His book is a collection of epitaphs by the inhabitants of Spoon River, not the epitaphs on their graves, but what they say about themselves in the frankness and freedom of death. They are like spirits speaking through a medium, sometimes with the malice and apparent irrelevance of spirits in such a case. They talk of this life as a boy who has gone to a public school talks of his private school. They are amused or bitter about their own misunderstood or wasted past, about the triviality of it all; or sometimes they have tender regrets. For Mr. Masters, luckily, is not always cynical. We feel that Spoon River, wherever it is, cannot be a pleasant place to live in, but there are some people in it that we like, and there is the beauty of the earth, which one would remember with regret even in heaven.

Dead men and women, talking about this life, would talk a very

naked language free of all airs and graces; and Mr. Masters has
made such a language for them, as if he had lived with them in
their other world. Sometimes he departs from it into a poetical
prose, and then at once we feel that it is he himself who is speaking, an ordinary literary man, and not his dead. But these lapses
are too rare to spoil the book. In most of it Mr. Masters has
found a style unlike any other, the style of the dead. He will be
compared, of course, to Walt Whitman, but it is only a formal
likeness. Whitman is personal and can rise at any moment into
poetry or fill a phrase with the richness of what is unsaid. Mr.
Masters cannot do that. At his best he is bare, cold, and utterly
detached, making the simplest statements of fact, which have a
dramatic power because it is the dead who speak. His irony is
always dramatic, not in the words so much as in the situation,
as in the case of Hamilton Greene, who does not know that his
mother was a German servant girl and who, even in death, boasts
of his parentage:

> I was the only child of Frances Harris of Virginia
> And Thomas Greene of Kentucky,
> Of valiant and honorable blood both.
> To them I owe all that I became,
> Judge, member of Congress, leader in the State.
> From my mother I inherited
> Vivacity, fancy, language,
> From my father will, judgment, logic.
> All honor to them for what service I was to the people.

This would be pointless but for the epitaph just before it of Elsa
Wertman, his real mother, who tells us the truth about his birth
and how

> At political rallies when sitters-by thought I was crying
> At the eloquence of Hamilton Greene,
> That was not it.
> No! I wanted to say:
> That's my son! That's my son!

Mr. Masters has been tempted, perhaps, to overuse the opportunities that his form gives him for irony and contempt and disillusionment. After all, he is still one of us and knows no better than we do that the dead think meanly of this life. Certainly among the living there is not so large a proportion of those for whom this life is a mere waste and error as among his dead; and we may believe that, in their detachment, they would not lay so much emphasis on old scandal, whether about themselves or about others, as he makes them lay. Life must be fuller and richer, even for Spoon River Philistines, than it appears in these bleak memoirs when they insist upon some single indignity or absurdity as if that were all that had happened to them. It is effective, but it seems sometimes a trick done for its effectiveness. It may be that the book has had its great success in America because of this, because it talks scandal about humanity so coldly; but it deserves a success for other reasons. It is full of pity for failure, which moves us all the more because it is expressed drily and without beauty, as in this epitaph:

> Out of a cell into this darkened space—
> The end at twenty-five.
> My tongue could not speak what stirred within me,
> And the village thought me a fool.
> Yet at the start there was a clear vision,
> A high and urgent purpose in my soul
> Which drove me on trying to memorize
> The Encyclopaedia Britannica.

At his best Mr. Masters is content to write without beauty; it is the writing of an age in which literature has exhausted all its arts, in which everything is stale but a bare statement of facts made interesting by circumstance. He leaves it to the reader to make beauty and passion for himself out of these bare statements. They are hints that arouse an activity in the mind, clues to a tragedy or a comedy that we can work out from our own experience. It could not be better done than Mr. Masters has done it, but the book is a masterpiece of self-denial rather than of self-expression.

Perhaps new beauties will come into literature this way, through this fastidious primitiveness; but Mr. Masters himself is not the new kind of poet, as he proves when he tries to be poetical.

EDGAR LEE MASTERS: *Spoon River Anthology*. (Reprinted from *The Times Literary Supplement* of January 27, 1916.)

THE BOYHOOD OF HOWELLS

THE OLDEST and the best-beloved of American living authors has continued to be so steadily prolific that it is startling to find, from his own confession, that within three months he will have completed his eightieth year. He has not slackened the steady output of his novels, which must, at this date, be close upon a hundred in number, and he has exercised his unresting pen on every species of subsidiary literature, verse and biography and criticism and morals. We hardly know why it is that during the last twenty years this tide of sensible, tender, and often humorous books has broken less and less vehemently against our British shores. Still we think of Mr. Howells as the author of *The Lady of the Aroostook* and the essayist of *Venetian Life*. Those exquisite productions continue to please, but they belong to a world of fifty years ago. When it is our good fortune to run up against one of Mr. Howells's latest novels we discover the same qualities of limpid English and exquisite narrative art, but they seem remote to us. Moreover, although the author has so valuable a knowledge of Europe and has so constantly visited it, he remains as an author almost querulously American. To read *Miss Bellard's Inspiration* and *A Hazard of New Fortunes* is to realize why the European world has been unable persistently to read Mr. Howells, in spite of his charm and value. He belongs to a world of Middle America from which everything but language more and more deeply divides us.

Mr. Howells has been no less lavish in autobiography than in other branches of literature. The volume before us deals with his childhood and adolescence, but this is not the first time on which we make with him the backward excursion. In *Literary Friends and Acquaintances,* in *My Literary Passions,* and above all in that very delightful book *A Boy's Town,* we have gone over the ground with Mr. Howells before. Meditation has brought up out of the wells of memory fresh anecdotes, and perhaps some of the old ones are subjected to a more careful analysis. We complain of nothing, but we have a fear that some of the events that enlivened Columbus, Ohio, seventy years ago may seem very small beer to European readers saturated with sensation.

It used to be a commonplace of criticism to bracket Mr. Howells with Henry James. They formed for many years, in their predominance on the stage of American letters, another set of heavenly twins, like Tennyson and Browning, or Ibsen and Björnson. Such parallels are fallacious, being mainly founded on the contemporary accident. The similarity of James and Howells was obvious, so long as criticism did not trouble itself to look below the surface. Each of them analyzed character very searchingly and preferred to select its types rather from ordinary than from exceptional groups. But the radical distinction—or one of the radical distinctions—between them lay in the deepest fiber of the nature of each. Henry James was aristocratic and European in his regard for the antique trappings of life. He felt America to be naked and negative, and he came away from it as from an atmosphere in which he could not breathe. Mr. Howells, on the other hand, has always been sincerely devoted to the bare democratic ideal. He has never ceased to prefer Venice, Pennsylvania, to the real Venice, and that in spite of his knowledge of the latter and his enforced appreciation of Italian art and history.

Both James and Howells have been what is vaguely termed "realists," but their attitude to reality was very dissimilar. Every careful reader of James is aware that, in spite of his elaborate discretion, he shrank from probing none of the darkest secrets of the soul. Mr. Howells, on the other hand, has willfully held his eyes averted from all the moral disease that leads to violent human action. His peculiarity as a novelist resides in his paradoxical relation to experience. No one has, within the sphere of his selection, kept closer than he to the formula of "naturalism" that Zola laid down. But he has restrained his attention from dwelling on anything unpleasant. He makes no secret of having done this on purpose. He describes, in this volume, how, when a youth, he was offered a lucrative job as the reporting correspondent of a Cincinnati journal, and how gladly he renounced this opportunity of learning "in the school of reality the many lessons of human nature which it could have taught me." One fancies that the night side of Columbus would not have been so very lurid, but Mr. Howells refused its advantages: "My longing was for the cleanly respectabilities, and I still cannot think that a bad thing; or, if experience cannot have more than the goodly outside of life, that this is not well worth having." This sentiment of the benefit of keeping to "the goodly outside of life" is repeated often in these reminiscences of a realistic novelist, but nowhere so emphatically as in the following remarkable passage. A certain Richard Realf had become the associate of Howells:

> While he was briefly with us a hapless girl, of those whom there is no hope for in this life, killed herself, and Realf went to the wicked house where she lay dead, out of some useless pathos, since she *was* dead. I reported the fact to my friend Dr. S. with a faltering tendency, I am afraid, to admire Realf for it, and the doctor said coldly, Yes, he had better kept away; his motive had already been scandalously construed. It was this world speaking at its best and wisest, but I am not sure that it altogether persuaded me.

If we consider for a moment, but with care, the contrast between this eminently candid and gentle paragraph and the treatment the same subject would have received from Charles Louis Philippe or from one of the younger Russians, the whole difference between Europe and the central United States stands revealed.

Mr. Howells has a chance word that is very significant in our consideration of sentiment in the United States: he speaks of "the comfort which now pervades our well-warmed American world."

His beautiful talent, through a long and most honorable life, has been occupied in illustrating the large monotonous interests, domestic and commercial, of a population protected against all the dangers of experience and sustained by no great idealism or enthusiasm. It is odd for us who seethe in the caldron of the biggest war in history to realize the cozy populations of the "well-warmed American world." What are they to Hecuba? Mr. Howells himself is neither ignorant of the sorrows of Europe nor insensible to them. His public utterances during these last two years have been inspired by a tender indignation, worthy of one who, as he simply tells us, has always had a lump in his throat whenever he has reflected on the cruelties of large birds to small ones. At his great age he is the most dignified figure in the intellectual world of America, and rarely has a country produced a man of letters more consistently representative of her qualities.

W. D. HOWELLS: *Years of My Youth*. (Reprinted from *The Times Literary Supplement* of December 7, 1916.)

MR. POUND AS CRITIC

THIS BOOK is a collection of things so diverse that it can be reviewed only in a series of notes. There are dialogues, in which Mr. Pound does not seem to be quite at ease; there is a satire in couplets written with the ostentatious roughness of Persius and Donne. There is a little catechism on religion, or rather on that pluralist, pagan religion that must always persist even though it has lost all its temples; there is a great deal of criticism; and there is also a great deal of provocation. We do not know why Mr. Pound issues so many challenges; perhaps it is to test his readers. He would say, no doubt, that those who are provoked by them are fools and may as well shut the book. But, after all, the aim of controversy is to convince, and with as little friction as possible. Mr. Pound likes friction as well as controversy.

He says that he takes no great pleasure in writing prose about aesthetic, and that one work of art is worth forty prefaces. But he continues to write prefaces and prose about aesthetic as if he liked doing it; and we confess we like reading him. He has learning, a grasp of principle, and a strong, willful taste of his own; and it is amusing to watch the conflict between his principles and his willfulness. He would like to curse Milton and Wordsworth altogether, but he cannot do it; he knows that they are great artists. He knows also that it is worth while to write prose about aesthetic, if it is well done, though he affects the careless impatience of the artist when he does it. He is himself part artist, part philosopher, part fanatic; and each of these elements in him is apt to inhibit or impede the others. He sees so clearly what the perfect poem would be, and then writes poems that are reactions against all kinds of sham poetry, and sometimes nothing more. And then he writes criticisms that are reactions against sham criticism, remembering all the time that he is himself an artist and anxious to avoid the wordiness and vagueness of the professional critic. He seems to be angry with a number of tiresome people, named or unnamed, all the time; we wish he would forget them and say what he has to say as if he were talking to a friend who understood him, not as if he were answering a cross-examining counsel in the witness box. For, when he does forget the world, the flesh, and the devil of commonplace, he says very good things.

> The first difficulty in a modern poem is to give a feeling of the reality of the speaker; the second, given the reality of the speaker, to gain any degree of poignancy in one's utterance. That is to say, you must begin in a normal, natural tone of voice, and you must, somewhere, express or cause a deep feeling.

Yes! it is so difficult now to begin poetry in a normal, natural tone of voice and not as if you were reading the Lessons or addressing a mass meeting in Hyde Park. And there are so many ways of affecting intimacy with your readers, so many methods of approach that prevent you from discovering what you have to say, if anything. Verse remains, for all except a few, a fancy dress in which they cannot behave naturally; and, if they give all their energy to behaving naturally, nothing happens but natural behavior; and they might as well not be writing at all. To write naturally and yet to say what is momentous, to have the inspiration of the Sibyl without her contortions—that is the task of the poet.

Mr. Pound gives us his Credo of art. He believes in an "absolute rhythm," a rhythm "in poetry which corresponds exactly to the emotion or shade of emotion to be expressed. A man's rhythm must be interpretative; it will be, therefore, in the end, his own, uncounterfeiting, uncounterfeitable." Yes! but the great mass of poetry has been written also in meters. That is a fact that the theorist has to deal with, as he has to deal with the fact that the great mass of painting has been representative. The poet who gives up meter, gives up pattern with its repetitions, must find an equivalent in the way of beauty; for beauty is the symptom of successful expression. It may be that free verse is too difficult in practice, however right in theory; and, if that is so, there is something wrong with the theory of it. At any rate the theory has to be proved in practice. "I think," says Mr. Pound, "there is a 'fluid' as well as a 'solid' content, that some poems may have form as a tree has form, some as water poured into a vase. That most symmetrical forms have certain uses. That a vast number of subjects cannot be precisely, and therefore not properly, rendered in symmetrical forms." According to this image it is the fluid content that needs the vase, the symmetrical form; and that, perhaps, is the justification of meter. The content of poetry, being mainly emotional, is fluid and needs the vase, the symmetrical form. The content of prose, being mainly intellectual, makes its own more logical form. The type of prose is an argument, which cannot be expressed in a pattern; its logic is the logic of its own process. But between the syllogism and the pattern there are many intermediate forms, according to the content; and, as any content has a right to exist, if it is content, so it is with any form.

We could annotate nearly every page of the book with eager agreement or dissent. This means that it is worth reading. You may wish that you had Mr. Pound before you in the flesh, to tell him what you think of him; but that, no doubt, is exactly the effect he wishes to produce on you.

EZRA POUND: *Pavannes and Divisions.* (Reprinted from *The Times Literary Supplement* of September 19, 1918.)

SMOKE AND STEEL:
THE POETRY OF CARL SANDBURG

AMERICAN POETS can be divided into those who stay in America and those who emigrate—a distinction equivalent to that applied to modern French poets by M. Georges Duhamel: acceptance or evasion of modern life. Carl Sandburg is one of those who have accepted Americanism. The book under review is the third large volume of poetry published by him since 1914. But his work is interesting apart from its bulk and worth some attention to its milieu, its tradition, its objects, and its achievements.

In considering realistic poetry like this the milieu, the kind of life from which it grows and which it purports to interpret, is of more importance than in other kinds of poetry. Since one of the primary claims of such poetry is that it is "true to life," true to its surroundings, we must know something about that life before we can judge if this object at least has been achieved. Now, the life that Mr. Sandburg wishes to express is, generally speaking, the life of the Middle West, which is different from that of the aristocratic South, ruined in the Civil War, different again from the Puritan New England that found expression in Lowell, Emerson, and Hawthorne, and yet again different from the life of the Coast. The distinguishing feature of the Middle West, to quote John Gould Fletcher, is "its immense flatness and monotony"; its population, after achieving a gigantic piece of pioneering, is isolated in farms or concentrated in small provincial towns, in either case with an attitude toward life that renders it indifferent or hostile to the arts. Yet in this monotony of landscape there are great stretches of beauty; in this worship of material success there is a stirring of the ideal; and Mr. Sandburg is, as it were, a mouthpiece for this inarticulate idealism to make itself heard.

One of the best poems in his new book is a description of a Middle Western town, whose sins are "neither scarlet nor crimson" but "a convict gray, a dishwater drab." This town, the poet continues, is

> . . . a spot on the map
> And the passenger trains stop there
> And the factory smokestacks smoke
> And the grocery stores are open Saturday nights
> And the streets are free for citizens who vote
> And inhabitants counted in the census.
> Saturday night is the big night.

and then:—

> Main Street there runs through the middle of the town,
> And there is a dirty post office
> And a dirty city hall
> And a dirty railroad station . . .

Not an inspiring home for poetry, one feels. But Mr. Sandburg sends into it a "loafer," who says some harsh things of the town and concludes:

> . . . you ain't in a class by yourself,
> I seen you before in a lot of places.
> If you are nuts America is nuts.

To smile over that as quaint or amusing is to miss its significance. This criticism from Mr. Sandburg, who is on the whole too easygoing, too easily satisfied with mere activity, is as significant as Arnold's "By the Ilyssus there was no Wragg." It is a recognition of an essential spiritual truth: mere material prosperity is not enough. "To blaspheme wealth" needs courage in any modern community; it needs especial courage in an Anglo-Saxon country.

But the significance of this is not that it comes from an exceptional and educated person—there are plenty such in the United States—but that Mr. Sandburg utters it as a feeling of the people.

These moments of dissatisfaction are rare and brief; more often we find Mr. Sandburg "celebrating" the vigor, usefulness, and supremacy of American commerce:

> Omaha, the roughneck, feeds armies,
> Eats and swears from a dirty face.
> Omaha works to get the world a breakfast,

or again he runs off on one of those excited catalogues dear to Walt Whitman:

Fire and wind wash at the slag.
Boxcars, clocks, steamshovels, churns, pistons, boilers, scissors—
Oh, the sleeping slag from the mountains, the slag-heavy pigiron will
    go down many roads.
Men will stab and shoot with it, and make butter and tunnel rivers,
    and mow hay in swaths, and slit hogs and skin beeves, and steer
    airplanes across North America, Europe, Asia, round the world.

We will not stay to discuss the merits of these lines, but will point out that they do explain Mr. Sandburg's milieu; he has used the materials that he found at hand. It would be unjust to omit saying that he has absorbed some of the natural beauty of his country, but he has a kind of predetermination to insist on the ugly, the materialistic side of his subject. At his best he uses this natural beauty to point a contrast; more frequently it is a mere reference, imperfectly "fused" by his talent. There is an absence of meditation in these poems that gives them an air of incompleteness. Like the French cubists, Mr. Sandburg tries "to confound himself with life."

No writer is without a literary tradition or literary influences of some sort, because no one writes without previously reading. The tradition of Mr. Sandburg is Whitman, journalism, and to a slighter extent modern *vers libre* poets, just as Whitman's tradition was journalism and prose translations of epic poetry. The value of a tradition is of course invaluable to the artist; at its best it is a sure foundation to build on, at its worst something to rebel against. We Europeans have an immense, an august tradition; even as Englishmen we have a considerable tradition. And since most Americans speak English and are descended from Europeans they also inherit our tradition. But, following Whitman, many American poets choose deliberately to ignore it, to forfeit its great benefits. Why? Whitman has explained his views in his prose works, but we do not need to go to them for an answer. These American poets desire their writings to possess above everything the qualities of vitality, novelty, and Americanism. Above all they wish to produce work that is emphatically American. They argue, like Whitman, that they are "out," not to follow any tradition, however great and splendid, but to create one, the tradition of America. They have therefore a distrust, almost a hatred, of the past and the beauty it created. Here is an interesting example from *Smoke and Steel:*

BRONZES

They ask me to handle bronzes
Kept by children in China
Three thousand years

Since their fathers
Took fire and molds and hammers
And made them.

The Ming, the Chou,
And other dynasties,
Out, gone, reckoned in ciphers,
Dynasties dressed
In old gold and old yellow—
They saw these.
Let the wheels
Of three thousand years
Turn, turn, turn on.

> Let one poet then
> (One will be enough)
> Handle these bronzes
> And mention the dynasties
> And pass them along.

What a perverse misunderstanding, we are tempted to exclaim, what a curious misapprehension of beauty, what a rejection of excellence! What an abyss between that and Renan's prayer on the Acropolis!

After the quotations made, no further example of Mr. Sandburg's debt to Whitman is needed. It is clear throughout his pages, even to the extent of his using phrases from *Leaves of Grass*—"hairy, hankering." More disturbing than Whitman is the journalism in Mr. Sandburg's style. We are referring not to his use of slang, his "crummy hobos" and "hoodlums" and "lousy doughboys," which are probably due to an overstrained sense of loyalty to one's own time, but to the tone of his poems, which so often read like a piece of newspaper writing. Look at the journalistic facetiousness in this:

> Let me count reminiscences like money; let me count Picnics, glad rags and the great bad manners of the Carlovingians breaking fresh eggs in the copper pans of their proud uncles.

Always that irritation with the past, that opposition of the live dog to the dead lion, that flattery of a living mediocrity. But there is the essence of Mr. Sandburg's writing: vitality, novelty, Americanism, at all costs. What does it matter (he seems to say) that the Parthenon is the supreme expression of a supreme wisdom, that Shakespeare is the supreme poet of tragedy and comedy, that anything supremely excellent and beautiful has been created *by the past?* The Parthenon is a ruin; Shakespeare is dust; excellence and beauty—what are they? Cowley said that there was no need to sing new songs but to say the old. These American poets would violently disagree. They are convinced that life, modern life, the "now" alone are important, that vitality, energy, truth to modern life, to the outward phenomena of modern life, are all that is asked of the poet.

How far have they succeeded in this? Have they achieved novelty, vitality, and truth to life? For Mr. Sandburg the answer is that to a great extent he has. He has introduced themes that have seldom, perhaps never, been treated before. There is an impressive display of energy in *Smoke and Steel*. His poems are true to a certain kind of life, they are undoubtedly American. They do succeed, then, in doing what they set out to do, but whether this in itself constitutes a high and right art is another question. Yet we ought to be sympathetic, as open-minded as possible to this kind of writing, remembering that one danger to poetry is always that it may become too bookish, preoccupied with formalities and dignities, and too little stirred by the rough energies of life. Mr. Yeats has said that modern poetry has two ways before it, one of increasing refinement and one "among the market carts." Mr. Sandburg has chosen the way among the market carts, and we are wrong if we refuse to accept what he has to give us. Yet, though European criticism must recognize these experiments and strive to understand them, European poetry may well reject them. Compare with Mr. Sandburg's poems these lines by a Renaissance poet:

Ut flos tenellus in sinu
Telluris almae lucidam
Formosus explicat comam,
Si ros et imber educat
Illum; tenella mens mea
Sic floret, almi Spiritus
Dum rore dulci pascitur.
Hoc illa si caret, statim
Languescit; ut flos arida
Tellure natus, eum nisi
Et ros et imber educat.

Between the two there can be no agreement; there you have two irreconcilables.

CARL SANDBURG: *Smoke and Steel*. (Reprinted from *The Times Literary Supplement* of December 9, 1920.)

AMERICAN DRAMATIST:
THE PLAYS OF EUGENE O'NEILL

EUGENE O'NEILL is a young writer—he is still in the thirties—
who has become well known in America only during the last two
years, thanks chiefly to the success of his play *Beyond the Horizon,* which ran for a considerable period in a New York theater and incidentally won for its author the Pulitzer prize of
$1,000, on the recommendation of Columbia University, as the
best American play of 1920. At the present moment two newer
plays of Mr. O'Neill's are running in New York, entitled *Emperor
Jones* and *Diff'rent.* Another play, *Gold,* is in preparation. The
last three plays, however, have not yet been published. *The Moon
of the Caribbees* and its companion one-act plays represent his
immature work, *Beyond the Horizon* his most popular style, while
Diff'rent is the most daring and *Emperor Jones* infinitely the most
interesting of these examples of his talent.

The seven little pieces in *The Moon of the Caribbees* deal
chiefly with seamen's life. The action in most of them deals with
the adventures of various members of the crew of a British tramp
steamer or of an American whaling vessel. They are dramatic
sketches rather than finished work, and not much description of
them is called for. In the first play, which gives its title to the
book, the tramp is lying at anchor off a West Indian island. Native women smuggle drink aboard, and in a drunken riot one of
the men is killed. *Bound East for Cardiff* describes the death of
another of the hands on board the ship. In *Where the Cross is
Made* Captain Bartlett is shown in the "cabin" he has built at
the top of his house as a lookout post for a vessel he sent out
three years before to search for a buried treasure. The vessel was
wrecked and lost, but the old man refuses to accept the ruin of
his hopes and still insanely waits for it to return. His son has

sent for a doctor to certify him as insane and have him removed to an asylum. Suddenly the old man is heard hailing his lost ship; the forms of its lost crew enter, carrying the treasure; the father and the son both see them, although they are invisible to other persons. The old man dies of heart failure, but his obsession takes hold of his son, who goes mad of it. The last playlet in the volume is a strange fragment, even by comparison with the others.

These gruesome little pieces are more remarkable for their promise than their actual merit; but Mr. O'Neill's next and more ambitious work, *Beyond the Horizon,* reveals greater dramatic gifts. Andrew and Rob Mayo are the sons of a farmer; their characters are very different; Rob is an impressionable and poetic youth who wishes only to travel and see the world that lies "beyond the horizon," whereas Andrew is a hard-headed farmer. Their uncle, a sea captain, arranges to take Rob on a three years' trip to the tropics with him, but on the day before he is to go Rob discovers that he loves his brother's sweetheart, Ruth, and that his love is returned. He decides to stay at home, and his brother goes away to sea in his place. The second act opens three years later; the farm has gone to ruin in Rob's impractical hands; his wife is a slut; and he is a disappointed man. Ruth declares that she preferred his brother all along and that she is eagerly awaiting his return. But Andy comes back only to go away again at once to the Argentine to make his fortune, leaving the unhappy couple together. In the last act Rob is dying of consumption, and his brother, who is known to have made good in the Argentine, returns again. But he has speculated on his way home and lost practically everything. To Ruth's disappointment he declares that he must go south once more and make another pile. Rob reviews their position: "I'm a failure, and Ruth's another— but we can both justly lay some of the blame for our stumbling on God. But you're the deepest-dyed failure of the three, Andy." He asks Andy to marry Ruth after he dies, and crawls out secretly to the highway to die. Andy and Ruth find him there dead and desperately agree to fulfill his last wish.

With *Emperor Jones* and *Diff'rent* Mr. O'Neill has greatly improved upon these earlier works. *Diff'rent* is a definitely unpleasant study of a woman's psychology. The first scene is laid in a
New England village in 1890. Emma Crosby is to marry Caleb
Williams, a young whaling skipper. On the eve of their wedding
she hears, through her brother, who tells her it as an amusing
story, that Caleb, while his boat was lying at anchor by a West
Indian Island, was visited in his cabin by a native woman who
had swum out to the boat for a joke. She tells Caleb that she
can now no longer agree to marry him; and the rough consola-
tions of her mother and friends, who endeavor to excuse his lapse,
are in vain. She agrees that it is human to err, but, she says, she
thought Caleb was "diff'rent." Caleb declares that he will wait for
her thirty years if need be. The second act takes place in 1920.
Emma is now an old maid of nearly fifty, but she has fallen in
love with Benny, the shameless young twenty-year-old nephew of
Caleb, a thief and a blackguard, who humors her for her money's
sake and offers to marry her. Caleb returns from a cruise and
pays Emma her usual visit; again he asks her to marry him. She
tells him that she is going to marry his nephew. After a terrible
scene, in which Caleb tells her that his nephew is making her the
laughingstock of the village, he insists that an offer of money
would make Benny desert her altogether. When the nephew returns, Emma repeats his uncle's offer to him and finds that he
is indeed willing to take the money and desert her. Then the news
is brought that Caleb has hanged himself in his barn; and the
curtain falls as Emma, too, goes off the stage to end her life.

We may turn now to *Emperor Jones*. The scene is set "on an
island in the West Indies as yet unself-determined by White Ma-
rines." It is one of those curious black empires in the Caribbean
seas. As the curtain rises on the "Emperor's" palace, a white
trader enters and meets a native woman. She tells him that she
is escaping to the hills to join the rest of her countrymen; the
trader, a sneering low-caste Englishman, comments gleefully on
the fact that trouble is breaking out. The old woman runs away,

and the Emperor enters. He is a tall, powerfully built Negro in
a fantastically bright uniform. Ridiculous as are his position and
appearance, he is clearly a man of great cunning and will. Smithers tells him that a revolution has broken out and takes a mean
delight in the disclosure. But the Emperor, in a mixture of shrewdness and bragging, declares that he is not afraid of any of these
"bush niggers," that he has made his plan to escape through the
forest to a bay on the other side, where a French gunboat is lying that will carry him to America, where he has put away most
of the wealth he has extorted from his foolish and superstitious
"subjects." He boasts of his former life in the United States as
porter on a Pullman car, murderer, convict, and prison breaker
and contrasts it with his present position, or rather this as it was
on the previous day. He knew that his rule could not last forever, but he had reckoned upon another six months of power; but
now, "I cashes in and resigns de job of Emperor right dis minute." He is sure that he can get away, with his carefully prepared
plans. Besides, he has persuaded the Negroes that he is invulner-
able to ordinary lead bullets.

SMITHERS: "But supposin' somethin' 'appens wrong, an' they
do nab you?"

JONES: "Dey don't—dat's de answer."

SMITHERS: "But, just for argyment's sake—what'd you do?"

JONES: "I'se got five lead bullets in dis gun good enuff fo' common
bush niggers—an' after dat I got de silver bullet left to cheat 'em
out o' gittin' me."

SMITHERS: "Ho, I was fergettin' that silver bullet. You'll bump
yourself orf in style, won't yer?"

JONES: "You kin bet yo' whole roll on one thing, white man.
Dis baby plays out his string to de end, and when he quits, he quits
with a bang de way he ought. Silver bullet ain't none too good for
him when he go, dat's a fact! Sho'! What is I talkin' about? Ain't
come to dat yit, an' I never will—not wid trash niggers like dese
yere. Silver bullet will bring me luck, anyway. I kin outguess, out-
run, outfight, an' outplay de whole lot o' dem all ovah de board
any time o' de day or night! You watch me!"

The tom-tom starts beating with a regular throb that is maintained to the very end of the play. "That's for you," says Smithers. The Negroes are holding a war dance and putting their wizards and ghost raisers on the track of Jones. The Emperor declares that he was a "member o' good standin' in de Baptist Church" when he was working on the Pullmans and is consequently not to be frightened by witchcraft; but actually he is a little uneasy in his inmost heart. However, he puts on a brave face—"I tells you I'se safe's 'f I was in New York City"—and starts off for the forest, not by any hidden door but by the main entrance to his palace.

> Does you think I'd slink out de back door like a common nigger? I'se Emperor yit, ain't I? And de Emperor Jones leaves de way he comes, and dat black trash don't dare stop him—leastways, not yit. Listen to dat rollcall, will yo'? Must be mighty big drum carry dat far. Well, if dey ain't got no whole brass band to see me off, I sho' got de drum part of it! So long, white man!

And whistling a tune he goes out into the plain, with three hours' start of sunset and his rebellious subjects.

The rest of the play, with the exception of a few lines at the end, is a monologue with ghostly interludes. First we see Emperor Jones reaching the forest at nightfall. He throws himself on the ground and talks to himself, with a strange mixture of satisfaction and nervousness. He pulls off his shoes and congratulates his feet on the excellent way they have so far supported him. "Feet, yo' is holding up yo' end fine, and I su'tinly hopes you ain't blistering none. It's time you git a rest. You is still in the pink—on'y a little mite feverish. Cool yo'selfs. Remember yo' done got a long journey yit befo' yo'." As he remarks, "Dat soft Emperor job ain't no training for a long hike ovah dat plain in de brilin' sun," he decides that all that is wrong with him is hunger and searches round for the food he had hidden in expectation of some such inevitable escape. He cannot find it, and, lighting a match to search for the place, remembers that he must not disclose where he is. Strange eyes peer at him through the dark-

ness, and he hears laughter. Scared, he pulls out his revolver and
fires at the nearest shape. It disappears, and again he tries to pull
himself together.

> Gorry, you give de game away when yo' fire dat shot. Dem niggers
> hear dat fo' su'tin. Time yo' beat it in de woods widout no long
> waits. Git in, nigger! What yo' skeered at? Ain't nothin' dere but
> de trees! Git in!

The next scene is three hours later, in the middle of the woods.
Jones enters, rather disheveled. "Dis am a long night fo' yo', yo'
Majesty," he says to himself. "Majesty! Der ain't much majesty
'bout dis baby now." He hears a rattling noise and, turning, sees
a Negro dressed in a Pullman attendant's uniform, rattling a dice-
box. It is a man whom he killed long ago in a gambling row. He
pulls out his revolver and shoots at the apparition. Once more he
realizes that he has given his position away; he turns and flees
among the trees. The next scene is two hours later. Jones is half
dead with exhaustion. He has lost his way, and his continual
chatter has become more frightened. He throws off his coat and
his spurs. Terror seizes him, and he vainly reminds himself that
the Baptist clergyman in the old days assured him that ghosts do
not exist. Suddenly we see before him the figures of a prison gang
in which he once worked. The white jailer lashes him with a whip.
Jones seizes his revolver and shoots him. "I kills you, you white
debil, if it's the last thing I evah does! Ghost or debil, I kill you
again!" The phantoms disappear. The noise of the tom-tom, which
has accompanied him throughout his flight, grows louder and more
insistent. Two hours later we find him worn out in another part
of the forest. He is calling upon the Lord to save him from his
fears. Suddenly a body of men and women in old-time dress sur-
round him, and he is motioned by one of them to ascend a tree
stump. In dumb show he is auctioned by a white auctioneer and
sold to one of the onlookers. He has passed in his hallucinations
from the memories of his own past to that of his race, the American Negroes. From this point on it is the "unconscious mind"
of his race that haunts him. He fires two shots at the auctioneer,

and the figures are blotted out. He has now used all his lead bullets and has only the silver one left. Again two hours pass. He is still in the forest, moaning with fear and weariness. A light appears at the back of the stage, and there is seen the hold of a slaveship, with half a dozen poor Negro wretches tugging at the oars. Jones takes his place among them and pulls at the oars in time with the others until he suddenly realizes that they are phantoms, and he rushes off among the trees. Another two hours pass and Jones stumbles into a curious landscape. It is the Congo, the original home of his race. A Congo witch dancer enters, whining and prancing. He points to a crocodile in the river and seems to order Jones to sacrifice himself to it. Jones cries out, "Mercy, O Lawd! Mercy! Mercy on this poor sinner. . . . Lawd, save me! Lawd Jesus, hear my prayer!" The crocodile opens its mouth to devour him; but he remembers the silver bullet and fires at the crocodile. The light dies out, with Jones lying cowed on the ground.

The next and last scene is at dawn. The trader Smithers is talking to the rebels who are tracking Jones. They are at the very place where he entered the forest twelve hours before. Shots are heard, and the tom-tom abruptly ceases. The headman tells Smithers that his men have been making silver bullets during the night to shoot Jones with, since lead ones would be useless against him. The men re-enter, bearing the dead body of the Emperor. Smithers salutes him mockingly and utters the last words of the play: "I s'pose you think it's yer charms and yer silly beatin' the drum that made 'im run in a circle when 'e'd lorst 'imself, don't yer? . . . Stupid as 'ogs, the lot of 'em! Blarsted niggers!"

This curious play is unlikely to make as strong an impression in print as when it is acted, especially when in New York so gifted a Negro actor as Charles Gilpin is in the role of Emperor Jones. But even from the inadequate description here one can see what an interesting experiment the play is. Whether Mr. O'Neill will follow his own lead further or develop his art rather on the lines of his *Diff'rent* is a matter of the greatest interest. If he can write more plays of the caliber of *Emperor Jones* he will rank high among living dramatists. But from *Diff'rent* to banality is not a far step. His next play, *Gold,* which is to be produced later in the year, is said to be to a large extent an amplification of *Where the Cross is Made,* referred to above. It will be impossible, therefore, to deduce from it which direction this author proposes to take in the future.

EUGENE O'NEILL: *The Moon of the Caribbees* and Six
other Plays of the Sea. *Beyond the Horizon.* (Reprinted from
The Times Literary Supplement of March 31, 1921.)

THE AMERICAN FRONTIER

HITHERTO THE story of the American frontier has given inspiration mainly to the romancer. Around the figures of the Red Indian and the backwoodsman has grown up quite a respectable library of fiction. But the abundant material it offers to the historian—and especially to the writer on what used to be called "the philosophy of history"—has been far from adequately explored. Of living authorities on this subject Professor F. J. Turner, of Harvard, stands in the front rank. It would be difficult to name anyone else who has made so extensive researches into the history of American expansion or who has revealed so clearly the significance of the various stages in the westward movement of the population. In this volume he has collected the more important of his contributions on this topic to the transactions of learned societies and to the magazines. Such a form of publication makes inevitable a certain amount of overlapping and repetition, but this defect is minimized by the excellence of the index, and the successive reading of the several papers and addresses leaves perhaps a deeper impression upon the mind than would be produced by a connected record.

In Professor Turner's opinion the larger part of what has been distinctive and valuable in America's contribution to the history of the human spirit has been due to her peculiar experience in extending her type of frontier into new regions. This experience has been fundamental in the economic, political, and social characteristics of the American people and in their conceptions of their destiny. Accordingly, this volume, though not ostensibly so, is virtually a history of American democracy. American democracy, Professor Turner holds, is not to be explained by reference to a "glorious Constitution" which has only to be copied by other nations in order that they may repeat America's career. The real clue is to be found in the story of her continually advancing frontier line and the consequent development of ever new areas.

The American frontier is to be sharply distinguished from the European—a fortified boundary line running through dense populations. It has always lain at the hither edge of free land. Whenever social conditions tended to crystallize in the East, whenever capital tended to press upon labor or political restraints to impede the freedom of the masses, there was always this gate of escape. Free lands meant free opportunities, and their existence has differentiated the American democracy from the democracies that have preceded it. What has actually happened was not in the least anticipated by early American statesmen. Professor Turner quotes a prediction of Monroe's in 1786 that the region of the prairies, the great plains, and the Great Lakes—the region of which Chicago is today the commercial center—was so "miserably poor" in the quality of its land that it would never contain a sufficient number of inhabitants to entitle them to membership in the Union.

In his introductory chapter, "The Significance of the Frontier in American History," the author traces the successive advances in the boundary line of occupied territory and points out their social and political consequences. In the chapters that follow he treats the subject in fuller detail, with specific investigations of the history of the Massachusetts Bay, the Old West, the Middle West, the Ohio valley, the Mississippi valley, and so on. No incident seems to be too small to escape his scrutiny. Professor

Turner gives us incidentally an admirable account of the types
of settlers in the various districts at various periods. He acutely
remarks that the New Englanders who went West, though they
acted as a leaven of great significance, did not spread an un-
mixed New England influence. These pioneers did not come from
the class that conserved the type of New England civilization pure
and undefiled. Compared with the New Englanders who stayed
at home, they were less contented, less conservative, less provincial, more adaptable and approachable, less rigorous in their
Puritan ideals, less men of culture and more men of action. And
as they traveled farther West their new environment made them
less and less representative of the section from which they came.

The historian of the American frontier has to investigate a
process of expansion that is now complete. According to the
Superintendent of the Census, there ceased in 1880 to be any
such thing as a frontier line. "Today," declared Professor Turner,
in an address as President of the American Historical Association
in 1910, "we must add that the age of free competition of individuals for the unpossessed resources of the nation is nearing
its end." In a paper of even earlier date he could speak of the
changed situation brought about by the exhaustion of the supply
of free land, the concentration of capital in the control of fundamental industries, and the political and commercial activity of the
United States in lands beyond the seas. A cycle of American development has been completed. Accordingly there arises the problem: What ideals persist from the democratic experiences of the
West, and have they acquired sufficient momentum to sustain
themselves under conditions so radically unlike those in the days
of their origin? On this question Professor Turner says much that
is enlightening and suggestive. He lays special stress upon the new
self-consciousness and revived self-assertion of the differing
geographical sections that make up the United States. He even
goes so far as to forecast the possibility of their ultimately replacing
the several states as the administrative and legislative units. Already, in his judgment, "the real federal aspect of the nation,

if we penetrate beneath constitutional forms to the deeper currents of social, economic, and political life, will be found to lie
in the relation of sections and nation, rather than in the relation
of States and nation." Meanwhile the old Western spirit, of which
he regards Tennyson's Ulysses as a symbol, is invoked by Professor Turner for new and nobler achievements. "In place of old
frontiers of wilderness, there are new frontiers of unwon fields of
science, fruitful for the needs of the race; there are frontiers of
better social domains yet unexplored."

FREDERICK J. TURNER: *The Frontier in American History.*
(Reprinted from *The Times Literary
Supplement* of August 25, 1921.)

SHERWOOD ANDERSON

SHERWOOD ANDERSON'S stories are as curiously uneven as any
stories well can be. The first of these books is the more striking
and has work of fine quality, and yet in a moment of impatience
it might be easily put aside. At the end of the little piece in free
verse with which it opens come the words, "I have a wonderful
story to tell, but know no way to tell it"; and though it is not Mr.
Anderson who speaks, but another, there is something a little
ominous in them. The next story, in which a boy's faith in life and
beauty is expressed in his passionate admiration of the beauty of
horses and marred by a sudden exposure of human viciousness,
just misses being a great thing; and if you then happen to read
the title story you find an attempt at starkly ironic humor that
fails to rise out of flatness and squalor. Yet to leave the book there
would be a grave mistake. Turn any other page, almost, and the
hard little facts and tight little houses of this typically American
scene in the Middle West—externals through which the people
seem to move like dreams or shadows—begin to thin away and a
peculiar, vivid kind of interest compels you to listen. Sherwood

Anderson undoubtedly has a quality of his own. In a sense his characters always remain dreamlike; their thoughts and gestures are more visible than their faces, and their actual dreams, as well as their reveries, unfold at times with a swift glimpse of meaning. Their inner life, a life much less of full consciousness than of half-shaped thoughts and impulses and restless cravings, is what vitalizes these stories; and Mr. Anderson can penetrate to those roots of emotion with a sureness that makes them profoundly real—more real than the cramping world outside them.

Sometimes, without sacrificing truth, he resolves the discord between inner and outer into a thing of beauty. In "Out of No- where into Nothing," for instance—a long story that fills a third of the first volume—not only Rosalind Wescott's dilemma but the girl herself, the other figures, and all the scenes are vivid and combine to make a whole. Rosalind, who has left a dreary little town to make a life for herself in Chicago and comes home to meditate on a crisis in her life, is a very real person; so is Walter Sayers, the employer who loves her and whose love she is on the point of returning; he is an interesting "failure" whose tempera- ment is subtly portrayed. Sayers's wife, who lives only for "growth" and her garden, and the young Negro who slaves for her are merely thumbnail sketches, but Mr. Anderson has condensed into them two personalities and one strange life history. Perhaps it is because he has given more scope to his faith in life that he is here, as his heroine was for a moment, a "creator of light." Else- where there is often a barrier hard to lift, and it seems even to shut out natural beauty; though in "The New Englander" a gray story is transfigured by the vast, forestlike cornfield. But the significance of Mr. Anderson lies in his handling of the currents and knots within the mind. His old people are gnarled and weighted with their past and apt to be grotesque; it is his young people who stay most in one's memory, because he gets to depths in them that more than make up for their triviality at times. A great many, if not most, of these stories hinge on the "problem of sex." Upon that subject, so vexed and yet hidden, Mr. Anderson repays attention. He can write with an absolute candor that wins its success in *The Other Woman,* his story of a man on the eve of marrying; and his frankness is persuasive because it springs from a true and sensitive intuition. What also makes it acceptable is that he sees this aspect of things calmly, imaginatively, and is not obsessed by it. It is an urgency, but it is not the whole of life; a far more vital thing to him, often expressed in his characters, is the achievement of some creative freedom or command of life that will subdue ugliness and set things in their right places.

His world is certainly peopled, perhaps almost indiscriminately, with individuals and types. He seems to believe in them as living outside himself with a real existence of their own; and though this is not the infallible mark of a creator, it is at least the probable sign of one. He provokes criticism not so much by occasional failures of technique—which are even refreshing at times as a protest against machinelike efficiency—but rather by apparent inability to distinguish a good story from a bad one. In the second of these books the monotony threatened by the title is successfully parried by several remarkable stories; but to write such a bit of melodrama as *The Strength of God* ought to have been repugnant to an artist. But having said much of his inequality, we prefer to insist on his merits. There is a generous flow of imagination in these stories that marks him out among American writers; and in that abundance there is something that abundance often misses: an original and interesting vision of experience. Apart from his setting, one might guess Mr. Anderson to be an American writer, because there seems to be a moral hovering in the distance; but we notice that he nearly always keeps it there and prefers to win or lose on the strength of his imaginative conception. These stories excite curiosity as to what he will do next, and as he has the kind of intuition that absorbs experience, they are probably far from marking the limit of his powers.

SHERWOOD ANDERSON: *The Triumph of the Egg.*
Winesburg, Ohio. (Reprinted from *The Times Literary Supplement* of July 13, 1922.)

EDWIN ARLINGTON ROBINSON

SOMETIMES, NEGLECTFUL of the metaphor involved, we speak of the body of a nation as of a mere bulk. This is to ignore a complex organization that passes through health and sickness, exuberant and exhausted periods, on its way from youth to senility, and has each condition reflected in the character of the individuals produced, as a fever makes itself known by a rash on the skin. But a metaphor is not an explanation, and often, as in the present instance, it is applicable from only one point of view; we are led astray if we attempt to interpret history in terms of physiology. Yet even a star, most isolated of things, moves to a tug from our hands like a kite on a string, and it is not good to forget, even if we cannot explain, the dependence of the artist, most starlike of men, on the efforts of the race to which he belongs. Every nation endeavors to be self-supporting, for its cultural as well as for its grosser needs; yet to ensure continuous fertility it is obliged to accept stimulation from outside, and the strongest impulse is generally received from a discordant union.

It may seem improper that such considerations should be allowed to influence aesthetic criticism. Such criticism is an art in itself and has its heroic artists, but for the majority our acceptance of a work of art depends on our national appetite. The relativity of criticism is absolute, and as we all hunger after strange fruits, we are likely to absorb much more readily a minor Latin than a minor Teutonic poet. We have seen the process occur in the last century in France, where the reverberation of a few American writers went much deeper, though on a small surface, than in this country. By a number of his countrymen that includes some of the most competent judges Mr. Robinson is esteemed not only as a poet, but as the most representative of the living American poets and as one whose work has most surely the qualities of endurance. This collected volume represents the work of about thirty years in nearly 600 pages and argues for a fair though not extraordinary fluency.

One of the first, not insignificant, details to catch the eye is the great number of proper names, standing either as titles or used in the body of the poem, in the early as well as in the later work; showing that the need for a dramatic protagonist has been a continuous part of this poet's character. With other poets, when used, it has generally been a feint, and hardly at that diverting the reader from the real subjectivity of the poem. As an instance to the contrary one thinks of Browning, whose persons do occupy a stage and, even when the poet is beside them and monopolizing the conversation, heighten the emotions by their presence. In many of his pieces Mr. Robinson entertains his audience from behind a screen, and the voices that penetrate to us have a peculiar shrouded tone, so that we hardly recognize the emotions to which they belong, and regret that the information on the program is so scanty. It is not mysterious, like a good Maeterlinck drama, but mystifying. He really is interested in the relations of men and women to one another and to the general scheme, and not, or hardly, in the way they affect him. This distinguishes him from most poets, who frankly or under a mask rhyme their own sentiments. It is perhaps merely a distinction of the surface; underneath he must be narrating his own experiences, though the way in which he does it is affected by this absence of an egotistical motive. The long colloquies, such as "Captain Craig" and "The Book of Annandale," in which someone worries over a past gradually but not very definitely built up, do not show Mr. Robinson at his best. They are diffuse, and we cannot help feeling that this lack of concentration is a defect, or rather that it springs from a deeper defect. However definite his intention may have been, he does not communicate to us the certainty, not even the certainty of uncertainty, that the words lead us to suppose he intended.

For what was his to live lives yet:
Truth, quarter truth, death cannot reach;

>   Nor is it always what we know
>   That we are fittest here to teach.

Such a stanza alone would mark Mr. Robinson as being on the main line of American tradition, the tradition of a serious pre-occupation with ethical values and the insistence on the superiority of transcendental experience. It is the instinct that has canalized into the great religions and for which such men as Emerson and Whitman attempted to drive other channels. Yet rather than a canal, such bodies as the Church are vast reservoirs of mystical experience into which one may dip one's cup of words certain to bring it up brimmed with meaning. The bulk of a nation's poetry when it is rich in this mystical or poetical experience answers the same purpose, for what a man can do with words depends so much on what has been done with them before him.

Mr. Robinson is not a writer from whom one can quote readily. His happiest effects, pictorial as well as verbal, are too intimately bound up with the poem to permit separating them alive. Perhaps this stanza, most fitting in its place, will yet stand by itself:

>   And all his wisdom is unfound,
>   Or like a web that error weaves
>   On airy looms that have a sound
>   No louder now than falling leaves.

That, written of the Unseeing Man, has the gentle melancholy characteristic of his later attitude. It is the sadness, not of despair, but of a man who probes too deep to hope greatly. His work lingers in the memory like something observed, something experienced in reflection; not less real but less insistent than the direct impact of the poetic giants.

EDWIN ARLINGTON ROBINSON: *Collected Poems.* (Reprinted from *The Times Literary Supplement* of October 12, 1922.)

JOHN CROWE RANSOM

In a poem entitled "Armageddon" Mr. Ransom daringly imagines Antichrist meeting Christ, the one "playing his lissome flute and merry," the other "brooding upon his frugal breviary": they exchange chivalrous courtesies and prepare to fight, but, remembering that originally they were one brotherhood, they are "loth to let the other's blood," and they retire instead to a white pavilion to "truce their honorable dispute." In this, by mutual accommodation, they admirably succeed, and it seems that at last the wolf is to lie down with the lamb and the ancient feud between "good" and "evil," life and morals, pagan gaiety and Christian self-immolation is to be ended. But

> It could not be: there was a patriarch,
> A godly liege of old malignant brood,
> Who could not fathom the new brotherhood
> Between the children of the light and dark.

He whispers the old "mad things" in the ear of Christ: he re-awakens suspicion, fear, and the crusading mania. Tolerance and understanding are banished, and Christ's trump

> recalls his own to right opinions,
> With scourge they mortify their carnal selves,
> With stone they whet the axheads on the helves,
> And seek the Prince Beelzebub and minions.

It is easy to see the kinship between such a poet and Mr. Graves, who has attributed "those darks misdeeds that shocked and deadened the sense of humanity for centuries" to this aggressive adoption of "good" and "evil" as rigid absolutes in eternal opposition. It is easy also to understand why Mr. Ransom's poems, when they appeared in America under the title *Poems about God,* fell completely flat, particularly if we are to believe Mr. Graves's theory that the literary editors, misled by the title, handed their review copies to the theological reviewers.

All the more is Mr. Graves to be praised for his rescue work. The selection that he has made from Mr. Ransom's poetry convinces us that he has discovered a poet of quite unusual significance, one more consistently skeptical and less rural in tone than Mr. Frost, but sharing with him both his revolt against the narrowness and complacency of commercial puritanism and his expression of a wider human tolerance based upon nature instead of creeds. In style, too, there is a likeness. For, as Mr. Graves remarks, "neither Frost nor Ransom had any local poetic tradition on which to build, and had each to evolve his own," a style that he happily describes as "an extremely fastidious art disguised by colloquialisms." In Mr. Ransom the colloquialism is less of the soil than in Mr. Frost. At present, too, he is more negative, more exclusively engaged in registering a critical reaction to easy, instinctive romanticism, although an example of the latest phase of his art, from which Mr. Graves quotes in his introduction, suggests that his irony is becoming less coldly analytical and consequently more imaginative. But the prevailing mood throughout this volume is one of vital cynicism, in which intelligence plays a mocking counterpoint upon emotion too aggressively for these impulses often to blend. Thus in "Ilex Priscus"

> a certain heart, too young, and mortally
> Yoked with an unbeliever of bitter blood,
> Observed, as an eminent witness of life, the tree,
> And she exulted—being given to crying,
> "Heart, heart; love is so firm an entity,
> It must not go the way of the hot rose dying."

Nevertheless the "unbeliever of bitter blood" shows her, by tapping the oak, that the tree which she took as a symbol of constancy was, despite its show of profuse spring greenery, hollow-trunked and rotten, that it too lied no less piteously than she. In "Moonlight" the irony is less stark, the poet half surrendering to the vague romanticism that he deplores:

When only moonbeams lit the dusk,
The world was somewhat set to right,
For all the piteous twisted things
Had lost the crooked marks of spite
Which seared the eyeballs to behold,
As man to man, in broad daylight.

But we forget so soon the shame,
Conceiving sweetness where we can,
Heaven the citadel itself
Illumined on the lunar plan,
And I the chief of sinners! I
The middlemost Victorian.

And in "The Lover" the cynic who in friendly company wags his
wicked tongue at woman's expense, playing a "loathly part" for
fear of being thought a sentimentalist, confesses to the secret adoration that is straining at his lips:

Do they not hear the burst of bells
Pealing at every step you take?
Are not their eyelids winking too,
Feeling your sudden brightness break?
O, too much glory shut with us,
O, walls too narrow and opaque!
O, come into the night with me
And let me speak, for Jesus' sake!

In Mr. Ransom, then, the critical spirit is keyed to a poetic pitch,
and his verse embodies very significantly the modern conflict between the desires for beauty and for truth. We see the refusal of
any merely sensuous acceptance of beauty implied in such a conflict most curtly expressed in the verses to the mannequin that
end:

I urge the moralists to thresh
(Indeed, the thing is very droll)
God's oldest joke, forever fresh:
The fact that in the finest flesh
There isn't any soul.

And although such an attitude, half wry, half humorous, and always on the watch against self-delusion, tempts Mr. Ransom occasionally into a too conscious and arid cynicism, we are generally conscious of a passionate impulse underlying his disintegrating analysis, inspiring it with a creative purpose.

JOHN CROWE RANSOM: *Grace After Meat.* (Reprinted from *The Times Literary Supplement* of January 15, 1925.)

THE GREAT GATSBY

F. SCOTT FITZGERALD, author of *The Great Gatsby,* is a young American novelist whose work has not hitherto reached England. We understand that with his previous novels, one of which had a university setting, he has won a large amount of popularity in his own country, and that the present novel, his latest, is an effort in a rather different direction from that of ordinary American popular fiction. However this may be, *The Great Gatsby* is undoubtedly a work of art and of great promise. Mr. Fitzgerald has grasped the economical construction of a story, and his power of telling conciseness enables him, without being obscure, to compass a great deal in a short space. He uses words like living things, instead of like dead counters.

Gatz, or Gatsby, is a Conradian hero—one of those beings, like Almayer or the hero of *Heart of Darkness,* who are lifted above all the evil that they do or seek, above all the dirty trails that shoddy souls leave over the world, and above all the tragedy or destruction in which they finally sink, by some great elemental loyalty to a dream that, in a different world, would have been beautiful. Mr. Fitzgerald has imagined a son of broken-down and shiftless farm folk who, in his youth, found a platonic conception of himself and "invented just the sort of Jay Gatsby that a seventeen-year-old boy would be likely to invent, and to this conception he was faithful to the end." His dream universe of "ineffable gaudiness," realized partially by five years of secretaryship to a dissolute old millionaire, is enriched by an experience of love when, as a young officer, he had had a month of Daisy Buchanan and known an almost superhuman ecstasy. Daisy, then unmarried, belonged to his dream universe of beauty, money, and ease; penniless Gatsby, having illicitly entered it in the disguise of uniform, comes back after brilliant service in the war to find himself still outside it and Daisy married. By the mouth of Mr. Carraway, who is related to Daisy and visits her home on Long Island, there is told what Gatsby did in order to enter into his dream again. All passes in one summer. Gatsby, wealthy through lending himself to nameless corruptions, keeps open house upon the shore of West Egg, because the green light of the Buchanans' dock, on the opposite shore of East Egg, twinkles to him in the darkness. All the lavish show of drunken vulgarity is simply kept up to bring that green light nearer. Through Carraway Gatsby meets Daisy again—the weak, shallow creature who loves only by moments—and their meeting, which culminates in Daisy's weeping over Gatsby's exhibition of multitudinous shirts in his wardrobe, is an admirable piece of writing. And so Gatsby, steadfast in all his corruption, becomes involved in the life of Daisy Buchanan and her sensual savage of a husband Tom, whose typical outing with his mistress, the wife of a seedy garage keeper, throws a queer light on the manners of New York. Tragedy is not long in coming, for Tom suspects Gatsby, and on the amazing afternoon when Gatsby tells him to his face that Daisy no longer loves him, it is Daisy's tawdriness that brings the dream to the ground with a crash. Daisy, having shattered Gatsby's life, can do no more than wrap him finally in death and dishonor. Mr. Fitzgerald finally maintains, besides his hard, sardonic realism, the necessary emotional intensity, but we must admit that it needs perhaps an excess of intensity to buoy up the really very unpleasant characters of this story.

F. Scott Fitzgerald: *The Great Gatsby*. (Reprinted from *The Times Literary Supplement* of February 18, 1926.)

AN AMERICAN TRAGEDY

THEODORE DREISER'S is an interesting case. He has written half a dozen very, very long novels, all of which have been highly praised by American critics. Until the publication of his most recent book, however, he was not widely read. It is not difficult to account for popular indifference to his work. He is without pretence of any kind, and he builds in a tremendously solid fashion; but his buildings are unlovely. No novelist has greater scorn for appearances and the arts of attraction. Mr. Dreiser has imagination and refinement in plenty, but his manner of saying what he wants to say can be as uncouth, as slipshod and bungling as the ramblings of an illiterate person. In short, for all his sincerity and power of analysis, he is hard to read. Now published as the first volume in an English uniform edition of his novels, *An American Tragedy* is the novel that has won remarkable favor with the reading public in America during the last few months. Why it should have made a greater appeal than *The Financier, The Genius,* or the comparatively short *Jennie Gerhardt* we cannot tell, unless it is simply that it contains elements of sensationalism flattering to public taste at the moment. At any rate, it has the same trying qualities as the rest of Mr. Dreiser's fiction. But it also has in a marked degree his sprawling strength.

That strength—of observation and of purpose—allows us to overlook many faults in him. *An American Tragedy* is a whale of a novel—there are more than 800 pages of close print in the book. Roughly speaking, its theme is the interaction of a religious and an industrial environment on character. When we are first introduced to Clyde Griffiths he is a boy of twelve, living with his parents in Kansas City. His father is a feckless itinerant preacher who compels his children to help him with his missionary labors. Clyde feels no religious emotion, is bored by having to sing hymns at street corners, and grows ashamed of his social inferiority and devoted to material things. At the first opportunity he gets a job at a cheap drugstore, eventually exchanging the work of an assistant to a soda water clerk for that of a bellhop at a large, dubious hotel. An ambitious, selfish, but moderately decent boy, he enjoys the use of money, kisses several girls, and entertains hopes of prosperity. A tragic escapade in the company of friends hurries him off to Chicago, where he again finds employment as a bellhop and again takes to kissing girls. At twenty or so he meets an uncle who has a shirt and collar factory in Lycurgus. He gets a job in the factory, makes full use of his ambiguous position, gets liked for his good looks, and begins to cherish the usual social ambitions. He falls in love with Roberta, a factory girl, and seduces her. But the high-stepping Sondra Finchley attracts his attention, and he falls for her. When Roberta tells him she is going to have a baby his longing for fortune and high society receives a shock. Threatened with her pitiful entreaties, afraid of being exposed and of losing his golden opportunity, and burying his head in Sondra's trailing cloud, he plays with the desperate thought of murdering Roberta. The planning of the murder inevitably brings Raskolnikov to one's mind. Mr. Dreiser undoubtedly makes a tense dramatic business of Clyde's probings and tortured vacillations, but he can put nothing heroic into his hero's desire to save his skin. Roberta dies by drowning; but, although Clyde has decided on the murder, it is by an accident that the boat capsizes. The trial follows. Mr. Dreiser describes it all in enormous detail. Then the execution. We are spared nothing. Mr. Dreiser makes it clear that the lights go out in the prison "as an idiotic or thoughtless result of having one electric system to supply the death voltage and the incandescence." And finally we get a brief picture of the Griffiths family in San Francisco. On the windows of the Mission Hall are written "God is Love" and "How Long Since You Wrote to Mother?"

It is a strange book, painstaking, honest, full of pity for human weaknesses, thoughtful, and moving—and awkward. When Mr. Dreiser writes, for instance, of the "anomalies of psychic and social reflex and motivation" he inspires little attention. But

the things like Clyde's aching curiosity about the dreadful little
Hortense, his ingenuous adoration of Sondra's cocksureness, his
queer humility and distrust of himself, his very zest for living—
these, however badly expressed, are real and disturbing. And their
cumulative effect does a great deal to justify Mr. Dreiser's plodding, graceless manner.

THEODORE DREISER: *An American Tragedy*. (Reprinted from
The Times Literary Supplement of October 7, 1926.)

MANHATTAN TRANSFER

ONE OF the most significant remarks made in John Dos Passos's
novel *Manhattan Transfer* is the reply of the philandering lawyer,
George Baldwin, to the question why he didn't go into politics:

> Why should I go up to Washington into that greasy backwater
> when I'm right on the spot where they give the orders? The terrible
> thing about having New York go stale on you is that there's nowhere
> else. It's the top of the world. All we can do is go round and round
> in a squirrel cage.

Really to understand this novel—whose title, being interpreted,
means "Manhattan Junction"—and a good deal of modern American fiction, it is probably necessary to take this estimate of New
York quite seriously as an opinion and even as a fact. New York
is the top of the world: the rest of America is only a stage toward it, and Europe is no more than an excursion ground easily
reached and quickly left. Mr. Dos Passos himself, we imagine,
records this view with complete disillusionment but without satire.
Jimmy Herf, the young reporter who represents the most negative attitude in the novel, crosses in the ferry at the close and
sets out vaguely westwards with three cents in his pocket, not
in angry rebellion but because he cannot go the pace. As he says
to the self-made French bootlegger millionaire, "You're going up

in the social scale, Armand, and I'm going down." Even without much personal experience of it, he gets no sensation out of the delusion of power, "the grand Babylonian stuff"; he has not even enough conviction to make a successful drunkard, so he drifts out of the story, and we should very much like to know whither. That, however, the author is not concerned to tell us: he confines himself to giving us a peep show of the "top of the world" from the days of the Russo-Japanese War to the present.

The picture is drawn in fragments, without connections or relations. Innumerable characters appear, of whom some recur and some vanish into the void; but throughout there is the sense of noise, particularly the noise of fire engines, of feverish haste, of imperious desire to be satisfied at almost any risk, of crowds and heat and an impossibility of standing still, much less of standing aloof. In this welter of blind energies men and women, like electrons, career and clash together and part again, falling and rising as far and as swiftly as the express elevators in the great buildings. For a moment, or moments, all the faces are vivid—they flash before our eyes in a kaleidoscope of motors, cars, offices, apartments, restaurants, beds, "lunches," bars, and hotels. Nothing stands still for a moment, nothing is final, nothing directive, nothing supremely important. No doubt the reader who knows New York has a great advantage over one who does not; but even that knowledge could hardly supply a corrective to this vivid and masterly impression of chaos.

JOHN DOS PASSOS: *Manhattan Transfer*. (Reprinted from *The Times Literary Supplement* of February 3, 1927.)

THE POEMS OF EZRA POUND

AT FIRST sight Ezra Pound gives the impression of a very literary poet. A large proportion of the work in this volume consists of translations or paraphrases from the Chinese, Greek, Latin, Provençal, Italian, German, and French. "Allusions," in the eighteenth-century sense, seems a more appropriate title than "Personæ," since only a few of these poems are dramatic monologues in the manner of Browning. Mr. Pound seems to have skimmed through half the poetical literature of the world and comes before us laden with strange and disparate spoil, like one of the barbarian conquerors returning from the sack of Imperial Rome. This does not mean that these poems have only a rhetorical value— that of redressing old themes in a garb of eccentrically new cut —because they often possess subtle beauty and quaint energy. It is not hard to produce examples of crudity and uncertain taste from these poems, but it is also easy to produce examples of delicate emotion and poetic felicity.

In his earlier poems Mr. Pound was a devotee of Romance, refining upon the already overrefined poets of Provence and Trecento Italy. His early diction is as romantic as his themes, and the abrupt, realistic mannerisms of Browning jostle oddly these memories of the Celtic twilight and ladies of Provence. Adventures among the classics and Renaissance poetry then apparently claimed this poet, and more perfect models of style produced happy effects. There is great purity of feeling and a rather beautiful rhythm in this little sentimental piece:

> The broken sunlight for a helm she beareth
> Who hath my heart in jurisdiction.
> In wildwood never fawn nor fallow fareth
> So silent light; no gossamer is spun
> So delicate as she is, when the sun
> Drives the clear emeralds from the bended grasses
> Lest they should parch too swiftly, where she passes.

Du Bellay, Leopardi, and Heine in turn were levied upon, and from these adaptations from Heine dates Mr. Pound's effort, seldom wholly successful, to introduce satire and irony into his work. Yet these translations certainly suggest that Heine wrote poetry, and not sentimental doggerel, as one gathers from most of his English translators. "Au Jardin" is one of his happiest efforts

in the Romantic mood treated in the manner of Browning. The
section headed "Ripostes" is a curious farrago of ancient and
modern, mysticism and realism, as if the poet were fumbling for
new themes. Yet this contains two of Mr. Pound's finest short
poems, as well as the daring "allusion" to the Anglo-Saxon "Sea-
farer," which may or may not depart from the text, but is undoubtedly spirited and energetic. A new, rather austere, but wholly
admirable dignity appears in the little poem called "Doria," which
is like a modern re-creation of an epigram from the Greek Anthology:

> Be in me as the eternal moods
>   of the bleak wind, and not
> As transient things are—
>   gaiety of flowers.
> Have me in the strong loneliness
>   of sunless cliffs
> And of gray waters.
>   Let the gods speak softly of us
> In days hereafter,
>   The shadowy flowers of Orcus
> Remember thee.

The same economy of phrase and curious, rare beauty of rhythm
is to be found in "The Return," while in "Apparuit" we have an
interesting attempt to reproduce in English the movement of sap-
phics:

> Crimson, frosty with dew, the roses bend where
> Thou afar, moving in the glamorous sun,
> Drinkst in life of earth, of the air, the tissue golden about thee.

The poems so far examined occupy fewer than eighty of the
230 pages in this book, and from this point onward there is a
very considerable change in Mr. Pound's manner. Reacting rather
violently from the Romantic delicacy of his earlier manner, he
made truculent efforts to be "modern," and the change was not
always happy.

From distant Cathay Mr. Pound now returned to the more familiar fields of Provence, with a brief excursion into the Greek Anthology and a still briefer visit to Ferney, where three of Voltaire's poems were paraphrased. Yet once again Mr. Pound showed his talent for writing "allusions" by his original reworking of Propertius. Willful anachronisms and not always willful misreadings of the text should not blind the reader to the curious felicities and quaint energy of these Propertius poems. While they must shock the classical scholar, they are a spirited effort to bring a Roman poet up to date and in harmony with transatlantic manners. And in the Envoi (1919), built upon a hint from Waller, Mr. Pound once more huddles on his singing robes and takes his leave with a beautiful stanza, just to show that he can do it when he chooses:

> Tell her that goes
> With song upon her lips
> But sings not out the song, nor knows
> The maker of it, some other mouth
> May be as fair as hers,
> Might, in new ages, gain her worshipers,
> When our two dusts with Waller's shall be laid,
> Siftings on siftings in oblivion,
> Till change hath broken down
> All things save Beauty alone.

Personæ: The Collected Poems of Ezra Pound. (Reprinted from *The Times Literary Supplement* of January 5, 1928.)

DODSWORTH

THE HERO of Sinclair Lewis's new novel, *Dodsworth,* was, at fifty years old, president of the Revelation Motor Company, which was about to be swallowed up by the Unit Automotive Company. Moreover, "he was none of the things which most Europeans and many Americans expect in a leader of American industry. He was not a Babbitt, not a Rotarian, not an Elk, not a deacon. . . .

He was common sense apotheosized," whatever this last phrase
may mean. As a creator of motor cars he was something of a
dreamer, but the merger of his company was going to cut that
particular dream short. His wife Fran suggested a voyage to Europe before any further decisions were made. A little doubting,
Sam Dodsworth agreed. And what happened to Sam and Fran in
Europe is the subject of this book.

The adventure was a revelation and, in some senses, a disaster. Husband and wife went in different spirits. Sam Dodsworth,
though he had romantic ideas of foreign scenes, meant only to
wander around a few months. He was "going on doing something
in life," and his place was in Zenith. Fran, having brought up
two children and been for twenty years the model wife of an
American business man, wished to cut free of everything, to go
to Europe without any responsibility for coming back, to begin,
at forty, a new life among interesting people. Trouble begins on
the ship and continues rhythmically throughout. Fran attracts men
and despises her husband. She plays the coquette, the snob, and
the spoiled darling tied to a dull boor, on the Atlantic, in London, in Paris, and in Berlin. At every rebuff due to her own fool-
ishness, she comes crying like a child to be comforted by the
long-suffering Sam.

Sinclair Lewis never drew characters better than he draws these
two. Sam Dodsworth, honest to the core, completely lost in the
alien world and values of Europe, yet striving to assimilate them
and, in the end, coming to terms with them, while understanding
life more deeply than he did before, is in every way but in surface quickness superior to his wife; but, as a study of a selfish,
conceited, superficial woman, completely contented by masculine
flattery, the easy prey of philanderers and adventurers, Fran is
admirable. Apart from these two admirable portraits, the reader
will find a great deal of interest and of color in the author's picture of the European scene, especially in the occasional halts for
a long monologue such as the excursus on Paris, Professor Braut's
speech on the essence of "Europe," and Ross Ireland's vigorous
denunciation of New York on the occasion when Sam and he

went back there, with disappointing results, for an interlude. In fine, Mr. Lewis predicts a great deal of humiliation, instruction and discomfort for those of his countrymen who think of traveling in middle age. In spite of a certain monotony of structure and the usual excess of detail, this novel shows the author's brilliant descriptive powers and his indignation at their height; but it is hardly safe reading for self-satisfied Europeans.

SINCLAIR LEWIS: *Dodsworth*. (Reprinted from *The Times Literary Supplement* of March 28, 1929.)

A FAREWELL TO ARMS

ERNEST HEMINGWAY'S *A Farewell to Arms* is a novel of great power. Though it adds one to the now many novels of war, it is unlike any other, for Mr. Hemingway's method and outlook are entirely his own. Though his mental processes, his language, and his subject matter are not what we in England should call "typically American," he is one of the few writers in the English language who are distinctively and absolutely American. To everything British he is foreign, and the British, though he likes them, are foreign to him. Nobody but an American could have his staccato style, his particular turn of dialogue, his power of rejecting everything that is extraneous to his keen but selective vision, his dismal animation, his unrationalized pessimism. It is always the same mind, the same man—one who finds no comfort but in vivid circumstance and pleasure of the senses—who tells the story: he tells it to himself, either in long passages of terse dialogue or in direct reflections of his own retina, hardly ever stopping to register a mental comment.

Here, at all events, he has found a theme more suited to him than any before. The events—ambulance work on the Isonzo, the bursting of a trench mortar shell in a dugout, a wound, hospital in Milan, return to the front, the great retreat after Caporetto, escape from shooting by the "Battle Police" at the Tagliamento, and a further escape at night in a boat from Stresa over the Swiss frontier—are episodes in a world agony, not merely the adventures of Bohemians; the characters depicted, with a masterly handling of dialogue (particularly the Italian surgeon Rinaldi), are more interesting than the drunkards of *Fiesta;* the love of Henry and Catherine Barkle, the English nurse, is rendered with an extraordinarily intense simplicity; and the peculiar hopelessness of Mr. Hemingway's humor finds an ideal scope in the contrasts and contradictions of war. The actual scenes of war are biting and brilliant: they are so vivid and yet effortless that it is hard to believe one is reading fiction. Mr. Hemingway's description of the retreating army—the blocking of the roads, the effort of the American Lieutenant Henry and his three mechanics to get a motor ambulance along, their failure when it is bogged in the mud, their flight on foot, the lost morale of the stragglers, the ruthless shooting of senior officers as they are singled out from the ruck crossing the Tagliamento, the American's plunge into the river, and his journey in a gun truck to Milan—has a note of complete authenticity and singularly corroborates a similar description in Riccardo Bacchelli's novel *La Città degli amanti.* Yet in these nearly identical descriptions there is an abyss between the two mentalities. The American, completely disillusioned, understands both the patriotism of an Italian officer and the innate opposition to war of an Italian soldier. The undisciplined talk of Henry's drivers is as masterly as that which reveals the Southern skepticism of Rinaldi, the faith of the chaplain, or the patriotism of his comrade Gino. Yet, while he understands, he accepts nothing. His only comments are to the effect that any glorification of life is false.

So drink deep and go a-whoring while you may, is the very plainly illustrated motto, and love truly, as Henry and Catherine loved, if you can; but the world will get you in the end, as it got Catherine, who died in childbirth with her child on a rainy night at Lausanne, leaving Henry with nothing. The frankly sensual love relation between Henry and Catherine is remarkable, not for any loftiness, but for its beautiful precision. Catherine is a stupid girl, with nothing but love and great courage to recommend her. Henry made love to her at first as a game, but when he came back wounded to Milan he fell passionately in love. In the simple, almost foolish exchanges of their conversation is built up a picture of a union that transcended difference, of a Phoenix and Turtle on the fleshly plane. The view of Catherine is purely a man's view, but as such it is unfalteringly delineated. After their happy days in Switzerland the end is unbelievably painful, for no horror of that tragic maternity is left to the imagination. And with that death and Henry walking back to the hotel in the rain this gripping story ends abruptly, leaving all its pain raw. Mr. Hemingway's pessimism is his own affair: we can only recognize that it animates an extremely talented and original artist.

ERNEST HEMINGWAY: *A Farewell to Arms.* (Reprinted from *The Times Literary Supplement* of November 28, 1929.)

SOLDIER'S PAY

WE MUST pay tribute to an English publisher's enterprise in introducing the work of a young American novelist who, as Richard Hughes says in his preface, is "not only unknown in England but practically unknown in America, also. . . . He is a Southerner from Mississippi; and young, prolific and unsuccessful." William Faulkner, author of *Soldier's Pay*—a tragedy of soldiers returned from the War—has a fertile invention, a power of illustrating and differentiating character, a force in depicting both tragic and comic incident, and a nostalgic sense of the poetry that can suffuse even so crude and fleshly a scene as he presents here in Charlestown, Georgia. This sense and what it suffuses may well be illustrated from the last lines of the novel, where two stricken but resigned men—the old rector who has buried his son and Joe Gilligan, who has not gained the love he waited for so patiently—stand listening to the singing in a Negro church:

Feed Thy Sheep, O Jesus. The voices rose full and soft. There was no organ: no organ was needed, as above the harmonic passion of bass and baritone soared a clear soprano of women's voices like a flight of gold and heavenly birds. They stood together in the dust, the rector in his shapeless black, and Gilligan in his new hard serge, listening, seeing the shabby church become beautiful with mellow longing, passionate and sad. Then the singing died, fading away along the mooned land inevitable with tomorrow and sweat, with sex and death and damnation; and they turned townward under the moon, feeling dust in their shoes.

Comparing this passage with the brilliant opening scene of drunken soldiers going South in a Pullman car, with the incursions into the story of the lustful satyr Januarius Jones, the sick ravings of George Farr after the body of the virgin who had willed him to seduce her, and the admirable scene of the dance that Mr. Hughes rightly compares to the last act of *The Silver Tassie,* one sees why Mr. Faulkner so heavily stresses the "sweat, with sex and death and damnation" that, to our mind, overburden his story.

This, in its main outlines, tells how the resourceful Joe Gilligan, a homeless common man with a heart of gold, Julian Lowe, a young air cadet who had had no time to win his wings, and Margaret Powers, young war widow, are brought together in the train by the helplessness of a countryman, Donald Mahon, an ex-officer in the British Air Force, who has been discharged from hospital with a lost memory, a hopelessly stricken body, and a hideous scar on his forehead. The hearts of both Gilligan and Margaret have been drained of so much in the war years that a passionate protection of the helpless one is the highest emotion they can rise to. Julian Lowe, being but a boy with an unspoiled heart, is quickly sent home to his mother by Margaret, and the story is punctuated by his pathetic letters from San Francisco assuring her that he is waiting to make a home and marry her. Meanwhile, Joe and Margaret carry the helpless, almost blind Donald to the small, sleepy Charlestown where an amiably philosophic rector is cherishing the memory of a beloved son, presumed dead, and the flighty sensual Cecily Saunders, Donald's fiancée, is already carrying on with another.

The characters pursue or flee from one another in a farandole of desire or repulsion, with the unspeakable Jones preying on them all. Crude desires, simple passions, loyalties, and hatreds, and harsh ironies dominate the dance, sometimes expressed in choric interlude from the hidden voices in the hearts. Death and departure end the turmoil; and Joe Gilligan, whose Margaret's heart had been too dead to take him in, is left learning from the rector that truth is unbearable, yet time steals even agony away. There is much ugliness as well as much beauty in this book.

WILLIAM FAULKNER: *Soldier's Pay*. (Reprinted from
The Times Literary Supplement of July 3, 1930.)

LOOK HOMEWARD, ANGEL

THOMAS WOLFE'S novel *Look Homeward, Angel* was obviously written as the result of tremendous internal pressure. It is a first novel and very long, following a boy's emergence from childhood and imprisonment in the bosom of an extraordinary family to manhood and independence. Such odysseys of youth are not uncommon; and by this time the crudities of the American scene are so familiar that the strange squalid-extravagant life of the Gant family in the hill town of Altamont, here described in profuse detail, will hold no particular surprise; what is amazing is the pressure under which this narrative is shot forth. To use a homely American metaphor, it might be called a "gusher"; for Mr. Wolfe's words come spouting up with all the force of a subterranean flood now at last breaking through the overlying strata of repression. Such native force is rare in England now; and it is impossible to regard this unstinting output of magnificent raw vigor without a thrill and a hope that it will be channeled to great art. The present book is not great art; but its promise and its power are so extraordinary that we dwell upon them rather than upon the details of its story.

Whether or no the family life of the Gants—the Bacchic flaming father everlastingly at odds with the tight-lipped avaricious mother nursing her secret pain in dumbness, the worthless Steve, the thwarted secretive Ben, the cheery go-getter Luke, and the passionately serving Helen—was Mr. Wolfe's own or no, there can be no doubt that he is Eugene, the last born, who saw the light while Gant the father was booming eloquent curses outside the bedroom door, and who grew up with the taints of the Gant and the Pentland blood in his body, in his soul the sensuality, the aimlessness of his mother's family, and the ache for wandering, the almost demoniac power of fantasy, and the sense of being a stranger in an alien world that stamped his drunken but gigantically molded father. It is the story of a boy's escape from a thralldom to which his own nature as much as circumstances subjected him. His mother's avarice, it is true, keeps him in the low boarding house that she, though rich in real property, keeps penuriously, forces him to sell newspapers at dawn before going to school, cuts short his school days, and sends him to the state university too soon. But it is the influence of the blood that makes him return again and again willingly to that home of strife and discomfort, bound together by its very hatreds, until its fibers are at last rent apart by the death from pneumonia of Ben—a passage of remarkable power—while Gant curses, Eliza purses her tight lips, and the others wrangle hideously around the dying man. The words of Ben's last moment give a measure of Mr. Wolfe's power over words when shaken, as he is often shaken, by a spasm of emotion:

Suddenly, marvellously, as if his resurrection and rebirth had come upon him, Ben drew upon the air in a long and powerful respiration; his gray eyes opened. Filled with a terrible vision of all life in the one moment, he seemed to rise forward bodilessly from his pillows without support—a flame, a light, a glory—joined at length in death to the dark spirit who had brooded upon each footstep of his lonely adventure on earth; and, casting the fierce sword of his glance with utter and final comprehension upon the room haunted with its gray pageantry of cheap loves and dull consciences and on all those uncertain mummers of waste and confusion fading now from the bright window of his eyes, he passed instantly, scornful and unafraid, as he had lived, into the shades of death.

This is not merely an eloquent passage, it is summary and judgment of what has been fairly set out with intense vividness before.

This intensity of apprehension, whether sensuous or imaginative, is Eugene's mark in the novel, as it is Mr. Wolfe's in the performance. We do not need the catalogues, remarkable in themselves, of the books on which Eugene fed his voracious fancy or the rich foods on which the elder Gant, in the great days, gorged his sons and daughters; Mr. Wolfe reveals himself as one who has fed upon honeydew and everything else under the sun. And his most astonishing passages, crammed though they are with the clangorous echoes of English poetry and prose, too often falling into sheer meter, come when, in contemplation of his past, he sends out a cry of lyrical agony for lost beauty. One might take to pieces the paragraph on spring that begins: "Yes, and in that month when Proserpine comes back and Ceres' dead heart rekindles, when all the woods are a tender smoky blur, and birds no bigger than a budding leaf dart through the singing trees"; or that other beginning: "In the cruel volcano of the boy's mind, the little brier moths of his idolatry wavered in to their strange marriage and were consumed"; one might trace the echoes and point out the faults, but the Marlowesque energy and beauty of them has already made such work vain. What is going to be done with this great talent, so hard, so sensual, so unsentimental, so easily comprehending and describing every sordidness of the flesh and spirit, so proudly rising to the heights? Knowing the times and the temptations of the times, we may well watch its fresh emergence with anxiety: for if Mr. Wolfe can be wasted, there is no hope for today.

THOMAS WOLFE: *Look Homeward, Angel.* (Reprinted from
The Times Literary Supplement of July 24, 1930.)

ROBERT FROST'S POEMS

IT IS some fifteen years since Mr. Frost's first book of poems, *A Boy's Will,* was published, but this volume represents considerably more than the labor of fifteen years, for Mr. Frost had to wait as many years for recognition. Even then it was left to England to recognize this very American poet. He came to that country in 1912, when he was thirty-seven, and soon found a publisher for his first and second books. When he returned to America in 1915 his literary reputation was already established in both countries.

Considering the length of time Mr. Frost must have had in which to shape his talent and select from his output, it is not surprising that his early work shows little of the hesitances of immaturity. In *A Boy's Will* that whimsical humor that is to become so dominant in his later work is not yet evident, and there is an exuberance—as in the lines "To the Thawing Wind" and "A Line Storm Song"—that is soon to disappear; but the author of "Mowing" and "October" is already confident of his direction and speaking with his own voice. The idiom of careful simplicity foreshadowed in *A Boy's Will* is fully developed in his second book, *North of Boston,* along with most of the qualities by which we recognize his poetry. The long, unrhymed monologues and dialogues that form the bulk of this book, as of Mr. Frost's work as a whole, are written throughout in the colloquial language and manner of casual conversation. It is Mr. Frost's peculiar talent to give to his most delicate utterance the air of a chance remark, never to stress in his verse a note that would not be stressed in the context of ordinary speech. Such a diction has dangers and disadvantages that Mr. Frost has not been able entirely to escape. In the shorter lyrical poems the narrowness of compass and restriction of rhyme serve to keep a balance between economy and Mr. Frost's natural discursiveness; but the balance is often lost in the longer poems, at the risk of tedium. The characters in the dialogues speak so unvaryingly with Mr. Frost's voice and accent, with such a flat, circumlocutory sameness, that the subtlety of his psychological delineation cannot always save them from monotony. Here and there, too, his simplicity defeats itself and obscures his meaning; such a passage as this from "Maple," though the subject is admittedly involved, needs to be more carefully unraveled than we feel should be necessary:

> It was as personal as he could be
> About the way he saw it was with you
> To say your mother, had she lived, would be
> As far again as from being born to bearing.

But at his best, in the short lyrics, his writing has an exquisite ease; the lines come as easily as one speaks, and the beauty that takes shape in them is all the more arresting for its fortuitous air. Consider, for example, the unassuming loveliness of the line that concludes "Our Singing Strength," a poem that describes how the birds in spring were driven by snow from the trees and fields to gather in the road. We quote the ending:

> Well, something for a snowstorm to have shown
> The country's singing strength thus brought together,
> That though repressed and moody with the weather
> Was none the less there ready to be freed
> And sing the wildflowers up from root and seed.

Mr. Frost is essentially a poet of nature; one feels that urban life is beyond the range of his interest or comprehension. The people in his poems, the country people of New England, live close to the earth, close enough to dread the menace of winter, to welcome the spring with more than poetic gladness. And Mr. Frost looks at Nature with the understanding of the farmer as well as the insight of the poet. As he bids good-by to the orchard in "Good-By and Keep Cold" his affection is quickened by the knowledge

> of all that can happen to harm
> An orchard away at the end of the farm
> All winter, cut off by a hill from the house.
> . . . No orchard's the worse for the wintriest storm;
> But one thing about it, it mustn't get warm.
> "How often already you've had to be told,
> Keep cold, young orchard. Good-by and keep cold. . . ."

And only one who is intimate with country things could tell with such tender precision how

> just as the soil tarnishes with weed,
> The sturdy seedling with arched body comes
> Shouldering its way and shedding the earth crumbs.

Mr. Frost's is always a quiet voice. One is aware of his emotional responses more by implication than by his admission. We have mentioned the lack of exuberance in his mature work; but though his reticence of feeling gives a certain air of moroseness to his poetry it is, we think, due less to the pessimism that has sometimes been ascribed to him than to his scrupulous refusal to falsify or poeticize the essential quality of what has moved him, his reluctance to testify to "anything more than the truth." And if there is a gesture of resignation in his attitude toward life, there is still an earnest faith in its courage and ability to endure—all that is implied in the assurance

> that winter death has never tried
> The earth but it has failed,

and a faith in the simple self-sufficiency of love that remains true to the youthful affirmations of *A Boy's Will,* achieving with maturity a more perfect expression:

> On snow and sand and turf, I see
> Where Love has left a printed trace
> With straining in the world's embrace.
> And such is Love and glad to be.

It is his ability to see that "printed trace" of love on the world about him that gives Mr. Frost's subdued utterance an inward

380 OPINIONS AT THE TIME

warmth and radiance that are rare enough in poetry today. His field of vision is perhaps limited, but within it his perception is penetratingly keen.

> *Collected Poems of Robert Frost*. (Reprinted from *The Times Literary Supplement* of January 29, 1931.)

LINCOLN STEFFENS

THE NAME of Lincoln Steffens is nothing like so well known in England as it deserves to be. American journalism has had in our time no representative of whom it has better reason to be proud. He is fond of describing himself as a "reporter," but he has really been a great deal more than that. He is by temperament a philosopher; and it has been largely because he has attempted to think out the problems of the day and to relate them to the history of the past that his dealing with contemporary affairs has amounted to so much more than a mere register of the events of his own time. His mastery of a vivid style, his keenness of observation, his courage in situations involving no little danger to reputation and even to life, and his determination not to be content until he has discovered the essential facts, whatever havoc they may make of his own or anyone else's preconceived theories, are qualities that have combined to make him one of the outstanding figures of his profession. He can now look back upon a journalistic career of nearly forty years, and his chronicle of it makes fascinating and stimulating reading. It would be hard to find a more useful book to put into the hands of a novice whom one wished to encourage to steer a straight course amid the many and subtle temptations that beset the writer for the press. Mr. Steffens will show him how it is possible to preserve youthful ideals and yet make one's influence effectively and even powerfully felt upon the life of one's time.

Perhaps the most conspicuous service Mr. Steffens has rendered to modern America has been his work in exposing the true nature and causes of political and civic corruption in the country. His interest in the subject was aroused early in the nineties, when, as a *New York Evening Post* reporter at police headquarters, he covered the successive stages of Dr. C. H. Parkhurst's crusade against Tammany. "What reporters know and don't report," he tells us, "is news—not from the newspapers' point of view, but from the sociologists'." The insight that he thus obtained into the practices of the underworld was of great value to him a few years later when, on behalf of *McClure's Magazine,* he undertook that investigation of municipal corruption in St. Louis, Minneapolis, Pittsburgh, Philadelphia, and New York, the results of which were subsequently published in *The Shame of the Cities.* That book, one regrets to learn, is now out of print, but it is one of the classics of American political literature. Most of the bosses and boodle politicians whose misdeeds Mr. Steffens exposed are now dead; but though the individuals immediately concerned may have passed away, the vile thing they exemplified still remains. And it remains the same. To understand how it has come about that gangsters and racketeers flourish today one cannot do better than study Mr. Steffens's account of the discoveries that he made nearly thirty years ago. *The Shame of the Cities* is the complete handbook, but the chapters on the subject in this autobiography are enough to provide all that it is really necessary to know. Its author's insistence on the responsibility of respectable business for the immunity of vice and crime is particularly relevant to present conditions; and in many other respects his revelations of 1902 and 1903 illuminate the civic scene of 1930 and 1931.

This investigation was only one of many phases of a career so diversified that its record will appeal to a great variety of readers. The psychologists of childhood will find useful material in the story of Mr. Steffens's early days on the Pacific coast. Educationists will be interested in his account of his life as a student, first at the University of California and afterwards at Berlin and Heidelberg, as well as in his frank comparisons between the academic methods of America and Europe. As a portrait gallery, too, this volume possesses exceptional merit. There are excellent character sketches of S. S. McClure, Judge Lindsey, the late Joseph Fels, E. A. Filene, Clarence Darrow, Senator Robert La Follette, and many other distinguished Americans with whom Mr. Steffens has at one time or another come in contact. Theodore Roosevelt, in particular, is depicted here to the life, from the time of his appointment as Police Commissioner of New York to his Presidency.

Not the least valuable section of the book is its account of the Paris Conference, on which it throws much new light, especially by its acute study of the mind and policies of Woodrow Wilson. According to Mr. Steffens, the President's instruction that his ship, the *George Washington,* should be made ready to take him home was by no means "bluff." He was deliberately intending by that means to arouse the public opinion of Europe to overthrow the ministries that were thwarting him; and he held fast to his purpose until he was assured by the British and the French that such action would not only cause the downfall of ministries but would also precipitate revolutions in all the Allied countries. While the peace negotiations were still in progress Mr. Steffens left Paris for a time in order to accompany W. C. Bullitt on his mission to Russia, and his narrative of that remarkable expedition will afford useful material to the future historian. His penetrating analysis of the character and ambitions of Mussolini, based on an unusually frank interview, will also repay the attention of everyone interested in the problems of contemporary Europe.

The Autobiography of Lincoln Steffens. (Reprinted from
The Times Literary Supplement of August 13, 1931.)

MAN AND THE MACHINE

THE MORE Mr. Mumford's nearly 500 large pages are reflected upon and assimilated, the more satisfyingly definitive appears his

title. It is simple, but it is precise. Technics *and* Civilization, the
total fact of the machine in its relation to total human living, social and individual—Mr. Mumford's subject is exactly that, no
more and no less. This totality of reference demands to be emphasized; it is one of the qualities, perhaps the most essential of
all, that make this work so immediately impressive and, we would
believe, so durably valuable. Mr. Mumford is a man of many
parts, well known as author of books on utopias, architecture,
American literary culture, and Herman Melville, and also lecturer
on sociology at Columbia University (and at one time editor of
the London *Sociological Review*), and for many years student of
technics and economics. He would, therefore, seem to come to
his subject, and proves himself, exceptionally well equipped, a
stranger in neither of the fields he purposes to regard together
and ultimately to unify.

He opens his study with a series of questions that it is his intention to answer in his succeeding chapters:

> During the last thousand years the material basis and the cultural
> forms of Western Civilization have been profoundly modified by
> the development of the machine. How did this come about? Where
> did it take place? What were the chief motives that encouraged this
> radical transformation of the environment and routine of life:
> what were the ends in view: what were the means and methods:
> what unexpected values have arisen in the process?

A new world has been brought into existence, but gains on one
hand have been offset by an indubitable impoverishment of life
in some respects on the other. "What has limited the beneficence
of the machine? Under what conditions may the machine be directed towards a fuller use and accomplishment?" Given that fuller
use, what would be the characteristic properties of the new order
which would emerge—

> its pattern, its planes, its angle of polarization, its color? Can one,
> in the process of crystallization, remove the turbid residues left
> behind by our earlier forms of technology? Can one distinguish
> and define the specific properties of a technics directed towards the

service of life: properties that distinguish it morally, socially, politically, esthetically from the cruder forms that preceded it?

Scarcely one of these questions is to be answered in terms of
a merely superficial survey. The issues are at bottom psychological. The machine in itself is nothing. It "makes no demands and
holds out no promises: it is the human spirit that makes demands
and keeps promises." The machine, Mr. Mumford further asserts,
could never have taken possession of European society had not
that society "by an inner accommodation" already surrendered itself. The book, consequently, falls into three distinct though in-
divisible parts. The first consists of an account of the development
during the later Middle Ages of an ideology making for that essential submission; the second describes at length each of the three
phases—Eotechnic, Paleotechnic, Neotechnic—into which he divides the machine's history; the third analyzes psychological attitudes to the machine, both actual and ideal, reactionary and creative.

For the first he looks back the better part of a thousand years,
to the dominant figures of that day, the monk in his monastery
routine embodying the will to order (and evoking the clock, which
Mr. Mumford terms "the key machine of the modern industrial
age"), the soldier taking his loot wherever he might find it, irrespectively of human cost, embodying the will to power. These,
it is asserted, but with much though always succinct elaboration
of the theme, are the two prime elements of the machine as we
know it to this day, growing and gathering influence throughout
the long seven centuries of the Dawn Age of modern technical
civilization, a period in Mr. Mumford's view one of the most brilliant in history, in which culture and technics were still in "relative harmony," in which, though "the rift between mechanization
and humanization" was already appearing, its consequences had
still to develop.

Only in the subsequent paleotechnic phase—from the mid-
eighteenth century forward—were the full depths of degradation
opened, when for the earlier wind and water power sources, oper-

ating upon mainly wooden constructions, was substituted a new "technological complex" of coal and iron. Both are essentially mine products, and from the mid-eighteenth century forward, suggests Mr. Mumford,

> the animus of mining affected the entire economic and social organism: this dominant mode of exploitation became the pattern for subordinate forms of industry. The reckless, get-rich-quick, devil-take-the-hindermost attitude of the mining rushes spread everywhere: the bonanza farms of the Middle West in the United States were exploited as if they were mines, and the forests were gutted out and mined in the same fashion as the minerals that lay in their hills. Mankind behaved like a drunken heir on a spree. And the damage to form and civilization through the prevalence of these new habits of disorderly exploitation and wasteful expenditure remained, whether or not the source of energy itself disappeared. The psychological results of carboniferous capitalism— the lowered morale, the expectation of getting something for nothing, the disregard for a balanced mode of production and consumption, the habituation to wreckage and debris as part of the normal human environment—all these results were plainly mischievous.

The passage is worth quoting as extremely typical alike in its suggestive generalization, its breadth of reference, its vividness of imagery, and its freshness of writing. But it should also be said that neither it nor any other such passage is allowed to stand unsupported. The account of each one of these three main phases is historical as well as critical, descriptive as well as analytic. To take that on the paleotechnic period as example, it opens with an account of the causes of England's leadership in industrial development, describes the consequences to society in terms of the lives of the workers, glances at the story of coal mining, and in greater detail at that of the steam engine, evidences the degree to which iron and coal (even to their very colors!) dominated the period, records the ruthless pollution of human environment and how, in such conditions, the worker, treated "solely as a means to cheaper mechanical production," was necessarily degraded, starved of anything like a full human life; how, in effect, society as a whole was poisoned from top to bottom. This, perhaps, is half the chapter, which goes on to treat, among other matters, of the doctrines of progress and the struggle for existence as intellectual rationalizations of evils men could not deny but were unprepared to eliminate, of power in relation to efficiency, and concludes with a semistatistical summary of "mechanical triumphs" and a brief summary in which the paleotechnic phase is declared to have explored the depths of the quantitative conception of life and to have shown that "mechanical improvements alone were not sufficient to produce socially valuable results—or even the highest degree of industrial efficiency."

But it is really only with the neotechnic chapter that the book's essential theme begins to emerge. This last phase, characterized by electricity applied to lighter metals and alloys, is described as if in being, though obviously it is only potentially so. Power here is united to mobility, the machine acquires both a new sensitiveness and a faculty of adjustment to human needs. Man at last is released from servitude to that paleotechnic prototype, the mine. Only, however, on conditions—a neotechnic civilization demands a neotechnic ideology. To apply, as we do today, neotechnic means to paleotechnic ends is but to walk the road to increasing disaster of which unemployment and overproduction are but preliminary warning signs.

It is therefore to the apprehension of such an ideology that Mr. Mumford devotes his last three chapters. First he gives his attention to man's paleotechnic reactions from the machine, but finds no outlet there; they were necessary but negative. What is needed is not a negative but a positive adjustment; not a rejection but an assimilation. A new type of individuality is demanded—impersonal, objective, precise, rational, at least in its social (and mechanical) dealings; so, too, is a new form of society. "The real social distinction of modern technics is that it tends to eliminate social distinctions. Its immediate goal is effective work. Its means are standardization; the emphasis of the generic and the typical; in short, conspicuous economy. Its ultimate aim is leisure—that is, the release of other organic

capacities." The final phrase is important, a reminder that Mr.
Mumford, insisting upon acceptance of the machine, is humanist
first and last. The spirit of Ruskin's phrase, "there is no Wealth
but Life," breathes upon every page that he writes.

> LEWIS MUMFORD: *Technics and Civilization*. (Reprinted from
> *The Times Literary Supplement* of October 11, 1934.)

MARIANNE MOORE'S POEMS

"MY CONVICTION," Mr. Eliot writes in his introduction, "has remained unchanged for the last fourteen years: that Miss Moore's
Poems form part of the small body of durable poetry written in
our time; of that small body of writings, among what passes for
poetry, in which an original sensibility and alert intelligence and
deep feeling have been engaged in maintaining the life of the
English language." He mentions also that he believes her to have
derived her sense of stringency in poetical composition from the
teaching of Ezra Pound, from his "repeated reminder that poetry
should be as well written as prose."

There is, we believe, an important element common to the
attitude of all three, different as their works appear in surface
and texture; but Miss Moore is certainly the most unapproach-
able, the most solitary. Mr. Eliot does something in his introduction to provide the common reader with an approach, but is
mainly engaged in offering tribute. Also, when he comes to his
quotations he is unfortunate; first, when he quotes to illustrate
sense, in joining two half sentences that make no sense together,
and again, when he quotes to illustrate rhyme, in choosing a
passage in which rhyme has been used ambiguously. To be candid,
he does not convince us that his admiration of Miss Moore's
poetry has been based on a sufficiently exact apprehension of its
principles.

Nevertheless, the first thing to be said about Miss Moore is that she has invented a technique, and the condition of appreciating her is to recognize it. You cannot read "The Testament of Beauty" or "The Wreck of the Deutschland" unless you can scan the lines. And of course it is not enough to know the principle of the scansion. It is rather as if you had to learn to play two different instruments. For Hopkins you must be a 'cellist with easy mastery of double stopping and the swing of the bow. For Bridges you must be a pianist, but abjure all pedal. For Miss Moore bow and keyboard must alike be discarded, you must learn to pluck one string, to be satisfied with one note at a time: one might almost say, so stringent is she, to be satisfied with one and the same note always. The rigor of her demands may best be shown by presenting the reader at once with an extreme example of her practice. Here, then, is stanza five of a seven-stanza poem about Peter, a tame cat. Since it both begins and ends in the middle of a word, the quotation necessarily includes a short introduction and coda:

Springing about with froglike accuracy, emitting jerky cries when taken in the hand, he is himself again; to sit caged by the rungs of a domestic chair would be unprofitable—human. What is the good of hypocrisy? It is permissible to choose one's employment, to abandon the wirenail, the roly-poly, when it shows signs of being no longer a pleasure, &c.

The key to reading is to remember simply that every syllable counts one. The verse is an apotheosis of syllabism. Each line has its selected number of syllables—long or short, accented or unaccented, is no matter, and there are no elisions. The first line has nineteen syllables, the second nineteen, the third fourteen, the fourth nineteen, the fifth sixteen: 19, 19, 14, 19, 16; it is a most subtle system of proportions, and naturally you cannot read the poem till you can somehow find means to register these proportions in music or rhythm to the ear. Notice, furthermore, that the importance of maintaining the imposed equality, the artificial metrical equivalence, of all the syllables is thrown into high relief by a touch of hidden rhyme—a touch so fleeting that it will escape you unless you are on high *qui vive,* are walking, as it were, on hot bricks to be ready for it. The second line (with intentional or unintentional preparations) rhymes with the third; and the tonelessness of the rhyme chosen is typical and important. Other rhymes in the same poem, always linking the second line to the third, are "say, a," "very, see," "either, stir," "to, pursue." You may judge from this how delicate the balance of your attention is required to be. You could not give it if any of the echoes and decorations our ear expects in poetry were suffered to compete. The test of the technique is to eliminate them. All is withdrawn; nothing rings; your brain has become a clock in which the undifferentiated syllables tick out their taste for you like time. Notice also that the indifference of the stanza to the sense points in the same direction. Only when we come to the last word of the last stanza do the two skeins of sense and syllables run off together.

A casual reader might be tempted to contend that Miss Moore's elaborate design was not after all an important technical triumph, since it required no more of her than to start a new line when her chosen number of syllables had run. But that would be a mistaken criticism. In other pieces she submits to technical limitations of a severity that all of us can recognize and leaves us in no doubt of her mastery over them. The most conclusive example of this is a poem "To Statecraft Embalmed," in which the syllabic design is 10, 10, 6, 1, the ones all rhyming together, the tens rhyming in their couplets, and the sixes connecting the eight stanzas in four pairs. Here again it is noticeable that the sentence disregards the stanza, while the meaning threads its way through the complicated rhyming system in a nonchalance that nothing disturbs. The conclusion of the poem (where the reference is to statecraft under the image of the Egyptian sacred Ibis) runs thus:

Slow
To remark the steep, too strict proportion
Of your throne, you'll see the wrenched distortion
Of suicidal dreams

>   Go
> Staggering towards itself and with its bill
> Attack its own identity until
>   Foe seems friend and friend seems
>   Foe.

Nothing could be more brilliant, more achieved. Obviously Miss Moore knows just what she is about, and whenever she seems casual (many of her poems are in free verse, and thick-sown with quotation from her incidental reading) the seeming casualness is part of a conscious plan. It would be superfluous, therefore, to emphasize the fact that her poems, emotionally and intellectually, are as distinct, and in their distinctiveness as elusive, as they are formally. Mr. Eliot's admiration of them makes it needless to labor the point, and our quotations illustrate it unmistakably.

There is, of course, a strong temptation to read the poems as if they were prose, hoping to get their meaning by itself and to be able to throw in the decoration afterwards. But that, again, will not do; the difficulties of thought and form are interlocked. What is said is too glancing, too disjointed, and generally too eccentric to pass as prose. It needs the dry artifice of the form to keep it from collapsing. In fact—to face an inevitable conclusion—there is no way of reading Miss Moore short of learning to play her cruelly difficult instrument:

> Those
> various sounds consistently indistinct, like intermingled echoes
> struck from thin glasses successively at random—the
> inflection disguised: your hair, the tails of two
> fighting-cocks head to head in stone—like sculptured scimitars re-
> peating the curve of your ears in reverse order: your eyes
>   flowers of ice.

We should be the last to wish to discourage experiments in technique or to underrate the value for poetry readers of understanding them. It is nevertheless important to recognize that experiments, especially when persevered in, reveal a poetic attitude. Miss Moore, Mr. Pound, Mr. Eliot have all been innovators, and behind their very different methods there seems to lie a similar aesthetic and intellectual revulsion from common life and common standards. Miss Moore carries revulsion to more elaborate lengths of exaltation. Her prosody flies full in the face of all the natural music of an English intonation, and of an American still more. Mr. Eliot is mistaken, we believe, in averring that the cosmopolitan aestheticism her work embodies is for the life of our language. It would, we think, be truer to say that its cultivated refusals and subtle detachment are poison to us. Much nearer to the heart of English are the crooners, the slang singers, the lumberjacks, in fact any men and women anywhere who are alive and immersed, and in whose language, therefore, there will be food and fire for our next Shakespeare when he wants them.

MARIANNE MOORE: *Selected Poems*. (Reprinted from *The Times Literary Supplement* of January 18, 1936.)

ALLEN TATE'S POEMS

MR. TATE is an American critic of unusual maturity and acuteness, and his power of critical concentration is evident in these poems, which are selected from three previous books, but which have been much revised and a few completely renovated. There is not a line in the whole volume, we feel, that has not been passed again and again under a close critical scrutiny or that indeed did not spring to life with a critical eye upon it. That he has in such critical circumstances generally maintained the tension of the poetic impulse is proof of an underlying force of feeling. But it is the mind that dominates his verse and makes much of it so esoteric that we are inclined to apply to it his own words from "Ignis Fatuus":

High in what hills, by what illuminations
Are you intelligible?

In an earlier "Monologue" he hints himself at the danger of intellectualizing experience, when he writes:

> Think about it at will; there is that
> Which is the commentary; there's that other,
> Which may be called the immaculate
> Conception of its essence in itself.
> It is necessary to distinguish the weights
> Of the two methods lest the first smother
> The second, the second be speechless (without the first).

And the tendency in his verse is for the mental commentary not so much to smother as to twist into obscure and peculiar shapes the essence. Sophistication rather than poetic wisdom dictates such lines as

> The essential wreckage of your age is different,
> The accident the same; the Annabella
> Of proper incest, no longer incestuous:
> In an age of abstract experience, fornication
> Is self-expression, adjunct to Christian euphoria,
> And whores become delinquents; delinquents patients;
> Patients, wards of society.

His own absorption in abstract experience is reflected in his habit of personifying abstractions, as when he writes:

> And abnegation folds hands, crossed like the knees
> Of the complacent tailor, stitches cloaks of mercy
> To the backs of obsessions.

And it leads him often to force his imagery, because it is of the mind rather than the imagination, as in the line "the bleak sunshine shrieks its chipped music," or to throw out phrases that are more cleverly pretentious than weighted with meaning, such phrases as "for death is morality touched with emotion" or "we are the eyelids of defeated caves." The mind, indeed, that speaks through his poetry is for the most part too feverishly alert to find meaning by resting in it. Several of his poems do in fact express the mental turnings and twistings of insomnia or the nightmare wakefulness that imagines wolves waiting in the next room or broods on skeletons "with naught but space within their eyes." And in the concluding stanzas of "Last Days of Alice" he cries out against the mental abstraction that has sucked reality out of experience:

> —We too back to the world shall never pass
> Through the shattered door, a dumb shade-harried crowd
> Being all infinite, function, depth and mass
> Without figure, a mathematical shroud
> Hurled at the air—blessèd without sin!
> O God of our flesh, return us to Your wrath,
> Let us be evil could we enter in
> Your grace, and falter on the stony path!

His verse then rather elucidates the bones of life than clothes them with poetic form. But there are poems, such as "Ode to the Confederate Dead," "The Cross," and "The Twelve," in which his mind strikes deep roots in imagination and gives memorable form to an experienced essence, while others trace the metaphysical pattern of love with remarkable subtlety.

ALLEN TATE: *Selected Poems*. (Reprinted from
The Times Literary Supplement of February 26, 1938.)

THE TROUBLE WITH TIGERS

DEFINITIONS OF the short story do not take us very far nowadays, if indeed they ever did. Butler's saying that definitions are a kind of scratching that generally leaves a sore place more sore than it was before seems to be uncommonly apt here. The great names still set an example, and some such topical conception as a Poe-Maupassant-Chekhov axis would doubtless comprehend the principal types—the fanciful, the realistic, the poetical. But the short story today, like so much else, exhibits a growing technical sophistication, and in the ordinary way classification is by varieties of structure. A dozen or so years ago, when the market for the "literary" as distinguished from the "commercial" product was considerably bigger than it is now, the name that cropped up most frequently in critical discussion was Katherine Mansfield, and argument labored the "emotional high light" or the "concentric moment." But time marches on, and today the emphasis falls elsewhere. Whether or not a shrinking market—a notable feature of present discontents—has something to do with it the structure of the short story seems to matter less and the imaginative point of view much more. The point of view, of course, may determine the structure; it is the mistaken notion that the converse is true that accounts for so much valueless experiment.

Mr. Saroyan has never entertained the notion. It was his droll and unexpected unliterariness that first made readers sit up and take notice. Only after the shock of surprise at his seeming ingenuousness and tricks of inconsequence had worn off was it evident how well these became his fresh and individual vision. And only then did it become obvious that the short story was necessarily Mr. Saroyan's medium for communicating his vision. Life as he images it is a thing of wonder, the theme of a brief rhapsody of sense and spirit. He sings, he chants, he almost bawls the praise of living, dancing as he goes. Everything temporarily intoxicates him; he reels off the wonders of life in a breathless Whitmanesque catalogue. This, needless to say, is no literary child of nature, no artless singing bird, but an exceptionally conscious and calculating poet of his sensations. Yet his song is always heartfelt, his gaze is unfaltering and uncorrupted. Only such impermanent or illusory things as factories, offices, governments, possessions, or the want of possessions prevent everybody else from feeling as he does. Good or bad, the adventure of living is always a miracle. He cannot keep it under his hat.

Mr. Saroyan, in brief, is what is called a serious artist, with something of the mystic's delight in his comic extravagance. This new collection of his stories is rich and diverting reading, though it is rather more of a miscellany than usual. The contents of one section of the book can barely be described as fiction; here are commentaries by and large upon politics, money, the cinema, the

American scene. But nobody would wish they were not there, since they cast a shining light upon the storyteller in Mr. Saroyan. This is his "Prayer for the Living": "God in heaven let them at least laugh once in a while, and if it isn't asking too much let them play a little before the flood comes, before the tigers come down from the mountains, before the black birds darken the sky." Here, as in "The People, yes, and then again, no," Mr. Saroyan's colloquialisms are weighted with tremendous imaginative simplicity. His purer exercises in fiction are not always satisfying. The title story, for instance, in which the tiger is his symbol of mortality, is of too sprawling a pattern to have the desired effect. Yet how swift and sure is his touch in such tales as that of the Italian boy beguiled by a pretty neighbor; or that of the young man in an office overcome by summer; or the tale of the two loafers who parted in mutual pity when one of them found a job. Mr. Saroyan's vision rests on everyday types and trivial incidents, but it is hard to think of anybody at the present day with a similar power of creating the commonplace anew.

WILLIAM SAROYAN: *The Trouble with Tigers.* (Reprinted from *The Times Literary Supplement* of January 21, 1939.)

THE THEORY OF INQUIRY

IT IS a striking fact, perhaps a paradoxical one, that logic, admitted on all hands (or nearly all) to be formal, methodological, and instrumental in most or all of the senses attaching to those debatable terms, has not only been one of the main philosophical battlegrounds but has also, as the names of Hamilton, Mill, Hegel, and Bradley may serve to attest, often been identified in a special sense with the entire system of many of the world's most prominent thinkers. This consideration, like most considerations bearing on his topic, does not indeed escape Professor Dewey's catholic survey; and if it is true, as it seems to be, that one has to wait to the very end for his explanation of this aspect of the case, the skill of the exposition itself makes ample amends.

The reason—if one may partially paraphrase the original—for what Professor Dewey calls this "two-way" relationship of logic to generalized philosophy is that every enduring synthesis must show that the formal patterns it exhibits are compatible with the vision of totality it expresses in two separate ways, first by rendering its underlying "logic" open to inspection and secondly by "borrowing its leading principles from some phase of the logical pattern of inquiry in order that its conclusions may seem to avoid *material* fallacies." There is much merit in that "seem"; and it is from this point that Professor Dewey passes in review the theories of the great historical traditions in order to show that each type "borrows" so selectively that while their strength lies in the fact that they borrow from the proper quarter their weakness consists in "arbitrary isolation of the elements selected from the inquiry-context in which they function." They are arraigned for the "failure to institute a logic based exclusively on the operations of inquiry" and for "not being conceived in terms of the operations by which in the continuum of experiential inquiry stable beliefs are progressively obtained and utilized." It is of course, recognized explicitly by the author that his final chapter is necessarily too short for critique to have its perfect work; but the quality as well as the importance of the argument calls for it to be noticed at the outset. As Aristotle put the matter, τὸ δὲ πρῶτον ἐν ἀναλύσει ὕστατον ἐν γενέσει, and it is convenient to invoke the august name of Aristotle to smooth the transition to a second and equally vital point.

In the last chapter of the first of his four sections Professor Dewey brilliantly develops the thesis that the restoration of logic to its position as the "material" and "procedural" factor in "rigorous" and "productive" inquiry is a true restoration in the sense that it comes not to destroy Aristotle but to fulfill. The argument, which is so masterly that one must dissent—if one should dare to dissent—on grounds independent of its intrinsic validity, is that the Organon represented the cosmology and metaphysics of the day, and that while its material content has for this very reason no value for us its formal content has abiding value just because the Aristotelian concepts involve the correct view of logic as sheerly instrumental. It is naturally insisted upon that the new creation must be fundamental, even to the extent of the repeated dictum that the very perfection of Aristotle's work in his own day actually augments its intrinsic inutility for ours; but it is none the less true that it is a new Aristotle, not a new Plato, who is to be the herald of the second dawn. And, for all the finish and subtlety of the reasoning, one may perhaps remain haunted by the impression that it is curious that Aristotle should be thus exalted, while Plato, who in the *Philebus* and elsewhere seems to have been standing on the threshold of the quantitative science so dear to Professor Dewey, should be excluded from the promised land.

Viewed as a whole, Professor Dewey's notable book is one of those major works of philosophy that are not patient of cursory criticism or rapid estimation and that raise anew, in a form that makes fresh demands on constructive thought, the perennial problems with which they deal. It may conduce but little to the further realization of the scale and scope of such a work to select for mention particular components in a whole of which every part is strictly organic; but within the compass of a review a partial eclecticism is inevitable, and it is perhaps permissible on this basis to compile a rather barren schedule of some of the more salient features of Professor Dewey's construction. At any rate, it is impossible not to be impressed with the arguments tending to show that the "true" is generally to be equated with the "warrantably assertible," that judgment is "individual" and is "a continuous process of resolving an indeterminate situation into a determinably unified one," that all knowledge is mediate, that propositions are formal components in ordered discourse imbued with the conditions of rigor and productivity, that singular terms exhibit intension at its maximum, that the problem of induction is that of the representative case, that the epistemological problem is or should be nonexistent, and that causation is a category that resolves itself into a functional means of regulating existential inquiry. These theses, stripped of the deliberate and unimpassioned calm of Professor Dewey's magisterial manner, may in some cases appear either implausible or trivial; but they are actually very far from being either the one or the other.

Professor Dewey proclaims his debt to that very great philosopher, Charles S. Peirce; and, although no two thinkers could be less alike temperamentally, their affinities from the doctrinal point of view are obvious enough, though never sufficiently so to detract from the essential originality of Professor Dewey's own patient and unremitting method. It must also be observed that Professor Dewey, whether or not he be thought to overvalue scientific method, is not desirous of idolizing science as such. There may be some whom even Professor Dewey may not convince that a methodology that (to date) has conducted "natural" science to practical control and fundamental nescience is of necessity omnicompetent; and there may be others who consider that to speak of "events previously experienced as separate becoming integral constituents of one experience" is less exact than to speak of them as "becoming experienced as" such integral constituents. But, be these things as they may, the book is one of prime importance for philosophy as a whole and is destined of its own right to occupy an honored place among the landmarks of speculative thought.

JOHN DEWEY: *Logic*. The Theory of Inquiry. (Reprinted from
The Times Literary Supplement of April 29, 1939.)

GRAPES OF WRATH

JOHN STEINBECK'S new novel is a campaign, and Mammon is the enemy. While lesser American writers complacently recall their country's past, Mr. Steinbeck is anxiously in touch with its present. He, too, describes an exodus to the West, but this is made in

ramshackle motorcars instead of lumbering wagons. Here there
are no battles to bring glory, and at the end the land of promise
is a bitter disappointment. There, sure enough, are the farms and
orchards and well-watered lands, but others are in possession of
them. Yet this the travelers expected: all they hoped for was work;
and the indecent exploitation of their need to work is shown with
cold and precise justice. Mr. Steinbeck's theme, indeed, is twofold. One part of it is the endurance of the common people in
conditions of great hardship; and the other is the tyranny over all
classes of economic laws that were framed only to record certain
movements and not, in fact, to be the pretext for compelling
them.

At their most wretched, Mr. Steinbeck's people have the refuge
of memory and humor, and in their recollections of past raciness
we are enabled to see the superior color and variety of a society
in which the owners lived on their land, worked it themselves, and
measured their prosperity directly against its prosperity. There
is, besides, the tedium inseparable from any long work pledged
to a single idea; but here the tedium is at its lowest. Against such
falling off as there is may be set those passages in which the
author makes still more transparent the barrier between his mind
and our own. We know his mind now for an original one. He has
passages in this book that restate the idea of the interlude in *To
the Lighthouse* in terms of another country; but his just understanding of character, the candor and forcefulness of his dialogue,
and his mastery of climaxes are all his own and inimitable.

> JOHN STEINBECK: *The Grapes of Wrath*. (Reprinted from
> *The Times Literary Supplement* of September 9, 1939.)

PALE HORSE, PALE RIDER

AFTER WAR consciousness, postwar consciousness, and crisis consciousness there is something like white war or near-war conscious-

ness. It seems to be the worst of the lot and the most damaging to novelists and novels. No doubt imaginative talent has almost always chosen the wrong time to be born; no doubt, too, there is seldom a crop of masterpieces in the space of a few months. But it is plain that the going has of late become rougher and more difficult for the novelist, plain that by comparison with even a year ago the present standard of performance is appreciably lower. Good novelists turn out inferior stuff or none at all, while the competent commercial product is more visibly in the ascendant. On the whole, the most interesting novels this year have come from America, or at any rate from over the sea and far away, where a near-war consciousness has less than the whole field to itself or can be indulged with an air of greater detachment.

In reserving the week's nosegay for *Pale Horse, Pale Rider* something more is intended than making the best of a bad job. The book consists of three long short stories—they are best described as short stories rather than *contes* or *novelles* or the "short novels" of the title page—by an American writer with a previous collection of attractive quality to her credit. What gives distinction to Mrs. Porter's work is the strain of poetry in it. The poetry is consistently elegiac and therefore of a vulnerable kind in prose narrative; but it is nevertheless very welcome, and for a good reason. Ordinarily, if as storyteller you are going to get away from the burning topicalities and agitations of the immediate hour, two ways seem open. One is through the humdrum realism of eternal verities such as catching the 9.05, being unhappily married, finding a new love, and watching the baby cut its first tooth. The other is through the doubtfully authentic thrill and glamour of the frozen North, the tropic sun, or, say, Wellington's Peninsula campaign. Both fashions, it must be said, are a little too much with us at the moment. The thing that comes all too rarely in fiction nowadays, the thing that is most sorely missed and that reconciles so-called escapism with literature, is the poetic vision— the seeing eye, the invocatory and evocative power of words. Prose is not poetry; but good fiction never lacks a quality that must ultimately be called poetic. It is this that appears perhaps rather more bravely than to discreet advantage in each of the three stories in Mrs. Porter's volume.

In the first, "Old Mortality," two small girls learn the history of Aunt Amy, a Texan beauty of the nineties, who had been much loved, who had been unhappy and died young. The past is delicately conjured in family legend, in the flaunting airs and graces of the South, in dove-colored velvet and eighteen-inch waists; the present materializes in the fat, shabby, and lugubriously sentimental person of Uncle Gabriel, whose bride Amy had been for a few weeks. The effect is too deliberate, but all the same something of enchantment hangs over Amy and her capricious duel with death. "Noon Wine" is the story of a Swede who turned up one day at a small Texan dairy farm asking for work and stayed there for nine years. The man was blankly, oppressively silent, shut in on himself. It is the discovery that he had escaped from a madhouse that brings murder and self-destruction into a tale that had seemed to grow to idyllic shape. Again the effect is both suddenly piercing and slightly manufactured. The title story, in which the child Miranda of "Old Mortality" has become a newspaper reporter, is an elegy-rhapsody of love in the last year of the war. It strikes tender and passionate notes, it captures vivid and arresting images, but it also cultivates beauty too assiduously.

That, indeed, is the failing of the book. The realistic and passionless transcript and the heroic romance are both being overdone just now, and it is a poetic sense such as Mrs. Porter tries to communicate in these stories that might best fortify the novelist not yet paralyzed by war fever or enslaved by Miss Literature. But as for beauty, almost the last way of achieving it in a novel is by cultivating it.

KATHERINE ANNE PORTER: *Pale Horse, Pale Rider*. (Reprinted from *The Times Literary Supplement* of May 27, 1939.)

THE IDES OF MARCH

The Ides of March is a novel without narrative or dialogue, but not without a hero. The hero is Julius Caesar, and among the letters, memoranda, and fragments of verse that make up this "fantasia on certain events and persons of the last days of the Roman republic" the essential documents are contributed by the Dictator. These are imaginary, as are all constituent parts of the book except Catullus's verses and a postscript. It is a study of individual processes that are not those of abstract thought or of self-expression for its own sake (diaries have practically no place in it), but are processes of communication between man and man. These people are under an obligation to say something definite; they speak in order to be heard and understood by the persons addressed. A style of formality is maintained or attempted; and their greater or less ability to make use of it is turned to clear account by Mr. Wilder as a measure of the integrity and character of each of them.

It is the book's most important achievement that Caesar's absolute command of the common style and thus his moral and mental pre-eminence are established. Whatever subject engages his attention we are made aware of Caesar's patience, his firmness, the high seriousness and the deep charitableness of his purpose. "Caesar," says his doctor, "embraces decision. It is as though he felt his mind to be operating only when it is interlocking itself with significant consequences." Mr. Wilder, with very strict economy of means, conjures up a variety of "consequences" and persuades us that each in its way is "significant." Even when the problems are insoluble by Caesar, as are the philosophical questions that he debates in correspondence with his old comrade Turrinus, the "interlocking" of his mind with the subject matter is shown; these passages, indeed, set the seal upon his character. Not only the stature of Caesar but also his tragedy is suggested, and the tragedy is the more impressive because it is never stated. It arises from the total impression of this short, witty, and extremely serious book.

> THORNTON WILDER: *The Ides of March.* (Reprinted from *The Times Literary Supplement* of July 31, 1948.)

AMERICAN UNIFICATION

THE TWO new volumes of Professor Nevins's great work fulfill the promise of the first two. Indeed, promise is not the word, the performance is already so impressive. Few periods in human history have been more thoroughly investigated than the years before the American Civil War. Faced with the evident failure of their institutions in one great crisis, conscious that the failure of the institutions only revealed a deeper failure in national life, the American people, as well as American scholars and polemical writers, have turned again and again to the question of how "the last, best hope of earth" was preserved in unity only by a very bloody war and by means that left wounds not yet wholly healed.

There are, of course, devil theories: the intrinsic wickedness of the "aggressive slavocracy," the hypocrisy and greed of Northern business men anxious (for rather obscure reasons) to ruin the South. There is personal ambition in Stephen Douglas, personal feebleness in President Buchanan; there are the needs of politicians to find an issue and of the homeless Whigs to find a new party. And more portentous theories of economic determinism or even a pessimistic Calvinism of the kind sketched by Lincoln in the Second Inaugural have their devotees. It is one of the chief merits of this book that Professor Nevins is not tempted by any short cuts and that, in the chain of events that led to the fatality, he can allow for human folly, incompetence, and pride as well as for great forces in history that would not be denied or evaded.

This is not to say that he thinks the Civil War, in a strict sense, inevitable. Even to the end some compromise might have been worked out, the cracks might have been papered over for a few more years; and, of course, with each decade the chances of the South's effectively resisting would have been less and less. But the more sagacious Southern leaders realized that, too. "They are fighting against the census of 1860," it was said at the time; and it would have been harder to fight against the census of 1870 and ludicrous to fight against the census of 1880, even if we allow for the distortion of the American economy in a sense favorable to the North that the war produced. Yet again and again we are reminded how needlessly the crisis was hastened on, by Douglas's forgetting in 1854 what *must* be the result in the North and West of appearing to reopen territory to slavery, by the failure to enact the Toombs Bill in 1856, by the folly of the Supreme Court in using the Dred Scott case to impose a judicial peace on the warring factions, by the double-dealing of Buchanan in Kansas, by the war against Douglas, by the folly of the Southern leaders in demanding federal legislation to protect the peculiar institution in territory controlled by the federal government, by the folly plus infamy of trying, in so many Southern states, to reduce the free Negroes to slavery, by the great crime of John Brown's raid on Harper's Ferry, and by the baseness of his wealthy and cowardly backers.

But all these crimes and stupidities occurred—and were disastrous—because America was faced with a problem of unexampled complexity, with material and moral aspects inextricably entwined. Lincoln, in his first famous speech, had been right: a house divided could not stand. It had to become all one thing or the other, not at once, not by mere legislation, but in a measurable period of time. And that unity could only come in one way. Slavery was dying, in the border states, in the world. One of the most effective chapters of this book puts American slavery in its world perspective, showing how it became more and more of an odious anomaly as the American share in the slave trade and support for filibustering in Central America saddened European democrats and gave grim pleasure to reactionaries as the one great republic then in existence lived in more and more flagrant contradiction with its own political religion.

It was this truth that Lincoln saw and that Douglas did not see, that the Southern leaders, even the most intelligent of them—men like Stephens, for example—did not see. On the other hand, as Professor Nevins makes plain, the North refused to see that it had its share in the guilt and in the problem. Yet there was no general scheme for spreading the losses of the slaveholders; no general scheme for gradual emancipation or for federal aid to the freedmen. American opinion was ready to sermonize, but that was all, and, of course, millions in the North were becoming ready to salve their consciences by putting all the loss on the slaveholders, as it was later put on the brewers and saloonkeepers in connection with prohibition.

It seems impossible today to understand how the South can have thought that it could maintain its increasingly Spartan republic in the late nineteenth century. Many Southern leaders must have stifled doubts, even though a refusal to change the status quo was evidently not enough, as the position of the Negro had to get quickly worse or better. And by 1860 it was getting quickly worse. Yet, as Professor Nevins shows in one of his most acute analyses, the unanimity with which the South, even the Deep South, seceded in 1861, has been much exaggerated; there were plenty of doubters if few unconditional Union men even in Alabama and Louisiana. That is only one of the many revisions of the standard story that Professor Nevins makes, revisions based on a prodigious knowledge of national and local archives, unprinted theses, unpublished diaries, obscure newspapers and pamphlets. That knowledge makes every page alive with relevant information, relevant local color.

In small matters and in great Professor Nevins knows his own mind. He does not think it proved, for instance, that the disastrous initiative in the Dred Scott case came from the Northern justices. He knows, too, that many things other than the slavery controversy excited America at this time. There was the movement of the economic tides, ebbing from time to time, but always rising higher. There were gold rushes and market crashes, new railways, new cities. It was the contrast between the fantastic material progress and the political and social cancer that angered and even maddened millions of Americans. And never has this been more completely or brilliantly demonstrated than in these volumes, from which it would be possible to excise one or two minor errors, but impossible to withhold the warmest admiration.

ALLAN NEVINS: *The Emergence of Lincoln*. (Reprinted from *The Times Literary Supplement* of January 12, 1951.)

Index

416 INDEX

Gentleman's Magazine, The, **177**
Geopolitics, 123
German Gothicism, 47
Germany, 55
Gesta Romanorum, 178
Gettysburg, 115, 116
Gibbon, Edward, 85
Gibbons, James Cardinal, The Life of, by John Tracy Ellis, 276
Gide, André, 37–38; *The Immoralist,* paperback edition, 270
Gill, Brendan, 258; *The Trouble of One House,* 170
Gilpin, Charles, 347
Gingertown, by Claude McKay, 101
Ginzberg, Eli, 109
Giordani, Igino, his *Pius X, a Country Priest,* 276
Gipson, Lawrence H., 123
"Girl with the Pimply Face, The," by William Carlos Williams, 185
Gladstone, William E., on the American Constitution, 222
Glamour magazine, book reviews in, 257
Glasgow, Ellen, 90, 107, 183, 213; *Barren Ground,* 107
Glass Key, The, by Dashiell Hammett, 171
Glendinning, Pierre, 206
Go Down Moses, by William Faulkner, 167, 208
God Without Thunder, by John Crowe Ransom, 77
Godey's Lady's Book, 177
God's Little Acre, by Erskine Caldwell, 240, paperback edition, 267
Goethe, Johann Wolfgang von, 34, 195, 198, 202
Gold, by Eugene O'Neill, 341
"Gold Bug, The," by Edgar Allan Poe, 49
Golden Apples, The, by Eudora Welty, 188
Golden Bowl, The, by Henry James, 198
Golden Boy, by Clifford Odets, 28
Golden Hawk, The, by Frank Yerby, 102
Goldsmith, Oliver, 195
Gone with the Wind, by Margaret Mitchell, 116
Good Man, A, by Jefferson Young, 219
"Good-By and Keep Cold," by Robert Frost, 378–379
Goodspeed, Edgar J., *As I Remember,* 276
Goofy, comic strip character, 319
Gordon, Adam Lindsay, 325
Gordon, Caroline, 75, 168, 185, 190, 210–211, 212, 218; *Old Red,* 185
Gothic tradition, 195–202
Gothicism, as used by Poe in his short stories, 49
Gourmont, Remy de, 37–38

Government positions, and writers, 237
Goyen, William, 169, 184, 190
Grace After Meat, by John Crowe Ransom, reviewed 1925, 357–360
Graduate students in literature, 150–153
Grammar of Motives, A, by Kenneth Burke, 39
Grapes of Wrath, The, by John Steinbeck, reviewed 1939, 398–399
Graphic arts, 278–288
Graphic Arts Research Foundation, 285
Graphic Forms: The Arts as Related to the Book, published by Harvard University Press, 279
Graves, Robert, 357, 358
Gravure printing, 287
Gravure Research, Incorporated, 282
Gray, Thomas, 4, 7
Great American novel, the, myth of, 160
Great Gatsby, The, by F. Scott Fitzgerald, 161; reviewed 1926, 360–361
Greatest Faith Ever Known, The, by Fulton Oursler, 271–272
Green, Anna Katharine, her *The Leavenworth Case,* 171
Green, Paul, his *In Abraham's Bosom,* 107; *The Scuffletown Outlaws,* 26
Greenville, Mississippi, 213
Greenwich Village, 230; still the true Bohemia, 19
Grotesque, school of the, 206
Ground We Stand On, The, by John Dos Passos, 68
Growing Spiritually, by E. Stanley Jones, 273
Guggenheim Foundation, 234

Hacker, Louis, 122
Hall, Basil, 93
Hall, James, 22
Haloid Company, 287
Hamilton, Alexander, 46, 119, 122
Hamilton, W. B., 213
Hamilton, Sir William, 395
Hamlet, The, by William Faulkner, 75
Hammett, Dashiell, and hard-boiled school of detective story, 172; most influential in development of detective story, 171–172; *The Glass Key,* 171; *The Maltese Falcon,* 172–173; *The Thin Man,* 171
Hammon, Jupiter, 96
Hampshire, Stuart, 270
"Hard-boiled" detective stories, 172–173
Hardin, John Wesley, 121
Hardy, Thomas, 70, 177; "Yellham Woods Story," 9
Harper, Frances, her *Iola Leroy,* 100
Harper's, book publishers, 273
Harper's magazine, 21, 89, 177, 187; book reviews in, 258
Harris, Joel Chandler, 213

COLOPHON

This book has been set in its entirety in TIMES RO-MAN, a face created for *The Times* (London) by Stanley Morison in 1932. Originally designed for newspaper and periodical work, it has become, by virtue of its strength, ease of reading, and economy of space, a current favorite for books and advertising as well.